SUBSTANCE ABUSE ASSESSMENT, INTERVENTIONS AND TREATMENT

# NICOTINE ADDICTION

## PREVENTION, HEALTH EFFECTS AND TREATMENT OPTIONS

# SUBSTANCE ABUSE ASSESSMENT, INTERVENTIONS AND TREATMENT

Additional books in this series can be found on Nova's website under the Series tab.

Additional e-books in this series can be found on Nova's website under the e-books tab.

SUBSTANCE ABUSE ASSESSMENT, INTERVENTIONS AND TREATMENT

# NICOTINE ADDICTION

## PREVENTION, HEALTH EFFECTS AND TREATMENT OPTIONS

GIUSEPPE DI GIOVANNI
EDITOR



Nova Science Publishers, Inc.
*New York*

**Library of Congress Cataloging-in-Publication Data**

Library of Congress Control Number : 2012933665
ISBN: 978-1-62081-290-7

*Published by Nova Science Publishers, Inc. † New York*

*To my son, Giulio Christopher Rocco,*
*wishing him a happy smoke-free life*

# CONTENTS

# PREFACE

Smoking tobacco presents serious social problems with major impacts on public health. It is estimated that 25-30% of the general population in western countries are currently smoking. Tobacco use is the major preventable cause of death in the United States, responsible for more than 400,000 deaths annually. Within the USA and Europe, 70% of all smokers have tried to quit smoking at least once, but only about 6% of these succeeded in maintaining abstinence. This book covers the latest nicotine-related research. The selection of chapters has a certain unity as physiologic, pathologic and psychological themes run through the book and supply the logical connections between the various authors. This work is intended as a contribution to the reversal of the current tobacco epidemic and thereby to preventing many of the deaths attributable to tobacco predicted in this century.

Drug abuse and the consequent phenomenon of drug addiction represent serious social problems with major impacts on public health. As reported by the World Health Organization, the extent of worldwide psychoactive substance is estimated at 2 million alcohol users, 1.3 billion smokers and 185 millions illicit drug users. Illicit substance use is predominantly a male activity, much more than cigarette smoking and alcohol consumption. Substance use, either legal or illegal, is also more prevalent among young people than in older age groups. The level of consumption of legal substances (tobacco and alcohol) is declining in developed countries but is increasing in developing countries. It is, however, estimated that 25-30% of the general population in western countries are currently smoking tobacco. Thus, it has been estimated that tobacco use is the major preventable cause of death in the United States, responsible for more than 400,000 deaths annually. Within the USA and Europe, 70% of all smokers have tried to quit smoking at least once, but only about 6% of these succeeded in maintaining abstinence. Thus, one of the major problems limiting the success of smoking cessations aids is that the great majority of abstinent people relapse. Since it has been estimated that smoking leads to an average loss of 12 healthy years and reduces the lifespan by 8 years, there is great interest in developing effective therapies that will help in facilitating smoking cessation and assist in maintaining abstinence.

Research on nicotine and related compounds has progressed at a rapid pace in the previous, and at the beginning of this, century. Therefore, this edited special volume, could serve the field and facilitate scientific progress.

While covering the latest nicotine-related research, for obvious reasons this book cannot be exhaustive and I am sorry indeed that it has been impossible to include a number of authors of obvious merit. The selection is intended, indeed, to be merely a very varied foretaste of contemporary research in the subject. I consider however, that the varied selection has a certain unity as physiologic, pathologic and psychological themes run through the book and supply the logical connections between the various authors. I believe this book is a reference that will be useful to researchers, students, health professionals, and to the growing number of people involved in efforts to regulate tobacco product contents and designs nationally and internationally. This work was intended as a contribution to the reversal of the current tobacco epidemic and thereby to preventing many of the deaths attributable to tobacco predicted in this century.

I want to end by thanking all the authors who have responded so willingly to contribute their time and expertise in preparing their individual chapters to a consistently high standard. My warmest thanks go to people at Nova Publishing who have helped to drive the book's development and eventual publication. My thanks go to everyone who has, in some way, contributed to the realization of this book.

*Professor Giuseppe Di Giovanni*
*Msida, Malta*
*December 2011*

In: Nicotine Addiction
Editor: Giuseppe Di Giovanni

ISBN: 978-1-62081-290-7


*Chapter 1*

# NICOTINE ADDICTION AND TREATMENT: RECENT ADVANCES

***Mostofa Jamal*, Kiyoshi Ameno, Naoko Tanaka, Mitsuru Kumihashi, and Hiroshi Kinoshita***
Department of Forensic Medicine, Faculty of Medicine,
Kagawa University, Ikenobe, Miki, Kita, Kagawa, Japan

## ABSTRACT

Nicotine is the most addictive substance in tobacco, and its action in humans is mediated by nicotinic acetylcholine receptors (nAChRs) present throughout the brain and peripheral nervous system. Stimulation of neuronal nAChRs releases various neurotransmitters, most importantly dopamine (DA). Glutamate and γ-aminobutyric acid are also important in the development of nicotine dependence. The endogenous cannabinoid and opioid systems have been suggested to be involved in several central effects of nicotine. Smoking may suppress monoamine oxidase, a DA clean-up enzyme, which allows satisfaction to linger far longer. Nicotine causes a temporary increase in pleasure and satisfaction. This mood-altering effect reinforces smoker's continued use of nicotine. Moreover, nicotine may cause a number of negative behavioral and psychological effects in human as well as in animals, although there exists some evidence that nicotine might have health benefits as well.

Repeated exposure to nicotine results in the development of tolerance, whereas stopping nicotine use may cause withdrawal symptoms. Breaking an addiction to nicotine is difficult due to the involvement of several biobehavioral processes of drug dependence, including reinforcement and withdrawal. In addition, relapse after quitting is common. A compelling motivation is essential in overcoming nicotine addiction. Thus, it could be a real challenge finding the best way to reduce nicotine dependence. There are several treatment options available such as nicotine replacement therapy, varenicline and bupropion. Of these three, varenicline has been found to be the most effective at preventing nicotine addiction, although some neuropsychiatric adverse events may impair

* Address for correspondence: Mostofa Jamal, Department of Forensic Medicine, Faculty of Medicine, Kagawa University, 1750-1, Ikenobe, Miki, Kita, Kagawa 761-0793, Japan; Phone: +81-87-891-2140; Fax: +81-87-891-2141; Email: jamal@kms.ac.jp.

smoker's satisfaction with this drug. Less is known about rimonabant; future research would be required to establish its long-term therapeutic implications. A nicotine vaccine has been achieved in development that might help to avoid nicotine addiction. All these medications seem to be most promising, but require further research to assess their effectiveness and safety. Although remarkable advances have been made in the understanding of nicotine addiction, the findings summarized in this chapter improve our understanding of nicotine addiction and suggest new possibilities in the treatment of this major public health disorder.

## INTRODUCTION

Millions of people smoke all over the world, despite the harmful health effects of various substances in tobacco. Of these, nicotine is the main addictive component. The basis of nicotine addiction is a combination of positive reinforcements such as enhancement of mood and avoidance of the negative emotional state produced by nicotine withdrawal [1]. Nicotine addiction produces a complex behavioral alteration, in which many neuronal pathways and neurotransmitters are involved. Nicotine-induced positive reinforcing effects [2, 3] occur by activating reward systems, including the mesolimbic dopamine (DA) system [4]. Nicotine targets the nicotinic acetylcholine receptors (nAChR) in the central nervous system (CNS), and DA is a potential neurotransmitter that mediates the rewarding effects of nicotine. In addition, a large number of studies have suggested that the endogenous cannabinoid and opioid systems play an overall modulatory effect on the reward circuitry and participate in the addictive properties of nicotine [5, 6].

Following inhalation of cigarette smoke, nicotine passes into the bloodstream and crosses the blood-brain barrier, reaching the brain within a few seconds [7]. The maximum brain levels of nicotine are reached in between three to five minutes, and accumulate more slowly in dependent smokers when compared to non-dependent subjects, because they have slower clearance of hepatic and lung nicotine [8, 9]. Cytochrome P450 2A6 (CYP2A6) is believed to play a major role in the systemic clearance of nicotine [10]. There are individual differences in the metabolism of nicotine due to variations in CY2A6 alleles [10].

Nicotine binds to neuronal nAChRs, principally the $\alpha 4\beta 2$ and $\alpha 7$ subtypes located on dopaminergic (DAergic), glutamatergic and $\gamma$-aminobutyric acid (GABA)-ergic neurons in the ventral tegmental area (VTA) of the midbrain, which in turn modulate the release of DA. Nicotine enhances GABAergic inhibition transiently [11, 12], followed by a persistent depression of these inhibitory inputs due to nAChR desensitization. Simultaneously, nicotine enhances glutamatergic excitation through nAChRs [13, 14] that desensitize less than those on GABA neurons, result in a greater overall increase in DA levels. This effect can cause pleasure, which may trick the brain into believing that it needs more of the stimulus to achieve the same effect, thus leading to addiction. Several lines of evidence suggest that cognitive enhancement may contribute to the addictive actions of nicotine [15-17]. Three principal factors that may contribute to addictive behaviors with nicotine: (1) neuroadaptation (i.e. tolerance) that occurs with the persistent use of nicotine, (2) dependence, and (3) withdrawal symptoms experienced when intake of nicotine is stopped. With repeated exposure to nicotine, neuroadaptation develops, which leads to reduce responsiveness to nicotine, requiring the continual presence of nicotine to be maintained. As a result, the number of binding sites on the nAChR in the brain increases [18], probably in response to nicotine-mediated desensitization of receptors [19]. It is proposed that the desensitization and upregulation of nAChRs following chronic nicotine exposure is the basis of tolerance to nicotine as well as the factors responsible for withdrawal symptoms on cessation.

If the brain stops getting the nicotine it wants, symptoms of craving and withdrawal begin, including depression, anxiety and stress (i.e. affecting signs) that are hard to overcome. The effects of nicotine withdrawal are mediated through nAChRs. Suggestive evidence that β2 nAChRs are involved in the affective signs of nicotine withdrawal has been found [20]. Researchers believe that these symptoms that cause quitters to take up smoking again may be the result of a decrease in DA overflow in the nucleus acumens (NAc) [21]. Besides DA, serotonin (5-HT) and norepinephrine (NE) can mediate the manifestations of withdrawal symptoms in rats due to perturbation of 5-HT and NE functions [22, 23]. There is evidence that the extrahypothalamic corticotropin-releasing factor (CRF)-CRF1 receptor system may contribute to the negative affect during nicotine withdrawal. A previous study supports the argument that the negative affective state associated with nicotine withdrawal is at least partly mediated by the release of CRF in the rat central nucleus of the amygdala and the NAc shell [24].

Additionally, anxiety-like behavior and the release of CRF in the central nucleus of the amygdala also occur during nicotine withdrawal in rats [25]. However, a blockade of CRF1 receptors has been shown to inhibit the anxiogenic effects of nicotine withdrawal as well as prevent the increase in self-administration of nicotine in experimental animals [24, 25]. Thus, both the underactivity of the DAergic system and activation of the CRF-CRF1 receptor system appear to contribute to the symptoms of nicotine withdrawal that often precipitate relapse.

Here, we summarize relevant research on nicotine addiction and its health effects, prevention and the treatment options. The first section of this chapter is focused on neuronal basis of nicotine addiction. Next, we address health effects, prevention and treatment options. Finally, this chapter also focuses on recent advances that could lead to the development of improved novel pharmacological treatments.

# Nicotine Addiction

## Involvement of Nicotinic Acetylcholine Receptors

Nicotine exerts its effects by activating neuronal nAChRs, which are found throughout animal and human brains, with the greatest number of binding sites for humans in the cortex, hippocampus, cerebellum and thalamus [26, 27]. Neuronal nAChRs appear to be located in many parts of the cells, including cell bodies and nerve terminals [28]. Nicotine binds to nAChRs, which are ligand-gated ion channels, allowing the entry of cations, including sodium and calcium. These cations further activate voltage-dependent calcium channels, allowing further calcium entry. One of the effects of the entry of calcium into a neuron is the release of DA and other neurotransmitters [29].

A large number of nAChR subtypes have been identified to date, including nine α-subunits (α2-α10) and three β-subunits (β2-β4 in the brain. Many of these nAChR subunits are reportedly expressed in the human brain as shown in Table1 [30].

**Table 1. Distribution of nAChR subtypes mRNA in the human brain**

| Brain region | β2 | β3 | β4 | α3 | α4 | α5 | α7 |
|---|---|---|---|---|---|---|---|
| Cortex | | + | + | | | + | |
| Prefrontal | + | | | ++ | + | | ++ |
| Motor | + | | | ++ | + | | +++ |
| Entorhinal | + | | | ++ | + | | + |
| Cingular | + | | | + | + | | |
| Temporal | + | | | + | + (+) | | |
| Thalamus | | + | + | | | + | |
| Dorsomedial | + | | | +++ | | | ++ |
| Lateroposterior | | | +++ | | | | |
| Reticular | | | ++ | | | + (+) | |
| Ventro-posterolateral | + | | | +++ | | | |
| Geniculate bodies | | | | | | ++ | |
| Hippocampus | + (+) | | | + | | | ++ |
| Dentate gyrus | + (+) | | | + | | | ++ |
| Caudate Putamen | + (+) | + | + | | | + | ++ |
| Cerebellum | + | + | + | + | + (+) | + | |

Sources: Paterson and Nordberg, 2000.

The α4β2 and α7 nAChRs subtypes are the most abundant in the human, and participate in important processes such as synaptic transmission, cognitive function, gene expression, and drug addiction [1, 31]. The α4β2 subunit has a high affinity for nicotine and is desensitized at low concentrations of nicotine, within the range of those found in the blood of smokers [32].

Compared with α4β2, the α7 subunit has low affinity for nicotine and is not desensitized at low nicotine concentrations [33, 34]. This delayed desensitization of the α7 subunit is believed to be what maintains DA activity after the α4β2 subunit has been desensitized [35]. Both these subtypes are specifically up-regulated after chronic nicotine administration in humans and animals [18, 31, 36].

The α3β4 unit is also present in the human brain, and has been shown to mediate the cardiovascular effects of nicotine [37]. The α4α6 unit has recently been shown to play a significant role in influencing DA release in the NAc and participates in nicotine reinforcement [38].

The *α*5 subunit is expressed in discrete regions of the mammalian CNS [39], and can control nicotine intake and brain reward function in mice [40]. The α6 subtype is present in midbrain DAergic neurons and has recently been shown to modulate the nicotine reward pathway [41, 42]. Previously, the α6 subunit is up-regulated in response to transient, high nicotine exposures [43].

The activation of nAChRs potentiates the release of a variety of neurotransmitters, most importantly DA as well as NE [44], acetylcholine [45], glutamate [46] and GABA [47]. Long-term exposure to nicotine results in an increased number of nAChRs in the brains of several species including humans [48, 49]. Thus, neuronal nAChRs could identify as a prime target for the development of nicotine addiction.

## Involvement of Neurotransmitters

### *Dopamine*

The mesocorticolimbic system mediates the rewarding properties of most drugs of abuse, including nicotine [50, 51]. This system originates from DA neurons in the VTA in the midbrain and projects to the prefrontal cortex (PFC) and the limbic structures, such as the NAc and amygdala. Nicotine increases DA by activating the firing of mesolimbic DA neurons [52]. This finding has been supported by various observations: namely, that infusion of neuronal nAChR antagonists into the cerebral ventricles, as well as systemic administration of DA receptor blockers and lesions of DA neurons with a selective DAergic neurotoxin 6-hydroxydopamine, impair nicotine self-administration in rats [53, 54]. Further, selective D1- and D2- DA antagonists can also attenuate some of the behavioral effects of nicotine, including stimulation of locomotor activity [55]. Effects of nicotine occur through excitatory actions at nAChRs on the mesolimbic DAergic neurons in both the VTA and the NAc [56]. The nAChRs in the VTA may in fact be of greater importance than those in the NAc in the effects of nicotine on the release of DA from the NAc [57]. Approximately one-third of $\alpha4\beta2$ nAChRs subunits are located on DA cells in the mesolimbic DA systems [58, 59]. The $\alpha4\beta2$ subtype has been thought to play a vital role in mediating nicotine reward [60, 61]. This is supported by the finding that a blockade of the $\alpha4\beta2$ subtype by dihydro-β-erythroidine inhibits nicotine self-administration in rats [62]. Genetic deletion of α4 or β2 subunits largely abolishes nicotine binding to the mouse brain and inhibits nicotine self-administration and nicotine-induced increases in NAc DA release [63, 64].

### *Glutamate*

Glutamate is the major excitatory neurotransmitter in the CNS. Considerable evidence indicates that glutamate is critically involved in the reinforcing properties of nicotine via N-methyl-D-aspartate (NMDA) receptors, possibly through stimulation of nAChRs localized presynaptically on glutamatergic afferents in the VTA [65]. Researchers have found that glutamate receptor antagonists largely prevent the stimulatory effect of nicotine in the NAc [66], suggesting that nicotinic upregulation of glutamatergic transmission contributes significantly to the enhancement of VTA DA output. Nicotine increases the release of glutamate through activation of nAChRs located on glutamatergic terminals in various brain regions, including the VTA [13, 14], NAc [67], PFC [68], and hippocampus [69]. Nicotinic α7 receptors have been proposed to be involved in presynaptic regulation of glutamate release [70]. In support of this hypothesis, *in vivo* focal injection of methyllycaconitine, an inhibitor of α7-containing nAChRs, into the VTA prevents nicotine-induced increases in DA release [71].

A substantial amount of preclinical research suggests the role of glutamatergic, particularly NMDA-receptor, neurotransmission in mediating the behavioral effects of drugs of abuse, including nicotine [72]. This is supported by the observation that stimulation of NMDA receptors on DA neurons in the VTA enhances the proportion of cells that exhibit burst firing [73]. The increases in DA efflux in both the NAc shell and core evoked by either acute or repeated nicotine injections are suppressed or abolished by the administration of NMDA receptor antagonists prior to the nicotine injection, suggesting a pivotal role of glutamate in nicotine's reinforcing effects [74].

### *GABA*

GABA is one of the major inhibitory neurotransmitter in the CNS, and acts via $GABA_A$, $GABA_B$, and $GABA_C$ receptors subtypes [75]. $GABA_A$ receptors are located predominantly on postsynaptic cells and hence, functionally lower their excitability. In contrast, $GABA_B$ receptors are predominantly located on presynaptic terminals, and inhibit presynaptic neurotransmitter release. $GABA_B$ receptors are widely distributed throughout the brain, and can regulate behavior and brain reward processes [76]. DAergic neurons receive descending inhibitory GABAergic input from the ventral pallidum and the NAc [77]. GABAergic neurons in the VTA inhibit mesocorticolimbic DA neurons [78] and nicotine stimulates GABA release transiently by activating mainly the α4β2 nAChRs [11, 12]. Chronic nicotine treatment increases the GABAergic input to projection neurons in the dorsal striatum of mice [79]. Thus, the increase in GABAergic transmission abolishes both the nicotine-induced DA increase in the NAc and the reinforcing effects of nicotine [80]. This is supported by the findings in mice that $GABA_B$ receptor agonists inhibit the reinforcing effects of drugs of abuse including nicotine [76]. The $GABA_B$ receptor agonist baclofen reduces the DA elevations produced by nicotine in the NAc [81] and inhibits the expression of nicotine-induced conditioned place preference in rats [82]. Moreover, activation of GABA receptors decreases nicotine self-administration in rats [83]. Taken together, these findings suggest that medications that increase GABAergic neurotransmission may have potential as anti-smoking treatments for humans.

### *Endocanabinoid System*

The endocannabinoid system has been fund to have an important contributory role in the motivational and reinforcing effects of nicotine [6, 84]. So far, two cannabinoid receptors (CBR) have been identified. CBR1, found mainly in the CNS, has been a significant pharmacological target for research in addiction to drugs including nicotine [85]. Chronic nicotine exposure appears to activate the brain endocannabinoid system in limbic regions, and this could remove the tonic inhibitory GABAergic control on VTA DA neurons via CBR1 [86]. Several lines of preclinical and clinical research indicate that CBR1 antagonists reduce nicotine self-administration behavior, an effect that may be related to the blockade of the DA-releasing effects of nicotine in the brain [87]. The CBR1 antagonist rimonabant abolishes nicotine-induced anxiolytic-like effects and increases the anxiogenic-like responses to nicotine of mice [88], suggesting the involvement of endocannabinoid system in the regulation of nicotine anxiety-like behavior in mice. This hypothesis was further confirmed using genetically modified CBR1 knockout mice [89]. These constitute new findings that support the use of cannabinoid antagonists in the treatment of nicotine addiction.

### *Endogenous Opioid System*

The endogenous opioid system has been suggested to participate in several central effects of nicotine [90]. Opioid receptors and their endogenous ligands are highly expressed in areas of the brain involved in reward such as the VTA, NAc, PFC and extended amygdala [91, 92]. Opioid compounds induce their pharmacological effects by activating three different receptors, μ-, δ-, and κ-opioid receptors [92]. Endogenous opioids seem to participate in mediating the reinforcing effects of nicotine; in particular, the μ-opioid receptor subtype may represent a potential target for selectively reducing nicotine-taking behavior [93].

Furthermore, several behavioral and physiological effects, including antinociception, rewarding properties, withdrawal, and physical dependence [94, 95], are shared by nicotine and opioids. These observations were further supported using knockout mice to reveal the involvement of μ-opioid receptors [96] and peptides derived from preproenkephalin [97] in the antinociceptive effects, rewarding properties and physical dependence induced by nicotine.

### *5-HT*

The serotonin (5-HT) system has been found to play an important role in nicotine dependence [98]. Nicotine not only stimulates the release of 5-HT [99], but also has direct effects on presynaptic re-uptake of 5-HT [100]. 5-HT neurons modulate the functioning of DA neurons in a complex fashion. Much of this complexity arises from the fact that 5-HT exerts its effects through multiple receptor subtypes, some of which even act in apparent functional opposition to each other.

There are several 5-HT subtypes, 5-HT1A, 5-HT2A and 5-HT2C being the most studied. The 5-HT1A receptor may play a role in the symptoms of nicotine withdrawal. There is evidence that a 5-HT1A receptor agonist increases some of the behavioral signs induced by nicotine withdrawal [101]. The 5-HT2C receptor may also play an inhibitory role in nicotine-induced locomotor activity and reward effects [102], suggesting the involvement of the 5-HT2C receptor in mediating mesolimbic DA functioning. The 5-HT2A receptor appears to play a role in potentiating nicotine-induced DA release as indicated by treatment with its receptor agonist [103]. A greater understanding of the 5-HT receptor's roles may lead to new 5-HT-based treatments for nicotine addiction.

### *Norepinephrine*

NE mechanisms have been identified as an additional target for nicotine dependence, but in general have received less attention. For example, NE may be relevant to the modulation of midbrain DA function [104]. Moreover, nicotine releases NE in various CNS regions [105, 106] through several nAChR subtypes [107].

The NE reuptake inhibitor reboxetine attenuates nicotine self-administration [108], an observation with added interest given that the smoking cessation treatment bupropion has an NE component to its action; namely, bupropion acts as an inhibitor of DA and NE transporters as well as nAChRs.

## Involvement of Monoamine Oxidase

Monoamine oxidase (MAO) is involved in the degradation of physiologically active monoamines including DA. Inhibition of MAO activity by MAO inhibitors contained in tobacco smoke may affect on nicotine addiction due to higher levels of DA in the reward circuit, but it is not clear to what extent the known MAO inhibitors in tobacco smoke cause this inhibition. MAO inhibition increases DAergic tone and facilitates the reinforcing effects of addictive drugs including nicotine. In rats, chronic MAO inhibitor treatment enhances the reinforcing effects as well as the motivational properties of nicotine [109], which lead to addiction. The behavioral study has demonstrated that nicotine self-administration was facilitated in rats pre-treated with the irreversible and non-selective MAO inhibitor tranylcypromine [110]. Researchers have found that MAO activity was lower in the brains of smokers; this may be largely due to MAOA inhibitors in tobacco smoke [111]. Several human studies demonstrated an association between high-activity alleles of MAOA and higher levels of nicotine addiction, suggesting a possible role of MAOA gene variants in nicotine dependence [112, 113]. Collectively, these findings may have important implications for addiction prevention and offers the potential for developing patient-specific therapies for smoking cessation.

## NEURONAL FUNCTION

Nicotine is a potent modulator of CNS function, producing a number of physiological, pharmacological and behavioral effects. Nicotine interacts with presynaptic nAChRs to facilitate the release of DA and other neurotransmitters including ACh, NA, 5-HT, GABA and glutamate, many of which have been implicated in mediating/modulating performance on a number of experimental behavioral tasks [114, 115]. The most obvious behavioral action mediated by nAChRs is the addiction to nicotine in tobacco smoke. Undoubtedly the mesolimbic dopaminergic system is central to nicotine addiction, where nicotine stimulates the release of DA [116]. Addiction to nicotine is motivated by both positive and negative reinforcing factors [117].

Positive factors are relaxation, reduced stress, increased vigilance, and improved cognition. Enhanced release of mesolimbic DA through activation of presynaptic nAChRs feasibly mediates these rewarding effects. Negative reinforcing factors are unpleasant withdrawal symptoms including nervousness, restlessness, irritability, anxiety, and impaired concentration and cognition, and may result from reduced stimulation of mesolimbic DA neurons. In a functional MRI study, nicotine induced a dose-dependent increase in several behavioral parameters and neuronal activity in the NAc, amygdala, cingulate, and frontal lobes [118], suggesting that nicotine can activate these brain regions and produce its reinforcing and dependence properties in humans.

## HEALTH EFFECTS

Nicotine has several adverse effects on physical health, but it is the other chemicals taken in along with nicotine that do much of the physiological damage. Nicotine produces a numbers of effects that include addiction and other behavioral and psychological effects in human as well as in animals, although there exists some evidence arguing that nicotine might be of benefit to relieve stress, anxiety, or panic and in therapy for some neurodegenerative diseases such as Alzheimer's disease and Parkinson's disease, and for attention deficit disorder [117].

Repeated exposure to nicotine results in the development of tolerance. Cessation of nicotine use is followed by a withdrawal syndrome that may last a month or more; it includes symptoms that can quickly drive people back to tobacco use. Indeed, nicotine's addictiveness is its primary negative health effect. Nicotine withdrawal symptoms include irritability, craving, cognitive and attention deficits, sleep disturbances, and increased appetite.

## PREVENTION

Nicotine is an addictive substance, and breaking an addiction to nicotine is difficult due to the involvement of several behavioral processes of drug dependence, including reinforcement and withdrawal [1]. In addition, relapse after quitting is very common. Obviously, prevention is the best treatment for nicotine addiction. Several treatment strategies have appeared to be promising interventions to prevent nicotine addiction. Although successful for some, currently available treatments including nicotine replacement strategies and bupropion-antidepressant treatment do not work for everyone. An ideal therapy would likely involve a combination of techniques including counseling and a variety of medicines that target diverse brain mechanisms and account for differences between tobacco users. Some new treatment strategies that are in development would be effective in both the treatment and prevention of nicotine addiction, as well as in the prevention of relapse. A genetic variant in the CYP2A6 enzyme may protect some individuals from nicotine addiction [119, 120]. CYP2A6 is the principal hepatic enzyme that degrades nicotine; however, inhibiting this enzyme decreases the craving felt by smokers, as less nicotine goes further. This strategy could help smokers trying to quit through nicotine replacement therapy (NRT) or any other method, by reducing the amount of replacement nicotine needed to very low doses.

## THERAPEUTIC OPTION

Nicotine substitutes reduce the withdrawal symptoms during the quitting process. Current first-line agents approved by the US Food and Drug Administration (FDA) for smoking cessation include NRT, bupropion, an atypical antidepressant, and varenicline, a partial agonist of $\alpha 4\beta 2$ nAChRs. Of these three, varenicline is the most effective for smoking cessation, followed by bupropion and NRT [121].

All these treatment options are focused on the following areas: (a) reducing withdrawal discomfort, (b) diminishing cravings, (c) blocking rewarding effects, and (d) treating comorbidities of nicotine withdrawal such as depression.

Recently, research has suggested that combining different forms of NRT or simultaneous administering NRT and non-nicotine medications (i.e. bupropion, varenicline) seems the most promising for effective therapy in nicotine addiction [122].

Nicotine vaccine is among newer products seeking approval from the FDA. Figure 1 illustrates the mechanism-based medication strategies for the treatment of nicotine dependence [123].

## NICOTINE THERAPY

NRT (i.e. lozenge, gum, patch, nasal spray, and inhaler) is the first-line treatment for nicotine dependence approved by the FDA. NRT gives smokers the benefit of weaning themselves off of nicotine in a gradual fashion, but it has the disadvantage of a risk for misuse and hypersensitivity.

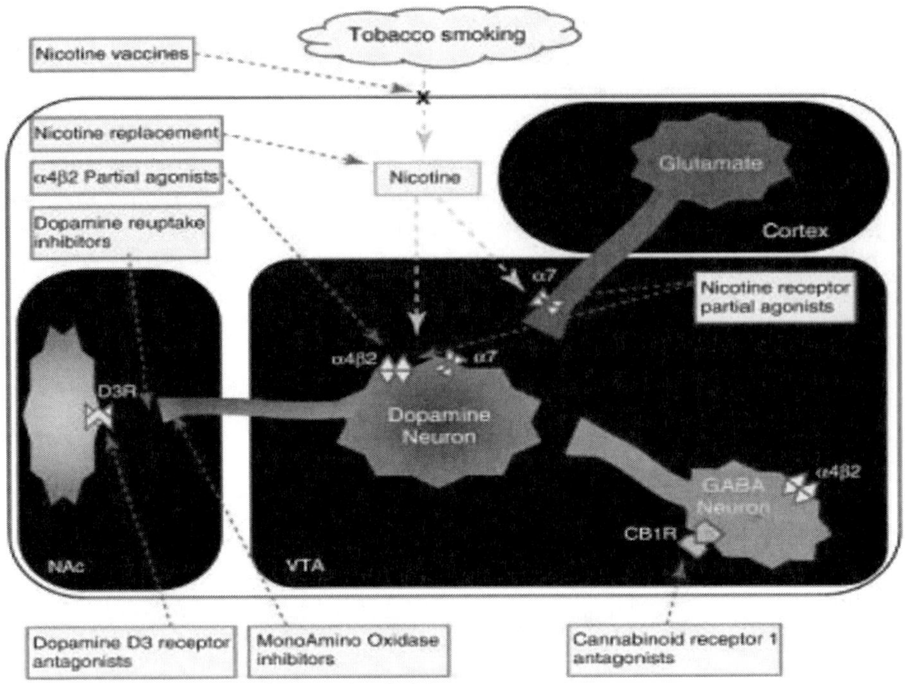


Source: modified from Polosa and Benowitz, 2011.

Figure 1. A simplified diagram of the mesolimbic dopamine projection pathway clearly illustrates the actions of nicotine on extracellular dopamine, glutamate and GABA in the ventral tegmental area, and the sites of action of various mechanism-based pharmacological agents for the treatment of nicotine dependence.

Moreover, it is safe for almost all patients, even those with cardiovascular symptoms [124-126]. There is little to no withdrawal discomfort when patients discontinue NRT use [127]. Its primary mechanism of action is to partially replace the nicotine formerly obtained from tobacco smoking, thereby reducing the severity of withdrawal symptoms and cravings [128]. Differences in formulations of NRT could have a distinct impact upon either withdrawal symptoms or urges to smoke, but there is little direct evidence that one nicotine product is more effective than another. Several lines of studies have demonstrated that all forms of NRT tested produced similar quit rates and were equally effective at reducing the frequency, duration, and severity of urges to smoke [124, 125, 129].

## NON-NICOTINE THERAPY

### Bupropion

Bupropion, an atypical antidepressant, has been approved by FDA as an aid to smoking cessation [130]. Depression is a common withdrawal symptom in people attempting to quit smoking; it is therefore logical that an antidepressant such as bupropion would provide a good basis for smoking cessation treatment. Although its exact mechanism of action is unknown, bupropion is thought to be a nonselective inhibitor of the DA transporter and NE transporter and a partial antagonist of nAChRs, suggesting that alteration of monoamine transporter function may modulate smoking addiction [131, 132]. It has been proposed that inhibition of the DA transporter and NE transporter functions alleviates negative withdrawal symptoms of abstinence; while nAChR antagonism attenuates the rewarding effects of cigarette smoking [133]. Multiple clinical trials have demonstrated that bupropion is an effective aid in facilitating smoking cessation, although, in the majority of cases, the abstinence from smoking was not maintained over the long term [134].

## Varenicline

Partial agonists of α4β2 nAChRs have recently been studied for various neurological disorders such as Alzheimer disease, dementia, [135] and attention deficit or hyperactivity disorder in adults [136]. Varenicline, an α4β2 nAChR partial agonist, has been approved by FDA for smoking cessation [137]. In addition to being an α4β2 nAChR partial agonist, varenicline is also a full α7 nAChR agonist [138]. Varenicline has been found to be more effective than NRT or bupropion in attenuating smoking satisfaction and in relieving craving and withdrawal symptoms after abstinence [115]. Nicotine, through stimulating α4β2 nAChRs, releases DA in the reward pathway. Varenicline elicits moderate and sustained release of DA, which is countered during the cessation attempts; it simultaneously blocks the effects of nicotine by binding with α4β2 nAChRs during smoking, thereby reducing the nicotine-induced DA increase in a dose-dependent manner [139]. This dual action likely creates a ceiling effect on DA release and stabilizes the DAergic status of the mesolimbic pathway, both in the presence and the absence of nicotine from tobacco. Varenicline has also been found to be effective in decreasing nicotine intake in rats [140]. Moreover, prolonged administration of varenicline has been shown to reduce relapse in smokers [141, 142]. The safety profile of varenicline is generally good, with the most commonly occurring adverse event being nausea, insomnia, and headache [143]. However, evidence suggesting a possible association between varenicline and increased psychiatric symptoms [144] prompted the FDA to issue a special warning regarding the use of varenicline in patients with pre-existing psychiatric illness [145].

## Nicotine Vaccine

The nicotine vaccine is a newer strategy being investigated for smoking cessation [146]. The principle of this strategy is to prevent nicotine from entering the brain. The vaccine is designed to bind to nicotine and slow its entry into the brain, thereby reducing the reinforcing effects of nicotine. The nicotine vaccine offers several advantages for those trying to quit: 1) it is safe because of its low cross-reactivity with compounds other than nicotine and only requires a brief series of monthly injections to maintain an adequate antibody titer, 2) The lack of major side effects and relatively minimal dosing requirements could be associated with improved patient compliance, 3) its unique mechanism of action makes it well suited for combination with other pharmacotherapy. Vaccines against nicotine are at an advanced stage of clinical evaluation in many places and three major pharmaceutical companies have reported promising results so far [146].

## Research Advances

Overcoming nicotine addiction can be difficult, due to the involvement of several biobehavioral processes of drug dependence. Nicotine withdrawal symptoms and undesirable effects such as depression serve as justification for those attempting cessation to resume smoking. Several new methods to fight this addiction are in the development stage. Scientists have made some progress in identifying the molecular components of nicotine addiction. Specifically, they have found a particular gene (*neurexin-1*) in the blood of smokers that is essential to the process of nicotine addiction [147, 148]. This finding thereby identifies a promising new site for targeted development of anti-nicotine addiction medications.

Several studies have revealed that some individuals carry a genetic mutation that may help protect them from nicotine addiction [119, 149, 150]. The *Cyp2A6* gene is involved in the metabolic inactivation of nicotine. Individuals with impaired nicotine metabolism, due to carrying a defective version of *Cyp2A6,* are less likely to become addicted to nicotine [119, 150, 151]. Thus, understanding the role of this enzyme in nicotine addiction will give a new target for developing more effective medications to help people stop smoking.

γ-Vinyl GABA (GVG, vigabatrin), an irreversible GABA-transaminase blocking agent, elevates GABA levels in the brain [152]. A large number of animal studies demonstrated that CVG dose-dependently attenuates nicotine-induced increase in extracellular DA in the NAc [80], and it also decreases nicotine self-administration [153] and abolishes both the acquisition and the expression of nicotine-conditioned place preference [154]. In addition, GVG dose-dependently reduces nicotine-induced increase in NAc DA in both naïve and chronically nicotine-treated rats, and blocks nicotine-induced increase in striatal DA in non-human primate (baboon) as measured by positron emission tomography [155]. These results suggest that GVG may have a potential utility as an anti-nicotine therapeutic medication.

Nicotine addiction can upset endocannabinoid system in the brain and numerous data provide evidence for the use CBR1 antagonists in treatment of nicotine addiction. Several clinical and animal studies have shown CBR1 antagonists rimonabant to be effective as an aid for smoking cessation by attenuating the hyperactivation of the endocannabinoid system and the mesolimbic DAnergic neuronal pathway [86, 156], but it has not been approved yet by the FDA owing to concerns about adverse neuropsychiatric effects [157]. Other potential future medications for smoking cessation are MAO inhibitors, which inhibit the metabolism of DA and therefore, increase DA levels in brain, and DA receptor D3 antagonists, which modulate activity of receptors involved in drug-seeking behaviors [158].

## Conclusion

The intent of this chapter is to update readers on research on nicotine addiction, including health effects, prevention and treatment options. Over the past several years, remarkable advances have been made in understanding nicotine addiction. Nicotine addiction is a complex behavioral and neurochemical process in which many neuroanatomical pathways and neurotransmitters are involved. Pathways of DA, glutamate, and GABA release are particularly important in the development of nicotine dependence, and CRF may play a key role in withdrawal. Interestingly, similar pathways and chemicals in the brain are involved in the effects of other addictive drugs. Study of the pleasure and reward pathways and of DA in the brain, for example, will increase understanding of other drugs of abuse as well as nicotine. The neurobiology of addiction not only explains in large part why people become addicted and what happens to the brain after a period of substance misuse, but it also illuminates the effects of current pharmacotherapies and potential new targets for drug development. The findings summarized in this chapter both improve our understanding of nicotine addiction and could suggest new possibilities in the treatment of this major public health disorder.

## ACKNOWLEDGMENT

The authors thank Dr. Haruki Kinoshita for his editorial assistance.

## REFERENCES

[1] Dani, J.A., Heinemann, S. (1996). Molecular and cellular aspects of nicotine abuse. *Neuron*, 16, 905-908.

[2] Pomerleau, C.S., Pomerleau, O.F. (1992). Euphoriant effects of nicotine in smokers. *Psychopharmacology (Berl)*, 108, 460-465.

[3] Grunberg, N.E. (1994). Overview: biological processes relevant to drugs of dependence. *Addiction,* 89, 1443-1446.

[4] Mansvelder, H.D., McGehee, D.S. (2002). Cellular and synaptic mechanisms of nicotine addiction. *J. Neurobiol.,* 53, 606-517.

[5] Zarrindast, M.R., Faraji, N., Rostami, P., Sahraei, H., Ghoshouni, H. (2003). Cross-tolerance between morphine- and nicotine-induced conditioned place preference in mice. *Pharmacol. Biochem. Behav.*, 74, 363-369.

[6] Lupica, C.R., Riegel, A.C. (2005). Endocannabinoid release from midbrain dopamine neurons: a potential substrate for cannabinoid receptor antagonist treatment of addiction. *Neuropharmacology,* 48, 1105-1116.

[7] Henningfield, J.E., Keenan, R.M. (1993). Nicotine delivery kinetics and abuse liability. *J. Consult. Clin. Psychol.*, 61, 743-750.

[8] Schoedel, K.A., Sellers, E.M., Palmour, R., Tyndale, R.F. (2003). Down-regulation of hepatic nicotine metabolism and a CYP2A6-like enzyme in African green monkeys after long-term nicotine administration. *Mol. Pharmacol.*, 63, 96-104.

[9] Rose, J.E., Mukhin, A.G., Lokitz, S.J., Turkington, T.G., Herskovic, J., Behm, F.M., Garg, S., Garg, P.K. (2010). Kinetics of brain nicotine accumulation in dependent and nondependent smokers assessed with PET and cigarettes containing 11C-nicotine. *Proc. Natl. Acad. Sci. USA*, 107, 5190-5195.

[10] Hukkanen, J., Jacob, P. III., Benowitz, N.L. (2005). Metabolism and Disposition Kinetics of Nicotine. *Pharmacol. Rev.*, 57, 79-115.

[11] Zhu, P.J., Chiappinelli, V.A. (1999). Nicotine modulates evoked GABAergic transmission in the brain. *J. Neurophysiol.*, 82, 3041-3045.

[12] Mansvelder, H.D., Keath, J.R., McGehee, D.S. (2002). Synaptic mechanisms underlie nicotine-induced excitability of brain reward areas. *Neuron*, 33, 905-919.

[13] Fu, Y., Matta, S.G., Gao, W., Brower, V.G., Sharp, B.M. (2000). Systemic nicotine stimulates dopamine release in nucleus accumbens: re-evaluation of the role of N-methyl-D-aspartate receptors in the ventral tegmental area. *J. Pharmacol. Exp. Ther.*, 294, 458-465.

[14] Grillner, P., Svensson, T.H. (2000). Nicotine-induced excitation of midbrain dopamine neurons in vitro involves ionotropic glutamate receptor activation. *Synapse*, 38:1-9.

[15] Rusted, J.M., Newhouse, P.A., Levin, E.D. (2000). Nicotinic treatment for degenerative neuropsychiatric disorders such as Alzheimer's disease and Parkinson's disease. *Behav. Brain Res.*, 113, 121-129.

[16] Lawrence, N.S., Ross, T.J., Stein, E.A. (2002). Cognitive mechanisms of nicotine on visual attention. *Neuron*, 36, 539-548.

[17] Kumari, V., Gray, J.A., ffytche, D.H., Mitterschiffthaler, M.T., Das, M., Zachariah, E., Vythelingum, G.N., Williams, S.C., Simmons, A., Sharma, T. (2003). Cognitive effects of nicotine in humans: an fMRI study. *Neuroimage,* 19, 1002-1013.

[18] Govind, A.P., Vezina, P., Green, W.N. (2009). Nicotine-induced upregulation of nicotinic receptors: underlying mechanisms and relevance to nicotine addiction. *Biochem. Pharmacol.,* 78, 756-765.

[19] Sokolova, E., Matteoni, C., Nistri, A. (2005). Desensitization of neuronal nicotinic receptors of human neuroblastoma SH-SY5Y cells during short or long exposure to nicotine. *Br. J. Pharmacol.*, 146, 1087-1095.

[20] Jackson, K.J, Martin, B.R., Changeux, J.P., Damaj, M.I. (2008). Differential role of nicotinic acetylcholine receptor subunits in physical and affective nicotine withdrawal signs. *J. Pharmacol. Exp. Ther.,* 325, 302-312.

[21] Hildebrand, B.E., Nomikos, G.G., Hertel, P., Schilström, B., Svensson, T.H. (1998). Reduced dopamine output in the nucleus accumbens but not in the medial prefrontal cortex in rats displaying a mecamylamine-precipitated nicotine withdrawal syndrome. *Brain Res.*, 779, 214-225.

[22] Slotkin, T.A., Seidler, F.J. (2007). A unique role for striatal serotonergic systems in the withdrawal from adolescent nicotine administration. *Neurotoxicol. Teratol.,* 29, 10-16.

[23] Bruijnzeel, A.W., Bishnoi, M., van Tuijl, I.A., Keijzers, K.F., Yavarovich, K.R., Pasek, T.M., Ford, J., Alexander, J.C., Yamada, H. (2010). Effects of prazosin, clonidine, and propranolol on the elevations in brain reward thresholds and somatic signs associated with nicotine withdrawal in rats. *Psychopharmacology (Berl)*, 212, 485-499.

[24] Marcinkiewcz, C.A., Prado, M.M., Isaac, S.K., Marshall, A., Rylkova, D., Bruijnzeel, A.W. (2009). Corticotropin-releasing factor within the central nucleus of the amygdala and the nucleus accumbens shell mediates the negative affective state of nicotine withdrawal in rats. *Neuropsychopharmacology,* 34, 1743-1752.

[25] George, O., Ghozland, S., Azar, M.R., Cottone, P., Zorrilla, E.P., Parsons, L.H., O'Dell, L.E., Richardson, H.N., Koob, G.F. (2007). CRF-CRF1 system activation mediates withdrawal-induced increases in nicotine self-administration in nicotine-dependent rats. *Proc. Natl. Acad. Sci. USA,* 104, 17198-17203.

[26] Hellström-Lindahl, E., Mousavi, M., Zhang, X., Ravid, R., Nordberg, A. (1999). Regional distribution of nicotinic receptor subunit mRNAs in human brain: comparison between Alzheimer and normal brain. *Brain Res. Mol. Brain Res.,* 66, 94-103.

[27] Adem, A., Jossan, S.S., d'Argy, R., Brandt, I., Winblad, B., Nordberg, A. (1988). Distribution of nicotinic receptors in human thalamus as visualized by 3H-nicotine and 3H-acetylcholine receptor autoradiography. *J. Neural. Transm.*, 73, 77-83.

[28] Xu, J., Zhu, Y. Heinemann, S.F. (2006). Identification of sequence motifs that target neuronal nicotinic receptors to dendrites and axons. *J. Neurosci.*, 26, 9780-9793.

[29] Dajas-Bailador, F., Wonnacott, S. (2004). Nicotinic acetylcholine receptors and the regulation of neuronal signalling. *Trends Pharmacol. Sci.*, 25, 317-324.

[30] Paterson, D., Nordberg, A. (2000). Neuronal nicotinic receptors in the human brain. *Prog. Neurobiol.,* 61, 75-111.

[31] Buisson, B. Bertrand, D. (2002). Nicotine addiction: the possible role of functional upregulation. *Trends Pharmacol. Sci.,* 23, 130-136.

[32] Gotti, C., Fornasari, D., Clementi, F. (1997). Human neuronal nicotinic receptors. *Prog. Neurobiol.*, 53, 199-237.

[33] Quick, M.W., Lester, R.A. (2002). Desensitization of neuronal nicotinic receptors. *J. Neurobiol.,* 53, 457-478.

[34] Wooltorton, J.R., Pidoplichko, V.I., Broide, R.S., Dani, J.A. (2003). Differential desensitization and distribution of nicotinic acetylcholine receptor subtypes inmidbrain dopamine areas. *J. Neurosci.*, 23, 3176-3185.

[35] Giniatullin, R., Nistri, A., Yakel, J.L. (2005). Desensitization of nicotinic ACh receptors: shaping cholinergic signaling. *Trends Neurosci.*, 28, 371-378.

[36] Alkondon, M., Albuquerque, E.X. (2005). Nicotinic receptor subtypes in rat hippocampal slices are differentially sensitive to desensitization and early in vivo functional up-regulation by nicotine and to block by bupropion. *J. Pharmacol. Exp. Ther.*, 313, 740-750.

[37] Aberger, K., Chitravanshi, V.C., Sapru, H.N. (2001). Cardiovascular responses to microinjections of nicotine into the caudal ventrolateral medulla of the rat. *Brain Res.*, 892, 138-146.

[38] Exley, R., Maubourguet, N., David, V., Eddine, R., Evrard, A., Pons, S., Marti, F., Threlfell, S., Cazala, P., McIntosh, J.M., Changeux, J.P., Maskos, U., Cragg, S.J., Faure, P. (2011). Distinct contributions of nicotinic acetylcholine receptor subunit alpha4 and subunit alpha6 to the reinforcing effects of nicotine. *Proc. Natl. Acad. Sci. U S A*, 108, 7577-7582.

[39] Jackson, K.J., Marks, M.J., Vann, R.E., Chen, X., Gamage, T.F., Warner, J.A., Damaj, M.I. (2010). Role of alpha5 nicotinic acetylcholine receptors in pharmacological and behavioral effects of nicotine in mice. *J. Pharmacol. Exp. Ther.*, 334, 137-146.

[40] Fowler, C.D., Lu, Q., Johnson, P.M., Marks, M.J., Kenny, P.J. (2011). Habenular α5 nicotinic receptor subunit signalling controls nicotine intake. *Nature*, 471, 597-501.

[41] Drenan, R.M., Grady, S.R., Steele, A.D., McKinney, S., Patzlaff, N.E., McIntosh, J.M., Marks, M.J., Miwa, J.M., Lester, H.A. (2010). Cholinergic modulation of locomotion and striatal dopamine release is mediated by alpha6alpha4 nicotinic acetylcholine receptors. *J. Neurosci.,* 30, 9877-9889.

[42] Quik, M., Perez, X.A., Grady, S.R. (2011). Role of α6 nicotinic receptors in CNS dopaminergic function: Relevance to addiction and neurological disorders. *Biochem. Pharmacol.,* doi:10.1016/j.bcp. 2011.06.001.

[43] Walsh, H., Govind, A.P., Mastro, R., Hoda, J.C., Bertrand, D., Vallejo, Y., Green, W.N. (2008). Up-regulation of nicotinic receptors by nicotine varies with receptor subtype. *J. Biol. Chem.*, 283, 6022-6032.

[44] Clarke, P.B., Reuben, M. (1996). Release of [3H]-noradrenaline from rat hippocampal synaptosomes by nicotine: mediation by different nicotinic receptor subtypes from striatal [3H]-dopamine release. *Br. J. Pharmacol.,* 117, 595-606.

[45] Wilkie, G.I., Hutson, P.H., Stephens, M.W., Whiting, P., Wonnacott, S. (1993). Hippocampal nicotinic autoreceptors modulate acetylcholine release. *Biochem. Soc. Trans.,* 21, 429-431.

[46] Gao, M., Jin, Y., Yang, K., Zhang, D., Lukas, R.J., Wu, J. (2010). Mechanisms involved in systemic nicotine-induced glutamatergic synaptic plasticity on dopamine neurons in the ventral tegmental area. *J. Neurosci.*, 30, 13814-13825.

[47] Yang, X., Criswell, H.E., Breese, G.R. (1996). Nicotine-induced inhibition in medial septum involves activation of presynaptic nicotinic cholinergic receptors on gamma-aminobutyric acid-containing neurons. *J. Pharmacol. Exp. Ther.,* 276, 482-489.

[48] Breese, C.R., Marks, M.J., Logel, J., Adams, C.E., Sullivan, B., Collins, A.C., Leonard, S. (1997). Effect of smoking history on [3H]nicotine binding in human postmortem brain. *J. Pharmacol. Exp. Ther.*, 282, 7-13.

[49] Benwell ,M.E., Balfour, D.J., Anderson, J.M. (1988). Evidence that tobacco smoking increases the density of (-)-[3H]nicotine binding sites in human brain. *J. Neurochem.,* 50, 1243-1247.

[50] Koob, G.F., Le Moal, M. (2008). Neurobiological mechanisms for opponent motivational processes in addiction. *Philos. Trans. R Soc. Lond. B Biol. Sci.*, 363, 3113-3123.

[51] De Biasi, M., Dani, J.A. (2011). Reward, addiction, withdrawal to nicotine. *Annu. Rev. Neurosci.,* 34, 105-130.

[52] Kleijn, J., Folgering, J.H., van der Hart, M.C., Rollema, H., Cremers, T.I., Westerink, B.H. (2011). Direct effect of nicotine on mesolimbic dopamine release in rat nucleus accumbens shell. *Neurosci. Lett.*, 493, 55-58.

[53] Corrigall, W.A., Coen, K.M. (1991). Selective dopamine antagonists reduce nicotine self-administration. *Psychopharmacology*, 104, 171-176.

[54] Corrigall, W.A., Franklin, K.B.J., Coen, K.M., Clarke, P.B.S. (1992). The mesolimbic dopaminergic system is implicated in the reinforcing effects of nicotine. *Psychopharmacology,* 107, 285-289.

[55] O'Neill, M.F., Dourish, C.T., Iversen, S.D. (1991). Evidence for an involvement of D1 and D2 dopamine receptors in mediating nicotine-induced hyperactivity in rats. *Psychopharmacology (Berl)*, 104, 343-350.

[56] Nisell, M., Nomikos, G.G., Svensson, T.H. (1995). Nicotine dependence, midbrain dopamine systems and psychiatric disorders. *Pharmacol. Toxicol.*, 76, 157-162.

[57] Nisell, M., Nomikos, G.G., Svensson, T.H. (1994). Infusion of nicotine in the ventral tegmental area or the nucleus accumbens of the rat differentially affects accumbal dopamine release. *Pharmacol. Toxicol.*, 75, 348-352.

[58] Clarke, P.B., Pert, A. (1985). Autoradiographic evidence for nicotine receptors on nigrostriatal and mesolimbic dopaminergic neurons. *Brain Res.*, 348, 355-358.
[59] Zhou, F.M., Wilson, C., Dani, J.A. (2003). Muscarinic and nicotinic cholinergic mechanisms in the mesostriatal dopamine systems. *Neuroscientist*, 9, 23-36.
[60] Jones, S., Sudweeks, S., Yakel, J.L. (1999). Nicotinic receptors in the brain: correlating physiology with function. *Trends Neurosci.*, 22, 555-561.
[61] Dani, J.A., De Biasi, M. (2001). Cellular mechanisms of nicotine addiction. *Pharmacol. Biochem. Behav.*, 70, 439-446.
[62] Watkins, S.S., Epping-Jordan, M.P., Koob, G.F. (1999). Blockade of nicotine self-administration with nicotinic antagonists in rats. *Pharmacol. Biochem. Behav.*, 62, 743-751.
[63] Picciotto, M.R., Zoli, M., Rimondini, R., Léna, C., Marubio, L.M., Pich, E.M., Fuxe, K., Changeux, J.P. (1998). Acetylcholine receptors containing the beta2 subunit are involved in the reinforcing properties of nicotine. *Nature*, 391, 173-177.
[64] Marubio, L.M., Gardier, A.M., Durier, S. (2003). Effects of nicotine in the dopaminergic system of mice lacking the alpha4 subunit of neuronal nicotinic acetylcholine receptors. *Eur. J. Neurosci.*, 17, 1329-1337.
[65] Liechti, M.E., Markou, A. (2008). Role of the glutamatergic system in nicotine dependence: implications for the discovery and development of new pharmacological smoking cessation therapies. *CNS Drugs*, 22, 705-724.
[66] Schilstrom, B., Nomikos, G.G., Nisell, M., Hertel, P., Svensson, T.H. (1998). N-methyl-D-aspartate receptor antagonism in the ventral tegmental area diminishes the systemic nicotine-induced dopamine release in the nucleus accumbens, *Neuroscience*, 82, 781-789.
[67] Reid, M.S., Fox, L., Ho, L.B., Berger, S.P. (2000). Nicotine stimulation of extracellular glutamate levels in the nucleus accumbens: neuropharmacological characterization. *Synapse*, 35, 129-136.
[68] Gioanni, Y., Rougeot, C., Clarke, P.B., Lepousé, C., Thierry, A.M., Vidal, C. (1999). Nicotinic receptors in the rat prefrontal cortex: increase in glutamate release and facilitation of mediodorsal thalamo-cortical transmission. *Eur. J. Neurosci.*, 11, 18-30.
[69] Bancila, V., Cordeiro, J.M., Bloc, A., Dunant, Y. (2009). Nicotine-induced and depolarisation-induced glutamate release from hippocampus mossy fibre synaptosomes: two distinct mechanisms. *J. Neurochem.*, 110, 570-580.
[70] Mansvelder, H.D. McGehee, D.S. (2000). Long-term potentiation of excitatory inputs to brain reward areas by nicotine. *Neuron* 27, 349-357.
[71] Schilström, B., Svensson, H.M., Svensson, T.H., Nomikos, G.G. (1998). Nicotine and food induced dopamine release in the nucleus accumbens of the rat: putative role of alpha7 nicotinic receptors in the ventral tegmental area. *Neuroscience*, 85, 1005-1009.
[72] Jain, R., Mukherjee, K., Balhara, Y.P. (2008). The Role of NMDA Receptor Antagonists in Nicotine Tolerance, Sensitization, and Physical Dependence: A Preclinical Review. *Yonsei Med. J.*, 49, 175-188.
[73] Chergui, K., Charléty, P.J., Akaoka, H., Saunier, C.F., Brunet, J.L., Buda, M., Svensson, T.H., Chouvet, G. (1993). Tonic activation of NMDA receptors causes spontaneous burst discharge of rat midbrain dopamine neurons in vivo. *Eur. J. Neurosci.*, 5, 137-144.

[74] Kosowski, A.R., Cebers, G., Cebere, A., Swanhagen, A.C., Liljequist, S. (2004). Nicotine-induced dopamine release in the nucleus accumbens is inhibited by the novel AMPA antagonist ZK200775 and the NMDA antagonist CGP39551. *Psychopharmacology (Berl),* 175, 114-123.

[75] Bormann, J., *Feigenspan, A. (1995).* GABA-C receptors. *Trends Neurosci.,* 18, 515-519.

[76] Vlachou, S., Markou, A. (2010). GABAB receptors in reward processes. *Adv. Pharmacol.*, 58, 315-371.

[77] Sugita, S., Johnson, S.W., North, R.A. (1992). Synaptic inputs to GABAA and GABAB receptors originate from discrete afferent neurons. *Neurosci. Lett.*, 134, 207-211.

[78] Steffensen, S.C., Svingos, A.L, Pickel, V.M., Henriksen, S.J. (1998). Electrophysiological characterization of GABAergic neurons in the ventral tegmental area. *J. Neurosci.*, 18, 8003-8015.

[79] Miura, M., Ishii, K., Aosaki, T., Sumikawa, K. (2006). Chronic nicotine treatment increases GABAergic input to striatal neurons. *Neuroreport,* 17, 537-540.

[80] Dewey, S.L., Brodie, J.D., Gerasimov, M., Horan, B., Gardner, E.L., Ashby, C.R. Jr. (1999). A pharmacologic strategy for the treatment of nicotine addiction. *Synapse*, 31, 76-86.

[81] Fadda, P., Scherma, M., Fresu, A., Collu, M., Fratta, W. (2003). Baclofen antagonizes nicotine-, cocaine-, and morphine-induced dopamine release in the nucleus accumbens of rat. *Synapse*, 50, 1-6.

[82] Le Foll, B., Wertheim, C.E., Goldberg, S.R. (2008). Effects of baclofen on conditioned rewarding and discriminative stimulus effects of nicotine in rats. *Neurosci. Lett.*, 443, 236-240.

[83] Paterson, N.E., Froestl, W., Markou, A. (2004). The GABAB receptor agonists baclofen and CGP44532 decreased nicotine self-administration in the rat. *Psychopharmacology (Berl),* 172, 179-186.

[84] Maldonado, R., Valverde, O., Berrendero, F. (2006). Involvement of the endocannabinoid system in drug addiction. *Trends Neurosci.*, 29, 225-232.

[85] Le Foll, B., Goldberg, S.R. (2005). Cannabinoid $CB_1$ receptor antagonists as promising new medications for drug dependence. *J. Pharmacol. Exp. Ther.*, 312, 875-883.

[86] Cohen, C., Kodas, E., Griebel, G. (2005). CB1 receptor antagonists for the treatment of nicotine addiction. *Pharmacol. Biochem. Behav.,* 81, 387-395.

[87] Le Foll, B., Forget, B., Aubin, H.J., Goldberg, S.R. (2008). Blocking cannabinoid CB1 receptors for the treatment of nicotine dependence: insights from pre-clinical and clinical studies. *Addict. Biol.*, 13, 239-252.

[88] Balerio, G.N., Aso, E., Maldonado, R. (2006). Role of the cannabinoid system in the effects induced by nicotine on anxiety-like behaviour in mice. *Psychopharmacology (Berl)*, 184, 504-513.

[89] Valverde, O., Karsak, M., Zimmer, A. (2005). Analysis of the endocannabinoid system by using CB1 cannabinoid receptor knockout mice. *Handb. Exp. Pharmacol.*, 168, 117-145.

[90] Balfour, D.J. (1982). The effects of nicotine on brain neurotransmitter systems. *Pharmacol. Ther.*, 16, 269-282.

[91] Delfs, J.M., Kong, H., Mestek, A., Chen, Y., Yu, L., Reisine, T., Chesselet, M.F. (1994). Expression of mu opioid receptor mRNA in rat brain: an in situ hybridization study at the single cell level. *J. Comp. Neurol.*, 345, 46-68.

[92] Mansour, A., Fox, C.A., Burke, S., Meng, F., Thompson, R.C., Akil, H., Watson, S.J. (1994). Mu, delta, kappa opioid receptor mRNA expression in the rat CNS: an in situ hybridization study. *J. Comp. Neurol.*, 350, 412-438.

[93] Ismayilova, N., Shoaib, M. (2010). Alteration of intravenous nicotine self-administration by opioid receptor agonist and antagonists in rats. *Psychopharmacology (Berl)*, 210, 211-220.

[94] Biała, G., Budzyńska, B., Kruk, M. (2005). Naloxone precipitates nicotine abstinence syndrome and attenuates nicotine-induced antinociception in mice. *Pharmacological Reports*, 57, 755-760.

[95] Watkins, S.S., Stinus, L., Koob, G.F., Markou, A. (2000). Reward and somatic changes during precipitated nicotine withdrawal in rats: centrally and peripherally mediated effects. *J. Pharmacol. Exp. Ther.*, 292, 1053-1064.

[96] Berrendero, F., Kieffer, B.L., Maldonado, R. (2002). Attenuation of nicotine-induced antinociception, rewarding effects, and dependence in mu-opioid receptor knock-out mice. *J. Neurosci.*, 22, 10935-10940.

[97] Berrendero, F., Mendizabal, V., Robledo, P., Galeote, L., Bilkei-Gorzo, A., Zimmer, A., Maldonado, R. (2005). Nicotine-induced antinociception, rewarding effects, and physical dependence are decreased in mice lacking the preproenkephalin gene. *J. Neurosci.*, 25, 1103-1112.

[98] Olausson, P., Engel, J.A., Söderpalm, B. (2002). Involvement of serotonin in nicotine dependence: processes relevant to positive and negative regulation of drug intake. *Pharmacol. Biochem. Behav.*, 71, 757-771.

[99] Li, X., Rainnie, D.G., McCarley, R.W., Greene, R.W. (1998). Presynaptic nicotinic receptors facilitate monoaminergic transmission. *J. Neurosci.*, 18, 1904-1912.

[100] Engberg, G. (1992). Citalopram and 8-OH-DPAT attenuate nicotine-induced excitation of central noradrenaline neurons. *J. Neural. Transm. Gen. Sect.*, 89, 149-154.

[101] Rasmussen, K., Czachura, J.F. (1997). Nicotine withdrawal leads to increased sensitivity of serotonergic neurons to the 5-HT1A agonist 8-OH-DPAT. *Psychopharmacology (Berl)*, 133, 343-346.

[102] Grottick ,A.J., Corrigall, W.A., Higgins, G.A. (2001). Activation of 5-HT(2C) receptors reduces the locomotor and rewarding effects of nicotine. *Psychopharmacology (Berl)*, 157, 292-298.

[103] Scarlota, L.C., Harvey, J.A., Aloyo, V.J. (2011). The role of serotonin-2 (5-HT2) and dopamine receptors in the behavioral actions of the 5-HT2A/2C agonist, DOI, and putative 5-HT2C inverse agonist, SR46349B. *Psychopharmacology (Berl)*, 213, 393-401.

[104] Linnér, L., Endersz, H., Ohman, D., Bengtsson, F., Schalling, M., Svensson, T.H. (2001). Reboxetine modulates the firing pattern of dopamine cells in the ventral tegmental area and selectively increases dopamine availability in the prefrontal cortex. *J. Pharmacol. Exp. Ther.*, 297, 540-546.

[105] Summers, K.L., Giacobini, E. (1995). Effects of local and repeated systemic administration of (-) nicotine on extracellular levels of acetylcholine, norepinephrine, dopamine, and serotonin in rat cortex. *Neurochem. Res.*, 20, 753-759.

[106] Fu, Y., Matta, S.G., Valentine, J.D., Sharp, B.M. (1997). Adrenocorticotropin response and nicotine-induced norepinephrine secretion in the rat paraventricular nucleus are mediated through brainstem receptors. *Endocrinology*, 138, 1935-1943.

[107] Fu, Y., Matta, S.G., James, T.J., Sharp, B.M. (1998). Nicotine-induced norepinephrine release in the rat amygdala and hippocampus is mediated through brainstem nicotinic cholinergic receptors. *J. Pharmacol. Exp. Ther.*, 84, 1188-1196.

[108] Rauhut, A.S., Mullins, S.N., Dwoskin, L.P., Bardo, M.T. (2002). Reboxetine: attenuation of intravenous nicotine self-administration in rats. *J. Pharmacol. Exp. Ther.*, 303, 664-672.

[109] Guillem, K., Vouillac, C., Azar, M.R., Parsons, L.H., Koob, G.F, Cador, M., Stinus, L. (2005). Monoamine oxidase inhibition dramatically increases the motivation to self-administer nicotine in rats. *J. Neurosci.*, 25, 8593-8600.

[110] Villégier, A.S., Lotfipour, S., McQuown, S.C., Belluzzi, J.D., Leslie, F.M. (2007). Tranylcypromine enhancement of nicotine self-administration. *Neuropharmacology*, 52, 1415-1425.

[111] Fowler, J.S., Volkow, N.D., Wang, G.J., Pappas, N., Logan, J., Shea, C., Alexoff, D., MacGregor, R.R., Schlyer, D.J., Zezulkova, I. (1996). Brain monoamine oxidase A inhibition in cigarette smokers. *Proc. Natl. Acad. Sci. USA*, 93, 14065-14069.

[112] McKinney, E.F., Walton, R.T., Yudkin, P., Fuller, A., Haldar, N.A., Mant, D., Murphy, M., Welsh, K.I., Marshall, S.E. (2000). Association between polymorphisms in dopamine metabolic enzymes and tobacco consumption in smokers. *Pharmacogenetics*, 10, 483-491.

[113] Ito, H., Hamajima, N., Matsuo, K., Okuma, K., Sato, S., Ueda, R., Tajima, K. (2003). Monoamine oxidase polymorphisms and smoking behaviour in Japanese. *Pharmacogenetics*, 13, 73-79.

[114] Wonnacott, S. (1997). Presynaptic nicotinic ACh receptors. *Trends Neurosci.*, 20, 92-98.

[115] McGehee, D.S., Role, L.W. (1995). Physiological diversity of nicotinic acetylcholine receptors expressed by vertebrate neurons. *Annu. Rev. Physiol.*, 57, 521-546.

[116] Pich, E.M., Pagliusi, S.R., Tessari, M., Talabot-Ayer, D., Hooft van Huijsduijnen, R., Chiamulera, C. (1997). Common neural substrates for the addictive properties of nicotine and cocaine. *Science*, 275, 83-86.

[117] Benowitz, NL. (1996). Pharmacology of nicotine: addiction and therapeutics. *Annu. Rev. Pharmacol. Toxicol.*, 36, 597-513.

[118] Stein, E.A., Pankiewicz, J., Harsch, H.H., Cho, J.K., Fuller, S.A., Hoffmann, R.G., Hawkins, M., Rao, S.M., Bandettini, P.A., Bloom, A.S. (1998). Nicotine-induced limbic cortical activation in the human brain: a functional MRI study. *Am. J. Psychiatry*, 155, 1009-1015.

[119] Audrain-McGovern, J., Al Koudsi, N., Rodriguez, D., Wileyto, E.P., Shields, P.G., Tyndale, R.F. (2007). The role of CYP2A6 in the emergence of nicotine dependence in adolescents. *Pediatrics*, 119, e264-274.

[120] Ho, M.K., Mwenifumbo, J.C., Zhao, B., Gillam, E.M., Tyndale, R.F. (2008). A novel CYP2A6 allele, CYP2A6*23, impairs enzyme function in vitro and in vivo and decreases smoking in a population of Black-African descent. *Pharmacogenet Genomics*, 18, 67-75.

[121] Sicras Mainar, A., Navarro Artieda, R., Díaz Cerezo, S., Martí Sánchez, B., Sanz De Burgoa, V. (2011). Abstinence rates with varenicline compared to bupropion and nicotine replacement therapy for quitting smoking in Primary Care. Aten Primaria, doi:10.1016/j.aprim. 2010.09.010.

[122] Raupach, T., van Schayck, C.P. (2011). Pharmacotherapy for smoking cessation: current advances and research topics. *CNS Drugs*, 25, 371-382.

[123] Polosa, R., Benowitz, N.L. (2011). Treatment of nicotine addiction: present therapeutic options and pipeline developments. *Trends Pharmacol. Sci.*, 32, 281-289.

[124] Joseph, A.M., Norman, S.M., Ferry, L.H., Prochazka, A.V., Westman, E.C., Steele, B.G., Sherman, S.E., Cleveland, M., Antonuccio, D.O., Hartman, N., McGovern, P.G. (1996). The safety of transdermal nicotine as an aid to smoking cessation in patients with cardiac disease. *N. Engl. J. Med.*, 335, 1792-1798.

[125] Hajek, P., West, R., Foulds, J., Nilsson, F., Burrows, S., Meadow, A. (1999). Randomized comparative trial of nicotine polacrilex, a transdermal patch, nasal spray, and an inhaler. *Arch. Intern. Med.*, 159, 2033-2038.

[126] Tønnesen, P. Mikkelsen, K.L. (2000). Smoking cessation with four nicotine replacement regimes in a lung clinic. *Eur. Respir. J.*, 16, 717-722.

[127] West, R., Hajek, P., Foulds, J., Nilsson, F., May, S., Meadows, A. (2000). A comparison of the abuse liability and dependence potential of nicotine patch, gum, spray and inhaler. *Psychopharmacology (Berl)*, 149, 198-202.

[128] Gross, J. Stitzer, M.L. (1989). Nicotine replacement: ten-week effects on tobacco withdrawal symptoms. *Psychopharmacology (Berl)*, 98, 334-341.

[129] Stead, L.F., Perera, R., Bullen, C., Mant, D., Lancaster, T. (2008). Nicotine replacement therapy for smoking cessation. *Cochrane Database Syst. Rev.*, 1:CD000146.

[130] Dwoskin, L.P., Rauhut, A.S., King-Pospisil, K.A., Bardo, M.T. (2006). Review of the pharmacology and clinical profile of bupropion, an antidepressant and tobacco use cessation agent. *CNS Drug Rev.*, 12, 178-207.

[131] Paterson, N.E., Balfour, D.J., Markou, A. (2007). Chronic bupropion attenuated the anhedonic component of nicotine withdrawal in rats via inhibition of dopamine reuptake in the nucleus accumbens shell. *Eur. J. Neurosci.*, 25, 3099-3108.

[132] Danielson, K., Truman, P., Kivell, B.M. (2011). The effects of nicotine and cigarette smoke on the monoamine transporters. *Synapse*, 65, 866-879.

[133] Paterson, N.E. (2009). Behavioural and pharmacological mechanisms of bupropion's anti-smoking effects: Recent preclinical and clinical insights. *Eur. J. Pharmacol.*, 603, 1-11.

[134] Hughes, J.R., Goldstein, M.G., Hurt, R.D., Shiffman, S. (1999). Recent advances in the pharmacotherapy of smoking. *JAMA*, 281, 72-76.

[135] Araki, H., Suemaru, K., Gomita, Y. (2002). Neuronal nicotinic receptor and psychiatric disorders: functional and behavioral effects of nicotine. *Jpn. J. Pharmacol.*, 88, 133-138.

[136] Wilens, T.E., Verlinden, M.H., Adler, L.A., Wozniak, P.J., West, S.A. (2006). ABT-089, a neuronal nicotinic receptor partial agonist, for the treatment of attention-deficit/hyperactivity disorder in adults: results of a pilot study. *Biol. Psychiatry*, 59, 1065-1070.

[137] Singh, J., Budhiraja, S. (2008). Partial nicotinic acetylcholine (alpha4beta2) agonists as promising new medications for smoking cessation. *Indian J. Pharmacol.*, 40, 191-196.

[138] Mihalak, K.B., Carroll, F.I., Luetje, C.W. (2006). Varenicline is a partial agonist at alpha4beta2 and a full agonist at alpha7 neuronal nicotinic receptors. *Mol. Pharmacol.*, 70, 801-805.

[139] Rollema, H., Coe, J.W., Chambers, L.K., Hurst, R.S., Stahl, S.M., Williams, K.E. (2007). Rationale, pharmacology and clinical efficacy of partial agonists of alpha4beta2 nACh receptors for smoking cessation. *Trends Pharmacol. Sci.*, 28, 316-325.

[140] George, O., Lloyd, A., Carroll, F.I., Damaj, M.I., Koob, G.F. (2011). Varenicline blocks nicotine intake in rats with extended access to nicotine self-administration. *Psychopharmacology (Berl)*, 213, 715-722.

[141] Stack, N.M. (2007). Smoking cessation: an overview of treatment options with a focus on varenicline. *Pharmacotherapy*, 27, 1550-1157.

[142] Hajek, P., Stead, L.F., West, R., Jarvis, M., Lancaster, T. (2009). Relapse prevention interventions for smoking cessation. *Cochrane Database Syst. Rev.*, 21:CD003999.

[143] Hays, J.T., Ebbert, J.O., Sood, A. (2008). Efficacy and safety of varenicline for smoking cessation. *Am. J. Med.*, 121, S32-42.

[144] Patterson, F., Jepson, C., Strasser, A.A., Loughead, J., Perkins, K.A., Gur, R.C., Frey, J.M., Siegel, S., Lerman, C. (2009). Varenicline improves mood and cognition during smoking abstinence. *Biol. Psychiatry*, 65, 144-149.

[145] Lorenz, R.A., Whitley, H.P., McCoy, E.K. (2010). Safety of Varenicline in Patients with Mental Illness. *Primary Psychiatry*, 17, 60-66.

[146] Escobar-Chávez, J.J., Domínguez-Delgado, C.L., Rodríguez-Cruz, I.M. (2011). Targeting nicotine addiction: the possibility of a therapeutic vaccine. *Drug Des. Devel. Ther.*, 5, 211-224.

[147] Nussbaum, J., Xu, Q., Payne, T.J., Ma, J.Z., Huang, W., Gelernter, J., Li, M.D. (2008). Significant association of the neurexin-1 gene (NRXN1) with nicotine dependence in European and African-American smokers. *Human Mol. Genetics*, 17, 1569-1577.

[148] Bierut, L.J, Madden, P.A.F., Breslau, N., Johnson, E.O., Hatsukami, D., Pomerleau, O.F, Swan, G.E., Rutter, J., Bertelsen, S., Fox, L., Fugman, D., Goate, A.M., Hinrichs, A.L., Konvicka, K., Martin, N.G., Montgomery, G.W., Saccone, N.L., Saccone, S.F., Wang, J.C., Chase, G.A., Rice, J.P., Ballinger, D.G. (2007). Novel genes identified in a high-density genome wide association study for nicotine dependence. *Human Mol. Genetics*, 16, 24-35.

[149] Kubota, T., Nakajima-Taniguchi, C., Fukuda, T., Funamoto, M., Maeda, M., Tange, E., Ueki, R., Kawashima, K., Hara, H., Fujio, Y., Azuma, J. (2006). CYP2A6 polymorphisms are associated with nicotine dependence and influence withdrawal symptoms in smoking cessation. *Pharmacogenomics J.*, 6, 115-119.

[150] Tyndale, R.F., Pianezza, M.L., Sellers, E.M. (1999). A common genetic defect in nicotine metabolism decreases risk for dependence and lowers cigarette consumption. *Nicotine Tob. Res., 1 Supp*l 2, S63-67.

[151] Mwenifumbo, J.C., Lessov-Schlaggar, C.N., Zhou, Q., Krasnow, R.E., Swan, G.E., Benowitz, N.L., Tyndale, R.F. (2008). Identification of novel CYP2A6*1B variants: the CYP2A6*1B allele is associated with faster in vivo nicotine metabolism. *Clin. Pharmacol. Ther.,* 83, 115-121.

[152] Jung, M.J., Lippert, B., Metcalf, B.W., Böhlen, P., Schechter, P.J. (1977). gamma-Vinyl GABA (4-amino-hex-5-enoic acid), a new selective irreversible inhibitor of GABA-T: effects on brain GABA metabolism in mice. *J. Neurochem.*, 29, 797-802.

[153] Paterson, N.E., Markou, A. (2002). Increased GABA neurotransmission via administration of gamma-vinyl GABA decreased nicotine self administration in the rat. *Synapse*, 44, 252-253.

[154] Dewey, S.L., Morgan, A.E., Ashby, C.R. Jr., Horan, B., Kushner, S.A., Logan, J., Volkow, N.D., Fowler, J.S., Gardner, E.L., Brodie, J.D. (1998). A novel strategy for the treatment of cocaine addiction. *Synapse*, 30, 119-129.

[155] Brebner, K., Childress, A.R., Roberts, D.C. (2002). A potential role for GABA(B) agonists in the treatment of psychostimulant addiction. *Alcohol Alcohol*, 37, 478-484.

[156] Cahill, K., Ussher, M.H. (2011). Cannabinoid type 1 receptor antagonists for smoking cessation. *Cochrane Database Syst. Rev.*, 16:CD005353.

[157] Nathan, P.J., O'Neill, B.V., Napolitano, A., Bullmore, E.T. (2010). Neuropsychiatric adverse effects of centrally ccting antiobesity drugs. *CNS Neurosci. Ther.*, DOI: 10.1111/j.1755-5949.2010.00172.x.

[158] Siu, E.C. Tyndale, R.F. (2007). Non-nicotinic therapies for smoking cessation. *Annu. Rev. Pharmacol. Toxicol.*, 47, 541-564.

In: Nicotine Addiction
Editor: Giuseppe Di Giovanni

ISBN: 978-1-62081-290-7


*Chapter 2*

# SEROTONIN-DOPAMINE INTERACTION IN NICOTINE ADDICTION: FOCUS ON 5-HT$_{2C}$ RECEPTORS

***Ennio Esposito[1,#], Vincenzo Di Matteo[1], Massimo Pierucci[2,3], Arcangelo Benigno[4], Mauro Pessia[5], Alessandro Pitruzzella[3,4], Christian Zammit[6], Mario Valentino[7], Richard Muscat[2], and Giuseppe Di Giovanni[2,3,4,8,*]***

[1]Istituto di Ricerche Farmacologiche "Mario Negri", Consorzio "Mario Negri" Sud, Santa Maria Imbaro (Chieti), Italy

[2]Department of Physiology and Biochemistry, Faculty of Medicine and Surgery, University of Malta, Msida, Malta

[3]Instituto Euro Mediterraneo di Scienza e Tecnologia, IEMEST, Palermo, Italy

[4]Dipartimento di Biomedicina Sperimentale e Neuroscienze Cliniche, Palermo Italy

[5]Department of Internal Medicine Section of Human Physiology University of Perugia Faculty of Medicine and Surgery Perugia, Italy

[6]Department of Anatomy, Faculty of Medicine and Surgery, University of Malta. Msida, Malta

[7]Department of Pathology, Faculty of Medicine and Surgery, University of Malta. Msida, Malta

[8]School of Biosciences, Cardiff University, Cardiff, UK

## ABSTRACT

Central dopaminergic systems play a critical role in the regulation of normal and abnormal behaviors. Recent evidence suggests that a dysfunction of dopamine (DA) and serotonin (5-HT) neurotransmitter systems contribute to various pathological conditions.

---

[#] Dr. E. Esposito died on the 23rd of October 2011.

[*] Corresponding author: Prof. Giuseppe Di Giovanni, Department of Physiology and Biochemistry, Faculty of Medicine and Surgery, University of Malta. Msida MSD 2080, Malta. Tel.: +356 23402776 (direct) +356 21316655 (department) +356 21310577 (fax); giuseppe.digiovanni @um.edu.mt.

Substantial evidence indicates that the mesolimbic pathway, particularly the DA cells innervating accumbal areas, is implicated in the reward value of both natural and drug reinforcers, such as sexual behavior or psychostimulants, respectively. Nicotine, the major psychoactive agent present in tobacco, acts as a potent addictive drug both in humans and laboratory animals. The locomotor activation and the reinforcing effects of nicotine may be related to its stimulatory effects on the mesolimbic dopaminergic function.

Thus, it is now well established that nicotine can increase *in vivo* DA outflow in the nucleus accumbens and the corpus striatum. The stimulatory effect of nicotine on DA release most probably results from its ability to excite neuronal firing rate and to increase bursting activity of DA neurons within the substantia nigra pars compacta (SNc) and the ventral tegmental area (VTA), together with its facilitatory activity on DA terminal release in the corpus striatum and the nucleus accumbens. The neurochemical data are consistent with neuroanatomical findings showing the presence of nicotinic acetylcholine receptors (nAChRs) in the SNc, VTA, and in projection areas of the central dopaminergic system such as the corpus striatum and the nucleus accumbens. Several lines of evidence indicate that the reinforcing properties of drugs of abuse, including nicotine, can be affected by the serotonergic system which may act by modulating central dopaminergic function.

In this paper, the effects of 5-$HT_{2C}$ receptors on DA function in relation to the neurobiological mechanisms underlying nicotine addiction will be reviewed, and the possible strategies with 5-$HT_{2C}$ agents for new pharmacological treatments of nicotine dependence will be examined.

## INTRODUCTION

There is now an extensive scientific literature regarding the functional interaction between serotonin (5-HT) and dopamine (DA) containing neurons in the brain [1-3]. In some cases, the nature of these interactions depends upon the baseline activity of DA and/or 5-HT systems, and whether they are activated. In addition, most of the effects of 5-HT on DA neurons are indirect, involving 5-HT modulation of complex neuronal circuitry, rather than direct effects on DA cell bodies. In recent years, research on this matter has been spurred by new important insights on the molecular biology of 5-HT receptor subtypes and by the availability of 5-HT receptor knockout mice [4, 5].

Central serotonergic and dopaminergic systems play an important role in regulating normal and abnormal behaviors [1, 6]. Dysfunctions of 5-HT and DA neurotransmission are involved in the pathophysiology of various neuropsychiatric disorders including schizophrenia, depression and drug abuse [1, 6, 7]. Thus, the development of a number of relatively selective pharmacological agents specific 5-HT receptor subtypes, has allowed investigators to better understand the functional role of these receptors in the control of central DA-ergic function [8-12].

In this chapter we will focus on the role of the 5-$HT_{2C}$ receptor subtype in nicotine addiction. Therefore, the physiology, pharmacology and anatomical distribution of the 5-$HT_{2C}$ receptors in the CNS, as well as experimental data regarding the effect of 5-$HT_{2C}$ selective agents on the nicotine central effects, will be reviewed after a brief description of the functional neuroanatomy of dopaminergic and serotonergic systems. Finally, the potential use of 5-$HT_{2C}$ agents in the treatment of nicotine addiction and as a tobacco smoking cessation aid will be also discussed.

## DOPAMINE SYSTEMS

Dopamine-containing neurons of the ventral mesencephalon have been denominated as A8, A9 and A10 cell groups: these neurons collectively constitute the mesotelencephalic DA system [13]. Historically, the mesolimbic DA system was defined as originating in the A10 cells of the ventral tegmental area (VTA) and projecting to structures closely associated with the limbic system. This system was considered to be separated from the nigrostriatal DA system, which originates from the more lateral substantia nigra pars compacta (SNc, A9 cell group) [13-16].

The mesolimbic and mesocortical DA systems appear critically involved in modulation of the functions subserved by cortical and limbic regions such as motivation, emotional control and cognition [17]. Substantial evidence indicates that the mesolimbic pathway, particularly in the DA cells innervating accumbal areas, is implicated in the rewarding value associated with both natural and drug reinforcers, such as sexual behavior, food and psychostimulants [6, 18]. Animal studies have shown that lesion of DA terminals in the nucleus accumbens reduces the exploratory activity, enhances the latency to the initiation of motor responses, induces disturbances in organizing complex behaviors and in switching from one to another behavioural activity [17]. Hence the mesolimbic DA system seems important for acquisition and regulation of goal-directed behaviours, established and maintained by natural or drug reinforcers [17, 19].

The medial prefrontal cortex is generally associated with cognitive functions including working memory, planning and execution of behaviours, inhibitory control of responses and maintenance of focused attention [17]. In addition, the mesolimbic DA pathway is sensitive to a variety of physical and psychological stressors [20].

The nigrostriatal DA system, which originates from the substantia nigra (A9 cell group), is one of the best studied, because of its involvement in the pathogenesis of Parkinson's disease [21] [22, 23]. In mammals, the substantia nigra (SN) is a heterogeneous structure that includes two distinct compartments: the SNc and the substantia nigra pars reticulata (SNr). The SNc represent the major source of striatal DA and its degeneration causes PD. On the contrary, the SNr mainly contains GABA-ergic neurons which constitute one of the major efference of the basal ganglia circuitry [22].

## SEROTONIN SYSTEMS

Virtually all parts of the central nervous system receive innervation from serotonergic fibers arising from cell bodies located in the the dorsal nucleus (DRN) and the median raphé nucleus (MRN), the two main subdivisions of the midbrain serotonergic nuclei [24-29]. Serotonin-containing neurons of the raphé nuclei send projections to dopaminergic cells of both the VTA and SN, and to their terminal fields in the nucleus accumbens, prefrontal cortex and striatum [25-29] (Figure1). Electron microscopy demonstrates the presence of synaptic contacts of [$^{3}$H]5-HT labeled terminals with both dopaminergic and non-dopaminergic dendrites in all subnuclei of the VTA, and in the SNc and SNr [15, 26, 29].

The precise nature of the interaction between 5-HT and DA is difficult to elucidate, in that both inhibitory and excitatory roles for 5-HT have been suggested. However, these discrepancies may be attributable to the differential distribution and to the diverse functional roles of 5-HT receptor subtypes within the dopaminergic systems [2, 30, 31]. Thus, much attention has been devoted to the role of 5-HT receptors in the control of central DA activity, because of their implication in the pathophysiology of the diseases that affect central DA systems, such as schizophrenia, depression, drug abuse and PD. In this review we will focus on the 5-$HT_{2C}$ receptor subtype that seems to play an inhibitory role in many nicotine-addiction related behaviors in animals.

## 5-HT Receptors Localization

The diverse physiological effects of serotonin in the brain are mediated by a variety of distinct receptors. These receptors are presently divided into seven classes (5-$HT_1$ – 5-$HT_7$), which are then subdivided into subclasses based upon their pharmacological profiles, cDNA-deduced primary sequences and signal transduction mechanisms, with a total of at least 14 different receptors [5, 30, 31]. With the exception of the ionotropic 5-$HT_3$ receptor, 5-HT receptors are G-protein coupled receptors (metabotropic) and act through intracellular signaling pathways to hyperpolarize, in the case of 5-$HT_1$ receptors, or depolarize, in the case of the remaining 5-HT receptor classes, their host cells [31]. In this chapter we will limit to the description of 5-$HT_2$ receptor family.

### The 5-$HT_2$ Receptor Family

5-$HT_2$ receptors form a closely related subgroup of G-protein-coupled receptors, functionally linked to the phosphatidylinositol hydrolysis pathway and currently classified as 5-$HT_{2A}$, 5-$HT_{2B}$ and 5-$HT_{2C}$ subtypes [30-32]. There is an high sequence homology (> 80% in the transmembrane regions) between the mouse, rat and human 5-$HT_{2C}$ receptors [31], and it is not surprising that many compounds bind with high affinity ?to all these three receptor subtypes.

5-$HT_{2C}$ receptors are widely distribuited throughout the brain and have been proposed to represent the main mediators of the different actions of 5-HT in the central nervous system [30-32]. High levels of 5-$HT_{2C}$ mRNA or protein expression have been found in the choroid plexus, the frontal cortex, limbic structures such as hippocampus, septum and hypotalamus, and also in the striatum, nucleus accumbens, rhombencephalon and spinal cord. The presence of these receptors has also been demonstrated on DA and non-DA cells in the VTA, SNc and the SNr [33-37]. The regional and cellular distribution of 5-$HT_{2C}$ receptors has also been investigated in the human brain. The main sites of mRNA 5-$HT_{2C}$ receptors or protein expression, were the choroid plexus, cerebral cortex, hippocampus, amygdala, some components of the basal ganglia and other limbic structures [38, 39], suggesting that this receptor might be involved in the regulation of different human brain functions, as well as in the pathophysiology of several mental disorders [8-12, 40, 41]. There is now evidence that the 5-$HT_{2C}$ receptor is mainly located postsynaptically within dopaminergic, GABA-ergic, cholinergic, substance P, dynorphin and other systems [31, 37, 42-44]. Interestingly, the studies by Eberle-Wang et al. [43] showed the presence of 5-$HT_{2C}$ mRNA within inhibitory

GABA-ergic interneurons making direct synaptic contact with SNc and VTA dopaminergic cell bodies. Other immunohistochemical and electrophysiological studies demonstrated an important role of 5-$HT_{2C}$ receptors, localized on non-DA neurons, presumably GABA-ergic, in the regulation of DA cells in the VTA [37, 45, 46], medial prefrontal cortex [47] and in the SNc [48, 49].

Recent studies found a somatodentritic localization of 5-$HT_{2A}$ receptors on DA neurons in both the parabrachial and paranigral subdivisions of the VTA [50, 51], which project mainly to the prefrontal cortex and nucleus accumbens, respectively. In addition, 5-$HT_{2A}$ immunoreactivity was also expressed on non-DA cells in the VTA, providing a potential anatomical basis for the modulation of DA neurons within this area, either directly, by 5-$HT_{2A}$ receptors localized on DA cell, or indirectly, through receptors present on non–DA (presumably GABA-ergic) neurons [50, 51]. These receptors were also found at high concentrations in various cortical regions [34, 50]. It is likely that 5-$HT_{2A}$ receptors could affect DA function by acting at the level of dopaminergic nerve terminals, although no direct evidence for the presence of 5-$HT_{2A}$ receptors on such terminals has been provided so far.

Using sensitive techniques, several groups have also shown the presence of both 5-$HT_{2B}$ receptor mRNA and protein [52] in the rat brain, including midbrain regions. Although there are regional differences in the distribution of these receptors, they are all expressed in the brain with extensive pharmacological and functional similarities, so that it is often difficult to ascribe particular functions to a specific receptor subtype.

## Effects of Nicotine on Central Dopaminergic Function

There is an extensive scientific literature indicating that nicotine can stimulate central dopaminergic function. Thus, it is now a paradigmatic assumption that the locomotor activation and the reinforcing effects of nicotine are related to its stimulatory effects on the mesolimbic dopaminergic function [53-59].

Although the exact mechanisms by which nicotine stimulates DA neuron activity are still not completely understood, there is evidence that it can directly depolarize DA-containing neurons by activating somatodendritic nicotinic receptors which, in this region, are mostly constituted by the assembly of $\alpha 4\beta 2$ subtypes [60-65]. Moreover, nicotine can indirectly increase DA activity by eliciting the release of glutamate (GLU) from nerve terminals synapsing on DA neurons, and by depressing the inhibitory GABA-ergic input to these neurons [64, 66]. Furthermore, various studies have suggested that nitric oxide (NO) functions as a neuronal messenger in nicotine effects subsequent to glutamatergic activation [67, 68]. Nevertheles, a direct NO/DA interaction is also plausible. Indeed, there is evidence that NO can be endogenously released by acute nicotine injection from nerve cells, acting at nAChRs increasing $Ca^{2+}$ intracellular concentration [69] independently from the well known NMDA GLU receptor-mediated NO release [70]. NO seems to be necessary for the hedonic nicotine-induced increase in firing rate and pattern of DA cells and consequent DA release in taget areas [67, 71].

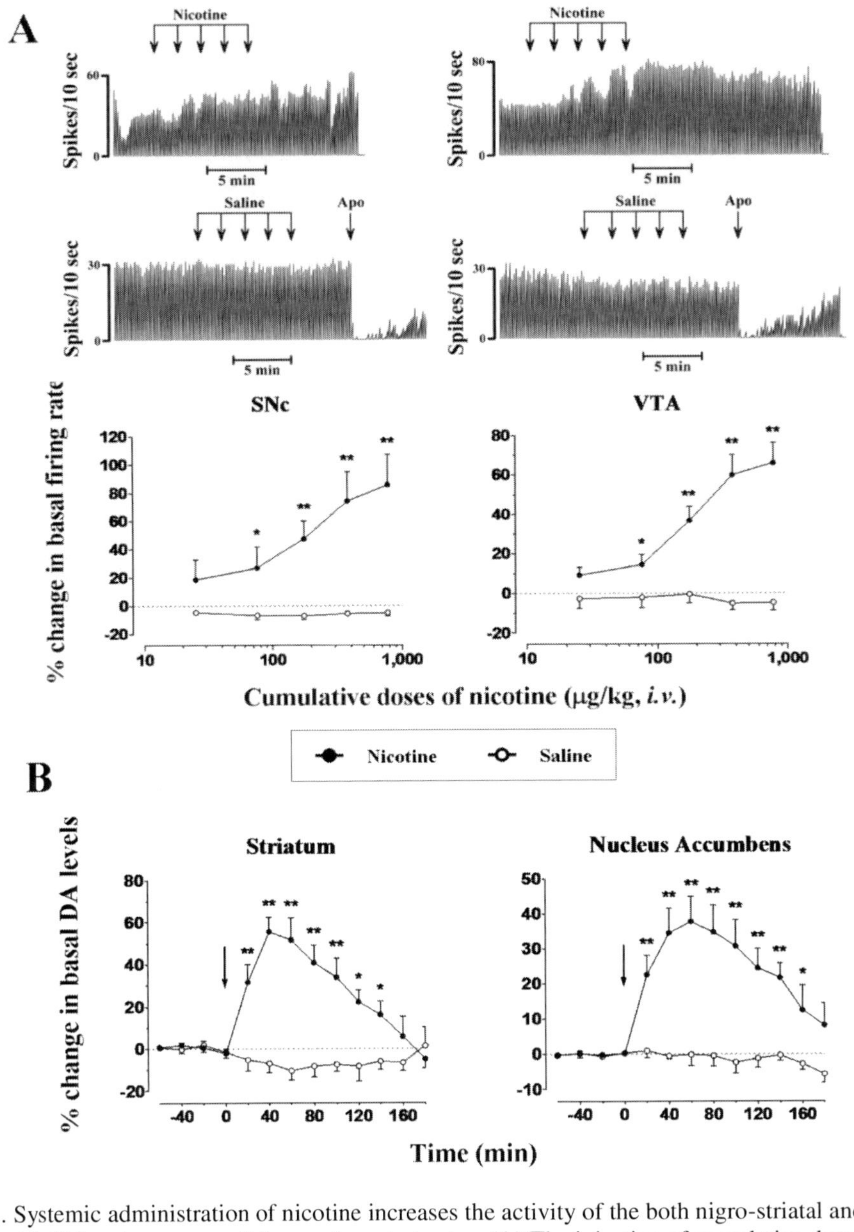


Figure 1. Systemic administration of nicotine increases the activity of the both nigro-striatal and meso-corticolimbic DAergic systems of drug-naïve rats *in vivo*. (A) The injection of cumulative doses of nicotine (25-775 µg/kg, i.v.) increased the firing rate of DA neurons recorded using *in vivo* single unit extracellular recording technique. The rate meters on top show the effect of nicotine administration on single DAergic neurons' firing rates compared to controls (saline, 100 µl i.v., at arrows), while the graphs below report the cumulative dose-response curves showing the mean percentage changes (±S.E.M.) in firing rate after either nicotine or saline administration. Arrows indicate the time of nicotine or saline injections; apomorphine (Apo), a D1/D2 receptors agonist, was injected (10-30 µg/kg, i.v.) at the end of most of experiments to confirm the DAergic identity of recorded neurons (adapted from [81]). (B) Time course of nicotine (1 mg/kg, i.p.) induced effect on DA terminal release in both the striatum and nucleus accumbens. Changes in DA extracellular levels were assessed using *in vivo* microdialysis on freely-moving animals. The arrows indicate the time of injection of either nicotine or saline (adapted from [78]).

In addition to its stimulatory effects on neuronal DA firing rate, nicotine has been shown to increase DA release from DAergic terminals in the corpus striatum and the nucleus accumbens [72-75] (Figure 1A).

It appears, however, that the action of nicotine on terminal areas of the mesolimbic DA system is less relevant as compared with the effect exerted by this drug in the VTA [74]. Thus, it has been shown that intra-VTA infusion of nicotine causes a more robust and prolonged increase of accumbal DA release as compared with intra-accumbens nicotine administration [74]. These neurochemical findings are consistent with behavioral data showing that nicotine-stimulated locomotor activity and self-administration are mediated by a direct action of this drug on DA neurons in the VTA [53, 56]. Although some studies claim no significant differences between the effects of nicotine on striatal and accumbal DA release, more compelling evidence shows that nicotine preferentially stimulates DA release in the nucleus accumbens [76, 77]. Nevertheless, we found that the peak effect of nicotine was more pronounced in the corpus striatum (+ 65%) than in the nucleus accumbens (+ 38%) [78] (Figure 1B). However, it is important to point out that nicotine was found to cause a preferential stimulation of DA release in the shell portion of the nucleus accumbens [79, 80], whereas in the Di Matteo et al. [78] study the microdialysis probes were mostly positioned at the transition border between shell and core. Neurochemical data are consistent with single-cell recordings showing that nicotine can increase the firing rate and the bursting activity of DA containing neurons in the SNc and the VTA [60-62, 81-85].

Several reports show that repeated nicotine exposure enhances its locomotor and reinforcing effects in rodents [54, 86-90], a phenomenon known as sensitization which is common to psychostimulant drugs [86, 91-93]. Moreover, repeated nicotine administration potentiates its stimulatory effects on DA overflow in the nucleus accumbens [86-88, 94] and increases the levels of mRNA for tyrosine hydroxylase (TH), the rate-limiting enzyme in DA biosynthesis, in the SN and the VTA [95]. This potentiation of nicotine effect might result, at least in part, from up-regulation of nAChRs following chronic exposure to nicotine [96-98]. Consistent with the data mentioned above, it has been shown that repeated administration of nicotine for 10 consecutive days caused a significant increase of basal DA outflow, which was particularly evident in the corpus striatum [78]. Those findings are in agreement with previously published data showing an enhanced basal DA outflow in the nucleus accumbens of rats treated daily with subcutaneous injections of nicotine (0.03–0.10 mg/kg) for 7 days [90].

These laboratory data might have clinical relevance since it has been shown that prior repeated nicotine exposure increases the control over behaviour by a conditioned reinforcer and enhances the ability of a conditioned stimulus to control behaviour in extinction [99]. Moreover, these findings may have important implications for studies investigating the consequences of repeated nicotine exposure on incentive motivational processes and expand our understanding of the mechanisms that mediate compulsive smoking behaviour and relapse, which may provide novel insight into treatments for smoking cessation [90]. In addition, repeated nicotine exposure augments the incentive salience of reward-associated cues in general. This effect of nicotine may be particularly important because nicotine is extensively co-abused with other addictive drugs and could thus promote the use of alcohol and illicit drugs by enhancing the vulnerability of cue-induced craving and relapse in general.

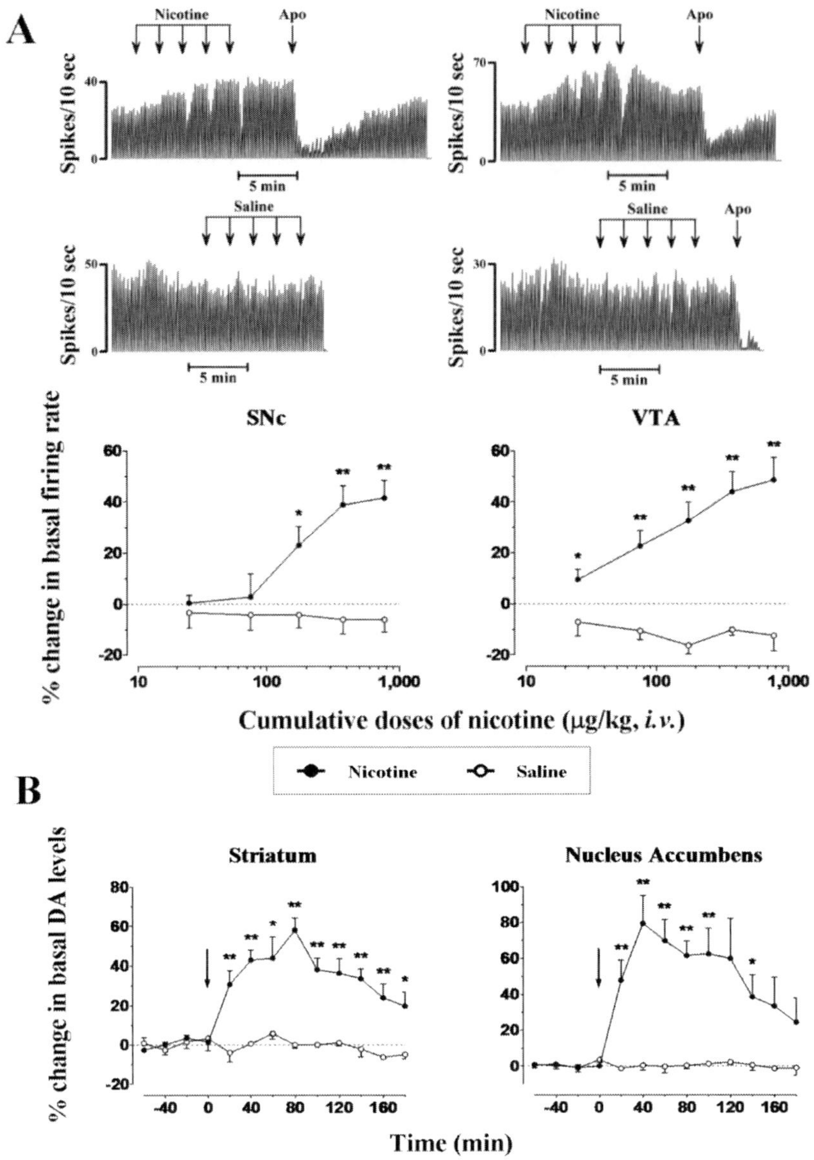


Figure 2. Systemic administration of nicotine increases the activity of the both nigro-striatal and meso-corticolimbic DAergic systems *in vivo* of rats chronically treated with nicotine (1 mg/kg, i.p.) for 10 consecutive days. (A) The injection of cumulative doses of nicotine (25-775 μg/kg, i.v.) increased the firing rate of DA neurons recorded using *in vivo* single unit extracellular recording technique. The rate meters on top show the effect of nicotine administration on single DAergic neurons' firing rates compared to controls (saline, 100 μl i.v., at arrows), while the graphs below report the cumulative dose-response curves showing the mean percentage changes (±S.E.M.) in firing rate after either nicotine or saline administration. Arrows indicate the time of nicotine or saline injections; apomorphine (Apo), a D1/D2 receptors agonist, was injected (10-30 μg/kg, i.v.) at the end of most of experiments to confirm the DAergic identity of recorded neurons (adapted from [81]). (B) Time course of nicotine (1 mg/kg, i.p.) induced effect on DA terminal release in both the striatum and nucleus accumbens. Changes in DA extracellular levels were assessed using *in vivo* microdialysis on freely-moving animals. The arrows indicate the time of injection of either nicotine or saline (adapted from [78]).

However, it does not seem that the potentiation of nicotine effect following its chronic administration is due to an increased firing activity of mesolimbic dopaminergic neurons in as much as no changes in nicotine-induced excitation of DA neurons in the VTA were found after repeated administration of this drug by Pierucci et al. [81] (Figure 2A).

In addition, acute challenge with nicotine in rats treated repeatedly with this drug was still capable of significantly increasing bursting activity of DA neurons in the VTA but not in the SNc [81]. These data are consistent with the hypothesis that tolerance to the stimulatory effect of nicotine occurs in the nigrostriatal but not in the mesolimbic dopaminergic system after repeated nicotine administration.

## EFFECTS OF NICOTINE ON CENTRAL SEROTONERGIC FUNCTION

Several lines of evidence indicate that the reinforcing properties of drugs of abuse, including nicotine, can be affected by a number of transmitter systems which may act by modulating central dopaminergic function. Among these, the role played by 5-HT seems particularly important. Serotonin contributes to mood, depression, and psychiatric illness, and several animal studies suggest that changes in serotonin transmission may also contribute to the affective symptoms of nicotine withdrawal [100]. Indeed, nicotine has an antidepressant action [101] and the prevalence of smoking is much higher amongst people suffering from depression [102]. Previous anatomic studies demonstrated the presence of α4, α7, and β2 subunit-containing nAChRs in the DRN [103-106]. The nAChR α7 subunit was found on large diameter DRN neurons (15–25 μm in diameter) that colocalized with tryptophan hydroxylase [107] and small-diameter neurons (5–10 μm), that are usually GABAergic [103]. The cholinergic input to the serotonergic DRN cells is substained by the pedunculopontine tegmentum [108]. Electrophysiological *in vitro* studies have revealed the influence of nicotine on 5-HT neuronal activity. The majority of serotonergic DRN neurons increase their action potential firing in response to nicotine administration, leading to an increased 5-HT release in target areas [109-111]. Nicotinic receptors also indirectly affect excitability of DRN neurons by modulating their synaptic drive. Nicotine enhances excitatory glutamatergic inputs to a subset of DRN-NAc projection neurons, while inhibitory GABAergic inputs are modulated either positively or negatively in a subset of these neurons. On the other hand, *in vivo* systemic nicotine was reported to decrease the firing rate in the majority of DRN neurons and increased firing in only a small subset [112]. Strikingly, nicotine failed to show any effect when locally applied within the DRN. The *in vivo* evidence does not agree with *in vitro* results, but it is important to note that serotonergic neurons are strongly influenced by the animal's arousal state (sleep-waking) [113]. Thus it is possible that the effect of nicotine on DRN neuron firing rate *in vivo* is influenced by anesthesia and/or the time of the day. Thus acute exposure to nicotine might excite DRN neurons by direct depolarization and indirect synaptic modulation. Given the excitatory effects of nicotine on DRN neurons, serotonin likely contributes to the rewarding effects of nicotine.

Moreover, there are also several behavioural actions of nicotine that seem to be mediated by the serotonergic system [100]. Thus, nicotine and the nAChRs agonist RJR-2403 significantly increased cortical 5-HT release in awake, behaving rats [114]. Nicotinic binding sites have not been observed on serotonergic axon terminals in the cortex [115]. It has thus been suggested that the increase in 5-HT release is likely due to stimulation of nAChRs on cortically projecting cell bodies in the DRN [114].

Acetylcholine, nicotine, and the potent nicotinic receptor agonists epibatidine and cytisine significantly increased [$^{3}$H]5-HT release from striatal synaptosomes, an effect blocked by the non-competitive nicotinic receptor antagonist, mecamylamine [116]. Moreover, the nicotine-stimulated increase in 5-HT release from striatal slices was significantly enhanced after 10 days of nicotine treatment [117] and the effects of chronic nicotine were enhanced by exposure to stress [118]. The nicotinic receptor agonists, 1,1-dimethyl-4-phenylpiperarazinium (DMPP),lobeline and nicotine have been shown to increase [$^{3}$H]5-HT release from rat hippocampal slices, although cytisine, epibatidine, and nicotine had no effect [119, 120] while Reuben and Clarke [116] found that nicotine had no effect. Contrasting data also exists on the effect of chronic treatment with nicotine on 5-HT concentrations in the dorsal hippocampus; both decrease [121] and increase has been described [122]. It is likely that the effect of nicotine on the brain serotonergic system depends on the duration of treatment. Both acute and chronic systemic administration of nicotine in rats increase 5-HT levels in the hypothalamus, although the rates of 5-HT synthesis were unaffected [100]. A series of experiments suggest the existence of multiple populations of functional nAChRs controlling, directly or indirectly, 5-HT release in the spinal cord. The first, activated by agonist application, has an excitatory effect and could be directly located on serotonergic terminals; the second, tonically activated by endogenous ACh and inhibited by nicotinic receptor antagonists, has an inhibitory outcome and is present in inhibitory neurons [100].

Overall, there is good evidence that nicotine increases 5-HT neuronal activity and its release in several brain regions and a serotonergic approach may hold promise as a novel avenue for smoking cessation treatment.

## Serotonin 2C (5-HT$_{2C}$) and Nicotine Rewarding Properties

Serotonin modulates the effect of many drugs of addiction on DAergic systems prevalently acting through the 5-HT$_{2C}$ receptor subtypes [123-125]. Thus, a series of studies has clearly shown that 5-HT$_{2C}$ receptors have a prominent role in the control of central DA function [11, 126, 127]. In fact, a series of *in vivo* electrophysiological and neurochemical studies showed that SB 206553, a selective 5-HT$_{2C/2B}$ receptor antagonist [128] and SB 242084, the most potent and selective 5-HT$_{2C}$ receptor antagonist available [129], increased the basal firing rate and the bursting activity of VTA DA neurons and enhanced DA release in both rat nucleus accumbens and prefrontal cortex [127, 130, 131]. On the other hand, RO 60-0175, a selective 5-HT$_{2C}$ receptor agonist [132] showed opposite effects on DA neurons activity [131, 133-135]. SB 242084 was also found to potentiate the phencyclidine-induced increase in accumbal DA release [136] and stress-stimulated DA outflow in the rat prefrontal cortex [137] while stimulation of 5-HT$_{2C}$ receptors by RO 60-0175 in the VTA suppressed it [137], suggesting a role of these receptors in controlling evoked DA release. In line with these data, it was recently found that SB 206553 administration potentiates both the enhancement of DA release in the nucleus accumbens and corpus striatum, and the increase in VTA and SNc DA neuronal firing rate induced by morphine [138]. Consistent with these findings, stimulation of central 5-$HT_{2C}$ receptors has been shown to inhibit morphine-induced increase in DA release in the nucleus accumbens of freely moving rats [139]. In addition, it was found that RO 60-0175 reduced cocaine-reinforced behaviour by stimulating 5-$HT_{2C}$ receptors [140]. Moreover, ketanserin [141], RO 60-0175 [89, 142] and lorcaserin [143], a relatively selective 5-$HT_{2C}$ agonist, reduced nicotine-induced self-administration and hyperactivity. Interestingly, RO 60-0175 not only reduced the operant responding for nicotine and the nicotine-induced hyperlocomotion in sensitized rats, but was also capable of blocking the sensitization to nicotine which occurs after repeated treatment with this drug [89]. Two recent studies found that WAY161503 [144] and WAY163909 [145] also blocked the effects of nicotine to stimulate locomotion in rats with prior nicotine exposure, and that these effect were reversed by SB242084.

An investigation conducted in our laboratory was designed as a neurochemical counterpart of Grottick et al. [89] study, with the aim of elucidating the possible involvement of DA in the behavioral effects of RO 60–0175 against nicotine-induced hyperlocomotion and reward [78]. Thus RO 60–0175, at doses of 1 and 3 mg/kg, was capable of preventing the increase in DA release induced by acute nicotine administration in the corpus striatum but not in the nucleus accumbens. On the other hand, 1 and 3 mg/kg RO 60–0175 dose-dependently prevented the enhancement of DA release induced by repeated nicotine administration, both in the corpus striatum and in the nucleus accumbens. The effects of RO 60–0175 were completely blocked by the selective 5-$HT_{2C}$ antagonists SB 242084 and SB 243213 [146]. Both SB 242084 and SB 243213 show high affinity for the cloned 5-$HT_{2C}$ receptors (p*Ki* 9.0) and a 100 to 160-fold selectivity over the closely related human 5-$HT_{2B}$ and 5-$HT_{2A}$ subtypes, respectively [129, 146]. In addition, SB 242084 and SB 243213 potently inhibit mCPP-induced hypolocomotion in rats, a model of *in vivo* central 5-$HT_{2C}$ receptor function, with an $ID_{50}$ of 0.11 mg/kg i.p. for SB 242084 [129] and an $ID_{50}$ of 0.7 mg/kg p.o. for SB 243213 [146]. Therefore, it is very likely that both SB 242084 and SB 243213 specifically block 5-$HT_{2C}$ receptors in the brain at the dose used. Thus, it is conceivable that the blockade by RO 60–0175 of the hyperlocomotive and rewarding effects of nicotine [140] are most probably mediated by its ability to inhibit mesolimbic DA function. The reasons for the differential effects of RO 60–0175 on acute and repeated nicotine-induced DA release in the nucleus accumbens are not readily apparent, but might be explained by the effect of nicotine on central 5-HT system [100]. Thus, acute nicotine administration has been shown to stimulate central 5-HT function increasing the firing rate of 5-HT-containing neurons in the DRN [147] and the 5-HT terminal release [116, 147, 148]. In contrast, repeated nicotine treatment was found to reduce brain 5-HT turnover [101, 149, 150], and hippocampal 5-HT concentration and release [100, 121]. Moreover, postmortem studies conducted on human brains showed a significant reduction in the concentrations of 5-HIAA (5-hydroxyindoleacetic acid), the main metabolite of 5-HT, in the hippocampus and the MRN of smokers [151]. Consistent with the above mentioned data, recent evidence indicates that repeated nicotine administration causes a reduced 5-HT turnover and increased 5-$HT_2$ receptor sensitivity [152]. Therefore, it is tempting to speculate that an up-regulation of 5-$HT_2$ might explain the finding described by Di Matteo et al [78] and indicating that RO 60–0175 can block nicotine-induced accumbal DA release only after repeated treatment with this alkaloid. Consistent with this hypothesis is the evidence that the unselective 5-$HT_2$ receptor agonist DOI can reduce nicotine-stimulated locomotor activity and accumbal DA release in nicotine-sensitized rats but not in animals treated acutely with nicotine [153] Moreover, repeated administration of the selective serotonin reuptake inhibitor citalopram counteracts the expression of nicotine-induced locomotor sensitization [54]. It thus seems that activation of the serotonergic system can counteract the development and expression of the mesolimbic DA system sensitization to nicotine which is typically induced by its repeated administration. This action can ultimately lead to the extinction of nicotine-induced rewarding effect on the DAergic system, an effect that would be beneficial to smoking cessation therapies. In this respect, it is interesting to note that bupropion, which is an effective drug in the treatment of nicotine dependence [154], causes a sustained increase in the basal firing activity of 5-HT neurons in the DRN [155]. Finally, there is evidence that gamma-vinyl GABA, which increases endogenous GABA, reduces nicotine-stimulated DA overflow in the nucleus accumbens and blocks the acquisition and expression of place preference induced by nicotine [156]. Consistent with these data, it has been also found that muscimol and baclofen, two GABA agonists, significantly reduce nicotine self-administration when infused into the VTA [157]. It is thus tempting to speculate that the inhibitory action of RO 60–0175 on nicotine-induced DA release reported in the present study might be mediated, at least in part, by stimulation of GABA-ergic neurons impinging on DA-containing neurons in the SN pars compacta and in the VTA, an effect which was previously associated with activation of 5-HT$_{2C}$ receptors [158].

## Serotonergic Drug Treatment for Smoking Cessation

Within the USA and Europe, 70% of all smokers have tried to quit smoking at least once, but only about 6% of these succeded in maintaining abstinence [159]. Thus, one of the major problems limiting the success of smoking cessations aids is that the great majority of abstinent people relapse [159]. Most relapses occur within three months of quitting, and half within the first two days [160]. Thus, it is important to consider that environmental and sensory stimuli associated with smoking can act as conditioned reinforcers in humans [161], so the exposure to such cues increase the motivation to smoke (i.e., produce cue-induced craving) both in active or former smokers [162, 163].

Since it has been estimated that smoking leads to an average loss of 12 healthy years and reduces the lifespan by 8 years [159], there is great interest in developing effective therapies that will help in facilitating smoking cessation and assist in maintaining abstinence. Two types of pharmacological therapies have been approved for smoking cessation by the US Food and Drug Administration. The first is nicotine replacement therapy (NRT), which enables the smoker to substitute the nicotine from cigarettes from other nicotine formulations that are safer than tobacco, such as chewing gum, transdermal patches or inhalers [164]. The second therapy is non-nicotine based represented mostly by the atypical antidepressant bupropion [165, 166] and the alpha4beta2* nAChRs partial agonist varenicline. Between these two, varenicline has been shown to be the most effective for smoking cessation, followed by bupropion and nicotine replacement therapies [167]. The improved varenicline's efficacy is likely due to its dual mechanism of action: when quitting smoking, varenicline can reproduce the subjective effects of smoking by partially activating $\alpha4\beta2$* nAChRs, and can prevent full activation of these receptors by nicotine when smoking again [168].

The phenylaminoketone atypical antidepressant agent buproprion, in the sustained-release formulation, was approved by Food and Drug Administration (FDA) in the USA in 1997 as the first non-nicotine pharmacotherapy for smoking cessation. Although the mechanism of action of bupropion in the treatment of nicotine dependence is still unclear, it is probably related to its modest capability to block DA and noradrenaline (NA) reuptake [166]. Moreover, the antagonistic activity of bupropion on nAChRs might also be relevant for its clinical efficacy as a smoking cessation aid [169]. The major metabolites of bupropion, hydroxybupropion and threohydroxybupropion produce equal or weaker inhibition of DA and NA reuptake than does bupropion [166]. Similar to tricyclic antidepressants, bupropion and hydroxybupropion were found to reduce the firing rate of noradrenergic neurons in the locus coeruleus in a dose-dependent manner – an action that is reversed by the $\alpha_2$-adrenergic antagonist yohimbine [170]. Bupropion dramatically reduced the effects of nicotine on DA neuron excitability and alone reduced GABAergic transmission to DA neurons, thereby diminishing tonic inhibition of these neurons *in vitro* [171]. This increased DA neuron excitability during bupropion treatment in the absence of nicotine may contribute to bupropion's antidepressant actions [171]. These findings suggest that a noradrenergic and dopaminergic component may contribute to the antidepressant effect of bupropion. Bupropion was also found to cause a sustained increase in the basal firing activity of 5-HT neurons in the DRN [155]. However, the relevance of the latter effect in the mechanism of clinical action of bupropion is presently unknown.

Varenicline (trade name Chantix in the USA and Champix in Canada, Europe and other countries) by Pfizer was introduced in 2006 as a novel efficacious smoking cessation aid that acts as an $\alpha 4\beta 2$ nAChR partial agonist [168, 172]. Varenicline affects monoaminergic neurotransmission modulating release of DA, NE, and 5-HT. Varenicline binds selectively with sub-nanomolar affinity to $\alpha 4\beta 2^*$ nAChRs and the varenicline-induced increase in DA release from rat nucleus accumbens [168, 172] is mediated via interactions with $\alpha 4\beta 2^*$ nAChRs in the VTA, similar to nicotine-evoked DA release [173]. Thus varenicline does not greatly increase the downstream release of DA. Due to its competitive binding on these receptors, varenicline blocks the ability of nicotine to bind and stimulate the mesolimbic DA system.

On the other hand, varenicline causes no significant changes in extracellular levels of 5-HT, NE, or DA in rat prefrontal cortex [174], while it produces robust increases in cortical DA and NE release after a high dose of 10 mg/kg [175]. This dose is associated with very high brain concentrations of >1 μM, which can interact with several other nAChR subtypes other than $\alpha 4\beta 2$ nAChRs. The lack of effects of varenicline on cortical monoamine release is also consistent with its *in vitro* properties, since varenicline has very low affinity for the 5-HT transporter or 5-HT receptors and thus cannot increase 5-HT either by blocking 5-HT reuptake or by interacting with central 5-HT receptors. Although varenicline has modest affinity for 5-$HT_{3A}$ receptors, at which it is a full agonist, the therapeutic unbound varenicline brain concentrations are predicted to be insufficient for activating central 5-$HT_{3A}$ receptors. Furthermore, varenicline does not bind to DA receptors that can modulate 5-HT release, and does not inhibit the enzyme that metabolizes 5-HT, MAO-A [174].

In recent meta-analyses varenicline resulted superior in effectiveness to bupropion and NRT [167, 176]. Nevertheless, the US FDA issued an alert concerning an the observed increase in serious neuropsychiatric symptoms in patients taking varenicline [177]. Such events can include changes in behavior, hostility, agitation, depressed mood, and suicidal thoughts or actions. FDA is continuing to evaluate the risk of neuropsychiatric events with Chantix. Pfizer is conducting a large safety clinical trial of Chantix to assess neuropsychiatric adverse events, and results from this study are expected in 2017.

Several tricyclic antidepressants (TCAs) which inhibit NA and 5-HT, such as nortriptyline [178-180] and doxepin [181], might facilitate smoking cessation in combination with behavioural treatment. Indeed, as a class, antidepressants are the most common non-nicotine drugs which have been shown to be of benefit in smoking cessation.

As already mentioned above, smokers are more likely than non-smokers to have symptoms of depression. In addition, smokers with a history of depression are more likely to be more dependent on nicotine and have a lower likelihood of successfully quitting. When they do quit, depression is more apt to be a prominent withdrawal. Cases of psychotic depression after smoking cessation have been reported.

Since TCAs have significant side-effects, such as anticholinergic activity and frequent lethality in overdose, a better tolerated and safer class of antidepressants, selective serotonin reuptake inhibitors (SSRIs), have also been studied, given the role of 5-HT in modulating nicotine reward and smoking behavior [78, 81, 89, 100]. Studies with the prototypical SSRI fluoxetine yielded equivocal results.

Fluoxetine might ameliorate of the most bothersome symptoms experienced during smoking cessation, in smokers with a history of major depression [182]. Another serotonergic agent used to treat nicotine addiction is buspirone, a 5-$HT_{1A}$ partial agonist which is provided with anxiolytic activity. Thus stimulation of 5-$HT_{1A}$ receptors by buspirone leads to a reduction in presynaptic release of 5-HT, which appears to mediate its anxiolytic effects. However, a placebo controlled clinical trial failed to support its efficacy in smoking cessation [183].

## CONCLUSION

It is now well established that nicotine can be considered an extraordinary psychotropic drug in that, by acting on nAChRs, it can stimulate the release of a number of neurotransmitters including ACh, GLU, DA, NA, 5-HT, and GABA. It is indeed difficult to find in the official pharmacopeia a psychotropic drug which is capable to exert such a wide range of effects on multiple neurotransmitters such as nicotine. The serotonin pathway has been implicated in nicotine dependence and may influence smoking cessation. The most promising receptor seems to be the 5-$HT_{2C}$. As far as the other 5-HT receptors are concerned, there is some evidence that 5-$HT_{1A}$ receptor stimulation inhibits behavioral sensitization to nicotine [54, 184] and may mediate nicotine withdrawal symptoms [184, 185]. Moreover, an inhibitory role of the 5-$HT_6$ and a facilitating role of the 5-$HT_3$ receptors have been described. However, 5-$HT_3$ receptor antagonism did not prove to be an effective treatment strategy in human smokers. Thus, these compounds are still at the stage of pre-clinical investigation and deserve further experimentantion to evaluate their potential usefulness as effective smoking cessation aids. Antidepressants such as nortriptyline, doxepin, fluoxetine, the reversible MAO-A inhibitor moclobemide, and the anxiolytic agent buspirone have been found to be helpful in the therapy of nicotine addiction. However, their efficacy as smoking cessation agents appears to be limited and it is still unclear if their clinical action in smoking cessation is specific or if it is simply linked to their therapeutic effect on the underlying depression and anxiety which are frequently associated with cigarette smoking.

Although basic research has provided a great deal of data on the neurobiological bases of nicotine action, dependence, and withdrawal, the pharmacotherapy of nicotine addiction can be still considered unsatisfactory. Serotonergic drugs may have some efficacy in supporting discontinuation of smoking. There is mounting evidence indicating that 5-HT neurotransmission is a critical neurological substrate for the process of smoking cessation per se or for a putative role in suppressing nicotine withdrawal in smokers administered NRT.

## ACKNOWLEDGMENTS

We wish to dedicate this chapter to Dr Ennio Esposito who unexpectedly died on the 23rd of October 2011. We will miss a brilliant and influential scientist with many fresh ideas, who was supportive and understanding, and a good friend. He leaves a big gap in my scientific life, but will remain in our thoughts as one who progressed the idea that 5-$HT_{2C}$ receptor modulation of dopaminergic function is a promising pharmacological intervention for many neuropsychiatric disorders.

## REFERENCES

[1] Di Giovanni, G., Di Matteo, V., Esposito, E. (2008) Serotonin–Dopamine Interaction: Experimental Evidence and Therapeutic Relevance *Prog. Brain Res.* ed. Vol. 172. Amsterdam: Elsevier. 1-665.

[2] Pessia, M., Jiang, Z.G., North, R.A., Johnson, S.W. (1994) Actions of 5-hydroxytryptamine on ventral tegmental area neurons of the rat in vitro. *Brain Res.,* 654 (2), 324-330.

[3] Prisco, S., Pessia, M., Ceci, A., Borsini, F., Esposito, E. (1992) Chronic treatment with DAU 6215, a new 5-HT3 receptor antagonist, causes a selective decrease in the number of spontaneously active dopaminergic neurons in the rat ventral tegmental area. *Eur. J. Pharmacol.,* 214 (1), 13-19.

[4] Bonasera, S.J., Tecott, L.H. (2000) Mouse models of serotonin receptor function: toward a genetic dissection of serotonin systems. *Pharmacol. Ther.,* 88 (2), 133-142.

[5] Hoyer, D., Hannon, J.P., Martin, G.R. (2002) Molecular, pharmacological and functional diversity of 5-HT receptors. *Pharmacol. Biochem. Behav.,* 71 (4), 533-554.

[6] Koob, G.F. (1992) Drugs of abuse: anatomy, pharmacology and function of reward pathways. *Trends Pharmacol. Sci.,* 13 (5), 177-184.

[7] Brown, A.S., Gershon, S. (1993) Dopamine and depression. *J. Neural. Transm. Gen. Sect.,* 91 (2-3), 75-109.

[8] Alex, K.D., Pehek, E.A. (2007) Pharmacologic mechanisms of serotonergic regulation of dopamine neurotransmission. *Pharmacol. Ther.,* 113 (2), 296-320.

[9] Higgins, G.A., Fletcher, P.J. (2003) Serotonin and drug reward: focus on 5-HT2C receptors. *Eur. J. Pharmacol.,* 480 (1-3), 151-162.

[10] Jenck, F., Bos, M., Wichmann, J., Stadler, H., Martin, J.R., Moreau, J.L. (1998) The role of 5-HT2C receptors in affective disorders. *Expert Opin. Investig Drugs,* 7 (10), 1587-1599.

[11] Di Matteo, V., De Blasi, A., Di Giulio, C., Esposito, E. (2001) Role of 5-HT2C receptors in the control of central dopamine function. *Trends Pharmacol. Sci.,* 22 (5), 229-232.

[12] Giorgetti, M., Tecott, L.H. (2004) Contributions of 5-HT(2C) receptors to multiple actions of central serotonin systems. *Eur. J. Pharmacol.,* 488 (1-3), 1-9.

[13] Dahlström, A., Fuxe, K. (1964) Evidence for the Existence of Monoamine-Containing Neurons in the Central Nervous System. I. Demonstration of Monoamines in the Cell Bodies of Brain Stem Neurons. *Acta Physiol. Scand. Suppl.,* SUPPL. 232, 1-55.

[14] Bannon, M.J., Roth, R.H. (1983) Pharmacology of mesocortical dopamine neurons. *Pharmacol. Rev.,* 35 (1), 53-68.

[15] Kalivas, P.W. (1993) Neurotransmitter regulation of dopamine neurons in the ventral tegmental area. *Brain Res. Brain Res. Rev.,* 18 (1), 75-113.

[16] White, F.J. (1996) Synaptic regulation of mesocorticolimbic dopamine neurons. *Annu. Rev. Neurosci.,* 19, 405-436.

[17] Le Moal, M., Simon, H. (1991) Mesocorticolimbic dopaminergic network: functional and regulatory roles. *Physiol. Rev.,* 71 (1), 155-234.

[18] Di Chiara, G., Imperato, A. (1988) Drugs abused by humans preferentially increase synaptic dopamine concentrations in the mesolimbic system of freely moving rats. *Proc. Natl. Acad. Sci. U S A,* 85 (14), 5274-5278.

[19] Kiyatkin, E.A. (1995) Functional significance of mesolimbic dopamine. *Neurosci. Biobehav. Rev.,* 19 (4), 573-598.

[20] Roth, R., Elsworth, J., *Biochemical pharmacology of midbrain dopamine neurons.*, in *Psychopharmacology: The fourth generation of progress*, F. Bloom and D. Kupfer, Editors. 1995, Raven Press: New York. p. 227-243.

[21] Deshpande, L.S., Khisti, R.T., Chopde, C.T. (2001) Cataleptic effect of neurosteroid 3[alpha]-hydroxy-5[alpha]-pregnan-20-one in mice: modulation by serotonergic agents. *Brain Res.,* 898 (1), 13-26.

[22] Esposito, E., Di Matteo, V., Di Giovanni, G. (2007) Death in the substantia nigra: a motor tragedy. *Expert Rev. Neurother.,* 7 (6), 677-697.

[23] Di Giovanni, G. (2008) Will it ever become possible to prevent dopaminergic neuronal degeneration? *CNS Neurol. Disord. Drug Targets,* 7 (1), 28-44.

[24] Azmitia, E.C., Segal, M. (1978) An autoradiographic analysis of the differential ascending projections of the dorsal and median raphe nuclei in the rat. *J. Comp. Neurol.,* 179 (3), 641-667.

[25] van der Kooy, D., Hattori, T. (1980) Dorsal raphe cells with collateral projections to the caudate-putamen and substantia nigra: a fluorescent retrograde double labeling study in the rat. *Brain Res.,* 186 (1), 1-7.

[26] Herve, D., Pickel, V.M., Joh, T.H., Beaudet, A. (1987) Serotonin axon terminals in the ventral tegmental area of the rat: fine structure and synaptic input to dopaminergic neurons. *Brain Res.,* 435 (1-2), 71-83.

[27] Van Bockstaele, E.J., Biswas, A., Pickel, V.M. (1993) Topography of serotonin neurons in the dorsal raphe nucleus that send axon collaterals to the rat prefrontal cortex and nucleus accumbens. *Brain Res.,* 624 (1-2), 188-198.

[28] Van Bockstaele, E.J., Cestari, D.M., Pickel, V.M. (1994) Synaptic structure and connectivity of serotonin terminals in the ventral tegmental area: potential sites for modulation of mesolimbic dopamine neurons. *Brain Res.,* 647 (2), 307-322.

[29] Moukhles, H., Bosler, O., Bolam, J.P., Vallee, A., Umbriaco, D., Geffard, M., Doucet, G. (1997) Quantitative and morphometric data indicate precise cellular interactions between serotonin terminals and postsynaptic targets in rat substantia nigra. *Neuroscience,* 76 (4), 1159-1171.

[30] Hoyer, D., Clarke, D.E., Fozard, J.R., Hartig, P.R., Martin, G.R., Mylecharane, E.J., Saxena, P.R., Humphrey, P.P. (1994) International Union of Pharmacology classification of receptors for 5-hydroxytryptamine (Serotonin). *Pharmacol. Rev.,* 46 (2), 157-203.

[31] Barnes, N.M., Sharp, T. (1999) A review of central 5-HT receptors and their function. *Neuropharmacology,* 38 (8), 1083-1152.

[32] Boess, F.G., Martin, I.L. (1994) Molecular biology of 5-HT receptors. *Neuropharmacology,* 33 (3-4), 275-317.

[33] Molineaux, S.M., Jessell, T.M., Axel, R., Julius, D. (1989) 5-HT1c receptor is a prominent serotonin receptor subtype in the central nervous system. *Proc. Natl. Acad. Sci. U S A,* 86 (17), 6793-6797.

[34] Wright, D.E., Seroogy, K.B., Lundgren, K.H., Davis, B.M., Jennes, L. (1995) Comparative localization of serotonin1A, 1C, and 2 receptor subtype mRNAs in rat brain. *J. Comp. Neurol.,* 351 (3), 357-373.

[35] Sharma, A., Punhani, T., Fone, K.C. (1997) Distribution of the 5-hydroxytryptamine2C receptor protein in adult rat brain and spinal cord determined using a receptor-directed antibody: effect of 5,7-dihydroxytryptamine. *Synapse,* 27 (1), 45-56.

[36] Clemett, D.A., Punhani, T., Duxon, M.S., Blackburn, T.P., Fone, K.C. (2000) Immunohistochemical localisation of the 5-HT2C receptor protein in the rat CNS. *Neuropharmacology,* 39 (1), 123-132.

[37] Bubar, M.J., Cunningham, K.A. (2007) Distribution of serotonin 5-HT2C receptors in the ventral tegmental area. *Neuroscience,* 146 (1), 286-297.

[38] Abramowski, D., Rigo, M., Duc, D., Hoyer, D., Staufenbiel, M. (1995) Localization of the 5-hydroxytryptamine2C receptor protein in human and rat brain using specific antisera. *Neuropharmacology,* 34 (12), 1635-1645.

[39] Pasqualetti, M., Ori, M., Castagna, M., Marazziti, D., Cassano, G.B., Nardi, I. (1999) Distribution and cellular localization of the serotonin type 2C receptor messenger RNA in human brain. *Neuroscience,* 92 (2), 601-611.

[40] Baxter, G., Kennett, G., Blaney, F., Blackburn, T. (1995) 5-HT2 receptor subtypes: a family re-united? *Trends Pharmacol. Sci.,* 16 (3), 105-110.

[41] Di Giovanni, G., Esposito, E., Di Matteo, V. (2010) Role of serotonin in central dopamine dysfunction. *CNS Neurosci. Ther.,* 16 (3), 179-194.

[42] Ward, R.P., Dorsa, D.M. (1996) Colocalization of serotonin receptor subtypes 5-HT2A, 5-HT2C, and 5-HT6 with neuropeptides in rat striatum. *J. Comp. Neurol.,* 370 (3), 405-414.

[43] Eberle-Wang, K., Mikeladze, Z., Uryu, K., Chesselet, M.F. (1997) Pattern of expression of the serotonin2C receptor messenger RNA in the basal ganglia of adult rats. *J. Comp. Neurol.,* 384 (2), 233-247.

[44] Esposito, E., Di Matteo, V., Pierucci, M., Benigno, A., Di Giovanni, G., Role of central 5-$HT_{2C}$ receptor in the control of basal ganglia functions, in *The Basal Ganglia Pathophysiology:* Recent Advances., G. Di Giovanni, Editor. 2007, Transworld research network: Trivandrum. p. 97-127.

[45] Van Bockstaele, E.J., Pickel, V.M. (1995) GABA-containing neurons in the ventral tegmental area project to the nucleus accumbens in rat brain. *Brain Res.,* 682 (1-2), 215-221.

[46] Steffensen, S.C., Svingos, A.L., Pickel, V.M., Henriksen, S.J. (1998) Electrophysiological characterization of GABAergic neurons in the ventral tegmental area. *J. Neurosci.,* 18 (19), 8003-8015.

[47] Liu, S., Bubar, M.J., Lanfranco, M.F., Hillman, G.R., Cunningham, K.A. (2007) Serotonin2C receptor localization in GABA neurons of the rat medial prefrontal cortex: implications for understanding the neurobiology of addiction. *Neuroscience,* 146 (4), 1677-1688.

[48] Di Giovanni, G., Di Matteo, V., La Grutta, V., Esposito, E. (2001) m-Chlorophenylpiperazine excites non-dopaminergic neurons in the rat substantia nigra and ventral tegmental area by activating serotonin-2C receptors. *Neuroscience,* 103 (1), 111-116.

[49] Invernizzi, R.W., Pierucci, M., Calcagno, E., Di Giovanni, G., Di Matteo, V., Benigno, A., Esposito, E. (2007) Selective activation of 5-HT(2C) receptors stimulates GABA-ergic function in the rat substantia nigra pars reticulata: a combined in vivo electrophysiological and neurochemical study. *Neuroscience,* 144 (4), 1523-1535.

[50] Doherty, M.D., Pickel, V.M. (2000) Ultrastructural localization of the serotonin 2A receptor in dopaminergic neurons in the ventral tegmental area. *Brain Res.,* 864 (2), 176-185.

[51] Nocjar, C., Roth, B.L., Pehek, E.A. (2002) Localization of 5-HT(2A) receptors on dopamine cells in subnuclei of the midbrain A10 cell group. *Neuroscience,* 111 (1), 163-176.

[52] Duxon, M.S., Flanigan, T.P., Reavley, A.C., Baxter, G.S., Blackburn, T.P., Fone, K.C. (1997) Evidence for expression of the 5-hydroxytryptamine-2B receptor protein in the rat central nervous system. *Neuroscience,* 76 (2), 323-329.

[53] Reavill, C., Stolerman, I.P. (1990) Locomotor activity in rats after administration of nicotinic agonists intracerebrally. *Br. J. Pharmacol.,* 99 (2), 273-278.

[54] Olausson, P., Engel, J.A., Soderpalm, B. (1999) Behavioral sensitization to nicotine is associated with behavioral disinhibition; counteraction by citalopram. *Psychopharmacology (Berl),* 142 (2), 111-119.

[55] Clarke, P.B.S., Fu, D.S., Jakubovic, A., Fibiger, H.C. (1988) Evidence that mesolimbic dopaminergic activation underlies the locomotor stimulant action of nicotine in rats. *J. Pharmacol. Exp. Ther.,* 246 (2), 701-708.

[56] Corrigall, W.A., Coen, K.M., Adamson, K.L. (1994) Self-administered nicotine activates the mesolimbic dopamine system through the ventral tegmental area. *Brain Res.,* 653 (1-2), 278-284.

[57] Corrigall, W.A., Franklin, K.B., Coen, K.M., Clarke, P.B. (1992) The mesolimbic dopaminergic system is implicated in the reinforcing effects of nicotine. *Psychopharmacology (Berl),* 107 (2-3), 285-289.

[58] Louis, M., Clarke, P.B.S. (1998) Effect of ventral tegmental 6-hydroxydopamine lesions on the locomotor stimulant action of nicotine in rats. *Neuropharmacology,* 37 (12), 1503-1513.

[59] Dani, J.A., De Biasi, M. (2001) Cellular mechanisms of nicotine addiction. *Pharmacology Biochemistry and Behavior,* 70 (4), 439-446.

[60] Calabresi, P., Lacey, M.G., North, R.A. (1989) Nicotinic excitation of rat ventral tegmental neurones in vitro studied by intracellular recording. *Br. J. Pharmacol.,* 98 (1), 135-140.

[61] Pidoplichko, V.I., DeBiasi, M., Williams, J.T., Dani, J.A. (1997) Nicotine activates and desensitizes midbrain dopamine neurons. *Nature,* 390 (6658), 401-404.

[62] Sorenson, E.M., Shiroyama, T., Kitai, S.T. (1998) Postsynaptic nicotinic receptors on dopaminergic neurons in the substantia nigra pars compacta of the rat. *Neuroscience,* 87 (3), 659-673.

[63] Klink, R., de Kerchove d'Exaerde, A., Zoli, M., Changeux, J.P. (2001) Molecular and physiological diversity of nicotinic acetylcholine receptors in the midbrain dopaminergic nuclei. *J. Neurosci.,* 21 (5), 1452-1463.

[64] Mansvelder, H.D., Keath, J.R., McGehee, D.S. (2002) Synaptic mechanisms underlie nicotine-induced excitability of brain reward areas. *Neuron,* 33 (6), 905-919.

[65] Picciotto, M.R., Zoli, M., Rimondini, R., Lena, C., Marubio, L.M., Pich, E.M., Fuxe, K., Changeux, J.P. (1998) Acetylcholine receptors containing the beta2 subunit are involved in the reinforcing properties of nicotine. *Nature,* 391 (6663), 173-177.

[66] Mansvelder, H.D., McGehee, D.S. (2000) Long-term potentiation of excitatory inputs to brain reward areas by nicotine. *Neuron,* 27 (2), 349-357.

[67] Schilstrom, B., Mameli-Engvall, M., Rawal, N., Grillner, P., Jardemark, K., Svensson, T.H. (2004) Nitric oxide is involved in nicotine-induced burst firing of rat ventral tegmental area dopamine neurons. *Neuroscience,* 125 (4), 957-964.

[68] Lallemand, F., Ward, R.J., Dravolina, O., De Witte, P. (2006) Nicotine-induced changes of glutamate and arginine in naive and chronically alcoholized rats: an in vivo microdialysis study. *Brain Res.,* 1111 (1), 48-60.

[69] Pogun, S., Demirgoren, S., Taskiran, D., Kanit, L., Yilmaz, O., Koylu, E.O., Balkan, B., London, E.D. (2000) Nicotine modulates nitric oxide in rat brain. *Eur. Neuropsychopharmacol.,* 10 (6), 463-472.

[70] Garthwaite, J. (1991) Glutamate, nitric oxide and cell-cell signalling in the nervous system. *Trends Neurosci.,* 14 (2), 60-67.

[71] Di Matteo, V., Pierucci, M., Benigno, A., Esposito, E., Crescimanno, G., Di Giovanni, G. (2010) Critical role of nitric oxide on nicotine-induced hyperactivation of dopaminergic nigrostriatal system: Electrophysiological and neurochemical evidence in rats. *CNS Neurosci. Ther.,* 16 (3), 127-136.

[72] Marshall, D.L., Redfern, P.H., Wonnacott, S. (1997) Presynaptic nicotinic modulation of dopamine release in the three ascending pathways studied by in vivo microdialysis: Comparison of naive and chronic nicotine-treated rats. *J. Neurochem.,* 68 (4), 1511-1519.

[73] Mifsud, J.C., Hernandez, L., Hoebel, B.G. (1989) Nicotine infused into the nucleus accumbens increases synaptic dopamine as measured by in vivo microdialysis. *Brain Res.,* 478 (2), 365-367.

[74] Ferrari, R., Le NovÃ¨re, N., Picciotto, M.R., Changeux, J.P., Zoli, M. (2002) Acute and long-term changes in the mesolimbic dopamine pathway after systemic or local single nicotine injections. *Eur. J. Neurosci.,* 15 (11), 1810-1818.

[75] Grady, S.R., Marks, M.J., Collins, A.C. (1994) Desensitization of nicotine-stimulated [3H]dopamine release from mouse striatal synaptosomes. *J. Neurochem.,* 62 (4), 1390-1398.

[76] Brazell, M.P., Mitchell, S.N., Joseph, M.H., Gray, J.A. (1990) Acute administration of nicotine increases the in vivo extracellular levels of dopamine, 3,4-dihydroxyphenylacetic acid and ascorbic acid preferentially in the nucleus accumbens of the rat: comparison with caudate-putamen. *Neuropharmacology,* 29 (12), 1177-1185.

[77] Imperato, A., Mulas, A., Di Chiara, G. (1986) Nicotine preferentially stimulates dopamine-release in the limbic system of freely moving rats. *Eur. J. Pharmacol.,* 132 (2-3), 337-338.

[78] Di Matteo, V., Pierucci, M., Esposito, E. (2004) Selective stimulation of serotonin2C receptors blocks the enhancement of striatal and accumbal dopamine release induced by nicotine administration. *J. Neurochem.,* 89 (2), 418-429.

[79] Cadoni, C., Di Chiara, G. (2000) Differential changes in accumbens shell and core dopamine in behavioral sensitization to nicotine. *Eur. J. Pharmacol.,* 387 (3), R23-25.

[80] Balfour, D.J., Wright, A.E., Benwell, M.E., Birrell, C.E. (2000) The putative role of extra-synaptic mesolimbic dopamine in the neurobiology of nicotine dependence. *Behav. Brain Res.,* 113 (1-2), 73-83.

[81] Pierucci, M., Di Matteo, V., Esposito, E. (2004) Stimulation of serotonin2C receptors blocks the hyperactivation of midbrain dopamine neurons induced by nicotine administration. *J. Pharmacol. Exp. Ther.,* 309 (1), 109-118.

[82] Grenhoff, J., Aston-Jones, G., Svensson, T.H. (1986) Nicotinic effects on the firing pattern of midbrain dopamine neurons. *Acta Physiol. Scand.,* 128 (3), 351-358.

[83] Lichtensteiger, W., Hefti, F., Felix, D., Huwyler, T., Melamed, E., Schlumpf, M. (1982) Stimulation of nigrostriatal dopamine neurones by nicotine. *Neuropharmacology,* 21 (10), 963-968.

[84] Clarke, P.B.S., Hommer, D.W., Pert, A., Skirboll, L.R. (1985) Electrophysiological actions of nicotine on substantia nigra single units. *Br. J. Pharmacol.,* 85 (4), 827-835.

[85] Mereu, G., Yoon, K.W., Boi, V., Gessa, G.L., Naes, L., Westfall, T.C. (1987) Preferential stimulation of ventral tegmental area dopaminergic neurons by nicotine. *Eur. J. Pharmacol.,* 141 (3), 395-399.

[86] Schoffelmeer, A.N., De Vries, T.J., Wardeh, G., van de Ven, H.W., Vanderschuren, L.J. (2002) Psychostimulant-induced behavioral sensitization depends on nicotinic receptor activation. *J. Neurosci.,* 22 (8), 3269-3276.

[87] Shim, I., Javaid, J.I., Wirtshafter, D., Jang, S.Y., Shin, K.H., Lee, H.J., Chung, Y.C., Chun, B.G. (2001) Nicotine-induced behavioral sensitization is associated with extracellular dopamine release and expression of c-Fos in the striatum and nucleus accumbens of the rat. *Behav. Brain Res.,* 121 (1-2), 137-147.

[88] Benwell, M.E., Balfour, D.J. (1992) The effects of acute and repeated nicotine treatment on nucleus accumbens dopamine and locomotor activity. *Br. J. Pharmacol.,* 105 (4), 849-856.

[89] Grottick, A.J., Corrigall, W.A., Higgins, G.A. (2001) Activation of 5-HT(2C) receptors reduces the locomotor and rewarding effects of nicotine. *Psychopharmacology (Berl),* 157 (3), 292-298.

[90] Iyaniwura, T.T., Wright, A.E., Balfour, D.J. (2001) Evidence that mesoaccumbens dopamine and locomotor responses to nicotine in the rat are influenced by pretreatment dose and strain. *Psychopharmacology (Berl),* 158 (1), 73-79.

[91] White, F.J., Kalivas, P.W. (1998) Neuroadaptations involved in amphetamine and cocaine addiction. *Drug Alcohol Depend.,* 51 (1-2), 141-153.

[92] Vanderschuren, L.J., Schmidt, E.D., De Vries, T.J., Van Moorsel, C.A., Tilders, F.J., Schoffelmeer, A.N. (1999) A single exposure to amphetamine is sufficient to induce long-term behavioral, neuroendocrine, and neurochemical sensitization in rats. *J. Neurosci.,* 19 (21), 9579-9586.

[93] Robinson, T.E., Berridge, K.C. (2001) Incentive-sensitization and addiction. *Addiction,* 96 (1), 103-114.

[94] Balfour, D.J., Benwell, M.E., Birrell, C.E., Kelly, R.J., Al-Aloul, M. (1998) Sensitization of the mesoaccumbens dopamine response to nicotine. *Pharmacol. Biochem. Behav.,* 59 (4), 1021-1030.

[95] Serova, L., Sabban, E.L. (2002) Involvement of alpha 7 nicotinic acetylcholine receptors in gene expression of dopamine biosynthetic enzymes in rat brain. *J. Pharmacol. Exp. Ther.,* 303 (3), 896-903.

[96] Buisson, B., Bertrand, D. (2001) Chronic exposure to nicotine upregulates the human (alpha)4((beta)2 nicotinic acetylcholine receptor function. *J. Neurosci.,* 21 (6), 1819-1829.

[97] Marks, M.J., Pauly, J.R., Gross, S.D., Deneris, E.S., Hermans-Borgmeyer, I., Heinemann, S.F., Collins, A.C. (1992) Nicotine binding and nicotinic receptor subunit RNA after chronic nicotine treatment. *J. Neurosci.,* 12 (7), 2765-2784.

[98] Dani, J.A., Heinemann, S. (1996) Molecular and cellular aspects of nicotine abuse. *Neuron,* 16 (5), 905-908.

[99] Olausson, P., Jentsch, J.D., Taylor, J.R. (2004) Repeated nicotine exposure enhances responding with conditioned reinforcement. *Psychopharmacology (Berl),* 173 (1-2), 98-104.

[100] Seth, P., Cheeta, S., Tucci, S., File, S.E. (2002) Nicotinic--serotonergic interactions in brain and behaviour. *Pharmacol. Biochem. Behav.,* 71 (4), 795-805.

[101] Balfour, D.J., Ridley, D.L. (2000) The effects of nicotine on neural pathways implicated in depression: a factor in nicotine addiction? *Pharmacol. Biochem. Behav.,* 66 (1), 79-85.

[102] Quattrocki, E., Baird, A., Yurgelun-Todd, D. (2000) Biological aspects of the link between smoking and depression. *Harv. Rev. Psychiatry,* 8 (3), 99-110.

[103] Bitner, R.S., Nikkel, A.L. (2002) Alpha-7 nicotinic receptor expression by two distinct cell types in the dorsal raphe nucleus and locus coeruleus of rat. *Brain Res.,* 938 (1-2), 45-54.

[104] Bitner, R.S., Nikkel, A.L., Curzon, P., Donnelly-Roberts, D.L., Puttfarcken, P.S., Namovic, M., Jacobs, I.C., Meyer, M.D., Decker, M.W. (2000) Reduced nicotinic receptor-mediated antinociception following in vivo antisense knock-down in rat. *Brain Res.,* 871 (1), 66-74.

[105] Cucchiaro, G., Chaijale, N., Commons, K.G. (2005) The dorsal raphe nucleus as a site of action of the antinociceptive and behavioral effects of the alpha4 nicotinic receptor agonist epibatidine. *J. Pharmacol. Exp. Ther.*, 313 (1), 389-394.

[106] Cucchiaro, G., Commons, K.G. (2003) Alpha 4 nicotinic acetylcholine receptor subunit links cholinergic to brainstem monoaminergic neurotransmission. *Synapse,* 49 (3), 195-205.

[107] Enkhbaatar, P., Murakami, K., Traber, L.D., Cox, R., Parkinson, J.F., Westphal, M., Esechie, A., Morita, N., Maybauer, M.O., Maybauer, D.M., Burke, A.S., Schmalstieg, F.C., Hawkins, H.K., Herndon, D.N., Traber, D.L. (2006) The inhibition of inducible nitric oxide synthase in ovine sepsis model. *Shock,* 25 (5), 522-527.

[108] Galindo-Charles, L., Hernandez-Lopez, S., Galarraga, E., Tapia, D., Bargas, J., Garduno, J., Frias-Dominguez, C., Drucker-Colin, R., Mihailescu, S. (2008) Serotoninergic dorsal raphe neurons possess functional postsynaptic nicotinic acetylcholine receptors. *Synapse,* 62 (8), 601-615.

[109] Li, X., Rainnie, D.G., McCarley, R.W., Greene, R.W. (1998) Presynaptic nicotinic receptors facilitate monoaminergic transmission. *J. Neurosci.,* 18 (5), 1904-1912.

[110] Mihailescu, S., Guzman-Marin, R., Drucker-Colin, R. (2001) Nicotine stimulation of dorsal raphe neurons: effects on laterodorsal and pedunculopontine neurons. *Eur. Neuropsychopharmacol.,* 11 (5), 359-366.

[111] Chang, B., Daniele, C.A., Gallagher, K., Madonia, M., Mitchum, R.D., Barrett, L., Vezina, P., McGehee, D.S. (2011) Nicotinic excitation of serotonergic projections from dorsal raphe to the nucleus accumbens. *J. Neurophysiol.,* 106 (2), 801-808.

[112] Engberg, G., Erhardt, S., Sharp, T., Hajós, M. (2000) Nicotine inhibits firing activity of dorsal raphe 5-HT neurones in vivo. *Naunyn. Schmiedebergs. Arch. Pharmacol.,* 362 (1), 41-45.

[113] Ranade, S.P., Mainen, Z.F. (2009) Transient firing of dorsal raphe neurons encodes diverse and specific sensory, motor, and reward events. *J. Neurophysiol.,* 102 (5), 3026-3037.

[114] Summers, K.L., Lippiello, P., Giacobini, E. (1996) A microdialysis study of the effects of the nicotinic agonist RJR-2403 on cortical release of acetylcholine and biogenic amines. *Neurochem. Res.,* 21 (10), 1181-1186.

[115] Schwartz, R.D., Lehmann, J., Kellar, K.J. (1984) Presynaptic nicotinic cholinergic receptors labeled by [3H]acetylcholine on catecholamine and serotonin axons in brain. *J. Neurochem.,* 42 (5), 1495-1498.

[116] Reuben, M., Clarke, P.B. (2000) Nicotine-evoked [3H]5-hydroxytryptamine release from rat striatal synaptosomes. *Neuropharmacology,* 39 (2), 290-299.

[117] Yu, Z.J., Wecker, L. (1994) Chronic nicotine administration differentially affects neurotransmitter release from rat striatal slices. *J. Neurochem.,* 63 (1), 186-194.

[118] Takahashi, H., Takada, Y., Nagai, N., Urano, T., Takada, A. (1998) Nicotine increases stress-induced serotonin release by stimulating nicotinic acetylcholine receptor in rat striatum. *Synapse,* 28 (3), 212-219.

[119] Lendvai, B., Sershen, H., Lajtha, A., Santha, E., Baranyi, M., Vizi, E.S. (1996) Differential Mechanisms Involved in the Effect of Nicotinic Agonists DMPP and Lobeline to Release [3H]5-HT from Rat Hippocampal Slices. *Neuropharmacology,* 35 (12), 1769-1777.

[120] Kenny, P.J., File, S.E., Neal, M.J. (2000) Evidence for a complex influence of nicotinic acetylcholine receptors on hippocampal serotonin release. *J. Neurochem.,* 75 (6), 2409-2414.

[121] Benwell, M.E., Balfour, D.J. (1979) Effects of nicotine administration and its withdrawal on plasma corticosterone and brain 5-hydroxyindoles. *Psychopharmacology (Berl),* 63 (1), 7-11.

[122] Takada, Y., Urano, T., Ihara, H., Takada, A. (1995) Changes in the central and peripheral serotonergic system in rats exposed to water-immersion restrained stress and nicotine administration. *Neurosci. Res.,* 23 (3), 305-311.

[123] Di Giovanni, G., Di Matteo, V., Pierucci, M., Benigno, A., Esposito, E. (2006) Central serotonin2C receptor: from physiology to pathology. *Curr. Top Med. Chem.,* 6 (18), 1909-1925.

[124] Di Giovanni, G., Esposito, E., Di Matteo, V., eds. *5-HT2C Receptors in the Pathophysiology of CNS Disease*. The Receptors. 2011, Springer/Humana Press: New York. 1-557.

[125] Fletcher, A., Higgins, G.A., *Serotonin and reward-related behaviour: focus on 5-HT2C receptors*, in *5-HT2C Receptors in the Pathophysiology of CNS Disease*, G. Di Giovanni, E. Esposito, and V. Di Matteo, Editors. 2011, Springer: New York. p. 293-324.

[126] Prisco, S., Pagannone, S., Esposito, E. (1994) Serotonin-dopamine interaction in the rat ventral tegmental area: an electrophysiological study in vivo. *J. Pharmacol. Exp. Ther.,* 271 (1), 83-90.

[127] Di Giovanni, G., De Deurwaerdere, P., Di Mascio, M., Di Matteo, V., Esposito, E., Spampinato, U. (1999) Selective blockade of serotonin-2C/2B receptors enhances mesolimbic and mesostriatal dopaminergic function: a combined in vivo electrophysiological and microdialysis study. *Neuroscience,* 91 (2), 587-597.

[128] Kennett, G.A., Wood, M.D., Bright, F., Cilia, J., Piper, D.C., Gager, T., Thomas, D., Baxter, G.S., Forbes, I.T., Ham, P., Blackburn, T.P. (1996) In vitro and in vivo profile of SB 206553, a potent 5-HT2C/5-HT2B receptor antagonist with anxiolytic-like properties. *Br. J. Pharmacol.,* 117 (3), 427-434.

[129] Kennett, G.A., Wood, M.D., Bright, F., Trail, B., Riley, G., Holland, V., Avenell, K.Y., Stean, T., Upton, N., Bromidge, S., Forbes, I.T., Brown, A.M., Middlemiss, D.N., Blackburn, T.P. (1997) SB 242084, a selective and brain penetrant 5-HT2C receptor antagonist. *Neuropharmacology,* 36 (4-5), 609-620.

[130] Di Matteo, V., Di Giovanni, G., Di Mascio, M., Esposito, E. (1998) Selective blockade of serotonin2C/2B receptors enhances dopamine release in the rat nucleus accumbens. *Neuropharmacology,* 37 (2), 265-272.

[131] Gobert, A., Rivet, J.M., Lejeune, F., Newman-Tancredi, A., Adhumeau-Auclair, A., Nicolas, J.P., Cistarelli, L., Melon, C., Millan, M.J. (2000) Serotonin(2C) receptors tonically suppress the activity of mesocortical dopaminergic and adrenergic, but not serotonergic, pathways: a combined dialysis and electrophysiological analysis in the rat. *Synapse,* 36 (3), 205-221.

[132] Martin, J.R., Bos, M., Jenck, F., Moreau, J., Mutel, V., Sleight, A.J., Wichmann, J., Andrews, J.S., Berendsen, H.H., Broekkamp, C.L., Ruigt, G.S., Kohler, C., Delft, A.M. (1998) 5-HT2C receptor agonists: pharmacological characteristics and therapeutic potential. *J. Pharmacol. Exp. Ther.,* 286 (2), 913-924.

[133] Di Matteo, V., Di Giovanni, G., Di Mascio, M., Esposito, E. (1999) SB 242084, a selective serotonin2C receptor antagonist, increases dopaminergic transmission in the mesolimbic system. *Neuropharmacology,* 38 (8), 1195-1205.

[134] Millan, M.J., Dekeyne, A., Gobert, A. (1998) Serotonin (5-HT)2C receptors tonically inhibit dopamine (DA) and noradrenaline (NA), but not 5-HT, release in the frontal cortex in vivo. *Neuropharmacology,* 37 (7), 953-955.

[135] Di Matteo, V., Di Giovanni, G., Di Mascio, M., Esposito, E. (2000) Biochemical and electrophysiological evidence that RO 60-0175 inhibits mesolimbic dopaminergic function through serotonin(2C) receptors. *Brain Res.,* 865 (1), 85-90.

[136] Hutson, P.H., Barton, C.L., Jay, M., Blurton, P., Burkamp, F., Clarkson, R., Bristow, L.J. (2000) Activation of mesolimbic dopamine function by phencyclidine is enhanced by 5-HT(2C/2B) receptor antagonists: neurochemical and behavioural studies. *Neuropharmacology,* 39 (12), 2318-2328.

[137] Pozzi, L., Acconcia, S., Ceglia, I., Invernizzi, R.W., Samanin, R. (2002) Stimulation of 5-hydroxytryptamine (5-HT(2C) ) receptors in the ventrotegmental area inhibits stress-induced but not basal dopamine release in the rat prefrontal cortex. *J. Neurochem.,* 82 (1), 93-100.

[138] Porras, G., Di Matteo, V., De Deurwaerdere, P., Esposito, E., Spampinato, U. (2002) Central serotonin4 receptors selectively regulate the impulse-dependent exocytosis of dopamine in the rat striatum: in vivo studies with morphine, amphetamine and cocaine. *Neuropharmacology,* 43 (7), 1099-1109.

[139] Willins, D.L., Meltzer, H.Y. (1998) Serotonin 5-HT2C agonists selectively inhibit morphine-induced dopamine efflux in the nucleus accumbens. *Brain Res.,* 781 (1-2), 291-299.

[140] Grottick, A.J., Fletcher, P.J., Higgins, G.A. (2000) Studies to investigate the role of 5-HT(2C) receptors on cocaine- and food-maintained behavior. *J. Pharmacol. Exp. Ther.,* 295 (3), 1183-1191.

[141] Levin, E.D., Slade, S., Johnson, M., Petro, A., Horton, K., Williams, P., Rezvani, A.H., Rose, J.E. (2008) Ketanserin, a 5-HT2 receptor antagonist, decreases nicotine self-administration in rats. *Eur. J. Pharmacol.,* 600 (1-3), 93-97.

[142] Tomkins, D.M., Joharchi, N., Tampakeras, M., Martin, J.R., Wichmann, J., Higgins, G.A. (2002) An investigation of the role of 5-HT(2C) receptors in modifying ethanol self-administration behaviour. *Pharmacol. Biochem. Behav.,* 71 (4), 735-744.

[143] Levin, E.D., Johnson, J.E., Slade, S., Wells, C., Cauley, M., Petro, A., Rose, J.E. (2011) Lorcaserin, a 5-HT2C agonist, decreases nicotine self-administration in female rats. *J. Pharmacol. Exp. Ther.,* 338 (3), 890-896.

[144] Hayes, D.J., Mosher, T.M., Greenshaw, A.J. (2009) Differential effects of 5-HT2C receptor activation by WAY 161503 on nicotine-induced place conditioning and locomotor activity in rats. *Behav. Brain Res.,* 197 (2), 323-330.

[145] Zaniewska, M., McCreary, A.C., Filip, M. (2009) Interactions of serotonin (5-HT)2 receptor-targeting ligands and nicotine: locomotor activity studies in rats. *Synapse,* 63 (8), 653-661.

[146] Bromidge, S.M., Dabbs, S., Davies, D.T., Davies, S., Duckworth, D.M., Forbes, I.T., Gaster, L.M., Ham, P., Jones, G.E., King, F.D., Mulholland, K.R., Saunders, D.V., Wyman, P.A., Blaney, F.E., Clarke, S.E., Blackburn, T.P., Holland, V., Kennett, G.A., Lightowler, S., Middlemiss, D.N., Trail, B., Riley, G.J., Wood, M.D. (2000) Biaryl-

carbamoylindolines are novel and selective 5-HT(2C) receptor inverse agonists: identification of 5-methyl-1-[[2-[(2-methyl-3-pyridyl)oxy]- 5-pyridyl]carbamoyl]-6-trifluoromethylindoline (SB-243213) as a potential antidepressant/anxiolytic agent. *J. Med. Chem.,* 43 (6), 1123-1134.

[147] Mihailescu, S., Palomero-Rivero, M., Meade-Huerta, P., Maza-Flores, A., Drucker-Colin, R. (1998) Effects of nicotine and mecamylamine on rat dorsal raphe neurons. *Eur. J. Pharmacol.,* 360 (1), 31-36.

[148] Ribeiro, E.B., Bettiker, R.L., Bogdanov, M., Wurtman, R.J. (1993) Effects of systemic nicotine on serotonin release in rat brain. *Brain Res.,* 621 (2), 311-318.

[149] Fuxe, K., Everitt, B.J., Hokfelt, T. (1979) On the action of nicotine and cotinine on central 5-hydroxytryptamine neurons. *Pharmacol. Biochem. Behav.,* 10 (5), 671-677.

[150] Balfour, D.J., Graham, C.A., Vale, A.L. (1986) Studies on the possible role of brain 5-HT systems and adrenocortical activity in behavioural responses to nicotine and diazepam in an elevated X-maze. *Psychopharmacology (Berl),* 90 (4), 528-532.

[151] Benwell, M.E., Balfour, D.J., Anderson, J.M. (1990) Smoking-associated changes in the serotonergic systems of discrete regions of human brain. *Psychopharmacology (Berl),* 102 (1), 68-72.

[152] Yasuda, K., Suemaru, K., Araki, H., Gomita, Y. (2002) Effect of nicotine cessation on the central serotonergic systems in mice: involvement of 5-HT(2) receptors. *Naunyn. Schmiedebergs. Arch. Pharmacol.,* 366 (3), 276-281.

[153] Olausson, P., Engel, J.A., Soderpalm, B. (2002) Involvement of serotonin in nicotine dependence: processes relevant to positive and negative regulation of drug intake. *Pharmacol. Biochem. Behav.,* 71 (4), 757-771.

[154] Jorenby, D.E., Leischow, S.J., Nides, M.A., Rennard, S.I., Johnston, J.A., Hughes, A.R., Smith, S.S., Muramoto, M.L., Daughton, D.M., Doan, K., Fiore, M.C., Baker, T.B. (1999) A controlled trial of sustained-release bupropion, a nicotine patch, or both for smoking cessation. *N. Engl. J. Med.,* 340 (9), 685-691.

[155] Dong, J., Blier, P. (2001) Modification of norepinephrine and serotonin, but not dopamine, neuron firing by sustained bupropion treatment. *Psychopharmacology (Berl),* 155 (1), 52-57.

[156] Dewey, S.L., Brodie, J.D., Gerasimov, M., Horan, B., Gardner, E.L., Ashby, C.R., Jr. (1999) A pharmacologic strategy for the treatment of nicotine addiction. *Synapse,* 31 (1), 76-86.

[157] Corrigall, W.A., Coen, K.M., Adamson, K.L., Chow, B.L., Zhang, J. (2000) Response of nicotine self-administration in the rat to manipulations of mu-opioid and gamma-aminobutyric acid receptors in the ventral tegmental area. *Psychopharmacology (Berl),* 149 (2), 107-114.

[158] Di Giovanni, G., Di Matteo, V., Pierucci, M., Benigno, A., Esposito, E. (2006) Serotonin involvement in the basal ganglia pathophysiology: could the 5-HT2C receptor be a new target for therapeutic strategies? *Curr. Med. Chem.,* 13 (25), 3069-3081.

[159] Anderson, J.E., Jorenby, D.E., Scott, W.J., Fiore, M.C. (2002) Treating tobacco use and dependence: an evidence-based clinical practice guideline for tobacco cessation. *Chest,* 121 (3), 932-941.

[160] Jain, A. (2003) Treating nicotine addiction. *BMJ,* 327 (7428), 1394-1395.

[161] Shahan, T.A., Bickel, W.K., Madden, G.J., Badger, G.J. (1999) Comparing the reinforcing efficacy of nicotine containing and de-nicotinized cigarettes: a behavioral economic analysis. *Psychopharmacology (Berl),* 147 (2), 210-216.

[162] Mucha, R.F., Geier, A., Pauli, P. (1999) Modulation of craving by cues having differential overlap with pharmacological effect: evidence for cue approach in smokers and social drinkers. *Psychopharmacology (Berl),* 147 (3), 306-313.

[163] Dols, M., Willems, B., van den Hout, M., Bittoun, R. (2000) Smokers can learn to influence their urge to smoke. *Addict. Behav.,* 25 (1), 103-108.

[164] Cryan, J.F., Gasparini, F., van Heeke, G., Markou, A. (2003) Non-nicotinic neuropharmacological strategies for nicotine dependence: beyond bupropion. *Drug Discov. Today,* 8 (22), 1025-1034.

[165] Rigotti, N.A. (2002) Clinical practice. Treatment of tobacco use and dependence. *N. Engl. J. Med.,* 346 (7), 506-512.

[166] Ascher, J.A., Cole, J.O., Colin, J.N., Feighner, J.P., Ferris, R.M., Fibiger, H.C., Golden, R.N., Martin, P., Potter, W.Z., Richelson, E., et al. (1995) Bupropion: a review of its mechanism of antidepressant activity. *J. Clin. Psychiatry,* 56 (9), 395-401.

[167] Eisenberg, M.J., Filion, K.B., Yavin, D., Belisle, P., Mottillo, S., Joseph, L., Gervais, A., O'Loughlin, J., Paradis, G., Rinfret, S., Pilote, L. (2008) Pharmacotherapies for smoking cessation: a meta-analysis of randomized controlled trials. *CMAJ,* 179 (2), 135-144.

[168] Rollema, H., Coe, J.W., Chambers, L.K., Hurst, R.S., Stahl, S.M., Williams, K.E. (2007) Rationale, pharmacology and clinical efficacy of partial agonists of alpha4beta2 nACh receptors for smoking cessation. *Trends Pharmacol. Sci.,* 28 (7), 316-325.

[169] Slemmer, J.E., Martin, B.R., Damaj, M.I. (2000) Bupropion is a nicotinic antagonist. *J. Pharmacol. Exp. Ther.,* 295 (1), 321-327.

[170] Cooper, B.R., Wang, C.M., Cox, R.F., Norton, R., Shea, V., Ferris, R.M. (1994) Evidence that the acute behavioral and electrophysiological effects of bupropion (Wellbutrin) are mediated by a noradrenergic mechanism. *Neuropsychopharmacology,* 11 (2), 133-141.

[171] Mansvelder, H.D., Fagen, Z.M., Chang, B., Mitchum, R., McGehee, D.S. (2007) Bupropion inhibits the cellular effects of nicotine in the ventral tegmental area. *Biochem. Pharmacol.,* 74 (8), 1283-1291.

[172] Coe, J.W., Brooks, P.R., Vetelino, M.G., Wirtz, M.C., Arnold, E.P., Huang, J., Sands, S.B., Davis, T.I., Lebel, L.A., Fox, C.B., Shrikhande, A., Heym, J.H., Schaeffer, E., Rollema, H., Lu, Y., Mansbach, R.S., Chambers, L.K., Rovetti, C.C., Schulz, D.W., Tingley, F.D., 3rd, O'Neill, B.T. (2005) Varenicline: an alpha4beta2 nicotinic receptor partial agonist for smoking cessation. *J. Med. Chem.,* 48 (10), 3474-3477.

[173] Reperant, C., Pons, S., Dufour, E., Rollema, H., Gardier, A.M., Maskos, U. (2010) Effect of the [alpha]4[beta]2* nicotinic acetylcholine receptor partial agonist varenicline on dopamine release in [beta]2 knock-out mice with selective re-expression of the [beta]2 subunit in the ventral tegmental area. *Neuropharmacology,* 58 (2), 346-350.

[174] Rollema, H., Wilson, G.G., Lee, T.C., Folgering, J.H., Flik, G. (2011) Effect of co-administration of varenicline and antidepressants on extracellular monoamine concentrations in rat prefrontal cortex. *Neurochem. Int.,* 58 (1), 78-84.

[175] Rollema, H., Hajos, M., Seymour, P.A., Kozak, R., Majchrzak, M.J., Guanowsky, V., Horner, W.E., Chapin, D.S., Hoffmann, W.E., Johnson, D.E., McLean, S., Freeman, J., Williams, K.E. (2009) Preclinical pharmacology of the alpha4beta2 nAChR partial agonist varenicline related to effects on reward, mood and cognition. *Biochem. Pharmacol.,* 78 (7), 813-824.

[176] Mills, E.J., Wu, P., Spurden, D., Ebbert, J.O., Wilson, K. (2009) Efficacy of pharmacotherapies for short-term smoking abstinance: a systematic review and meta-analysis. *Harm. Reduct. J.,* 6, 25.

[177] US Food and Drig Administration, C.f.D.E.a.R. Varenicline (marketed as Chantix) information. Washington (DC): US Department of Health and Human Services. 2008 [cited 2011 December 12th ]; Available from: www.fda.gov/CDER/Drug/infopage/ varenicline/default.htm.

[178] Prochazka, A.V., Weaver, M.J., Keller, R.T., Fryer, G.E., Licari, P.A., Lofaso, D. (1998) A randomized trial of nortriptyline for smoking cessation. *Arch. Intern. Med.,* 158 (18), 2035-2039.

[179] Hall, S.M., Humfleet, G.L., Reus, V.I., Munoz, R.F., Hartz, D.T., Maude-Griffin, R. (2002) Psychological intervention and antidepressant treatment in smoking cessation. *Arch. Gen. Psychiatry,* 59 (10), 930-936.

[180] Hall, S.M., Reus, V.I., Munoz, R.F., Sees, K.L., Humfleet, G., Hartz, D.T., Frederick, S., Triffleman, E. (1998) Nortriptyline and cognitive-behavioral therapy in the treatment of cigarette smoking. *Arch. Gen. Psychiatry,* 55 (8), 683-690.

[181] Edwards, N.B., Murphy, J.K., Downs, A.D., Ackerman, B.J., Rosenthal, T.L. (1989) Doxepin as an adjunct to smoking cessation: a double-blind pilot study. *Am. J. Psychiatry,* 146 (3), 373-376.

[182] Dalack, G.W., Glassman, A.H., Rivelli, S., Covey, L., Stetner, F. (1995) Mood, major depression, and fluoxetine response in cigarette smokers. *Am. J. Psychiatry,* 152 (3), 398-403.

[183] Schneider, N.G., Olmstead, R.E., Steinberg, C., Sloan, K., Daims, R.M., Brown, H.V. (1996) Efficacy of buspirone in smoking cessation: a placebo-controlled trial. *Clin. Pharmacol. Ther.,* 60 (5), 568-575.

[184] Olausson, P., Akesson, P., Engel, J.A., Soderpalm, B. (2001) Effects of 5-HT1A and 5-HT2 receptor agonists on the behavioral and neurochemical consequences of repeated nicotine treatment. *Eur. J. Pharmacol.,* 420 (1), 45-54.

[185] Cheeta, S., Irvine, E.E., Kenny, P.J., File, S.E. (2001) The dorsal raphe nucleus is a crucial structure mediating nicotine's anxiolytic effects and the development of tolerance and withdrawal responses. *Psychopharmacology (Berl),* 155 (1), 78-85.

In: Nicotine Addiction
Editor: Giuseppe Di Giovanni

ISBN: 978-1-62081-290-7


*Chapter 3*

# DEFINING THE ROLE OF THE HIPPOCAMPUS IN NICOTINE ADDICTION

***Robin A. J. Lester****
Department of Neurobiology and The McKnight Brain Institute,
University of Alabama at Birmingham, Alabama, US

## ABSTRACT

The associative storage of information, in addition to subject categorization, provides a powerful means of recalling a significant amount of related information with little input. The subcortical limbic system devotes a good deal of processing power and anatomy to correctly associate information, both for species and self-survival, using reward-driven learning via the projections of dopaminergic midbrain neurons and the hippocampus. These two systems are continuously and largely subconsciously updating this information based on experience, so that animals don't have to be overly occupied about predictable events. As humans, like other animals, it is advantageous that our brains care more about the unexpected. The drug nicotine, when consumed in its many forms, is constantly paired with a variety of sensory and environmental cues, and this associated information is stored using operant and classical conditioning mechanisms for future retrieval. These nicotine-induced associations are obviously not advantageous for survival. However, because addictive drugs greatly activate the reward pathway, they are repeated and any associatively-stored contextual information becomes a strong secondary predictor of drug expectation, perhaps inducing motivationally driven-states that facilitate drug-seeking behavior, and trigger the craving and withdrawal which ultimately may be responsible for the chronic relapsive nature of this disease. Initially, the brain seems to be able to adapt homeostatically to the presence of the drug, such that it can function normally with the drug on board. However, when the drug is absent, perhaps during cessation attempts, activating anti-reward systems, notably stress, may induce further brain changes, such that the nicotine-affected brain can never return to its naïve state even following a prolonged absence from the drug. During the abstinent period,

* Mailing address for correspondence: Robin A.J. Lester - Department of Neurobiology, SHEL 1006, University of Alabama at Birmingham, 1825 University Boulevard, Birmingham AL 35294, US. FAX: (205) 934-6571. TEL: (205) 934-4483. Email: nicotine@uab.edu.

secondary associative contexts or sensory cues may become the major trigger for a lifetime of an induced predisposition to nicotine by providing the drive for eventual nicotine relapse and abuse. In this review, I will discuss what is known about changes, induced by chronic nicotine use, in the hippocampus on the cellular and circuit levels. Furthermore, I attempt to link these changes to the rest of the reward system with the goal of ultimately working towards a model of how exposure to a small amount of nicotine can lead to the addictive behavior that affects 1 in 5 of the world's population – over 1 billion people. Specifically, the functional role of the hippocampus, traditionally associated with the relapse stage of addiction, will be re-analyzed in the broader context of the entire addiction process, much of which will involve assembling data that has been viewed largely in isolation, and will, by necessity, involve a certain amount of speculation.

## INTRODUCTION

The overarching, largely unanswered question that underlies the discussion in this chapter might be simply phrased as, "Exactly how does the hippocampus contribute to nicotine addiction?"

"Quitting smoking is easy, I've done it thousands of times", the quotation attributed, perhaps incorrectly, to Mark Twain exemplifies the relapse to nicotine-related products. Relapsing to drug seeking or abuse is extremely common, even following prolonged periods of abstinence. This hallmark of drug abuse perhaps contributes more than any other aspect to the difficulties of treating or curing nicotine addiction and, to some extent, all abused compounds [1]. Although, not necessarily the entire explanation, it seems somewhat intuitive that the neuroanatomical basis for this is based on dysfunctional learning and likely resides in the numerous cognitive processing areas of the brain, including the hippocampus [2-5]. While other mechanisms, such as acute stress and emotional episodes, also contribute (as discussed below), it seems that a "memory of nicotine" is likely crucial to making tobacco abuse a lifelong disease.

Despite the numerous reviews written on the neurobiology of addiction, much of what I will discuss is based on the premise that the hippocampus has not received due credit for its crucial role in this disease. This is somewhat odd considering the major role that the hippocampus plays in both the consolidation of associative memory and its recall (for a recent review see [6]), and in terms of drug addiction transferring smoking-related contexts (and perhaps other sensory cues) to numerous subconscious limbic structures, in addition to its role in enabling these signals to reach conscious areas of the brain such as the prefrontal cortex (PFC). Moreover, because its circuitry is ideally suited to recognize novel sensory stimuli, a process routed in its dual anatomical circuitry (see Figure 1), it is enabled to compare past experiences with new sensory input [7, 8]. Therefore, the hippocampus is potentially poised to function in a much more holistic manner than it has usually been assigned, perhaps allowing it to detect the novelty associated with the initial exposure to drugs of abuse, although it is appreciated that the detection of novel stimuli does not necessarily equate with rewards or reinforcements (see references in [7]). Furthermore, over the last decade or so, the connectivity of the hippocampus with the central dopaminergic (DA) reward circuitry has become much more widely appreciated. Moreover, because of the functional interplay between the hippocampus and the canonical motivation brain areas (not forgetting aversive and anti-reward systems) in the survival of self and species - an aspect of motivation that critically depends on prior experience and learning [9] - it is surprising that the hippocampus does not feature at the forefront of addiction research. That is not to say that many authors have completely downplayed the importance of this limbic region, or that other memory systems and their associated plasticity to abused drugs are not equally relevant.

More specifically, in terms of addiction to nicotine products, it is fair to say that the exact function of the many neuroadaptations occurring within the hippocampus remain obscure [10], a declaration that is partly confounded by the complexity of nicotinic acetylcholine receptors (nAChRs) in this region and their contribution to synaptic transmission and plasticity [11, 12]. However, the role of nicotine as a cognitive enhancer [13] and the marked hippocampal memory deficits known to occur, at least during the early stages of nicotine withdrawal [14, 15], imply that some of the addictive potential of nicotine must be associated with this limbic structure.

This article will begin by addressing the general, functional, and anatomical arrangement of the hippocampus with respect to the better researched DA components of the reward "pleasure center" circuit [16], based largely on drugs of abuse other than nicotine because a great deal more is known about the addictive nature of these compounds. This will be followed by a more in depth examination of the status associated with the interplay between the various anatomical substrates, focusing on the hippocampus, specifically in regard to nicotine addiction. Finally, the potential for therapeutic intervention in the hippocampus will be discussed, and I will attempt to begin assembling a model that takes into account nAChRs, the hippocampus and the traditional reward circuitry. Up front, I would like to acknowledge the published literature from many authors that have made writing this chapter possible. Obviously, complete details concerning every aspect of nAChRs, the hippocampus, and addiction will not be covered, and I apologize in advance to the authors of those studies not included.

## Canonical View of Reward and Addiction

At a simplistic level the majority of species can be regarded as sensory-input, motor-output devices. In higher animals like humans, an extreme reductionist view of the nervous system, in particular the central nervous system (CNS), positions it as an integrator making sure that, under variable conditions, sensory input is appropriately linked to motor output (of course, motor output could be replaced by other forms of cognitive processing). Notwithstanding the obvious need for complexity in order for it to optimally function, it can be useful to view the CNS (especially the brain) as a rather simple piece of apparatus. Thus, it is not unrealistic to propose that it is programmed (and modified by evolution and self-experience) to perform a series of seemingly simple behavioral tasks. For example, one could argue that one of its most important functions is in providing the necessary drive and motivation in order to keep the self and species in existence [9]., In humans, although distinguished from most other mammals by their large and deeply folded cortex, the cortex from this vantage point would not necessarily be the most important part of the brain (aside from being able to store, manipulate and utilize massive amounts of data). Rather, the pleasure and aversion centers become much more central to existence, as brought to light by the experiments of James Olds and colleagues [16]. Such studies demonstrated that rats would lever-press in order to receive low threshold, electrical self-stimulation into areas of the brain colloquially known as the "pleasure centers", even to the point of ignoring normal life-sustaining behaviors. These experiments rightly positioned the dopaminergic ventral tegmental area (VTA) (corticomesolimbic pathway) nucleus accumbens at the forefront of addiction theories. Subsequently, many studies have shown that animals will self-administer drugs of abuse, including nicotine [17], directly into this pathway [1], although it should be noted (as discussed below) that the VTA seems like the most essential structure for initiating the nicotine reinforcement [18]. Importantly, the hippocampus is involved and is essential for learning such an operant conditioning task (see references in [19, 20]), especially in the early stages of the behavior.

A somewhat naïve view of the DA pathway considers that, at a very minimum, it must provide the "wanting" incentive and motivational drive for humans (or rodents, for that matter) to get out of bed in the morning, eat breakfast, and go to work (earn money) so that they are able to maintain a family and home. In this overly simplistic take on the reward system, the drive could be thought of as largely independent of consciousness: it keeps us going despite what we may prefer to do otherwise (i.e., no override function). Such a system must be intrinsically dominant and reinforcing (rewarding), and it must coordinate the brain to repetitively perform actions despite the potentially boring nature of the task. Although we may have automated (by balancing reward with anti-reward) the regulation of these reward pathways, it is also reasonable that we have conscious override and decision-making inputs. Furthermore, as humans, we may be uniquely (or somewhat better adapted than lower mammals) at doing this. Based on experience, memory and emotion signals arise in the PFC and nucleus accumbens, informing us of the intrinsic value of the reward. Nonetheless, without entering a debate on free will, we still have the ability to decide whether to seek it out or not [21]. Should I play the mega millions lottery tonight? However, addictive behaviors appear to override these regulatory mechanisms and, as a consequence, the "reward" becomes self-perpetuating. Indeed, many theories of drug abuse imply that an inadequate PFC top-down control of these subcortical and limbic structures is at the heart of many, if not all, addictive and risk-taking behaviors [22]. However, (as discussed below) projections from the hippocampus are an essential link coupling the PFC and the DA pathway, ultimately making these behaviors possible.

It has been argued through the "incentive-relevance" theory that the main VTA-accumbens DA pathway is the most important for "wanting" the reward or drug. Thus, there is an increased firing in the VTA when the reward is initially detected [23] along with PFC activation which couples this motivational incentive to the behavioral goal of obtaining the reward [24, 25]. Consequently,, a straightforward explanation is provided for drug-seeking behavior involving a simple neuroanatomical circuit. Furthermore, through both experimental observations and theoretical modeling, this same circuit can be modified by experience, such that the animals can predict, using associated cues, whether to expect a reward. After the animal has learned the prediction, the VTA neurons increase their firing rate only to the cue, but not to the reward, as long as the expected reward occurs [23]. Because the system works in a bidirectional fashion, producing a decreased firing in the VTA if the reward does not occur, it has been generalized to an "error-detection" device. This fits well with the idea that animals, including humans, do not like uncertainty, enabling them to be much more attentive to unexpected or novel signals [7, 26], such as the first exposure to a drug, use of an established drug in a new context, or induction of a homeostatic drive-state if the drug is not delivered following an appropriate cue. Thus, the brain, utilizing temporal lobe regions such as the hippocampus and amygdala, is constantly collecting associations (incorporating emotional significance), building up pictures of our likes and dislikes, and consolidating this information in our massive cortex. Because of the continuous nature of our interactions with the environment, one can readily see the need for a huge amount of ROM [27]. However, as discussed by Di Chiara and North [28], there has to be a consummatory "liking" phase in addition to the incentive "wanting" phase in order for a reward to be fully reinforcing, implying that additional brain circuitry, which may be both common and specific to certain drugs, is likely involved in addiction.

The addiction cycle, from first exposure through escalation and ultimately to uncontrolled abuse, has been divided into a series of sequential stages: acute binging and intoxication, withdrawal and negative affect, and preoccupation and anticipation, gradually moving the behavioral nature of addiction from impulsivity to thatof a more compulsive act [1, 29]. The hippocampus is most often associated with the withdrawal and relapse stage of addiction, not surprisingly because of its ability to recall associated drug contexts and cues, which likely trigger the incentive and motivation to seek drugs via activating the DA-PFC system. By necessity, the progression towards full addiction involves multiple areas of the CNS (brainstem; limbic systems; sensory, motor and cognitive cortical areas), some acting specifically during different phases and others in a more synchronous manner. According to the simplistic input-output integration model of the nervous system proposed earlier, the behavior called addiction probably involves the coordination of massive amounts of brain volume. In his book *Descartes' Error* [30], Antonio Damasio takes a similar view when discussing how the brain processes emotion and reasoning, implying that many areas of the brain must function together to produce logical decision-making. Thus, the brain may use much of its power (similar circuitry) to accomplish complexly similar, but distinct, behavioral tasks. In addition, it is to be expected that many areas, not just the hippocampus, undergo cognitive adaptations during the different phases of drug abuse, including, but not restricted to: the central DA reward pathway (ventral striatum), dorsal striatum, amygdala and the PFC [31]. Plasticity in these other areas is beyond the scope of the current chapter, but has been extensively discussed in a number of excellent reviews (e.g., [25, 32, 33]). Here we will focus on the mechanisms of drug addiction in the hippocampus. However, as can be seen below from the functional anatomical connectivity of this region, it is not possible to consider the hippocampus in complete isolation.

To date, while much is known about reinforcement and reward systems, the precise roles of various components, how they interact with one another and exactly what functions they perform is still not fully understood, especially when it comes to the dysregulation experienced during the addiction process. This is especially true for the hippocampus. In summary, motivation is viewed as the key to the survival of self and species, requiring the ability to detect novel information, decide whether it is worth paying attention to, and then place it in storage for later use. In such a scenario, certainty about future events is desired because "not knowing" would put the species at a disadvantage. Conversely, being able to predict the future would be very useful, and thus the long-term storage of pertinent information about upcoming rewarding (or adverse) events through associative learning would have to be an essential feature of this system; therefore it is also not surprising that such a system is highly evolutionarily conserved [9]. In terms of forming sensory associations (especially drug-context links), a substantial amount is known about hippocampal connectivity and its interactions with the reward pathway, but much of this information has not been consolidated and is distributed throughout the literature. In the next section I will attempt to provide a clearer picture of the anatomical basis associated with the hippocampus in terms of addictive behavior.

## CONNECTIVITY BETWEEN THE HIPPOCAMPUS AND THE REWARD CIRCUITRY

Ever since the loss of long-term anterograde memory, following bilateral temporal lobe resection, in the infamous patient HM [34], the hippocampus has been viewed largely as a major anatomical substrate for consolidating short-term memories, especially spatial learning [6]. This function gels well with its importance in environmentally and contextually driven relapses to drug seeking behavior in addiction [1, 3]. However, as discussed by Cooper et al., [26] the involvement of the hippocampus in reward and motivation, and indeed drug addiction, may be much more extensive.

As beautifully illustrated by Anne Kelley (see Figure 2 in ref [9]) in her review on the similarities between memory and reward systems, the hippocampus does not purely reside on the side-lines, looking over at the central dopaminergic VTA-nucleus accumbens pathway: it is intricately hooked up, both directly and indirectly, to many of the more well-known structures in this circuitry. This connectivity has been discussed in terms of encoding novelty, schizophrenia [7, 35-37], and drug addiction [26]. The dual input, direct and indirect, from the entorhinal cortex, allows the CA1 region (see Figure 1) to act as a comparator between incoming and stored information, giving it the ability to detect novel sensory information [7]. A bidirectional relay between the dopaminergic system and the hippocampus is then used to gauge relevance and subsequent encoding if warranted [7]. The anatomical circuitry underlying the first part of the relay occurs via the ventral subiculum projection to the nucleus accumbens [38].

However, until recently, this pathway alone provided an unsatisfactory explanation for complete circuit functioning because the excitation or inhibition of the ventral subiculum produced changes in the firing patterns of VTA neurons, seeming to be absolutely necessary for altered dopamine output in the nucleus accumbens [35, 36], and the anatomical link between the hippocampus and the VTA had not been fully established. Floresco et al. [37] suggested that the missing link in the subiculum-induced excitation of the VTA occurred via the ventral pallidum in what would be a disynaptic inhibitory pathway. Although not shown in Figure 1, projection of the GABAergic medium spiny neurons in the accumbens directly to the VTA could influence dopaminergic cells via local VTA inhibitory neurons [26]. Continuing with the disinhibitory theme, a recent study has demonstrated that an additional part of the hippocampus, the CA3 region, is functionally hooked up to the VTA via the lateral septum [39] and is essential for a context-induced reinstatement of cocaine seeking (Figure 2). Together, these studies suggest that novel sensory cues and or drug context signals, originating in the hippocampus, may exert specific (or perhaps a more generalized) increased activity of the main reward circuitry [26, 40].

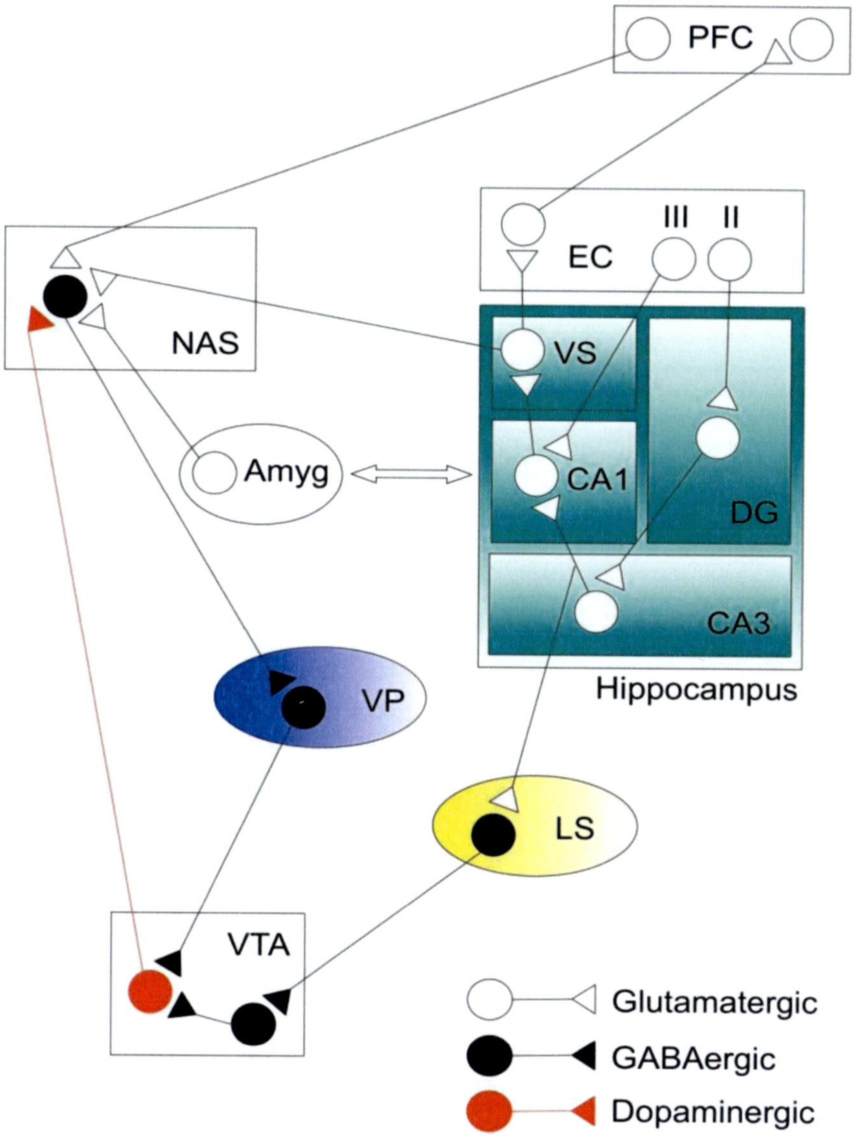


Figure 1. Hippocampal connectivity with the dopaminergic reward circuitry. Schematic representation of some of the major (functional) anatomical connectivity between the hippocampus (*green*) and the major dopaminergic circuit from the ventral tegmental area (VTA) to the nucleus accumbens (NAS). The main projections from the hippocampus are from the ventral septum (VS) to the NAS [37], which in turn, via medium spiny GABAergic neurons, is proposed to reach the VTA via the ventral pallidum (VP *blue*; [7, 38]). A second pathway from the CA3 region of the hippocampus also projects to the VTA through the lateral septum (LS *yellow*; [39]). There are additional hippocampal efferents (and reciprocal afferents; not shown) to the prefrontal cortex (PFC) utilizing the neighboring entorhinal cortex and other temporal cortical structures ([129, 130]; for review see [131]), Reciprocal connections also exist between most regions of the hippocampus and the amygdala (Amyg; [132, 133]). The dual intrinsic connectivity through the direct temporoammonic and the canonical trisynaptic hippocampal circuitry, originating from entorhinal cortex (EC) layers III and II, respectively, is also illustrated.

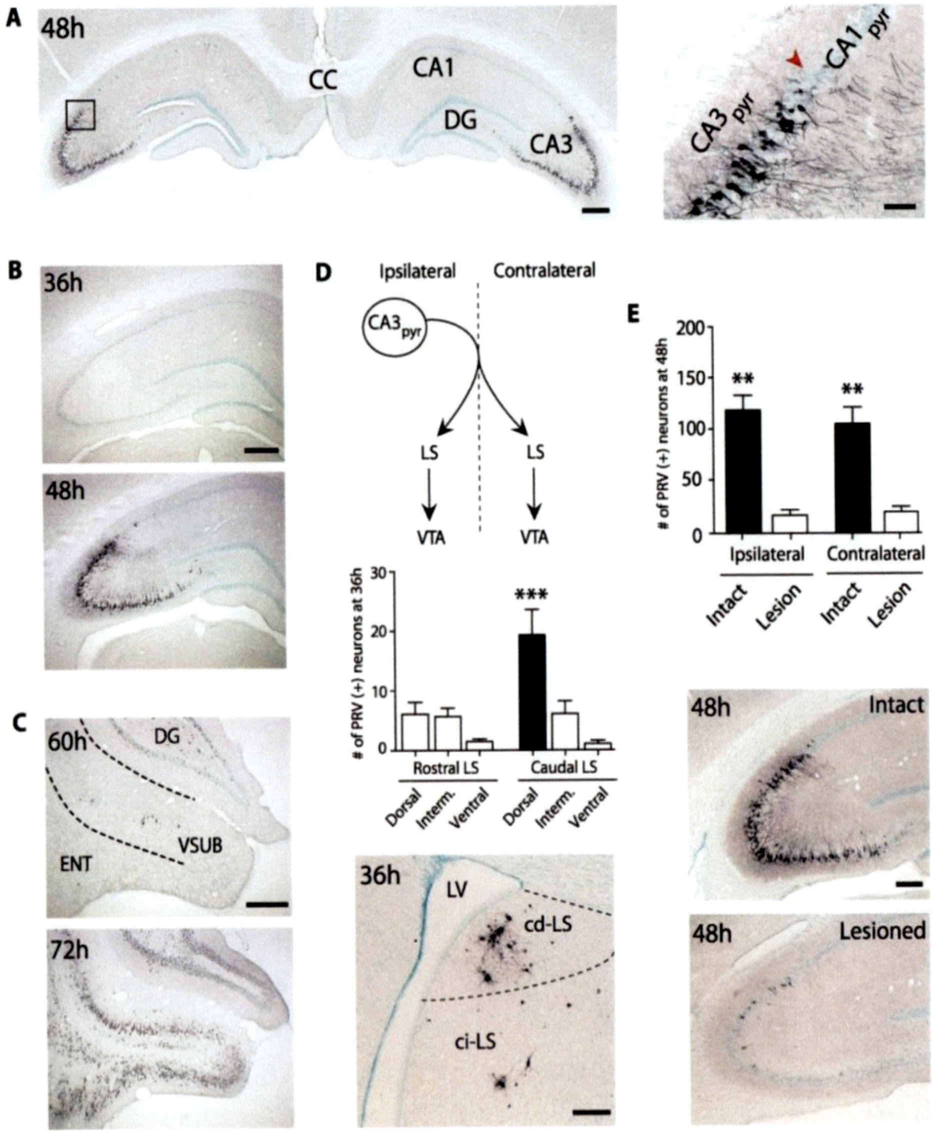


Figure 2. A dorsal CA3-cd-LS-VTA Pathway. (A) Photomicrographs of PRV immunoreactivity in the dorsal hippocampus 48 hours after PRV injection in VTA. Area delineated by rectangle is magnified at right. Red arrowhead indicates approximate boundary between CA1 and CA3. (B) Photomicrographs of PRV labeling in dorsal hippocampus and (C) vSUB at increasing postinjection times. (D) (Top) **Schematic of projections from CA3 to LS and LS to VTA; (middle) PRV (+) cell counts (Dunn's post** hoc test, $***P \leq 0.0001$); **(bottom) photomicrograph of lateral septum** subregions at 36 hours postinjection. (E) Cell counts and photomicrographs of dorsal CA3 PRV (+) neurons from intact and cd-LS–lesioned animals (Newman-Keuls post hoc test, $**P = 0.0005$). Hemisphere ipsilateral to PRV injection is shown in all photomicrographs with one hemisphere and left in (A). Dorsal is up for all panels. Tissue sections are coronal. $CA1_{pyr}$, CA1 pyramidal layer; $CA3_{pyr}$, CA3 pyramidal layer; CC, corpus callosum; ci-LS, caudointermediate-lateral septum; DG, dentate gyrus; ENT, entorhinal cortex; Interm, intermediate; LV, lateral ventricle; VSUB, ventral subiculum. Scale bars: (A) (left), (B), and **(C), 500 μm; (D) and (E), 250 μm; (A) (right), 100 μm.** From Alice H. Luo, Pouya Tahsili-Fahadan, Roy A. Wise, Carl R. Lupica, and Gary Aston-Jones. Linking Context with Reward: A Functional Circuit from Hippocampal CA3 to Ventral Tegmental Area *Science 15 July 2011: 353-357. [DOI:10.1126/science.1204622]*. Reprinted with permission from AAAS.

The PFC, while implicated in many aspects of addiction, including drug reinstatement [1, 33], does not appear to be required for subiculum-induced dopaminergic activity [37], implying that the hippocampal-VTA-accumbens circuitry could function in isolation, at a subconscious level, to influence addictive behaviors. Dysregulation of both the PFC and glutamatergic projections to the nucleus accumbens are thought to be essential for the increased motivation towards drug-seeking [22]. However, the activation of hippocampal glutamatergic efferents, but not amygdala projections, is necessary for PFC inputs to engage with medium spiny neurons in the accumbens by switching them into an active depolarized state, implying a "gating" role for the hippocampus in the coupling of the PFC and the DA system [41]. It is important to note that others do not make such a clear distinction between these three sets of inputs to the nucleus accumbens [42].

Voorn et al. [43] have considered the pattern of innervation to the striatum in more detail, illustrating that hippocampal and amygdala inputs, and cortical inputs differentially innervate the ventral (nucleus accumbens) and dorsal striatum, respectively. (Although these authors strongly stress that the functional anatomical patterns in the striatum, taken as a whole, do not readily allow for a strict division of input between dorsal and ventral areas.) Ballard et al. [44] recently suggested that the dorsolateral PFC is the initial sensor of an anticipated reward in humans followed by the VTA and accumbens. Although activation of the left hippocampus was mentioned, its role in the timing of information transfer was not further discussed. Moreover, other studies indicate that the hippocampus is activated *prior* to the dopaminergic system (discussed in [7, 26]), which could be expected in light of the above discussed hippocampal gating of PFC-induced nucleus accumbens activity (see also [31]).

Although DA pathways have been the favored route for the self-administration of drugs of abuse [45], it is noteworthy that other areas of the brain, including the hippocampus, are also amenable to both electrical self-stimulation (see references in [46]) and drug self-administration [47]. For example, in addition to the VTA, morphine is also readily self-administered directly into the hippocampus [48], although this has not been demonstrated for nicotine as of yet. Interestingly, as discussed by Shoaib [49], when animals are trained to discriminate nicotine from saline in order to obtain a food reward, this effect appears to be critically dependent on CNS structures such as the hippocampus [50, 51].

Thus, the hippocampus may have a more central role in the entire addiction process, determining whether a drug is a novel stimulus (or associated with a novel context), providing the signal to allow the DA reward system to engage with the PFC in order to assess goal worthiness, while also linking emotional significance through connectivity with the amygdala. Throughout the entire drug-seeking and taking experience, the hippocampus must surely be associating sensory cues and environmental contexts, continually updating this information. Upon withdrawal from a drug, secondary predictions registered in the hippocampus will not be met again, leading to a "craving" and the future motivation for a reward. Although much of this information remains speculative to some extent, if true, then it implies that the hippocampus may be involved from the initial drug experience through to uncontrolled addiction [1].

It should be further noted that multiple (independently functioning) parts of the CNS have been implicated in drug reinstatement. Kalivas et al. [52] favor a mechanism largely involving an altered PFC signaling to the nucleus accumbens, whereas the newly discovered connectivity between the hippocampus and VTA also seems to be essential [38]. How these multiple areas coherently function in drug-seeking remains to be resolved, and whether any one area is necessary and sufficient for certain aspects of drug addiction will require further research.

## Nicotine-Associated Contexts and Cues

As introduced earlier, in the three-stage model of addiction, the role of the hippocampus appears most prevalent in the last phase, the relapse to addiction [1]. Drug-associated contexts and cues can become powerful secondary reinforcers that trigger drug cravings and a relapse or reinstatement to drug-seeking and use, including in humans [28, 42, 53, 54].

With respect to nicotine addiction, as with other drugs, relapse can occur several years after the drug abuse has ceased [55, 56], implying that altered brain states are powerful sensors (and transmitters) of information that has become associated with prior drug use. Furthermore, likely because of these brain changes, the reinstatement of nicotine use is faster than observed in a naïve subject [56]. The neurobiological substrates underlying the secondary-induced reinforcement are not completely understood and, similar to other aspects of drug addiction, appear to involve multiple interconnected regions including the PFC, amygdala and hippocampus [42], and that a single region, i.e., the hippocampus, is unlikely to be involved in all aspects of cue-induced, reinstatement behavior [57]. Davies et al. [14] demonstrated an important separation between the effects of chronic nicotine treatment on context- and cue-induced fear conditioning, concluding an essential role for the hippocampus in terms of contextual (environmental) stimuli, but not sensory cues. While these latter data conveniently correlate the hippocampus and context with chronic nicotine-mediated cognitive deficits, it does not definitively eliminate a further role for the hippocampus in terms of a cue-induced reinstatement of nicotine use in the addiction process.

Conditioned place preference (CPP), in which an animal learns to form associations between a drug and a specific environment, is a generally well accepted model of drug addiction, although self-administration may better mimic drug abuse in humans [45]. CPP, basically a Pavlovian, classical conditioning model, has been studied for all classes of abused drugs, including nicotine, and can be used to assess relapse and reinstatement following extinction [58]. Nicotine-induced CPP has produced mixed results [59], and its dependency on specific dopaminergic receptors in the central reward pathways is somewhat controversial [58], although cFos and pCREB expressions are found throughout the extended reward circuitry [9], including the hippocampus, during both the acquisition and reinstatement of CPP [60]. Conversely, Koob and Volkow [1] discuss the idea that nicotine-induced CPP does not involve the traditional reward circuitry based on the observation that lesions of the tegmentum prevents the rewarding effects of nicotine as assessed with CPP [61]. However, it should be noted that the tegmentum does send important cholinergic projections to the VTA [9, 62] that are known to be involved in the nicotine-induced regulation of DA neurons [63].

Caggiula et al. [64] discuss the idea that associated sensory cues are as important as nicotine in smoking behavior. Several studies have documented that the hippocampus is activated in humans in response to smoking-related cues [65-67], implying that this limbic region, in addition to other parts of the reward circuitry, are very important in producing cue-induced "cravings" and the subsequent motivation towards seeking nicotine. Overall, it can be stated with certainty that environmental contexts and sensory cues become strongly associated with nicotine use and develop into major motivational factors in the drive for nicotine [68].

## HIPPOCAMPAL NICOTINIC ACETYLCHOLINE RECEPTORS, PLASTICITY AND ADDICTION

The history of tobacco and its addictive properties have been long recognized, notwithstanding that much of the evidence from pre-Columbian times is largely anecdotal [69, 70]. The timeline of nicotine usage has been discussed in a recent review [68], but perhaps one of the earliest and pertinent scientific experiments (although likely not possible to conduct under current research standards) was performed by Lenox Johnston and documented in *The Lancet* [71]. These experiments, involving self-injection into human smokers, demonstrated that nicotine could temporally replace cigarette use to some extent and, in some subjects, even produce a more profound effect than tobacco itself. Shortly after its isolation from tobacco, the paralytic action of nicotine at the neuromuscular junction was recognized [72]. Although its effects have been studied ever since in various parts of the nervous system, it wasn't until the late 1980's that scientific studies formally demonstrated that animals could self-administer nicotine and linked this action to the central dopaminergic reward circuitry [17], thereby confirming that nicotine, of all the constituents in tobacco leaves, was the main addicting compound. With respect to relapse, an early review of the tobacco and nicotine literature by Stewart [73] led her to hypothesize that because of its "medicinal use" for a rather large number of ailments, patients were simply returning to their doctors for repeat prescriptions in order to eliminate the pain associated with withdrawal, implying that relapse to nicotine was a dependent behavior. In retrospect, this indirectly linked for the first time, although not by name, the importance of the hippocampus to nicotine addiction.

nAChRs are a diverse family of ligand-gated ion channels [74-76], distributed non-uniformly throughout the central nervous system [77]. Within the hippocampus, several major subtypes of nicotinic receptors are expressed on principle glutamate neurons and many classes of interneurons, both pre- and post-synaptically, where their physiological role, although well-documented, still remains an ongoing area of exploration [11, 12]. Stepping aside from the hippocampus and back into the dopaminergic reward pathway, some fairly recent, exquisite experiments, performed by re-expressing certain nAChR subunits selectively into the VTA, on an otherwise subunit null background, have demonstrated that just three subunits, $\alpha4$, $\alpha6$ and $\beta2$, are necessary and sufficient for the self-administration of nicotine in mice [78]. These data appear to eliminate an essential role for nAChRs within the hippocampus (at least with respect to the initiation and maintenance of addiction). Nonetheless, the latter data should be taken with some caveats for two reasons: 1) certain existing difficulties that are associated with the self-administration of nicotine in mice [79]; 2) the roles for other subunits may become more apparent when certain nAChRs subunits are knocked-out [80], e.g., it is known that $\alpha7$ subunit containing-receptors contribute to the cellular firing and plasticity in the VTA [81]. Thus, it is possible that changes in many nAChR subtypes in different areas of the brain are important for the complete nicotine addiction process [82]. Moreover, as discussed earlier, although novelty recognition in the hippocampus could be involved in early stages of addiction [7, 26], full drug reinforcement likely requires goal-relevant information from the PFC [24]. Areas such as the hippocampus, which likely contribute to the interactions between the incentive-salience DA system and the PFC, may have auxiliary roles collecting information about contexts and cues associated with nicotine, even in the absence of certain nAChRs.

In many ways, addiction can be viewed as an aberrant form of learning, usurping the hippocampal and other pathways known to make useful associations, forming who we are and how we interact with our environment [4, 8]. Thus, it is not surprising that many of the long-lasting plastic mechanisms that encode and consolidate these "normal" forms of memory [82] are also induced by drugs of abuse, including nicotine [4, 84, 85]. The cognitive enhancing potential of nicotinic ligands is largely consistent with the general ability of nicotine to facilitate synaptic plasticity in the hippocampus [5, 9]. Early studies focused on acute applications of nicotinic compounds in the *in vitro* hippocampal slice preparation [86], concluding that α7 nAChRs were important for enhancing long-term potentiation (LTP) and are very similar to other studies in the dopaminergic regions [81], but additional experiments in the VTA have delineated roles for the high affinity α4β2 receptor [87]. Due to the distribution of nAChRs, multiple subtypes, and differential effects on plasticity, it has been difficult to establish exactly what the overall effect of nicotine is on hippocampal functioning [10]. At a minimum, however, the presence of nicotine clearly influences neuronal excitability at many levels, and will therefore likely disrupt information storage in this region.

Next, I will attempt to focus the discussion on studies that have administered nicotine *in vivo*. The well established (and so-called paradoxical upregulation) of nAChRs in the CNS, following administration [88], formed the basis for many original theories of how nicotine may initiate the addiction process, possibly through receptor desensitization [89-92]. The desensitization-upregulation theory, however, never made complete sense, partly because an increased nAChR number would potentially push the system away from homeostasis. More recent findings from several research groups have concluded that the upregulation of nAChRs, principally the α4β2 receptor, arises from the stabilization of receptors during the assembly process and may not be a starting point for nicotine addiction (for a discussion see [93]). On the other hand, such changes may not be an entirely epiphenomena, but could be central to the initiation of downstream changes in circuit function. Autoradiographs show that nAChRs in human smokers are dramatically increased in the dentate gyrus of the hippocampus. Furthermore, although these sites were labeled with the non-specific radioligand epibaditine, they most likely represent α4β2 nAChRs [94]. Further confirmation associated with the prominent effects of the nicotine-induced upregulation of α4β2 nAChRs in this region of the hippocampus comes from a similar increase in the magnitude of fluorescently-tagged α4 nAChR subunits in the perforant path (and temporoammonic pathway) following chronic exposure to nicotine in mice [95]. These studies and those of Penton et al. ([96]; see below) clearly establish the relevance of dentate gyrus α4β2 nAChRs in the addiction process. Nashmi et al. [95] additionally showed an increased sensitivity of LTP to acute nicotine in the dentate gyrus after the upregulation of nAChRs, implying that these receptors were also functionally enhanced. Such data contrast with *in vitro* studies from the Anwyl lab [97] in the same region that showed that the *acute* nicotine enhancement of

LTP in the dentate gyrus appears to require the α7 nAChR. Thus, both acute and chronic nicotine may facilitate plastic change, but likely involve different types of nicotinic receptors.

With respect to the upregulation of α4β2 receptors in various regions of the brain, including the hippocampus, it is likely important (at least during withdrawal) that they induce more permanent downstream effects, since these nAChRs return to normal levels only a week or so after cessation of nicotine treatment [98]. Furthermore, any behavioral effects associated with the upregulation of nAChRs (possibly including those in the hippocampus) are normalized by counter-adaptations within a very short time after chronic nicotine is initiated [14], implying that their direct impact within the hippocampus may be limited, at least while nicotine is present.

The research of Sumikawa and colleagues has greatly contributed to our understanding of the *in vivo* effects of nicotine on synaptic plasticity in the hippocampus. In their initial studies, the threshold for the induction of LTP in CA1 was significantly reduced following chronic nicotine treatment and discussed in terms of the cognitive influence of nicotine in addition to its potential therapeutic usefulness in Alzheimer's disease [99]. The precise receptor mechanism was further investigated with the authors concluding that the major receptor involved after *in vivo* nicotine exposure, based on additional LTP facilitation by the agonist A85380, was likely to be α4β2, and differed from the acute nicotine augmentation of plasticity, which benefited from the additional desensitization of α7 nAChRs ([100]; also see above). Again, these latter results are somewhat in conflict with those of Welsby et al. [97] in the dentate gyrus, in which LTP was facilitated by α7 activation, implying that the role of this receptor subtype may differ depending on region, and it has been argued that there remains insufficient knowledge about the distribution of nAChR subtypes in the hippocampus [100]. After prolonged withdrawal (4 days to 1 month), both the decreased threshold for LTP and the nicotine-enhancement of LTP are mostly lost, although plasticity does not return to its baseline in a straightforward manner [101]. Such data are consistent with cocaine-induced synaptic plasticity in the VTA, which also may not persist following the removal of the drug for more than a week or so [102, 103].

Sumikawa and colleagues [104] additionally report changes in glutamatergic functioning, including increased AMPA and *N*-methyl-D-aspartate receptor activity, which could theoretically contribute to the facilitated LTP. The upregulation of AMPA receptor functioning has also been observed in dopaminergic regions (see [105]). In sum, it can be argued that the majority of studies imply that both acute and, more importantly, chronic nicotine can enhance synaptic plasticity within hippocampal circuitry, although the exact nAChR mechanisms are yet to be resolved.

Penton et al. [96] report a long-lasting two-phase increase (up to 9-months) in the excitability of CA1 neurons in the hippocampus following withdrawal from a 1-week treatment with nicotine *in vivo* that does not involve conventional LTP-like plasticity, as observed in the VTA [84]. Rather, it is expressed as a facilitated EPSP-population spike (EPSP-pSpike) potentiation [106]. At early times of withdrawal, this type of plasticity requires an intact hippocampal circuitry and originates in the dentate gyrus where most of the major changes in hippocampal nAChRs have been observed in rodents [95] and humans [94] (see earlier discussion), and may correlate with nicotine-induced changes in stem cells, intermediate early gene induction, cell death and additional molecular changes within the dentate gyrus and other regions of the hippocampus (see references in [93, 96]). In addition, these novel forms of plasticity [95] have been discussed in terms of a potential cellular and circuit correlate of the cognitive behavioral deficit observed by the Gould lab [14], partly because the behavioral and circuitry changes observed upon the initial withdrawal from the drug can be fully reversed by acute nicotine and involve α4β2 nAChRs [107]. Interestingly, opposite changes in the excitability of ventral subiculum cells have been described in response to chronic treatment with amphetamine [108]. The differential changes seen with these two drugs may point to contrasting mechanisms, but, at least in the case of nicotine, one should also take into account the influence of adaptations in local hippocampal interneurons [109].

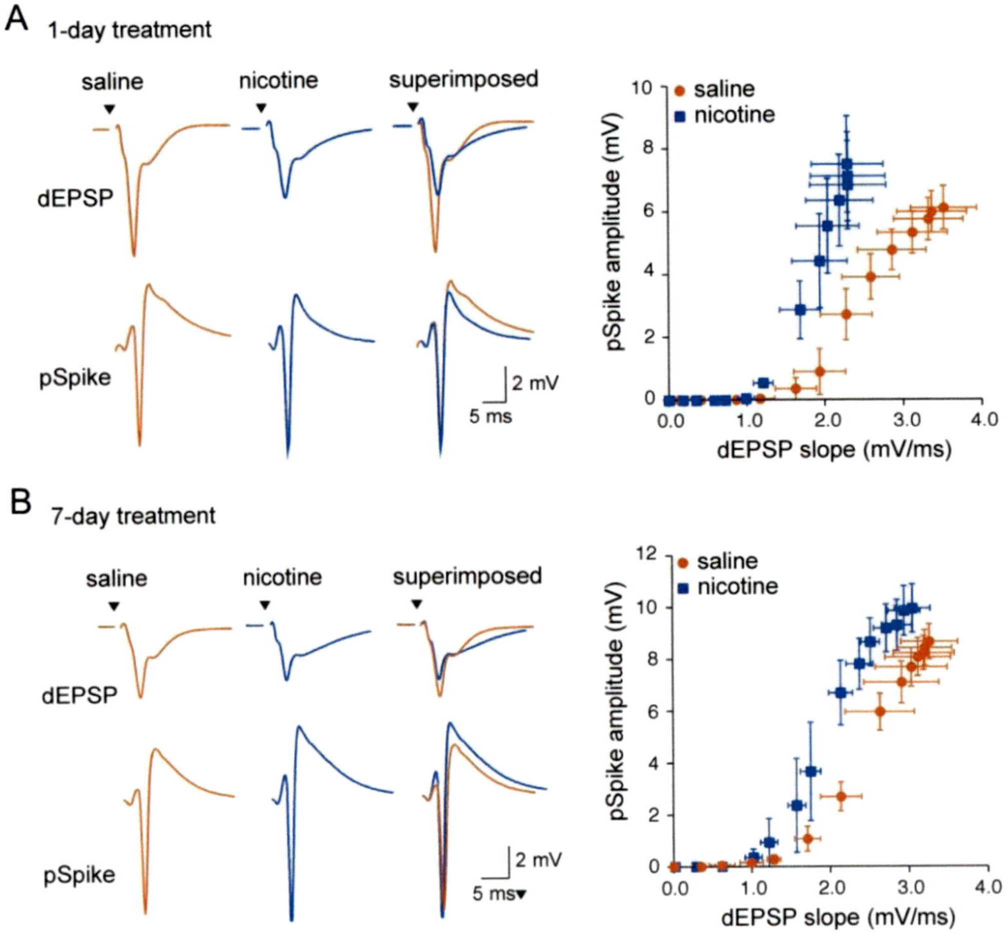


Figure 3. Rapid Induction of Hippocampal Neuroadaptations to Nicotine. Brief continuous nicotine (equivalent to 3.15 mg/kg/d nicotine base) exposure *in vivo* induces changes in CA1 excitability. Both a 1-day (*A*) or a 1-week (*B*; [96]) treatment with nicotine, produced a leftward shift in the dEPSP-pSpike curve, after a 1-day withdrawal period, indicating an increased excitability of CA1 neurons. Example traces of the dEPSPs recoded in the *stratum radiatum* with their corresponding pSpikes measured in the *stratum pyramidale* are shown (*left traces*), along with the mean data for the dEPSP-pSpike curves (*right*).

Interestingly, many of the reported nicotine-induced changes in nAChRs *in vitro* can be observed within the first 24-48 hours of treatment [91, 110, 111), agreeing with the idea that the process towards full addiction may be induced relatively quickly [56]. Indeed, a retrospective analysis of smoking behavior has been used to argue that just a few cigarettes may be sufficient to set up a lifelong predisposition to nicotine addiction [55]. Bearing this in mind, we recently obtained preliminary data showing that, even following withdrawal from a 1-day *in vivo* treatment with nicotine, we can reproduce the increase in hippocampal excitability, measured again by a leftward shift in the EPSP-pSpike curve (Figure 3), as originally observed after a 7-day treatment [96]. Persistent late term (4 weeks to 9 months) changes in the EPSP-pSpike curve, as described above [95], imply that, unlike canonical synaptic plasticity in hippocampal CA1 cells, these types of neuronal excitability changes could underlie the prolonged predisposition to tobacco relapse.

## Hippocampus, Stress and Withdrawal

It is becoming more appreciated that stress is a major factor in the maintenance and relapse to drug addiction [112]. Stress and acute drug application, including nicotine, initiate a similar type of synaptic plasticity in the dopaminergic (VTA) reward pathways [4, 84]. The stress response, originally described as forming part of the opposing anti-reward pathway [113] and which may become hypersensitive during the addiction process [56, 114], ultimately leads to persistent allostatic changes in the brain. Such allostatic changes keep a variety of CNS processes out of their homeostatic ranges, and may prevent the return of certain behaviors to their normal state, thereby making stress, via increased cravings, an easy path back to drug use, even following prolonged abstinence.

While the stress response has been discussed in global terms [112], certain areas of the CNS, because of their susceptibility to stress-related hormones, may be more sensitive than others. For example, Francesconi et al. [115] show that, following prolonged withdrawal from alcohol, cocaine and heroin, there are secondary plastic changes in the *stria terminalis* that can be prevented by blocking those receptors that respond to the canonical corticotropin-releasing factor (CRF). These findings imply that anti-stress agents may be therapeutically useful during cessation from addictive behaviors not only in terms of directly reducing patient stress, but also in preventing additional brain alterations. In theory, this could make return to drug use less likely.

The hippocampus and other regions of the limbic system, including the amygdala, have been discussed with respect to stress and drug relapse [116]. These authors describe the relationship between stress and environmental contexts, specifically referring to the subiculum of the hippocampus (see Figure 1) with respect to the influence of norepinephrine provided by the locus coeruleus. The hippocampus is also very sensitive to a variety of stress-induced corticosteroid hormones, presumably due to high levels of glucocorticoid receptors, particularly in the dentate gyrus and CA1 areas [117]. The glucocorticoid receptor antagonist, RU486, is effective at reversing stress, but not drug (including nicotine) induced plasticity in VTA neurons [84]. However, in the hippocampus, the same antagonist was effective at reversing morphine-induced changes in plasticity and *some* forms of stress-induced behavior during withdrawal [118], although it should be appreciated that regions other than the hippocampus may also be important targets for inappropriate glucocorticoid signaling that occurs during drug use and withdrawal [119].

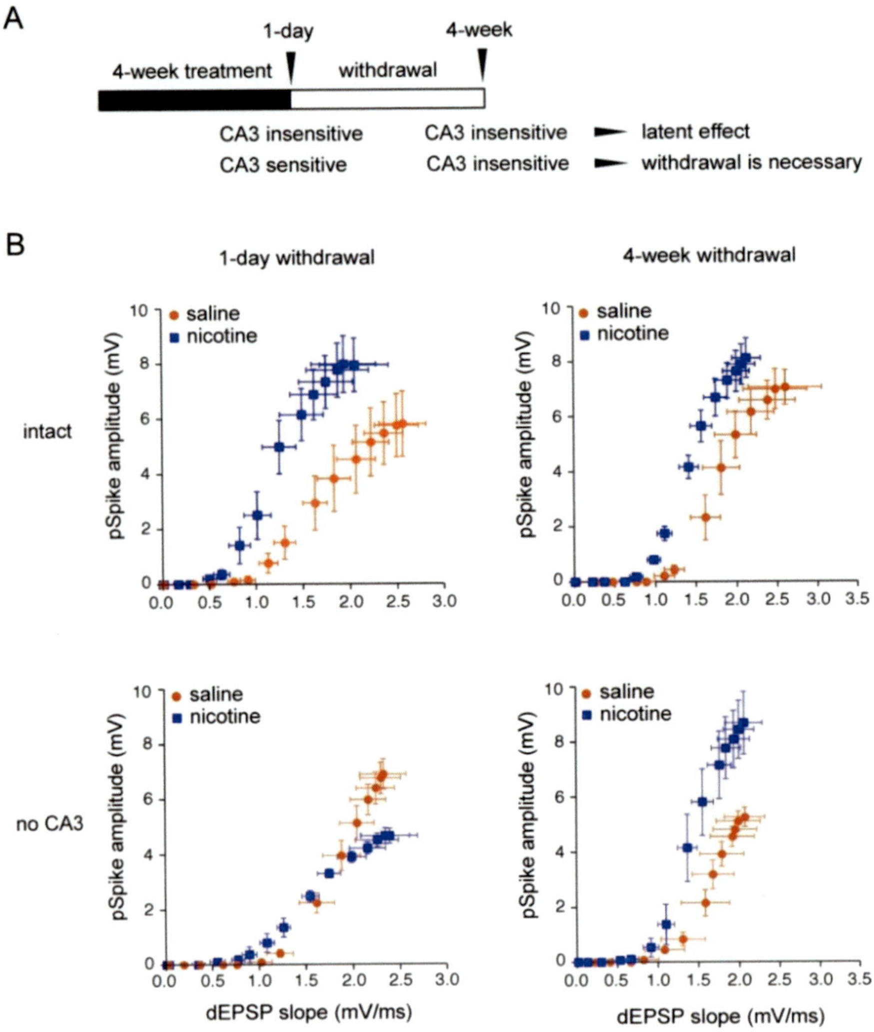


Figure 4. Withdrawal from nicotine is critical for late-term plasticity. *A*, Schematic representation of the nicotine treatment paradigm. After a 1-day (see Figure 2) or 1-week treatment with nicotine *in vivo*, the leftward shift in the dEPSP-pSpike curve is sensitive to removal of the CA3 at a 1-day withdrawal but not at a 4-week withdrawal [96]. If the CA3-insensitive change at 4-weeks is a latent effect of nicotine treatment that simply requires more time, then it should be observed immediately after a 4-week nicotine treatment (*latent effect*). However, if the period of withdrawal is necessary in order to induce the CA3-insensitive phase, then even after prolonged treatment with nicotine, the initial change at 1 day should be sensitive to removal of CA3, and the insensitive phase should only appear after a protracted period of withdrawal (*withdrawal is necessary*). *B*, dEPSP-pSpike curves following a 4-week treatment with nicotine (blue) or saline (red) at a 1-day (*left graphs*) or 4-week withdrawal (*right graphs*), in intact hippocampal slices (*upper graphs*) or in slices with the CA3 region removed (*lower graphs*).

As discussed above, Penton et al. [96] demonstrated that during the early phase (1 day) of withdrawal from a 7-day continuous exposure to nicotine *in vivo,* rodents express specific changes throughout the canonical DG-CA3-CA1 pathway resulting in an increased excitability of CA1 pyramidal neurons (see Figure 3). All of these adaptations to nicotine are fully reversed by the acute application of low (500 nM) concentrations of nicotine *in vitro*, implying that they are fully homeostatic and that nicotine intake may restore "normal" brain function (at least within the hippocampus). These data provide a potential explanation for the maintenance of everyday drug use, even following a nighttime period of abstinence [120]. However, following protracted withdrawal (4 weeks), the neuroadaptations to nicotine were found to be isolated to just the CA1 region (insensitive to either dentate gyrus or CA3 surgical removal), and were no longer entirely homeostatic [96]. Interestingly, it was additionally found that these secondary late withdrawal phase adaptations were not just a latent effect of nicotine, but rather critically depended on the protracted period of withdrawal because, following longer periods (4 weeks compared with 1 week) of exposure to nicotine, the initial (1 day) changes in hippocampal excitability were still dependent on a fully intact circuitry (Figure 4). Overall, it then appears that protracted withdrawal from the drug may be *necessary* for the induction of secondary plasticity in multiple brain regions, including the hippocampus, that are potentially related to a prolonged stress response and glucocorticoid receptor changes [112].

At present, nicotine replacement therapy (NRT) is the major intervention used to facilitate attempts to quit smoking, but it is estimated that these methods, on average, are only about 1.5-fold better than stopping cold turkey, measured six months to a year after nicotine cessation [121]. Since there are around a billion smokers worldwide [122], the majority of who have expressed a strong desire to quit, current NRT treatments still leave the vast majority (≈ 80 %) without a good pharmacological intervention strategy for quitting. Thus, it can be speculated that anti-stress drugs may offer an additional therapeutic strategy that not only will aid in the process of smoking cessation, but also may prevent some of the hippocampal neuroadaptations that could in part make it easier to relapse [56, 114]. Indeed, the anxiety associated with nicotine withdrawal is mediated through the CRF system in the amygdala [123] and results in an elevated drive for nicotine [124].

## Towards a Hippocampus Model for Nicotine Addiction

The functional circuitry underlying addictive behaviors is extensive and not fully understood [1]. One of the likely reasons is that the motivational systems, because of their evolutionary importance [9] and now hijacked by drugs of abuse, involve regions of the CNS from brainstem to cortex. Thus, many studies have focused on defining independent elements of the brain circuitry necessary to support such behaviors. Often, this can be to the detriment of areas such as the hippocampus, that are barely discussed, partly because of the known dominance of the cortical-dopaminergic system in the addiction process and the subsequent development of theories that minimize the limbic system once addiction has been established [33]. However, based on both the bidirectional anatomical connectivity of the hippocampus to other key areas subserving reinforcement [7], the known role of the hippocampus as a detector of novelty, and its special participation in environmental context, it could be argued, as I have attempted here, that the hippocampus should be appreciated as a much more central part of the addiction circuitry than traditionally viewed. In this respect, nicotine administration in awakened rodents induces plasticity within the hippocampal dentate gyrus; a process that depends on dopamine signals originating from the VTA [125], thereby, demonstrating the importance of the reciprocal connectivity between the hippocampus and the chief dopaminergic reward pathway for nicotine (not shown in Figure 1; but see [7]). Such studies imply that nicotine, through its actions in the hippocampus, could be aiding in establishing the contingencies needed for a context-induced reinstatement and relapse to drug addiction, although not as yet fully demonstrated for nicotine compared with other drugs of abuse [40]. In addition, recent studies show that a transient treatment of the nucleus accumbens with nicotine can restore the altered signal-to-noise dopaminergic signaling on withdrawal from nicotine [126]. Thus, it is possible that the many forms of plasticity induced by nicotine *in vivo* in the hippocampal circuitry contribute to the maintenance of and relapse to smoking behavior by sending secondary contextual nicotine-associated cues back to the reward pathway through the now several proposed routes (Figure 1). In particular, it has been shown that at early phases of withdrawal from continuous nicotine, the CA3 region is strongly excited, i.e., shows an increase in spontaneous firing [96]. Such a dramatic change could transmit either specific or generalized signals that produce increased motivation of the dopaminergic pathway through the newly established CA3 to the lateral septal pathway, as shown to be essential for reinstatement of cocaine seeking (Figure 2; [39]).

During withdrawal from drugs of abuse, especially nicotine, emphasis has been on somatic signs and has been useful for evaluating the nAChR subtypes involved in somatic withdrawal behaviors [127, 128]. Due to the powerful cognitive effects of nicotine, and its apparent usefulness in the self-medication of many psychiatric disorders [13], it is likely that cognitive dysfunction is a key component of nicotine addiction [10]. Davis et al. [14] have demonstrated a key role for the hippocampus in the context-dependent learning of nicotine-induced associations, and more importantly the profound deficit in cognition upon drug withdrawal. Penton et al. [96] have provided a possible hippocampal circuit correlate of this behavior (discussed above), and because nicotine can both alleviate the behavioral deficit and normalize the *in vivo* induced changes in synaptic plasticity in *isolated* hippocampal slices upon drug cessation, these studies suggest that the altered hippocampal circuitry may be able to function somewhat autonomously in setting up the conditions for cognitive dysfunction and its restoration by nicotine [107].

Self-administration of nicotine is dependent upon nAChR activation in the VTA, but not the nucleus accumbens [18], lending additional significance to the plasticity induced in this area by nicotine [85]. Desensitization of $\alpha4\beta2$ receptors on VTA GABAergic interneurons contributes to enhanced excitability of the principal dopaminergic neurons by nicotine *in vitro*, presumably by diminishing the cholinergic tegmental drive to these interneurons [87]. These same $\alpha4\beta2$ nAChRs are powerfully and selectively upregulated by chronic nicotine *in vivo* and lead to diminished dopaminergic activity (in the absence of nicotine) giving rise to the theory that "cravings" could be due to an enhanced endogenous tone of the local VTA GABAergic cells [95]. Although these mechanisms remain under development, such clear evidence for plasticity in the VTA provides a serial pathway (see Figure 1) through which nicotine-induced changes in the hippocampus could lead to a further dysregulation of the reward system.

Much is still unknown about nicotine addiction and the precise neurobiological substrates that underlie this disorder. It is evident that nicotine is poised to interact with nAChRs at key positions throughout the reward circuitry, including the hippocampus, but exactly how plasticity in each of these brain regions can be incorporated into a single working model of tobacco abuse still seems out of reach [82, 128].

## ACKNOWLEDGMENTS

This research was supported by Public Health Service National Institute on Drug Abuse Grant DA11940. I thank Dr. Rachel E. Penton and Jessica H. Chancey for generating, analyzing and commenting on the data used to create Figs. 3 and 4; Dr. Alice Luo Clayton and colleagues; and the AAAS for permission to republish their data. Ms. Jan C. Phillips has been an enormous help, especially in compiling the bibliography.

## REFERENCES

[1] Koob GF, Volkow ND (2010). Neurocircuitry of addiction. *Neuropsychopharmacol.* 35:217-238.

[2] Kauer JA (2004). Learning mechanisms in addiction: synaptic plasticity in the ventral tegmental area as a result of exposure to drugs of abuse. *Annu. Rev. Physiol.* 66: 447-475.

[3] Robbins TW, Ersche KD, Everitt BJ (2008). Drug addiction and the memory systems of the brain. *Ann. N. Y. Acad. Sci.* 1141:1-21.

[4] Hyman S, Malenka R, Nestler E (2006). Neural mechanisms of addiction: The role of reward-related learning and memory. *Annu. Rev. Neurosci.* 29:565-598.

[5] Placzek AN, Zhang TA, Dani JA (2009). Nicotinic mechanisms influencing synaptic plasticity in the hippocampus. *Acta Pharmacol. Sin.* 30:752-760.

[6] Wang SH, Morris RG (2010). Hippocampal-neocortical interactions in memory formation, consolidation, and reconsolidation. *Annu. Rev. Psychol.* 61:49-79, C1-4.

[7] Lisman JE, Grace AA (2005). The hippocampal-VTA loop: controlling the entry of information into long-term memory. *Neuron* 46:703–713.

[8] Colgin LL, Denninger T, Fyhn M, Hafting T, Bonnevie T, Jensen O, Moser MB, Moser EI (2009). Frequency of gamma oscillations routes flow of information in the hippocampus. *Nature* 462:353-357.

[9] Kelley AE (2004). Memory and addiction: shared neural circuitry and molecular mechanisms. *Neuron* 44:161-179.

[10] Kenney JW, Gould TJ (2008). Modulation of hippocampus-dependent learning and synaptic plasticity by nicotine. Mol. Neurobiol. 38:101-121.

[11] Yakel JL, Shao Z (2004). Functional and molecular characterization of neuronal nicotinic ACh receptors in rat hippocampal interneurons. *Prog. Brain Res.* 145:95-107.

[12] Alkondon M, Albuquerque EX (2004). The nicotinic acetylcholine receptor subtypes and their function in the hippocampus and cerebral cortex. *Prog. Brain Res.* 145: 109-120.

[13] Levin ED (2002). Nicotinic receptor subtypes and cognitive function. *J. Neurobiol.* 53:633-640.

[14] Davis JA, James J, Siegel SJ, Gould TJ (2005). Withdrawal from chronic nicotine administration impairs contextual fear conditioning in C57BL/6 mice. *J. Neurosci.* 25:8708-8713.

[15] Davis JA, Gould TJ (2009). Hippocampal nAChRs mediate nicotine withdrawal-related learning deficits. *Eur. Neuropsychopharmacol.* 19:551-561.

[16] Olds J (1956). Pleasure center in the brain. *Sci. Am.* 195:105-116.

[17] Corrigall WA, Coen KM (1989). Nicotine maintains robust self-administration in rats on a limited-access schedule. *Psychopharmacol.* (Berl) 99:473-478.

[18] Corrigall WA, Coen KM, Adamson KL (1994). Self-administered nicotine activates the mesolimbic dopamine system through the ventral tegmental area. *Brain Res.* 653: 278-284.

[19] Grossberg S, Merrill JW (1992). A neural network model of adaptively timed reinforcement learning and hippocampal dynamics. *Brain Res. Cogn. Brain Res.* 1:3-38.

[20] Rapanelli M, Frick LR, Zanutto BS (2011). Learning an operant conditioning task differentially induces gliogenesis in the medial prefrontal cortex and neurogenesis in the hippocampus. *PLoS One* 6:e14713.

[21] Breiter HC, Aharon I, Kahneman D, Dale A, Shizgal P (2001). Functional imaging of neural responses to expectancy and experience of monetary gains and losses. *Neuron* 30:619-639.

[22] Kalivas PW, Volkow ND (2005). The neural basis of addiction: a pathology of motivation and choice. *Am. J. Psychiatry* 162:1403-1413.

[23] Schultz W, Dayan P, Montague PR (1997) A neural substrate of prediction and reward. *Science* 275:1593-1599.

[24] Berridge KC, Robinson TE (1998). What is the role of dopamine in reward: hedonic impact, reward learning, or incentive salience? *Brain Res. Brain Res. Rev.* 28:309-369.

[25] Montague PR, Hyman SE, Cohen JD (2004). Computational roles for dopamine in behavioural control. *Nature* 431:760-767.

[26] Cooper DC, Klipec WD, Fowler MA, Ozkan ED (2006). A role for the subiculum in the brain motivation/reward circuitry. *Behav. Brain Res.* 174:225-231.

[27] Lehrer J (2009). How we decide. Houghton Mifflin Harcourt Publishing Company, New York.

[28] Di Chiara G, North RA (1992). Neurobiology of Opiate Abuse. *Trends Pharmacol. Sci.* 13:185-193.

[29] Le Moal M (2009). Drug abuse: vulnerability and transition to addiction. *Pharmacopsychiatry* 42 Suppl 1:S42-55.

[30] Damasio A (1994) "Descartes' Error": Emotion, Reason, and the Human Brain. Harper Perennial, New York, London, Toronto, Sydney.

[31] Everitt BJ, Robbins TW (2005). Neural systems of reinforcement for drug addiction: from actions to habits to compulsion. *Nat. Neurosci.* 8:1481-1489.

[32] Gerdeman GL, Partridge JG, Lupica CR, Lovinger DM (2003). It could be habit forming: drugs of abuse and striatal synaptic plasticity. *Trends Neurosci.* 26:184-192.

[33] Kalivas PW (2009). The glutamate homeostasis hypothesis of addiction. *Nat. Rev. Neurosci.* 10:561-572.

[34] Scoville WB, Milner B (1957). Loss of recent memory after bilateral hippocampal lesions. *J. Neurol. Neurosurg. Psychiatry* 20:11-21.

[35] Legault M, Rompré PP, Wise RA (2000). Chemical stimulation of the ventral hippocampus elevates nucleus accumbens dopamine by activating dopaminergic neurons of the ventral tegmental area. *J. Neurosci.* 20:1635-1642.

[36] Legault M, Wise RA (2001). Novelty-evoked elevations of nucleus accumbens-dopamine: dependence on impulse flow from the ventral subiculum and glutamatergic neurotransmission in the ventral tegmental area. *Eur. J. Neurosci.* 13:819–828.

[37] Floresco SB, Todd CL, Grace AA (2001). Glutamatergic afferents from the hippocampus to the nucleus accumbens regulate activity of ventral tegmental area dopamine neurons. *J. Neurosci.* 21:4915–4922.

[38] Groenewegen HJ, Vermeulen-Van der Zee E, te Kortschot A, Witter MP. Organization of the projections from the subiculum to the ventral striatum in the rat (1987). A study using anterograde transport of Phaseolus vulgaris leucoagglutinin. *Neurosci.* 23: 103–120.

[39] Luo AH, Tahsili-Fahadan P, Wise RA, Lupica CR, Aston-Jones G (2011). Linking context with reward: a functional circuit from hippocampal CA3 to ventral tegmental area. *Science* 333:353-357.

[40] Vorel SR, Liu X, Hayes RJ, Spector JA, Gardner EL (2001). Relapse to cocaine-seeking after hippocampal theta burst stimulation. *Science* 292:1175-1178.

[41] O'Donnell P, Grace AA (1995). Synaptic interactions among excitatory afferents to nucleus accumbens neurons: hippocampal gating of prefrontal cortical input. *J. Neurosci.* 15:3622–3639.

[42] Crombag HS, Bossert JM, Koya E, Shaham Y (2008). Context-induced relapse to drug-seeking: a review. *Phil. Trans. R Soc. Lond B Biol. Sci.* 363:3233-3243.

[43] Voorn P, Vanderschuren LJ, Groenewegen HJ, Robbins TW, Pennartz CM (2004). Putting a spin on the dorsal-ventral divide of the striatum. *Trends Neurosci.* 27: 468-474.

[44] Ballard IC, Murty VP, Carter RM, MacInnes JJ, Huettel SA, Adcock RA (2011). Dorsolateral prefrontal cortex drives mesolimbic dopaminergic regions to initiate motivated behavior. *J. Neurosci.* 31:10340-10346.

[45] Stolerman IP, Shoaib M (1991). The neurobiology of tobacco addiction. *Trends Pharmacol. Sci.* 12:467-473.

[46] Ricoy UM, Martinez JL Jr (2009). Local hippocampal methamphetamine-induced reinforcement. *Front Behav. Neurosci.* 3:47.

[47] Vetulani J. Drug addiction (2001). Part II. Neurobiology of addiction. *Pol. J. Pharmacol.* 53:303-317.

[48] Self DW, Stein L (1993). Pertussis toxin attenuates intracranial morphine self-administration. Pharmacol Biochem Behav 46:689-695.

[49] Shoaib M (1998). Is dopamine important in nicotine dependence? *J. Physiol. Paris* 92:229-233.

[50] Meltzer LT, Rosecrans JA (1981). Investigations on the CNS sites of action of the discriminative stimulus effects of arecoline and nicotine. *Pharmacol. Biochem. Behav.* 15:21-26.

[51] Shoaib M, Stolerman IP (1996). Brain sites mediating the discriminative stimulus effects of nicotine in rats. *Behav. Brain Res.* 78:183-188.

[52] Kalivas PW, Volkow ND, Seamans J (2005). Unmanageable motivation in addiction: a pathology in prefrontal-accumbens glutamate transmission. *Neuron* 45:647-650.

[53] Wikler A (1973). Dynamics of drug dependence. Implications of a conditioning theory for research and treatment. *Arch. Gen. Psychiatry* 28:611-616.

[54] O'Brien CP, Childress AR, McLellan AT, Ehrman R (1992). Classical conditioning in drug-dependent humans. *Ann. N Y Acad. Sci.* 654:400-415.

[55] Russell MA (1990). The nicotine addiction trap: a 40-year sentence for four cigarettes. *Br. J. Addict.* 85:293-300.

[56] DiFranza, J.R. (2008). Hooked from the first cigarette. *Sci. Am.* 298:82-87.

[57] Holland PC, Bouton ME (1999). Hippocampus and context in classical conditioning. *Curr. Opin. Neurobiol.* 9:195-202.

[58] Liu Y, Le Foll B, Liu Y, Wang X, Lu L (2008). Conditioned place preference induced by licit drugs: establishment, extinction, and reinstatement. *Sci. World J.* 8:1228-1245.

[59] Le Foll B, Goldberg SR (2006). Nicotine as a typical drug of abuse in experimental animals and humans. *Psychopharmacol.* (Berl) 184:367-381.

[60] Pascual MM, Pastor V, Bernabeu RO (2009). Nicotine-conditioned place preference induced CREB phosphorylation and Fos expression in the adult rat brain. *Psychopharmacol.* (Berl) 207:57-71.

[61] Laviolette SR, Alexson TO, van der Kooy D (2002). Lesions of the tegmental pedunculopontine nucleus block the rewarding effects and reveal the aversive effects of nicotine in the ventral tegmental area. *J. Neurosci.* 22:8653-8660.

[62] Blaha CD, Allen LF, Das S, Inglis WL, Latimer MP, Vincent SR, Winn P (1996). Modulation of dopamine efflux in the nucleus accumbens after cholinergic stimulation of the ventral tegmental area in intact, pedunculopontine tegmental nucleus-lesioned, and laterodorsal tegmental nucleus-lesioned rats. *J. Neurosci.* 16:714-722.

[63] Fagen ZM, Mansvelder HD, Keath JR, McGehee DS (2003). Short- and long-term modulation of synaptic inputs to brain reward areas by nicotine. *Ann. N Y Acad. Sci.* 1003:185-195.

[64] Caggiula AR, Donny EC, White AR, Chaudhri N, Booth S, Gharib MA, Hoffman A, Perkins KA, Sved AF (2001). Cue dependency of nicotine self-administration and smoking. *Pharmacol. Biochem. Behav.* 70:515-530.

[65] Due DL, Huettel SA, Hall WG, Rubin DC (2002). Activation in mesolimbic and visuospatial neural circuits elicited by smoking cues: evidence from functional magnetic resonance imaging. *Am. J. Psychiatry* 159:954-960.

[66] Smolka MN, Bühler M, Klein S, Zimmermann U, Mann K, Heinz A, Braus DF (2006). Severity of nicotine dependence modulates cue-induced brain activity in regions involved in motor preparation and imagery. *Psychopharmacol.* 184:577–588.

[67] Franklin T, Wang Z, Wang J, Sciortino N, Harper D, Li Y, Ehrman R, Kampman K, O'Brien C, Detre J, Childress A (2007). Limbic activation to cigarette smoking cues independent of nicotine withdrawal: a perfusion fMRI study. *Neuropsychopharmacol.* 32:2301-2309.

[68] Dani JA, Balfour DJ (2011). Historical and current perspective on tobacco use and nicotine addiction. *Trends Neurosci.* 34:383-392.

[69] Billings ER (1875). *Tobacco; Its History, Varieties, Culture, Manufacture and Commerce*. American Publishing Company, Hartford.

[70] Goodman J (1993) *Tobacco history: The culture of dependence.* Routledge, London, New York.

[71] Johnston LM (1942). Tobacco smoking and nicotine. *Lancet* 243:742.

[72] Bernard C (1850). Action physiologique des venins (curare). *C R Soc. Biol.* t.1 1949, p. 90.

[73] Stewart GG (1967). A history of the medicinal use of tobacco. *Med. Hist.* 11:228-268.

[74] Role LW (1992). Diversity in primary structure and function of neuronal nicotinic acetylcholine receptor channels. *Curr. Opin. Neurobiol.* 2:254-262.

[75] Colquhoun LM, Patrick JW (1997). Pharmacology of neuronal nicotinic acetylcholine receptor subtypes. *Adv. Pharmacol.* 39:191-220.

[76] Cordero-Erausquin M, Marubio LM, Klink R, Changeux JP (2000). Nicotinic receptor function: new perspectives from knockout mice. *Trends Pharmacol. Sci.* 21:211-217.

[77] Jones S, Sudweeks S, Yakel JL (1999). Nicotinic receptors in the brain: correlating physiology with function. *Trends Neurosci.* 22:555-561.

[78] Pons S, Fattore L, Cossu G, Tolu S, Porcu E, McIntosh JM, Changeux JP, Maskos U, Fratta W (2008). Crucial role of a4 and a6 nicotinic acetylcholine receptor subunits from ventral tegmental area in systemic nicotine self-administration. *J. Neurosci.* 28:12318-12327.

[79] Fowler CD, Kenny PJ (2011). Intravenous nicotine self-administration and cue-induced reinstatement in mice: effects of nicotine dose, rate of drug infusion and prior instrumental training. *Neuropharmacol.* 61:687-698.

[80] Besson M, Granon S, Mameli-Engvall M, Cloëz-Tayarani I, Maubourguet N, Cormier A, Cazala P, David V, Changeux JP, Faure P (2007). Long-term effects of chronic nicotine exposure on brain nicotinic receptors. *Proc. Natl. Acad. Sci. USA* 104:8155-8160.

[81] Mansvelder HD, McGehee DS (2000). Long-term potentiation of excitatory inputs to brain reward areas by nicotine. Neuron 27:349-57.

[82] Markou A (2008). Neurobiology of nicotine dependence. *Philos. Trans. R Soc. Lond B Biol. Sci.* 363:3159-3168.

[83] Bliss TV, Collingridge GL (1993). A synaptic model of memory: long-term potentiation in the hippocampus. *Nature* 361:31-39.

[84] Saal D, Dong Y, Bonci A, Malenka R (2003). Drugs of abuse and stress trigger a common synaptic adaptation in dopamine neurons. *Neuron* 37:577-582.

[85] Mansvelder H, McGehee DS (2002). Cellular and synaptic mechanisms of nicotine addiction. *J. Neurobiol.* 53:606-617.

[86] Hunter BE, de Fiebre CM, Papke RL, Kem WR, Meyer EM (1994). A novel nicotinic agonist facilitates induction of long-term potentiation in the hippocampus. *Neurosci. Lett.* 168:130-134.

[87] Mansvelder H, Keath JR, McGehee DS (2002). Synaptic mechanisms underlie nicotine-induced excitability of brain reward areas. *Neuron* 33:905-919.

[88] Wonnacott S (1990). The paradox of nicotinic acetylcholine receptor upregulation by nicotine. *Trends Pharmacol. Sci.* 11:216-219.

[89] Marks MJ, Burch JB, Collins AC (1983). Effects of chronic nicotine infusion on tolerance development and nicotinic receptors. *J. Pharmacol. Exp. Ther.* 226:817-825.

[90] Schwartz RD, Kellar KJ (1983). Nicotinic cholinergic receptor binding sites in the brain: regulation in vivo. *Science* 220:214-216.

[91] Fenster CP, Whitworth TL, Sheffield EB, Quick MW, Lester RA (1999). Upregulation of surface a4b2 nicotinic receptors is initiated by receptor desensitization after chronic exposure to nicotine. *J. Neurosci.* 19:4804-4814.

[92] Picciotto M, Addy NA, Mineur YS, Brunzell D (2008). It is not "Either/or": Activation and desensitization of nicotinic acetylcholine receptors both contribute to behaviors related to nicotine addiction and mood. *Prog. Neurobiol.* 84:329-342.

[93] Penton RE, Lester RA (2009). Cellular events in nicotine addiction. *Sem. Cell Dev. Biol.* 20:418-431.

[94] Perry DC, Dávila-García MI, Stockmeier CA, Kellar KJ (1999) Increased nicotinic receptors in brains from smokers: membrane binding and autoradiography studies. *J. Pharmacol. Exp. Ther.* 289:1545-1552.

[95] Nashmi R, Xiao C, Deshpande P, McKinney S, Grady SR, Whiteaker P, Huang Q, McClure-Begley T, Lindstrom JM, Labarca C, Collins AC, Marks MJ, Lester HA (2007). Chronic nicotine cell specifically upregulates functional a4* nicotinic receptors: Basis for both tolerance in midbrain and enhanced long-term potentiation in perforant path. *J. Neurosci.* 27:8202-8218.

[96] Penton RE, Quick MW, Lester RAJ (2011). Short- and long-lasting consequences of in vivo nicotine treatment on hippocampal excitability. *J. Neurosci.* 31:2584-2594.

[97] Welsby P, Rowan M, Anwyl R (2006). Nicotinic receptor-mediated enhancement of long-term potentiation involves activation of metabotropic glutamate receptors and ryanodine-sensitive calcium stores in the dentate gyrus. *Eur. J. Neurosci.* 24:3109-3118.

[98] Collins AC, Romm E, Wehner JM (1988). Nicotine tolerance: An analysis of the time course of its development and loss in the rat. *Psychopharmacol.* 96:7-14.

[99] Fujii S, Ji Z, Morita N, Sumikawa K (1999). Acute and chronic nicotine exposure differentially facilitate the induction of LTP. *Brain Res.* 846:137-143.

[100] Fujii S, Ji Z, Sumikawa K (2000). Inactivation of a7 ACh receptors and activation of non-a7 ACh receptors both contribute to long term potentiation induction in the hippocampal CA1 region. *Neurosci. Lett.* 286:134-138.

[101] Yamazaki Y, Fujii S, Jia Y, Sumikawa K (2006a) Nicotine withdrawal suppresses nicotinic modulation of long-term potentiation induction in the hippocampal CA1 region. *Eur. J. Neurosci.* 24:2903-2916.

[102] Thomas MJ, Beurrier C, Bonci A, Malenka RC (2001). Long-term depression in the nucleus accumbens: a neural correlate of behavioral sensitization to cocaine. *Nat. Neurosci.* 4:1217-1223.

[103] Ungless MA, Whistler JL, Malenka RC, Bonci A (2001). Single cocaine exposure in vivo induces long-term potentiation in dopamine neurons. *Nature* 411:583-587.

[104] Yamazaki Y, Jia Y, Wong JK, Sumikawa K (2006b). Chronic nicotine-induced switch in Src-family kinase signaling for long-term potentiation induction in hippocampal CA1 pyramidal cells. *Eur. J. Neurosci.* 24:3271-3284.

[105] Chen BT, Hopf FW, Bonci A (2010). Synaptic plasticity in the mesolimbic system: therapeutic implications for substance abuse. *Ann. NY Acad. Sci.* 1187:129-139.

[106] Bliss TV, Lomo T (1973). Long-lasting potentiation of synaptic transmission in the dentate area of the anaesthetized rabbit following stimulation of the perforant path. *J. Physiol.* 232:331-356.

[107] Lester RA (2011). Cognitive mechanisms underlying relapse to nicotine. *Rev. Neurosci.* 22:467-470.

[108] Cooper DC, Moore SJ, Staff NP, Spruston N (2003). Psychostimulant-induced plasticity of intrinsic neuronal excitability in ventral subiculum. *J. Neurosci.* 23:9937–9946.

[109] Zhang TA, Tang J, Pidoplichko VI, Dani JA (2010). Addictive nicotine alters local circuit inhibition during the induction of in vivo hippocampal synaptic potentiation. *J. Neurosci.* 30:6443-6453.

[110] Peng X, Gerzanich V, Anand R, Whiting PJ, Lindstrom J (1994). Nicotine-induced increase in neuronal nicotinic receptors results from a decrease in the rate of receptor turnover. *Mol. Pharmacol.* 46:523-530.

[111] Alkondon M, Albuquerque E (2005) Nicotinic receptor subtypes in rat hippocampal slices are differentially sensitive to desensitization and early in vivo functional up-regulation by nicotine and to block by bupropion. *J. Pharmacol. Exp. Ther.* 313: 740-750.

[112] Koob GF, Le Moal M (2008). Neurobiological mechanisms for opponent motivational processes in addiction. *Phil. Trans. R Soc. Lond B* 363:3113-3123.

[113] Koob GF, Bloom FE (1988). Cellular and molecular mechanisms of drug dependence. *Science* 242:715-723.

[114] DiFranza JR, Wellman RJ (2005). A sensitization-homeostasis model of nicotine craving, withdrawal, and tolerance: integrating the clinical and basic science literature. *Nicotine Tob. Res.* 7:9-26.

[115] Francesconi W, Berton F, Repunte-Canonigo V, Hagihara K, Thurbon D, Lekic D, Specio SE, Greenwell TN, Chen SA, Rice KC, Richardson HN, O'Dell LE, Zorrilla EP, Morales M, Koob GF, Sanna PP (2009). Protracted withdrawal from alcohol and drugs of abuse impairs long-term potentiation of intrinsic excitability in the juxtacapsular bed nucleus of the stria terminalis. *J. Neurosci.* 29:5389-53401.

[116] Belujon P, Grace AA (2011). Hippocampus, amygdala, and stress: interacting systems that affect susceptibility to addiction. *Ann. N Y Acad. Sci.* 1216:114-121.

[117] Joëls M, Krugers H, Karst H (2008). Stress-induced changes in hippocampal function. *Prog. Brain Res.* 167:3-15.

[118] Dong Z, Han H, Wang M, Xu L, Hao W, Coa J (2006). Morphine conditioned place preference depends on glucocorticoid receptors in both hippocampus and nucleus accumbens. *Hippocampus* 16:809-816.

[119] Mantsch JR, Li SJ, Risinger R, Awad S, Katz E, Baker DA, Yang Z (2007). Levo-tetrahydropalmatine attenuates cocaine self-administration and cocaine-induced reinstatement in rats. *Psychopharmacology* (Berl) 192:581-591.

[120] Dani JA, Heinemann S (1996). Molecular and cellular aspects of nicotine abuse. *Neuron* 16:905-908.

[121] Stead LF, Perera R, Bullen C, Mant D, Lancaster T (2008). Nicotine replacement therapy for smoking cessation. *Cochrane Database Systematic Reviews:* CD000146.

[122] WHO Report on the Global Tobacco Epidemic, 2008: the MPOWER package (2008). Geneva: World Health Organization.

[123] Aydin C, Oztan O, Isgor C (2011). Vulnerability to nicotine abstinence-related social anxiety-like behavior: molecular correlates in neuropeptide Y, Y2 receptor and corticotropin releasing factor. *Neurosci. Lett.* 490:220-225.

[124] George O, Ghozland S, Azar MR, Cottone P, Zorrilla EP, Parsons LH, O'Dell LE, Richardson HN, Koob GF (2007). CRF-CRF1 system activation mediates withdrawal-induced increases in nicotine self-administration in nicotine-dependent rats. *Proc. Natl. Acad. Sci. U S A* 104:17198-17203.

[125] Tang J, Dani JA (2009). Dopamine enables in vivo synaptic plasticity associated with the addictive drug nicotine. *Neuron* 63:673-682.

[126] Zhang L, Dong Y, Doyon WM, Dani JA (2011). Withdrawal from Chronic Nicotine Exposure Alters Dopamine Signaling Dynamics in the Nucleus Accumbens. *Biol. Psychiatry* [Epub ahead of print].

[127] De Biasi M, Salas R (2008). Influence of neuronal nicotinic receptors over nicotine addiction and withdrawal. Exp Biol Med 233:917-929.

[128] De Biasi M, Dani JA (2011). Reward, addiction, withdrawal to nicotine. *Annu. Rev. Neurosci.* 34:105-30.

[129] Swanson LW (1981). A direct projection from Ammon's horn to prefrontal cortex in the rat. *Brain Res.* 217:150-154.

[130] Jay TM, Witter MP (1991). Distribution of hippocampal CA1 and subicular efferents in the prefrontal cortex of the rat studied by means of anterograde transport of Phaseolus vulgaris leucoagglutinin. *J. Comp. Neurol.* 313:574–586.

[131] Rolls ET (2007). An attractor network in the hippocampus: theory and neurophysiology. *Learn Mem.* 14:714-731.

[132] Pitkänen A, Pikkarainen M, Nurminen N, Ylinen A (2000). Reciprocal connections between the amygdala and the hippocampal formation, perirhinal cortex, and postrhinal cortex in rat. A review. *Ann. N Y Acad. Sci.* 911:369-91.

[133] Kealy J, Commins S (2011). The rat perirhinal cortex: A review of anatomy, physiology, plasticity, and function. *Prog. Neurobiol.* 93:522-548.

In: Nicotine Addiction
Editor: Giuseppe Di Giovanni

ISBN: 978-1-62081-290-7


*Chapter 4*

# NICOTINE, NEURODEGENERATION, AND NEUROPROTECTION IN NEUROPSYCHIATRIC DISORDERS

***Susan E. Maloney[1,2,*], Kuryn M. Kroutil[1], and George T. Taylor[1]***
[1]Behavioral Neuroscience Program, Department of Psychology, University of Missouri - St. Louis, Missouri, US
[2]Department of Psychiatry, Washington University School of Medicine, St. Louis, Missouri, US

## ABSTRACT

This chapter reviews the relation of nicotine to brain function and dysfunction. The emphasis is on the influences of nicotine on neurodegeneration and neuroprotection of consequent psychopathology. Topics covered include data from animal models and human patients on behavioral consequences on disorders of memory, traumatic brain injury, mood disorders, and schizophrenia. For example, cigarette smoking is related to a reduced incidence and severity of the symptoms of Parkinson's disease. The neuroprotective mechanism of acute and chronic exposure appears to involve the genes that regulate nicotinic cholinergic receptors. Laboratory evidence suggests nicotine facilitates cognitive recovery and attenuates synaptic disruptions following brain injury. Nicotine may be an effective agent in modifying the progression of the cognitive correlates of schizophrenia. Indeed, the percentage of schizophrenia patients who choose to smoke is remarkably high. The same is found in bipolar mood disorders. However, bipolar patients who smoke experience a worse outcome than non-smoking patients. These data call into question the often-stated hypothesis that psychiatric populations self-medicate with nicotine. In conclusion, evidence is equivocal, but nicotine appears to be neuroprotective under certain pathological conditions. Therefore, nicotine analogues may be useful in the treatment of behavioral deficits of some neurodegenerative diseases, various types of neural injury, or certain psychiatric disorders.

[*] Corresponding Address: Susan E. Maloney, M.A. Department of Psychiatry Washington University, School of Medicine, Campus Box 8134, 660 South Euclid Avenue, St. Louis, MO 63110 US. FAX: (314) 516-5397. E-mail: sem885@mail.umsl.edu.

## INTRODUCTION

The nicotine in tobacco is a much maligned drug, and certainly there is no question smoking is associated with cancer and likely other life threatening diseases. However, as with most other malign drugs, for example thalidomide [1], nicotine may have beneficial effects. Our interest is the potential benefits to normal and psychopathological behavior [2].

Nicotine has been shown to improve various types of memory [3, 4, 5] and may improve the symptoms of certain psychiatric conditions [6, 7, 8]. Cigarette smoking is prevalent in schizophrenia patient populations and there is evidence that those that smoke are less affected by the disease. Cigarette smoking reduces incidences of certain neurodegenerative diseases such as Alzheimer's disease (AD), and especially Parkinson's disease (PD) and relieves symptoms in PD patients [9, 10, 11, 12].

The question these data immediately raise is the mechanism. Nicotine is the most biologically active ingredient in tobacco smoke and has neuroprotective properties in the central nervous system (CNS). Nicotine influences the cholinergic system in the brain by binding to and activating the nicotinic receptor (nAChR). Manipulations of this receptor have demonstrated its importance in cognition. Nicotine induces structural and functional changes responsible for the neuroprotection and consequent cognitive improvements. Human and animal research suggests that nicotine or non-addictive nicotine analogs may be a beneficial pharmaceutical therapy for behavioral deficits of some neurodegenerative diseases, various types of neural injury, or certain psychiatric disorders.

## NICOTINE NEUROPROTECTION IN NEURODEGENERATIVE DISEASES

### Nicotine and Alzheimer's Disease

It seems counterintuitive to suggest that smoking is inversely associated with disease. More likely data would indicate that smoking increases the risk of a disease, such as lung cancer or cerebrovascular disease. However, smoking has been suggested to decrease the risk of developing AD [9, 11]. There is evidence of an inverse relationship between smoking history and AD (Figure 1) [13, 14, 15], although studies exist contesting this relationship [16, 17].

Nevertheless, this association warranted further investigation. Genetic studies demonstrated this relationship is independent of a suggested genetic predisposition to AD. That is, no increased prevalence of smoking exists in people possessing the APO e4 gene, which has been linked to AD [18], suggesting that it is not the case that smokers are genetically or epigenetically less at risk of developing AD. The explanation seems to be that nicotine, the ingredient in tobacco smoke that is most biologically active in the CNS, has neuroprotective properties. This neuroprotection may extend directly to AD pathology and the consequent declines in cognition.

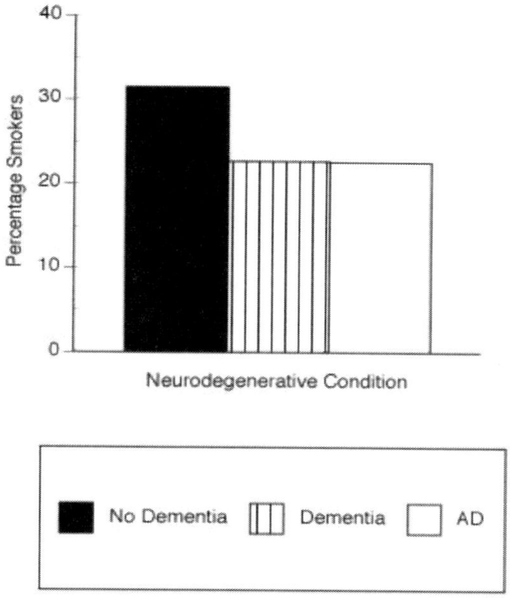


Adapted from Wang et al., 1999 [15].

Figure 1. Percentage of smokers at baseline measurement of the longitudinal study of smoking and Alzheimer's disease (AD) prevalence and incidence over the 3 year study period. At the beginning of the study, a greater percentage of smokers existed within the non-demented, healthy control group than within the group of patients with dementia, including those that have the Alzheimer's disease diagnosis. This illustrates the negative association between smoking and prevalent dementia, including Alzheimer's disease.

### *Nicotine Influence on Cognitive Impairment*

Memory disturbances are the hallmark of AD and typically the first clinical symptoms of dementia. Consequently, considerable research with animal models has been directed towards cognitive deficits and agents that can eliminate these deficits. Most commonly, old animals are used to model dementia in this literature. One can question the logic of this choice because simple aging is not responsible for AD or any form of dementia. However, until we know more about the neuropathology of AD, there are no clearly preferable animal models.

Data in the literature points to nicotine as having a positive influence on neurotransmitter and brain regions underlying certain aspects of cognition. Both human and animal studies have demonstrated learning and memory enhancements with nicotine exposure. Working memory improvement has been seen in smokers relative to non-smokers or ex-smoker controls [19, 20]. The possibility that nicotine can enhance learning and memory has attracted the attention of animal researchers. Most of the studies with animal models have employed hippocampal-based spatial memory tasks, such as the radial arm maze (RAM) or Morris water maze (MWM) tasks. Positive results also have been reported in other hippocampal-dependent paradigms, for example a visual spatial orientation paradigm and even non-spatial working memory tasks that are hippocampus-dependent, such as the object recognition task [2, 21].

Both spatial working and reference memory ability can be measured easily in the RAM, and improvements have been observed in both domains with nicotine administration. Acute administration of nicotine with a dose within the typical dosage range (0.2 – 0.7 mg/kg bwt) improves both working and reference memory performance in the RAM in young adult rats [22]. Chronic exposure to higher dosages (2.5 – 12.0 mg/kg bwt) of nicotine in young adult rats also improves RAM performance, even after nicotine cessation [4, 5, 23]. Aged rats perform significantly worse in the RAM compared to young adult rats, one reason aged rats are used as an animal model for dementia research. Acute and chronic nicotine administration within the typical dosage range improves working and reference memory performance in aged rats in the RAM [24, 25]. Chronic administration of higher nicotine dosages, however, failed to improve RAM performance in aged rats [26], indicating nicotine improvement in cognitively compromised rats is dosage and duration-dependent.

The MWM is more commonly used to evaluate reference memory performance that is akin to episodic memory of humans. For this reason, this paradigm is often used in AD rodent studies as aged rodents exhibit impaired performance relative to young adult rodents [27, 28]. While nicotine does not improve the already outstanding acquisition performance of young adult rats when administered chronically, it does bolster retention memory. In aged rats, chronic nicotine treatment improves impaired acquisition, but not impaired retention performance [28]. The same results have been reported in a transgenic mouse model of AD. The transgenic mouse expressing neuron-specific enolase-controlled APPsw exhibits increased AD pathology in the brain and cognitive impairments at 12 months of age. Chronic treatment with high dosages of nicotine (5.0, 30, 180 mg/kg bwt) improved acquisition performance in the MWM in a dose-dependent fashion in these mice [29], that is, the greater the nicotine dose, the greater the enhancement. Retention memory was not influenced. The animal research suggests both acute and chronic nicotine administration can improve age-related memory declines with particular support for improvement of compromised learning in the pathological aged-brain.

More importantly, nicotine has been reported to enhance cognition in human AD populations. In AD patients chronically administered nicotine through a transdermal patch improvement has been observed on a repeated acquisition test demonstrating improved learning, although memory and global cognitive functioning were unaffected in this study [30]. However, improvements on a verbal fluency test designed to assess semantic memory have been observed following chronic transdermal nicotine administration in AD patients [31]. Taken together with animal studies, these findings suggest that nicotine has a greater influence over compromised learning than it does over memory retention.

The beneficial effects on cognition, however, extend beyond the hippocampus. A common finding in the animal and human literature is increased acute attention [32]. Patients with AD exhibit an increase in reaction time and better sustained visual attention and visual short-term memory when administered nicotine either acutely by intravenous or subcutaneous injections or chronically through transdermal skin patches [33,34,35,36]. The influence of nicotine on attention may also underlie the improvements observed in learning. An increased attention span could lead to greater acquisition of information.

### *Nicotine, the Cholinergic System and Alzheimer's Disease*

The mechanism responsible for the enhancements of cognitive function by nicotine appears to be its influence on the cholinergic system in the CNS. The two main subtypes of cholinergic receptors are the muscarinic and nicotinic receptors. Nicotine binds to and activates the nicotinic receptor (nAChR). Manipulations of this receptor have demonstrated its importance in cognition. Nicotinic agonists, such as nicotine or lobeline, enhance cognitive performance, whereas nAChR blockers, such as mecamylamine, inhibit cognitive performance [22, 37, 38, 39]. Not only does nicotine acutely activate these receptors, but chronic nicotine exposure actually upregulates, or increases, the density of nAChRs in the CNS [40, 41, 42].

A number of nAChR variants exist. Five subunits assemble in different and complex ways to create nAChR subtypes [43]. Particular variants are involved in cognitive performance. The $\alpha7$ subunit is related to attention and working memory performance [44]. Interestingly, the $\alpha7$ subunit does not upregulate.

However, it is responsible for the maintenance of homeostasis within the cholinergic system following the alterations of other subunits caused by chronic nicotine exposure [41]. The subunits $\alpha4$ and $\beta2$ combine to create the subunit complex $\alpha4\beta2$, which also is related to attention and working memory function [39, 43, 46]. This combined subunit does upregulate following chronic nicotine exposure. It is the most common combination of subunits and nicotine binds to it with the highest efficacy of all subunit combinations. Both the $\alpha7$ and $\alpha4\beta2$ subunits are widely distributed throughout the mammalian CNS. However, the $\alpha7$-nAChRs are found in high concentrations within the hippocampus while $\alpha4\beta2$-nAChRs are only moderately represented in that area [39, 43, 47].

Although the density of $\alpha4\beta2$-nAChRs is not high in hippocampus, upregulation of these receptors does occur here, along with other areas of the CNS. The hippocampus is largely involved in learning and memory. Learning and memory performance in the animal model paradigms discussed above (e.g. MWM, RAM) is dependent on hippocampal function [48, 49]. This area is also largely damaged in neurodegenerative diseases that present with large memory declines, such as AD [50]. Nicotine action to upregulate and activate $\alpha4\beta2$-nAChRs may increase hippocampal function and, therefore, learning and memory performance. Although nicotine does not upregulate $\alpha7$-nAChRs within the hippocampus, this subunit is already present in large numbers. Increased activation of this subunit by nicotine may activate some compensatory mechanism in pathological brains to help improve function.

Damage within the cholinergic system is a consistent finding in the human dementia literature (figure 2). In both AD and PD, neuron loss is found in the nucleus basalis area of the basal forebrain [51, 52, 53]. Cholinergic neurons in nucleus basalis area send projections to the hippocampus and widespread areas of the cortex. It is notable that the hippocampal and cortical regions are the ones that show the most AD pathology, senile plaques and neurofibrillary tangles. That AD patients present with significant memory impairments is not surprising given that these areas are heavily involved in learning and memory processes.

Not only has cholinergic neuron loss been observed in AD brains, but this disease affects other aspects of the cholinergic system, as well. Significant losses of nAChRs, both in subcortical and cortical regions, have been observed through imaging studies of brain tissue following the autopsy of AD brains [54, 55, 56, 57]. A decline in density and activity of nAChRs in AD brains is likely related to the observed cognitive dysfunction. Indeed, the severity of AD at the time of death has consistently correlated with nAChR loss [58]. Experimentally induced hippocampal degeneration, as well as accompanying cognitive impairments, is protected by nicotinic activation of nAChRs [59]. This protection is likely given by enhanced synaptic transmission in the hippocampus caused by nicotine activation of nAChRs [60].

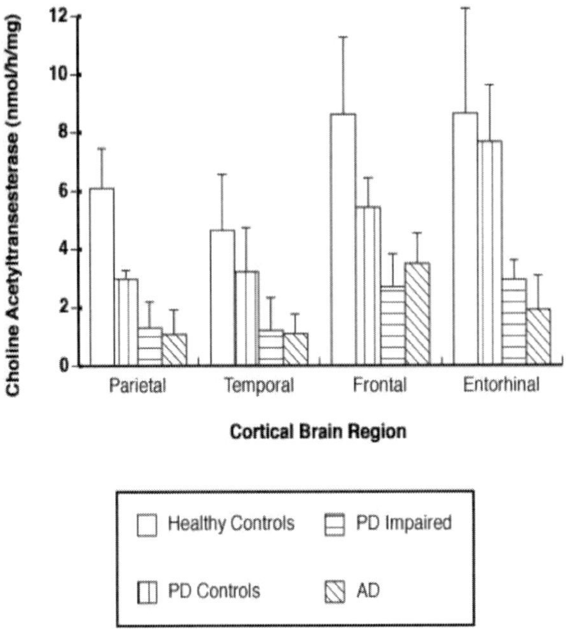


Adapted from Perry et al., 1985 [85].

Figure 2. Activity of the cholinergic system, as measured by amount of choline acetyltransferase, in four areas of the cortex. Clearly, healthy controls exhibit greater cholinergic activity than all other groups within the parietal, frontal, and temporal cortices. However, within the entorhinal cortex, the area within the temporal lobe which connects between the cortex and the hippocampus and which plays a major role in memory function, both the healthy controls and Parkinson's disease patients with no obvious cognitive impairment (PD Controls) exhibit greater cholinergic activity than either Parkinson's disease patients with obvious cognitive impairment (PD Impaired) and Alzheimer's disease (AD) patients. This demonstrates the decline of the cholinergic system within each of these diseases and indicates a relationship between the declining cholinergic system and impaired cognitive functioning in both Parkinson's disease and Alzheimer's disease.

Nicotine has a direct influence on pathology in the AD brain. The AD brain is plagued with senile plaques and neurofibrillary tangles which kill neurons from the outside or the inside, respectively. Senile plaques are a buildup of Aβ amyloid peptide deposits surrounding the neuron and neurofibrillary tangles consist of hyperphosphorylated tau protein filaments that accumulate within the neuron [61]. Nicotine and its metabolite, nornicotine, have been demonstrated to protect against the neurotoxicity of Aβ amyloid [62, 63, 64, 65]. Nicotine appears to inhibit the formation of this protein as well as disrupt already formed deposits [66]. Suggested mechanisms underlying this neuroprotection include reduction of amyloid beta-protein precursor enzyme, upregulation of proteins that inhibit neuronal death processes, and regulation of copper concentrations [67, 68, 69]. Antioxidant mechanisms also have been suggested, as well as involvement of the neurotrophic agent fibroblast growth factor [70, 71].

Whether one or all of these mechanisms are at play, it is likely the activation of the nAChRs that initiates the neuroprotective process [72]. The evidence lies not only in nicotine and nicotinic agonist protection, but that the administration of nicotinic receptor antagonists, alone or in combination with nicotine, block any neuroprotective effect [72, 73, 74]. Neuroprotection appears is specific to activation of the α7-nAChR and α4β2-nAChR subtypes

[73, 74, 75]. This is not surprising given that these two subtypes are so heavily involved in learning and memory function.

Behavioral research has also confirmed the specificity of these two receptor subtypes to nicotine neuroprotection in AD. Aged rats acutely administered a α7-nAChR agonist demonstrated improved working memory performance in the MWM and in the object recognition paradigm, two hippocampus-dependent tasks [76]. Chronic administration of α7-nAChR agonists also improves cognition. Rats are administered a saline solution containing β amyloid into the fourth ventricle of the brain to create an animal model of Alzheimer's type dementia (ATD).Chronic administration of a α7-nAChR agonist expunged the memory deficits observed in untreated ATD rats [77]. Evidence also exists for α4β2-nAChR agonist-induced cognitive enhancement. AD patients acutely administered a α4β2-nAChR agonist improved on a verbal learning task and a non-verbal spatial learning and memory task [78]. Chronic administration of a α4β2-nAChR agonist to AD patients improved cognitive performance as measured by the Mini Mental State Examination [79]. Taken together, these studies suggest these receptor subtypes are specifically relevant to nicotine cognitive protection in AD. An interesting counter to this idea is a study that assessed cognition in mice over-expressing the human amyloid precursor protein (APP) and that were missing the gene for the α7-nAChR subtype. The APP mice without the α7-nAChR subtype performed better than those with the α7-nAChR subtype. The authors of this study suggest the interruption of α7-nAChR function may be beneficial to the treatment of AD cognitive declines [80].

Nicotinic receptor agonists that work at these receptor subtypes have been developed in an effort to capture the neuroprotective influence nicotine has against AD. Research with humans and animal models is promising. These agents have been demonstrated to enhance attention, learning and memory capabilities, and decrease aspects of AD pathology in the brain [45, 78, 81, 82].

Nicotine benefits cognition in old animals and likely young adults, too, although the latter may be so good at certain cognitive tasks a ceiling effect occurs. Attention is the primary cognitive feature that benefits from nicotine treatment, and this occurs with both acute and chronic nicotine exposure.

However, it is not simply that nicotine is a stimulant that makes the subject more attentive, and thus improved learning and memory performance occurs. It is the structural (increased nAChRs) and functional (increased cholinergic and other neurotransmitter activity) changes induced by nicotine responsible for the neuroprotection and consequent cognitive improvements.

The early reports were that smokers are less likely to develop AD and other neuro-degenerative diseases, but more recent work has questioned the association and more studies are needed to determine the actual relationship. It can be said with some certainty that simply administrating nicotine to AD patients doesn't do much. However, it is likely that by the time AD symptoms arise it is too late; the cholinergic and other neurotransmitter systems have lost too many neurons for nicotine to be effective. No one in the medical community would advocate smoking because of its overall detrimental health effects. However, the results suggest that nicotine administered alone, or, better, non-addictive nicotine analogs may provide the benefits without the risks.

## Nicotine and Parkinson's Disease

Three decades ago epidemiology studies of smoking habits reported fewer cigarette smokers among PD patients than other patients, indicating cigarette smoking and PD may be inversely related [83, 84]. A study of long-term smokers indicated a statistically significant reduction in PD compared to non-smokers. Moreover, the acute benefits of nicotine were suggested in a study demonstrating that smoking a cigarette relieved PD symptoms in patients [10, 12]. After reviewing over 40 published reports on the, nicotine – PD relations, researchers concluded there was enough evidence to warrant further research into the therapeutic benefits of nicotine [12]. Among other findings supporting possible therapeutic benefits were an apparent dose-response relation, the lack of an explanation by confounding variables, and that a similar relationship existed between smoking and AD.

A central question subsequently facing researchers was determining if the mechanisms for neuroprotection observed in AD are the same in PD patients. While sharing some neurodegenerative features, the neuropathology and presentation of symptoms differ quite extensively between these two neurodegenerative diseases. For example, the most obvious clinical expression of PD is in motor movements. The suggestion is that the beneficial influences of nicotine may also differ in the PD brain.

### *Nicotine and the Pathology of Parkinson's Disease*

PD is a neurodegenerative disease that primarily influences functioning of the dopaminergic system by destroying the dopaminergic neurons originating from the substantia nigra [51]. These neurons send projections to the basal ganglia, an area of the brain involved in motor learning and motor control. PD is considered a progressive movement disorder. As the degeneration of the neurons of the substantia nigra neurons progresses, the severity of the symptoms worsens.

The main impairment is that of starting and sustaining voluntary movements. This is due to the compromised function of the basal ganglia. Cognitive decline is also observed in PD patients, as the basal ganglia is involved in certain aspects of cognition. Dopamine is not the only transmitter system undergoing neurodegeneration in PD. Cholinergic neuronal loses in the basal forebrain may account for most of the cognitive declines with PD (figure 2) [53, 54, 85].

Nicotine therapy has shown promise as a treatment for the cognitive declines associated with PD, and evidence exists for nicotine protecting against motor deficits, as well [86]. Nicotine studies with human PD patients primarily administer nicotine acutely. Therefore, the short-term influences of nicotine therapy are better understood than that of long-term, chronic therapy. The main long-term influence of nicotine exposure appears to be the decreased risk of developing PD [12]. Chronic nicotine treatment also improved several motor measures in PD patients [86]. This suggests some other mechanism is required beyond simply the activation of nAChRs to influence motor function. Perhaps the upregulation of nAChRs with chronic nicotine treatment has a beneficial effect on the depleted dopaminergic systems of the PD brain.

The cholinergic system interacts with the dopaminergic system through activation of nAChRs. These receptors are located on the substantia nigra neurons, which project to the basal ganglia. Activation of the nAChRs, either by the endogenous acetylcholine neurotransmitter or a nicotinic-agonist, enhances the synaptic transmission of these dopaminergic neurons [87]. This results in an increase in dopamine activity within the basal ganglia. The enhanced neurotransmitter activity is likely the mechanism behind nicotine-induced benefits in the PD brain.

Nicotine-induced improvement in cognitive domains occurs following short-term exposure. Acute nicotine exposure has improved reaction times, central processing speeds, and decreased tracking errors [86]. Semantic processing improvement also has been observed [88, 89]. These studies suggest that direct activation of nAChRs by nicotine restores cognitive processing, perhaps by boosting function of subcortical – cortical circuits.

Research with animal models has demonstrated similar neuroprotection. Animal models of PD rely on the chemical destruction of the dopaminergic system, primarily the neurons of the substantia nigra. Two substances are typically used – rotenone and 1-methyl-4-phenyl-1,2,5,6-tetrahydropyridine (MPTP). Rotenone is a pesticide that has been linked to PD and which causes PD-like symptoms in rodents. MPTP is a chemical that causes the death of dopaminergic neurons in the CNS in both rodents and primates, including humans [51].

Administration of either of these agents to a rodent will cause dopaminergic neuronal degeneration as well as Parkinson-like cognitive and motor deficits. Chronic nicotine exposure inhibits motor deficits and influences locomotor activity in rotenone-treated and MPTP-treated mice [90, 91]. The suggested mechanism here is a long-term increase in dopaminergic activity within the nigrostriatal pathway produced by nicotine binding to nAChRs on the dopaminergic neurons, as outlined above.

Nicotine, acutely administered, also improves attention and central executive functioning in monkeys chronically exposed to MPTP [92]. This improvement appears to be independent of stimulation of the dopaminergic system. This was observed in rats when a haloperidol infusion, a dopamine receptor antagonist, failed to attenuate memory improvements exhibited by acute nicotine administration [93]. This suggests, as with human data, that cognitive improvements are more likely a result of direct nAChR activation by nicotine in other areas of the brain, likely within cholinergic pathways.

More evidence for the involvement of nAChRs in the performance declines of PD patients is the significant loss of nicotinic receptors with disease progression [55]. Receptor losses have been observed in both the cortex and subcortical areas [54, 57]. The loss of nAChRs in the midbrain, specifically in the substantia nigra, has important implications for PD-related functional deficits.

The loss of the receptors has been suggested to precede the neurodegeneration [94], indicating a possible neuroprotective role of nAChRs in this area against neuronal loss in the substantia nigra. If the density of the receptors was stable, it would seem the neurons would remain protected and delay the development of PD.

Research with animal models has demonstrated a significant decrease in neurodegeneration within the nigrostriatal pathway with nicotine exposure [95]. Nicotine protected against MPTP-induced nigrostriatal neurodegeneration in mice, rats, and monkeys [96, 97, 98, 99, 100, 101]. As in AD, the neuroprotective influence of nicotine is relegated to the activation of certain nAChR subtypes. The $\alpha4\beta2$, $\alpha6\beta2$, and $\alpha7$ subtypes have all been linked to this neuroprotection [95, 102, 103]. It is a clear possibility that the upregulation of nAChRs caused by nicotine exposure is playing a large role in the decreased frequency of PD observed in smokers.

Upregulation of nAChRs results in a number of downstream effects that may contribute to neuroprotection. These include an increase in the activity of the ubiquitin-proteasome system, the decrease of which is thought to play a role in the pathology of PD [104]. Also, nicotine is thought to increase the neurotrophic factor fibroblast growth factor – 2, preserve mitochondrial function, and restore gene expression that is influenced by PD pathology [105, 106, 107].

Nicotine has also been suggested to increase enzymes in the brain that metabolize neurotoxins associated with PD [108]. Perhaps most importantly, nicotine inhibits the formation of α-synuclein, a pathological hallmark of PD [109].

Whether one or all of these mechanisms are responsible, the therapeutic implications of nicotinic agonists in PD are clear. Smoking would never be advised as a preventative measure against PD. However, these findings tell an obvious neuroprotective story that will help researchers and clinicians to understand the pathology behind PD and develop new and better pharmacological therapies.

### Nicotine and other Memory Disorders

Nicotine protects against memory impairments related to other conditions that are not considered neurodegenerative diseases. In fact, nicotine has been observed to attenuate help with memory declines related to normal aging [110]. However, studies of smokers have demonstrated a decrease in performance in recall tasks in older smokers, but not in younger smokers [111].

Many health issues are related to smoking, outside of the nicotine exposure, such as breathing problems and cardiovascular effects. These other health problems could indirectly influence learning and memory function.

Researchers have investigated nicotine influence on substance-induced amnesia. The nootrophic effects of nicotine have been demonstrated in carbon monoxide-induced, morphine-induced, and ethanol-induced memory impairment [112, 113, 114, 115].

Based on nicotine neuroprotection in neurodegenerative diseases, the upregulation of nAChRs is plausible for the memory improvements. The cholinergic system is known to be a key system in learning and memory performance. It would not be surprising if nicotine improved some aspect of cognition in any disorder that affects ACh and nAChRs.

## Nicotine Neuroprotection in Neural Injury

Smoking is not associated with a reduced risk of occurrence or severity of traumatic brain injury (TBI). However, evidence exists that nicotine can play a neuroprotective and therapeutic role in the recovery of function following TBI.

There are two types of traumatic brain injury: open and closed. Open head injury occurs with penetration of the brain parenchyma, as with a gunshot wound. Closed head injury occurs without penetration, but most damage is due to the impact of the brain hitting the skull or from the shearing of tissue when the brain is stretched. This would occur following a blow to the head, for example [116].

The resulting TBI damage can be both in focal and diffuse areas of the brain. Focal damage occurs in the cortex by mechanical forces and may include a contusion, hematoma formation, neuronal loss and edema, all of which can produce neuronal death at the impact site [117, 118]. The neurons surrounding the impact site are also at risk. An excess of release of the excitatory neurotransmitter glutamate occurs in the cortical areas adjacent to the impact site [119]. The glutamate excessively activates the NMDA receptors resulting in overstimulation of the neurons and eventually killing the neurons secondary to the initial impact trauma. This process is known as excitotoxicity [120].

Initial diffuse damage is usually in the form of diffuse axonal injury in the subcortical white matter due to movement of the brain within the skull. The permeability of the axonal membrane is altered, allowing the influx of normally external ions. This result is excitotoxic to surrounding neurons due to an increase of glutamate neurotransmitter release. This also is toxic to the affected neurons as a cascade of intracellular events is activated leading to the death of that neuron [117, 121]. Other secondary injuries follow the initial cascade of negative events. Further neuronal losses result from swelling of tissue, blood clots, and hypoxic and ischemic events due to vascular disturbances [122].

TBI damage causes a variety of cognitive disturbances. Attentional disturbances are most often reported. Patients experience difficulty concentrating, multitasking, and impaired speed of thinking [122]. Anterograde memory impairment is often observed. Difficulty learning new information and creating new memories is present in most TBI patients regardless of severity of damage. Attention and memory deficits are likely due to hippocampal and cortical damage. Decreases in procedural learning are often observed subsequent to impairment of frontal-striatal functions [123]. Executive functioning deficits appear following moderate to severe TBI. Executive function is higher-order cognition necessary to successfully prepare and execute goal-oriented, independent behaviors. This impairment causes TBI patients to have difficulty performing daily tasks [122]. These deficits result from damage to the frontal cortex and its connections. Impairment of these cognitive domains can occur with direct injury to cortical, subcortical or brainstem areas that support these processes.

The involvement of nicotine in TBI is suggested by findings of dysfunction in the cholinergic system following TBI despite the area of direct mechanical impact [121, 124, 125]. Diffuse axonal injury often affects cholinergic neurons and can lead to the death of these and surrounding neurons. Dysfunctions most often observed are reductions in choline acetyltransferase, deficits in cholinergic presynaptic terminals, and lower acetylcholinesterase activity [124, 125]. It is not surprising that attention and memory are among the most frequent cognitive functions impaired, given the impact of TBI on the cholinergic system.

The ability of nicotine to increase cholinergic function suggests it as a possible therapy for the injured brain. TBI research with animal models use controlled cortical impact (CCI) to model a closed head injury in humans. Studies using the CCI paradigm have demonstrated nicotine administration to be beneficial. Chronic nicotine administration attenuates deficits in nAChRs following CCI in the cortex and hippocampus [126, 127]. This is not surprising considering nicotine upregulates nAChRs in healthy brain tissue [40]. Cognitive improvements have also been reported in studies with lab animals. For example, nicotine attenuated acquisition deficits in the MWM following CCI [126, 128]. This is probably a consequence of the facilitating influence of nicotine within the compromised cholinergic system.

Nicotine as a neuroprotective agent in TBI patients is more promising with regard to neuronal loss from excitotoxicity. *In vivo* and *in vitro* rodent models have demonstrated nicotine to protect against excitotoxicity in the hippocampal, striatal, and cortical neurons

[129, 130, 131, 132, 133]. This form of neuroprotection works through a calcium-dependent mechanism, possibly mediating calcium influx observed following overstimulation of NMDA receptors [134, 135].

Secondary injuries may be delayed for several hours to days later, providing a window of therapeutic opportunity. Nicotine or nicotinic agonist administration during this window may help increase neuronal survival and protect against further cognitive declines by protecting against excitotoxic damage.

# Nicotine Neuroprotection in Psychiatric Disorders

## Nicotine and Schizophrenia

Schizophrenia is an intractable neurological disease often first diagnosed in the late teens and early twenties. Characterizing the symptoms of schizophrenia into positive and negative symptoms has proven useful for treatment and prognosis. Positive symptoms include delusions, hallucinations, and disorganized speech and behavior. Negative symptoms include affective flattening, anhedonia, avolition, and cognitive impairments. Schizophrenia has a lifetime prevalence of 4.0/1000 [136] and results in impairments in every aspect of day to day functioning.

Neurotransmitter systems have been a particular focus of research in underlying mechanisms of schizophrenia. Dopamine (DA) was the neurotransmitter initially implicated in the disorder. The predominant model proposed abnormally low prefrontal DA activity leading to abnormally high DA activity in mesolimbic regions [137]. The DA model accounted for the negative symptoms from prefrontal hypoactivity and the positive symptoms from striatal hyperactivity. More recently, hypoactivity of glutamate has been associated with schizophrenia, specifically the NMDA subtype of glutamate receptor. Blockade of this receptor leads to less stimulation of $\gamma$-aminobutyric acid (GABA) interneurons, increasing DA release in mesolimbic areas and causing symptoms characteristic of schizophrenia in nonpsychiatric participants [138, 139]. Observations of the effects of second generation antipsychotics have led researchers to examine the role of serotonin (5-HT), and the many receptor subtypes of 5-HT, in schizophrenia. Atypical antipsychotics, unlike older neuroleptics, can provide improvement of negative symptoms. Reductions in negative symptoms are thought to result from increased DA release in the prefrontal cortex by a variety of mechanisms including agonism of the 5-HT1A receptor and antagonism of the 5-HT2A receptor [140]. The involvement of ACh, especially nAChRs, is now a focus of research because nAChRs are found on GABA interneurons. Another reason to focus on nicotine is the high rates of smoking among schizophrenic patients [141] that has led to the popular self-medication hypothesis.

It has been widely reported that there is a high prevalence of smoking among schizophrenia patients (figure 3). Although the astronomically high 80-90% frequently cited in the literature and in popular media is contestable [142], the more reasonable figure of 62% worldwide [143] is still significantly higher than the approximately 23% prevalence rate among the general population worldwide [144]. Smoking prevalence among schizophrenic patients is also significantly higher than in non-schizophrenic psychiatric patients [145]. With the well-known health consequences from long-term use, smoking is a concern for families and care providers of patients. Yet, smoking cessation rates among schizophrenic patients are markedly lower than among both the general population and non-schizophrenic psychiatric patients [145], even though the majority of patients who smoke would like to quit [7, 146, 147]. Despite both internal and external motivations to quit, continuing to smoke suggests patients are accruing benefits. The prevailing hypothesis is that schizophrenic patients use smoking to self-medicate with nicotine for relief both of the side effects of anti-psychotic medications and the symptoms of schizophrenia.

Schizophrenic patients report that they smoke for many of the same reasons stated by non-psychiatric smokers [6, 7, 8, 147]. However, when ranking reasons for smoking in order of salience to the decision to smoke, schizophrenic patients give more weight to those reasons that they associate with relief from schizophrenia symptoms and medication side effects than do non-psychiatric smokers. Non-psychiatric smokers rate reasons associated with social activity and addiction as being prominent reasons to smoke, whereas schizophrenic smokers rate calmness or relief from anxiety, and alertness and attention or stimulation as prominent reasons to smoke [6, 7, 8]. Emerging research is furthering our understanding of the mechanisms by which nicotine can provide partial amelioration from disease symptoms and drug side effects.

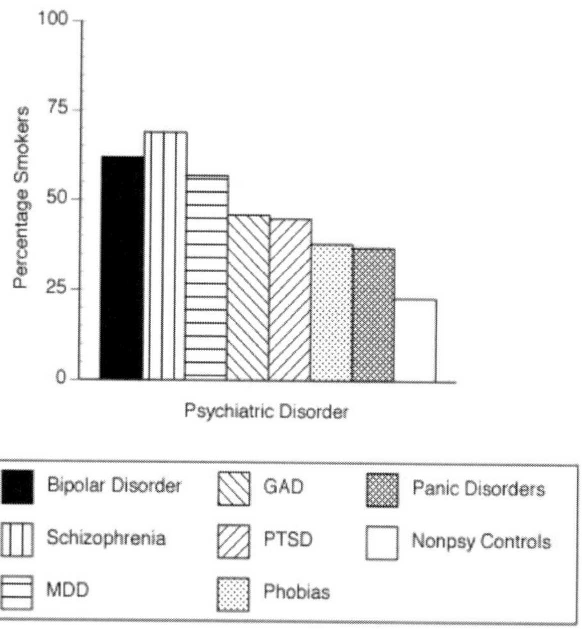


Adapted from Lasser et al., 2000 [205].

Figure 3. Percentage of smokers according to psychiatric diagnosis at any time in their lives. A clear trend exists for a greater prevalence of smoking among psychiatric populations than among the nonpsychiatric control population, with the greatest percentage of reported smokers within schizophrenia, bipolar mood disorder, and major depressive disorder (MDD) populations (general anxiety disorder, GAD; posttraumatic stress disorder, PTSD).

***Nicotinic Acetylcholine Receptors in Schizophrenia***

Nicotine binds nAChRs. There are two families of subtypes of nAChRs. The α4β2-nAChR subtype is the most common in the CNS and is representative of the family of nAChRs that have a high affinity for nicotine and a long desensitization latency. The α7-nAChR subtype is representative of the family of nAChRs that have a low affinity for nicotine and short desensitization latency [148]. Postmortem studies of brain tissue reveal schizophrenic patients to have reduced numbers of the low affinity α7-nAChR in the hippocampus [149], frontal cortex [150], and the reticular nucleus of the thalamus [151] when compared to non-psychiatric control participants. Moreover, tissue from schizophrenic patients who smoke have reduced numbers of high affinity nAChRs in the hippocampus and cortex [141], indicating a failure to upregulate these nAChRs [152], as is often observed in postmortem studies of other smokers [141]. Attempts to attain a level of cognitive functioning consistent with normal nAChR stimulation in the circumstance of low levels of nAChRs may be a cause of increased smoking rates among schizophrenic patients. As may be expected, low levels of both high and low affinity nAChRs in such varied brain regions results in varied pathophysiological and behavioral outcomes.

***Auditory Evoked Potential Inhibition Deficits in Schizophrenia***

Sensory processing deficits are commonly observed in schizophrenia. One of the sensory gating abnormalities frequently observed in patients [153], as well as their first-degree relatives [154, 155, 156], is diminished inhibition of the electroencephalographic hippocampal auditory evoked response to repeated stimuli. Briefly, electrodes attached to the scalp record an electrically positive evoked potential which occurs 50 ms after an auditory stimulus is presented (P50). An identical stimulus is presented 500 ms after presentation of the first stimulus. Normally, there is a significant decrease in the amplitude of the second P50 in relation to the amplitude of the first. The decrease is from an inhibitory response by the hippocampus triggered by the first stimulus. In the normal response, inhibition results from cholinergic stimulation of inhibitory GABA interneurons leading to GABA-ergic inhibition of glutamate activation of pyramidal neurons of the CA3 region of the hippocampus [156].

The role of the inhibitory response is to ignore unimportant, repeated stimuli such as traffic noise or the furnace running, so that attention can be focused elsewhere. Low levels of nAChRs in the hippocampus of schizophrenic patients can reduce the amount of possible cholinergic activation of GABA interneurons, thereby decreasing the ability to inhibit the hippocampal response to the second stimulus. An impaired inhibitory response results in a reduced ability to filter extraneous or intrusive input, explaining the state of sensory overload and distractible hypervigilance characteristic of schizophrenia [149, 153, 156, 157]). The motivation to mitigate this overwhelmed, anxious state is understandable, and supports the self-medication hypothesis.

An interesting empirical test of the hypothesis that nicotine can normalize the P50 inhibition deficit examined nonsmoking relatives of schizophrenic patients. Nonsmoking, unaffected relatives were used to avoid confounds of nicotine withdrawal and medication side effects possible in a typical schizophrenic sample. Those individuals showing the P50 inhibitory deficit were administered nicotine gum and the results were normalization of the evoked potential response [158].

Early genetic studies of schizophrenic patients determined that no single gene responsible for the disease. This conclusion does not come as a surprise; genetics studies often have concluded psychiatric conditions have a complex polymorphic and epigenetic etiology. Although studies of schizophrenic patients do not reveal a unique set of genes, the research has yielded interesting associations among P50 gating deficits, α7-nAChR, and smoking among schizophrenic patients. Linkage and association studies have examined CHRNA7, the gene that codes for the neuronal α7-nAChR. Findings have indicated that mutations in the promoter regions of CHRNA7 are associated with the P50 gating deficit observed in schizophrenic patients and their relatives [155, 156, 159], and associated with smoking in schizophrenic patients [160, 161]. The implication is that mutations in the CHRNA7 gene may be the mechanism responsible for the irregularities in α7-nAChR expression often observed in schizophrenic patients.

Pharmacological studies with animal models provide further support for the mediating effects of α7-nAChRs on the P50 gating deficit. A variety of cholinergic antagonists were administered to rats to examine the possible role of cholinergic neurons in hippocampal inhibitory responses [162]. Evoked responses were recorded by an electrode in the CA3 layer of the hippocampus to detect any change in evoked P20-N40 response inhibition, a rodent analogue of the P50 inhibition response in humans. Neither the muscarinic AChR antagonists nor antagonists of the high affinity nAChRs caused a decline in the P20-N40 response. Antagonists of the low affinity nAChRs, however, effectively–produced impairments in inhibitory responses. These results suggest a role specifically for α7-nAChRs in auditory gating.

Stevens and colleagues [163] extended this research in a series of experiments using DBA/2 mice, a strain that exhibits both extremely low numbers of low affinity nAChRs in the hippocampus and a marked impairment of P20-N40 gating. A variety of nicotinic agonists were administered to the DBA/2 mice, including nicotine, a novel mixed α7 and α4β2 nAChR agonist [164], and novel α7-nAChR partial agonists [165]. All of the drugs significantly improved P20-N40 gating. The improvements were eliminated in all groups by the administration of a selective α7-nAChR antagonist, but not by the administration of a selective α4β2-nAChR antagonist. Interestingly, the α7-nAChR partial agonist DMXB was able to improve the P20-N40 gating response over sequential injections. Unlike DMXB, nicotine does not continuously produce its beneficial effects on auditory gating after initial administration, probably as a result of desensitization due to occupation of the receptor.

### *Smooth Pursuit Eye Movement Deficits in Schizophrenia*

Another sensory processing deficit common in schizophrenia is abnormality of smooth pursuit eye movement (SPEM). As the definition suggests, SPEM is visual tracking of a moving target to stabilize the retinal image of the target on the fovea. Smooth pursuit is initiated by slippage of the image of the target on the retina, which provides information on the target's movement such as velocity and direction. In people without a psychiatric diagnosis the eye velocity usually closely matches the velocity of the target, [166]. When the movement of the target is predictable, such as a sinusoidal pattern, extraretinal motion signals such as anticipation of that movement plays an important role in successfully maintaining SPEM [167]. Smooth pursuit is a complex visual function involving several cognitive and ocular motor processes including visual attention, processing of visual motion information, integration of visual information to formulate a motor response, and generation of smooth pursuit eye movements.

Research on smoking and SPEM among schizophrenic patients has used a variety of different methods to administer nicotine, from nicotine in gum or a nasal spray, [168, 169, 170] to a transdermal patch [171], to the chosen smoking habits of the participant [172, 173]. Different delivery methods could account for differences across the studies in both the pharmacokinetics and pharmacodynamics of nicotine.

Although route of administration differed in the relevant literature, nicotine seems to have a generally positive effect on precision of SPEM in schizophrenia patients, as expressed by a ratio of eye velocity to target velocity, the gain ratio. Olincy and colleagues have consistently found an increase in gain ratio for schizophrenic patients [172, 173], but results have been mixed for controls. Dépatie and colleagues [171], in agreement with one Olincy study [172], found nicotine to significantly increase gain ratio in both schizophrenic patients and controls, but the Dépatie study examined both monitoring and no-monitoring conditions. The no-monitoring condition was a standard, computerized sinusoidal smooth pursuit task. The monitoring condition included extra instructions to enhance attention in the form of a randomly changing target which the participants were to indicate with a button press. There was an increase in gain ratios in both patients and controls after nicotine administration, but surprisingly only in the no-monitoring condition [171].

Studies of SPEM have also been conducted using neuroimaging methods such as functional magnetic resonance imaging (fMRI). A study by Tanabe, Tregellas, Martin, and Freedman [170] had participants perform a smooth pursuit task while undergoing an MRI. Taking into consideration the effects nicotine has on the inhibitory processes in the hippocampus, it is not surprising that both schizophrenic patients and controls exhibited a decrease in hippocampal activity after nicotine administration. The findings from the anterior cingulate gyrus raise some interesting questions. After nicotine administration there was decreased activity in the cingulate in controls, but increased activity in schizophrenic patients. There has been research indicating that nicotine has a modulating effect on activity in the cingulate gyrus, an area implicated in attention and behavioral inhibition [174]. Given these functions of the cingulate, an increase in activity in schizophrenia patients seems reasonable. However, if the modulatory effect nicotine is having in controls is a decrease in activity that would seem to suggest that the average person has an overactive cingulate gyrus. This decreased functioning may give some clue as to why some studies find no improvement in SPEM among controls after nicotine administration.

### *Prepulse Inhibition of Startle Response Deficits in Schizophrenia*

In addition to auditory and visual sensory processing impairments, schizophrenic patients also display sensorimotor gating impairments. Most commonly, prepulse inhibition (PPI) of the startle reflex is used to test sensorimotor gating. PPI is the reduction in response to a strong startling stimulus, or pulse, if preceded by 30-500 ms by a stimulus of subthreshold intensity, the prepulse. One major advantage of startle response paradigms is that the response can be studied across many sensory modalities and many species [175]. In humans, the blink reflex of the startle response is measured, and in rats, the whole-body flinch is measured. Similar to the P50 inhibition response and suggesting a genetic link, both schizophrenic patients [176, 177, 178, 179] and unaffected biological siblings show a deficit in PPI [180]. As with other sensory processing deficits in schizophrenia, PPI is affected by nicotine.

Animal studies of PPI have reported an increased PPI after nicotine administration [181, 182]. Human studies of non-psychiatric smokers have confirmed the increase in PPI upon smoking after an overnight period of no smoking [183, 184]. Smokers in one study had comparable gating to non-smokers after a period of no smoking, and smoking reinstatement produced a significant improvement in PPI such that gating in the smokers exceeded that of the non-smokers [183]. Nicotine administration by subcutaneous injection in healthy non-smokers has also been shown to improve PPI [185].

Improvements in sensorimotor gating in non-psychiatric participants and the improvements in P50 response inhibition with nicotine in schizophrenic patients predict improvement of PPI in schizophrenic patients. Indeed, studies have borne out this prediction [186, 187, 188]. A study by George and colleagues [186] resulted in comparable PPI for non-psychiatric and schizophrenic smokers when normal smoking habits were allowed. Overnight smoking abstinence significantly reduced PPI in schizophrenic patients, while smoking reinstatement reversed this worsening of PPI deficits. However, overnight abstinence and reinstatement did not significantly affect PPI in control smokers. Another experiment extended these findings with non-deprived schizophrenic smokers. Their PPI increased but only when tested within 10 min of smoking a cigarette [187]. Collectively, these results point to nicotine enhancing sensory gating deficits as is also observed in the P50 gating deficit in schizophrenia.

Postma et al. [188], investigated brain regions associated with the effects of nicotine on PPI in a fMRI study of non-psychiatric and schizophrenic participants. The study employed a placebo controlled, double blind design with subcutaneous injections of nicotine. The electrodes used to record eyeblink cannot be used in the MRI scanner, so this study correlated PPI performance in a paradigm performed outside the scanner with neuroresponse to the same paradigm performed in the scanner. Hippocampal gyrus and thalamus activation was observed during the PPI testing with increased activity after nicotine injection. Activation in these areas was significantly greater in the patient group relative to controls. These data are consistent with evidence of the involvement of the same brain areas in auditory P50 evoked potential inhibition and the effects of nicotine on the P50 response [156, 162]. Indeed, consistency in the data lends strong support for the hypothesis that the cholinergic system, and especially nicotinic receptors, plays a central role in the gating deficits found in schizophrenia.

### *Neuropsychological Impairments in Schizophrenia*

Impairments in cognition and attention frequently accompany the sensory processing irregularities common in schizophrenia. Attentional dysregulation is frequently implicated as a major factor in some of the thought disturbances observed in schizophrenia, including deficits in some types of memory. In a study of patients experiencing their first psychotic episode, smokers performed better on neuropsychological tests of attention and working memory than nonsmoking patients [189]. This study is notable for findings of smoking benefits while including controls for the effects of chronic schizophrenia and long-term pharmacotherapy. Harris et al. [190] also conducted a study with smoker and non-smoker schizophrenic patients. They used a battery of neuropsychological tests to assess the influence of direct administration of nicotine. Across the domains of immediate memory, visuospatial construction, language, attention, and delayed memory, the only domain to show improvement from nicotine was attention. There was a small decline in performance among the smokers in the study. The likely explanation is that the participants had a period of forced smoking abstinence prior to drug administration and testing, and withdrawal symptoms influenced their performance.

Another experiment examined smoking and cognitive deficits in schizophrenia to establish the role of nAChRs in mediating nicotine–related cognitive enhancements [191]. Smokers who were schizophrenic or non-patients were tested over three levels of treatment with a non-competitive nAChR antagonist. The drug, mecamylamine hydrochloride, was chosen because of its greater affinity for the high affinity receptors and less affinity for the α7-nAChR [162]. Baseline testing was performed, followed by a night of abstention from cigarettes. A second test session was performed the next morning when the participants were in a state of withdrawal. Following the morning testing participants were instructed to smoke to satiety and tested again after smoking reinstatement. The nAChR antagonist blocked the usual reinstatement-induced reversal of abstinence-related deficits in visuospatial working memory and sustained attention. These data suggest that the high affinity nAChRs play a central role in enhancement of visuospatial working memory and sustained attention that schizophrenic patients experience from smoking.

***Pharmacologic Interventions Targeting the Nicotinic Acetylcholine System***

All these things taken together suggest a possible therapeutic role for pharmaceuticals targeting of the nAChRs. The most obvious approach to activating the cholinergic receptor is to increase availability of endogenous ACh. One method is to block the ACh metabolism by acetylcholinesterase (AChE) with an AChE inhibitor (AChEI). This class of drug is commonly prescribed as a treatment for AD.

One such AChE inhibiting drug is galantamine. In addition to inhibiting AChE, galantamine is an allosteric modulator of several nAChRs, including both the high affinity α4β2 and the low affinity α7. Galantamine treatments yielded significant improvements in tests of processing speed and verbal memory in schizophrenic patients [192]. However, a behavioral side effect of the drug was disrupted performance on an attention task. A subsequent experiment replicated the negative effects of galantamine on attention but also found significant reductions of inhibitory processing in stable, nonsmoking schizophrenic patients [193]. The conclusion of the authors was that galantine may harm cognitive functioning, at least at the doses they used [193].

Another AChEI, rivastigmine, does not have the same nAChR allosteric modulatory effects as galantamine. A 24 week, placebo-controlled trial of rivastigmine as an add-on therapy in schizophrenia included measures of executive functioning, verbal skills, verbal and spatial working memory, attention, and psychomotor speed. The study results failed to replicate the positive results of some preliminary studies of the drug, and failed to find benefits to cognition among schizophrenic patients [194]. A 12 week, placebo-controlled trial of donepezil, another AChEI, as an adjunctive therapy to risperidone also failed to show any significant improvement in any of the cognitive domains tested [195]. Whether the lack of success with these drugs is due to receptor desensitization or an unknown neurobiological feature of schizophrenia is not known.

Atypical antipsychotics are arguably better than the older neuroleptics, if only for their reduced side effect profile. However, it is generally accepted that, similar to the first generation drugs, the atypical medications do not provide effective resolution of the cognitive symptoms of schizophrenia [196,197,198]. On the other hand, there is evidence that clozapine may be an exception to the general rule. In a small study of clozapine treatment for neuroleptic refractory schizophrenic patients, the patients who showed clinical improvements to clozapine, also showed normalization of the P50 auditory gating response [157]. Experiments with DBA/2 mice have indicated that the neurobiological effects of clozapine include activation of α7-nAChRs, and result in a normalization of the P20-N40 evoked potential [199]. Interestingly, patients being treated with clozapine also show increased rates of smoking cessation [200].

The novel α7-nAChR partial agonist 3-(2,4-dimethoxybenzylidene)-anabaseine (DMXB-A) is being evaluated clinically for treatment of the sensory gating and cognitive deficits in schizophrenic patients. In phase 2 trials, schizophrenic patients receiving the drug rated their negative symptoms as being significantly better than did the patients on placebo [201]. Participants in the drug group also displayed better attention and working memory [201].

Imaging studies were also done during the phase 2 trials to determine whether the drug had the intended effect on hippocampal inhibitory interneurons [202], and default network changes were evaluated in the context of a polymorphism in CHRNA7 [203]. Patients performed a SPEM task while having an fMRI. Only the higher of the two studied doses of DMXB-A reduced the activity of the hippocampus during the SPEM task [202]. Both dose levels did alter default network activity, including a reduction in posterior cingulate, inferior parietal cortex, and medial frontal gyrus activity and an increase in precuneus activity [203]. The pattern of reduced activity in the posterior cingulate and increased activity in the precuneus suggests normalization from the overactivity of the posterior cingulate and underactivity of the precuneus observed in schizophrenia patients [203]. The posterior cingulate activity reduction was affected by CHRNA7 genotype [203].

Dysfunctions of the DA and glutamate systems are most frequently implicated in schizophrenia. Yet, genetic, behavioral, and pharmacological evidence indicate the nicotine-sensitive components of the cholinergic system play an important role in both the pathophysiological processes underlying schizophrenia, and their treatment.

## Nicotine and Bipolar Mood Disorder

Bipolar disorder is a psychiatric disorder characterized by major depressive episodes alternating with hypomanic or manic episodes. Major depressive episodes involve persistent depressed mood, anhedonia, and feelings of worthlessness. Hypomanic and manic episodes involve persistent elevated or irritable mood, increased energy, and excessive involvement in risky activities. Substance use, including smoking, is common in bipolar patients.

Smoking prevalence rates among U.S. patients with bipolar disorder is approximately 69%, well above the national average (figure 3) [204, 205]. Smoking cessation rates among bipolar patients are also lower than those of the general population [204, 205]. As with schizophrenia, these increased rates of smoking in the face of the associated health consequences suggests a powerful incentive to initiate and maintain smoking behaviors. Again, as with schizophrenia, self-medication is generally thought of as a likely cause.

The effects of nicotine and the cholinergic system on major depressive disorder are more thoroughly quantified and documented than their effects on bipolar disorder (for review see: 206, Vázquez-Palacios, this volume). The focus here will remain on bipolar disorder because smoking, nicotine, and depression are reviewed elsewhere in this text (Vázquez-Palacios, this volume).

### *Symptom Progression in Smoking Bipolar Patients*

Nicotine can moderate symptoms of the depressive phase of bipolar disorder such as anhedonia, attentional deficits, and fatigue [207]. Unfortunately, nicotine only has acutely positive effects due to desensitization of nAChRs [152]).

Although nicotine can ease some of the symptoms of depression in patients with major depressive disorder, it seems to have a detrimental effect on the course of bipolar disorder. In a retrospective study, bipolar patients with lifetime smoking were more likely than non-smoker patients to have earlier age at onset of mood disorder, greater severity of symptoms, poorer functioning, history of a suicide attempt, and a lifetime history of comorbid anxiety and substance use disorders [208].

In a large cross-sectional study, bipolar patients with rapid cycling, comorbid psychiatric disorders, and/or substance abuse, and those experiencing a current mood episode were more likely to be smokers [209]. More lifetime depressive and manic episodes, as well as greater severity of depressive and manic symptoms, were associated with smoking. Use of atypical antipsychotic medications was also more prevalent among smokers.

In an Australian observational study over 24 months, daily smokers experiencing bipolar and schizoaffective disorder had significantly worse scores on measures of depressive and overall symptoms and longer hospital stays over the duration of the study compared to non-smokers [210].

A longitudinal drug study by Berk and colleagues [211] observed treatment outcomes of smokers and non-smokers who presented with bipolar mania and were treated with a series of common anti-mania medications. The two groups initially displayed manic symptoms of comparable severity, but then diverged in their treatment outcomes, with those who were current smokers showing overall poorer clinical outcomes compared to those who did not smoke.

There were significant differences on both mania severity measures used, for both treatment phases of the 12 week active comparison trial, and in one of the two treatment phases of the 47 week active comparison trial. In addition, there was a significantly shorter duration in the trial for the smoking group compared with the nonsmoking group after discontinuation of drug treatment. The first phase of the study did not show a significant difference in treatment response between smoking and nonsmoking patients. The authors speculated that this delayed response could be due to smoking-related dysregulation of the DA system [211].

Ostacher et al. [212] conducted a nine month, prospective study of smoker and non-smoker bipolar patients to examine possible relationships to suicidality. They also assessed impulsivity. Smoking was associated with higher baseline suicidality scores, and also significantly predicted higher scores at nine months. Smokers made more suicide attempts during the study compared to the non-smokers. The authors concluded that current cigarette smoking was a predictor of current and nine-month suicidal ideation and behavior. They attributed some of the observed relations between smoking and suicidal ideation to impulsivity, which they propose may be a factor in the decision to smoke.

### *Genetics of Bipolar Disorder and Nicotinic Acetylcholine Receptors*

The genetic underpinnings of bipolar disorder are poorly understood, although it does seem to cluster in families, suggesting that there is at least a vulnerability that is heritable [213]. Twin and family studies of bipolar patients with a history of psychosis have shown a deficit in the electrophysiological P50 measure of auditory inhibition similar to that seen in schizophrenia [213, 214]. Similar to schizophrenia, a large percentage of unaffected first degree relatives of these patients also show a deficit in the P50 gating response [213, 214]. Studies that compared bipolar patients with a history of psychosis to non-psychotic bipolar patients reported that both the non-psychotic bipolar patients and their families do not display the P50 gating deficit [214] A study of patients with schizoaffective disorder-bipolar type reported that many of these patients had mutations in the promoter regions of the CHRNA7 gene that codes for α7-nAChRs [215]. Interestingly, both the patients and non-patient controls who had these allelic mutations showed deficits in P50 gating, whereas both patients and controls without the mutations had normal P50 auditory gating [215]. This suggests that there may be a genetic risk for psychosis that extends across psychotic and affective disorders, and this risk is associated with the α7-nAChRs.

Postmortem, prefrontal cortical been used to investigate this possible involvement [160]. Levels of α7-nAChRs were not significantly different across groups, but the schizophrenia and bipolar patients displayed lower ratios of α7 to α7- like mRNA levels, with bipolar patients displaying the lowest ratios. The suggestion of a link between altered CHRNA7:CHRFAM7A ratio and bipolar disorder, raises the question as to what role it plays in the pathophysiology of the disorder.

The high smoking prevalence among bipolar patients, association of CHRNA7 polymorphisms to P50 gating deficits in bipolar patients, and the observed behavioral benefits to major depressive disorder patients would all seem to lend support to the investigation of drugs targeting nAChRs for the treatment of bipolar disorder. However, worsening of outcomes in smoking bipolar patients suggests a fundamental difference between major depressive disorder and bipolar disorder. Worsening of symptoms in smoking bipolar patients also suggests that addiction may offer a better explanation for high smoking prevalence among patients than a self-medication hypothesis. Due to the consistently negative effects of smoking observed in studies of psychological history, symptom progression, and drug treatment outcomes in bipolar patients, any experimentation with drugs specific to the nicotinic system would need to be undertaken with the utmost caution.

## Conclusion

Considering the clear adverse health consequences of smoking it comes as a surprise to many that nicotine has beneficial effects. Conditions in which nicotine may have a positive impact include neurodegenerative disorders with a strong memory decline presentation, various types of neural injury, and certain psychiatric disorders. Here, we examined the literature with both animal models and humans on these various beneficial influences of nicotine.

AD is the classic example of a neurodegenerative disorder that affects millions of people with evidence that nicotine may be related to lower incidence and slower progression of this disease. Memory disturbances are the hallmark of AD and typically the first clinical symptoms of dementia. A review of the effects of nicotine on memory in AD patients and non-patients suggests that nicotine improves aspects of cognition. Indeed, there is general agreement that the greatest cognitive benefits are on attention. The subsequent improvements in memory could be simply due to a more alert brain.

However, the molecular biology data suggest that the mechanism lies in the nAChR dynamics of the cholinergic system. The α7 and α4β2 nAChR subunits are found in the brain region critical to memory function, the hippocampus, and appear to play an important role in the neuroprotective influences of nicotine.

The obvious translation of these data is to the treatment of AD patients with nicotine, yet the clinical studies have not been as effective as expected. One reason, surely, is that by the time treatment is required for an AD patient, that individual likely has extensive loss of cholinergic neurons and activation of the cholinergic receptors is unlikely to have a great influence on cognitive performance.

Many of the same conclusions can be applied to PD in that smokers appear to accrue some neuroprotection from the disease. Indeed, the evidence is that nicotine may be more effective in the treatment of PD than that of AD. The reason behind this is that the cholinergic system, in the PD brain, is probably having a significant effect on the dopaminergic system that is critically involved in the motor responses of the basal ganglia. Also, the cholinergic system, largely responsible for cognitive performance, is not as compromised in the PD brain as in the AD brain.

Nicotine neuroprotection for brain tissue loss that is acute rather than neurodegenerative and progressive is less clear. Smoking is not associated with a reduced severity of TBI. However, evidence exists that nicotine can play a neuroprotective and therapeutic role in the recovery of function following TBI. Nicotine has neuroprotective influence against secondary neuronal injuries following initial TBI. The mechanism of the behavioral recovery benefits of nicotine following TBI is likely an increase in cholinergic function.

In the final two sections we reviewed the literature of smoking and nicotine on two psychiatric disorders with clear organic bases. The initial most striking feature of these disorders is the high percentage of schizophrenia and bipolar patients who smoke. The popular explanation is that the patients are deriving some relief of symptoms, that is, they are self-medicating. Much of the research on schizophrenia and nicotine is electrophysiological differences between smoking and nonsmoking patient populations and non-psychiatric participants. The data indicate a clear relation of sensory gating to deficits experienced by schizophrenic patients in processing incoming sensory information, but it is not entirely clear how the P50 evoked potential is related to sensory gating.

Nicotine seems to moderate the severity of symptoms of schizophrenia, which is certainly supportive of ideas of self-medication from smoking. However, studies of bipolar patients challenge the veracity of the self-medication concept applied broadly in psychiatry. Acute exposure seems to benefit symptoms, but chronic exposure worsens bipolar symptoms. The suggestion is that there are other factors that are influencing high rates of smoking in psychiatric populations.

It is clear, however, that the benefits accrued from nicotine have received solid support in neurodegenerative diseases, various types of neural injury, and certain psychiatric disorders.

## REFERENCES


[1] da Fonseca, M.J., Casamassimo, P. (2011). Old drugs, new uses. *Pediatr. Dent.,* 33(1), 67-74.

[2] Taylor, G.T., Maloney, S. (2010). Gender differences and the role of estrogen in cognitive enhancements with nicotine in rats. *Pharmacol. Biochem. Behav.,* 95, 139-145.

[3] Taylor, G.T., Bassi, C.J. Weiss, J. (2005). Limits of learning enhancement with nicotine in old male rats. *Acta Neurobiol. Exp.,* 65(2), 125-136.

[4] Levin, E.D., Briggs, S.J., Christopher, N.C., Rose, J.E. (1992). Persistence of chronic nicotine-induced cognitive facilitation. *Behav. Neural. Biol.,* 58, 152-158.

[5] Levin, E.D., Briggs, S.J., Christopher, N.C., Rose, J.E. (1993). Chronic nicotinic stimulation and blockade effects on working memory. *Behav. Pharmacol.,* 4, 179-182.

[6] Barr, A. M., Procyshyn, R. M., Hui, P., Johnson, J. L., Honer, W. G. (2008). Self-reported motivation to smoke in schizophrenia is related to antipsychotic drug treatment. *Schizophr. Res.,* 100(1-3), 252-260.

[7] Green, M.A. Clarke, D.E. (2005). Smoking reduction and cessation: A hospital-based survey of outpatients' attitudes. *J. Psychosoc. Nurs. Ment. Health Serv.*, 43(5), 18-25.

[8] Gurpegui, M., Martínez-Ortega, J. M., Jurado, D., Aguilar, M. C., Diaz, F. J., De Leon, J. (2007). Subjective effects and the main reason for smoking in outpatients with schizophrenia: A case-control study. *Compr. Psychiatry,* 48(2), 186-191.

[9] Brenner, D.E., Kukull, W.A., van Belle, G., Bowen, J.D., McCormick, W.C., Teri, L., Larson, E.B. (1993). Relationship between cigarette smoking and Alzheimer's disease in a population-based case-control study. *Neurology,* 43(2), 293-300.

[10] Ishikawa, A., Miyatake, T. (1993). Effects of smoking in patients with early-onset Parkinson's disease. *J. Neurol. Sci.,* 117(1-2), 28-32.

[11] Lee, P.N. (1994). Smoking and Alzheimer's disease: a review of the epidemiological evidence. *Neuroepidemiology,* 13(4), 131-144.

[12] Morens, D.M., Grandinetti, A., Reed, D., White, L.R., Ross, G.W. (1995). Cigarette smoking and protection from Parkinson's disease: false association or etiologic clue? *Neurology,* 45(6), 1041-1051.

[13] van Duijn, C.M., Hofman, A. (1991). Relation between nicotine intake and Alzheimer's disease. *Br. J. Med. Med.,* 302(6791), 1491-1494.

[14] van Duijn, C.M., Clayton, D.G., Chandra, V., Fratiglioni, L., Graves, A.B., Heyman, A., et al. (1994). Interaction between genetic and environmental risk factors for Alzheimer's disease: a reanalysis of case-control studies. EURODEM risk factors research group. *Genet. Epidemiol.,* 11(6), 539-551.

[15] Wang, H.X., Fratigloioni, L., Frisoni, G.B., Viitanen, M., Winblad, B. (1999). Smoking and the occurrence of Alzheimer's disease: cross-sectional and longitudinal data in a population-based study. *Am. J. Epidemiol.,* 149 (7), 640-644.

[16] Fratiglioni, L., Wang, H. X. (2000). Smoking and Parkinson's and Alzheimer's disease: Review of the epidemiological studies. *Behav. Brain Res.,* 113, 117-120.

[17] Letenneur, L., Larrieu, S., Barberger-Gateau, P. (2004). Alcohol and tobacco consumption as risk factors of dementia: a review of epidemiological studies. *Biomed. Pharmacothe.r,* 58, 95-99.

[18] van Duijn, C.M., Havekes, L.M., Van Broeckhoven, C., de Knijf, P., Hofman, A. (1995). Apolipoprotein E genotype and association between smoking and early onset Alzheimer's disease. *Br. J. Med.,* 310 (6980), 627-631.

[19] Ernst, M., Matochik, J.A., Heishman, S.J., Van Horn, J.D., Jons, P.H., Henningfield, J.E., et al. (2001). Effect of nicotine on brain activation during performance of a working memory task. *Proc. Natl. Acad. Sci. U S A,* 98 (8), 4728-4733.

[20] Pineda, J.A., Herrera, C., Kang, C., Sandler, A. (1998). Effects of cigarette smoking and 12-h abstention on working memory during a serial-probe recognition task. *Psychopharmacology, 139,* 311-321.

[21] Puma, C., Deschaux, O., Molimard, R., Bizot, J. (1999). Nicotine improves memory in an object recognition task in rats. *Eur. Neuropsychopharmacol.,* 9, 323-327.

[22] Brown, R.W., Beale, K.S., Frye, J. (2002). Mecamylamine blocks enhancement of reference memory but not working memory produced by post-training injection of nicotine in rats tested on the radial arm maze. *Behav. Brain Res.,* 134, 259-265.

[23] Poincheval-Fuhrman, S., Sara, S.J. (1993). Chronic nicotine ingestion improves radial arm maze performance in rats. *Behav. Pharmacol.,* 4 (5), 535-539.

[24] Arendash, G.W., Sanberg, P.R., Sengstock, G.J. (1995). Nicotine enhances the learning and memory of aged rats. *Pharmacol. Biochem. Behav.,* 52 (3), 517-523.

[25] French, K.L., Granholm, A.E., Moore, A.B., Nelson, M.E., Bimonte-Nelson, H.A. (2006). Chronic nicotine improves working and reference memory performance and reduces hippocampal NGF in aged female rats. *Behav. Brain Res.,* 169, 256-262.

[26] Levin, E.D., Torry, D. (1996). Acute and chronic nicotine effects on working memory in aged rats. *Psychopharmacology,* 123 (1), 88-97.

[27] Bryan, K.J., Lee, H., Perry, G., Smith, M.A., Casadesus, G. (2009). Transgenic mouse models of Alzheimer's disease: Behavioral testing and considerations. In J.J. Buccafusco (Ed.), *Methods of Behavior Analysis in Neuroscience* (Second edition, 1-18). Boca Raton, FL: Taylor Francis Group.

[28] Socci, D.J., Sanberg, P.R., Arendash, G.W. (1995). Nicotine enhances Morris water maze performance of young and aged rats. *Neurobiol. Aging,* 16 (5), 857-860.

[29] Shim, S.B., Lee, S.H., Chae, K.R., Kim, C.K., Hwang, D.Y., Kim, B.G. (2008). Nicotine leads to improvements in behavioral impairment and an increase in the nicotine acetylcholine receptor in transgenic mice. *Neurochem. Res.,* 33 (9), 1783-1788.

[30] Wilson, A.L., Langley, L.K., Monley, J., Bauer, T., Rottunda, S., McFalls, E., et al. (1995). Nicotine patches in Alzheimer's disease: a pilot study on learning, memory, and safety. *Pharmacol. Biochem. Behav.,* 51 (2-3), 509-514.

[31] Parks, R.W., Becker, R.E., Rippey, R.F., Gilbert, D.G., Matthews, J.R., Kabatay, E., et al. (1996). Incrased regional cerebral glucose metabolism and semantic memory performance in Alzheimer's disease: a pilot double blind transdermal nicotine positron emission tomography study. *Neuropsychol. Rev.,* 6 (2), 61-79.

[32] Rezvani, A.H., Bushnell, P.J., Levin, E.D. (2002). Effects of nicotine and mecamylamine on choice accuracy in an operant visual signal detection task in female rats. *Psychopharmacology, 164*(4), 369-375.

[33] Jones, G.M., Sahakian, B.J., Levy, R., Warburton, D.M., Gray, J.A. (1992). Effects of acute subcutaneous nicotine on attention, information processing and short-term memory in Alzheimer's disease. *Psychopharmacology,* 108 (4), 485-494.

[34] Newhouse, P.A., Sunderland, T., Tariot, P.N., Blumhardt, C.L., Weingartner, H., Mellow, A., et al. (1988). Intravenous nicotine in Alzheimer's disease: a pilot study. *Psychopharmacology,* 95 (2), 171-175.

[35] Sahakian, B., Jones, G., Levy, R., Gray, J., Warburton, D. (1989). The effects of nicotine on attention, information processing, and short-term memory in patients with dementia of the Alzheimer type. *Br. J. Psychiatry,* 154, 797-800.

[36] White, H.K., Levin, E.D. (1999). Four-week nicotine skin patch treatment effects on cognitive performance in Alzheimer's disease. *Psychopharmacology,* 143 (2), 158-165.

[37] Katner, S.N., Davis, S.A., Kirsten, A.J., Taffe, M.A. (2004). Effects of nicotine and mecamylamine on cognition in rhesus monkeys. *Psychopharmacology,* 175 (2), 225-240.

[38] Decker, M.W., Majchrzak, M.J., Arneric, S.P. (1993). Effects of lobeline, a nicotinic receptor agonist, on learning and memory. *Pharmacol. Biochem. Behav.,* 45 (3), 571-576.

[39] Felix, R., Levin, E.D. (1997). Nicotinic antagonist administration into the ventral hippocampus and spatial working memory in rats. *Neuroscience,* 81 (4), 1009-1017.

[40] Abreu-Villaca, Y., Seidler, F.J., Qiao, D., Tate, C.A., Cousins, M.M., Thillai, I., et al. (2003). Short-term adolescent nicotine exposure has immediate and persistent effects on cholinergic systems: critical periods, patterns of exposure, dose thresholds. *Neuropsychopharmacology,* 28, 1935-1949.

[41] Besson., M., Granson, S., Mameli-Engvall, M., Cloëz-Tayarani, I., Maubourguet, N., Cormier, A., et al. (2007). Long-term effects of chronic nicotine exposure on brain nicotinic receptors. *Proc. Natl. Acady. Sci. U S A,* 104 (19), 8155-8160.

[42] Collins, S.L., Wade, D., Ledon, J., Izenwasser, S. (2004). Neurochemical alterations produced by daily nicotine exposure in periadolescent vs. adult male rats. *Eur. J. Pharm.,* 502, 75-85.

[43] Dani, J.A. (2000). Nicotine mechanisms in Alzheimer's disease: Overview of nicotinic receptors and their roles in the central nervous system. *Biol. Psychiatry,* 49, 166-174.

[44] Young, J.W., Crawford, N., Kelly, J.S., Kerr, L.E., Marston, H.M., Spratt, C., et al. (2007). Impaired attention is central to the cognitive deficits observed in alpha 7 deficient mice. *Eur. Neuropsychopharmacol.,* 17 (2), 145-155.

[45] Buccafusco, J.J., Jackson, W.J., Terry A.V. Jr., Marsh, K.C., Decker, M.W., Arneric, S.P. (1995). Improvement in performance of a delayed matching-to-sample task by monkeys following ABT-418: a novel cholinergic channel activator for memory enhancement. *Psychopharmacology,* 120 (3), 256-266.

[46] Hahn, B., Sharples, C.G., Wonnacott, S., Shoaib, M., Stolerman, I.P. (2003). Attentional effects of nicotinic agonists in rats. *Neuropharmacology,* 44 (8), 1054-1067.

[47] Rezvani, A.H., Levin, E.D. (2001). Cognitive effects of nicotine. *Biol. Psychiatry,* 49, 258-267.

[48] Sharma, S., Rakoczy, S., Brown-Borg, H. (2010). Assessment of spatial memory in mice. *Life Sci.,* 87 (17-18), 521-536.

[49] Wenk, G.L. (2004). Assessment of spatial memory using the radial arm maze and Morris water maze. *Current Protocols in Neuroscience, Chapter 8:*Unit 8.5A.

[50] Dhikav, V., Anand, K. (2011). Potential predictors of hippocampal atrophy in Alzheimer's disease. *Drug Aging,* 28 (1), 1-11.

[51] Thompson, R.F. (2000). *The Brain: A Neuroscience Primer* (Third edition), New York, NY; Worth Publishers.

[52] Whitehouse, P.J., Price, D.L., Struble, R.G., Clark, A.W., Coyle, J.T., Delon, M.R. (1982). Alzheimer's disease and senile dementia: loss of neurons in the basal forebrain. *Science,* 215 (4537), 1237-1239.

[53] Whitehouse, P.J., Hedreen, J.C., White, C.L. 3rd, Price, D.L. (1983). Basal Forebrain neurons in the dementia of Parkinson disease. *Ann. Neurol.,* 13 (3), 243-248.

[54] Aubert, I., Araujo, D.M., Cécyre, D., Robitaille, Y., Gauthier, S., Quirion, R. (1992). Comparative alterations of nicotinic and muscarinic binding sites in Alzheimer's and Parkinson's diseases. *J. Neurochem.,* 58 (2), 529-541.

[55] Nordberg, A. (1994). Human nicotinic-receptors—their role in aging and dementia. *Neurochem. Int.,* 25 (1), 93-97.

[56] Paterson, D., Nordberg, A. (2000). Neuronal nicotinic receptors in the human brain. *Prog. Neurobiol.,* 61 (1), 75-111.

[57] Whitehouse, P.J., Martino, A.M., Wagster, M.V., Price, D.L., Mayeux, R., Atack, J.R., et al. (1988). Reductions in [3H]nicotinic acetylcholine binding in Alzheimer's disease and Parkinson's disease: an autoradiographic study. *Neurology,* 38 (5), 720-723.

[58] Albuquerque, E.X., Pereira, E.F.R., Samochocki, M., Alkondon, M., Ullmer, C., Maelicke, A. (2004). Nicotinic receptor modulation: implications for treatment of Alzheimer's disease and other neurological disorders. In I. Silman, H. Soreq, L. Anglister, D. Michaelson, A. Fisher (Eds.), *Cholinergic Mechanisms: Function and Dysfunction* (297-308). Boca Raton, FL: Taylor Francis.

[59] O'Neill, A.B., Morgan, S.J., Brioni, J.D. (1998). Histological and behavioral protection by (-)-nicotine against quinolinic acid-induced neurodegeneration in the hippocampus. *Neurobiol. Learn Mem.,* 69 (1), 46-64.

[60] Gray, R., Rajan, A.S., Radcliffe, K.A., Yakehiro, M., Dani, J.A. (1996). Hippocampal synaptic transmission enhanced by low concentrations of nicotine. *Nature,* 383 (6602), 713-716.

[61] Kandel, E.R., Schwartz, J.H., Jessell, T.M. (2000). *Principles of Neural Science* (fourth edition), St. Louis, MO: McGraw-Hill.

[62] Court, J.A., Johnson, M., Religa, D., Keverne, J., Kalaria, R., Jaros, E., et al. (2005). Attentuation of Abeta deposition in the entorhinal cortex of normal elderly individuals associated with tobacco smoking. *Neuropathol. Appl. Neurobiol.,* 31 (5), 522-535.

[63] Dickerson, T.J., Janda, K.D. (2003). Glycation of the amyloid beta-protein by a nicotine metabolite: a fortuitous chemical dynamic between smoking and Alzheimer's disease. *Proc. Natl. Acad. Sci. U S A,* 100 (14), 8182-8187.

[64] Nordberg, A., Hellström-Lindahl, E., Lee, M., Johnson, M., Mousavi, M., Hall, R., et al. (2002). Chronic nicotine treatment reduces beta-amyloidosis in the brain of a mouse model of Alzheimer's disease (APPsw). *J. Neurochem.,* 81 (3), 655-658.

[65] Zanardi, A., Leo, G., Biagini, G., Zoli, M. (2002). Nicotine and neurodegeneration in ageing. *Toxicol. Lett.,* 127 (1-3), 207-215.

[66] Ono, K., Hasegawa, K., Yamada, M., Naiki, H. (2002). Nicotine breaks down preformed Alzheimer's beta-amyloid fibrils in vitro. *Biol. Psychiatry,* 52 (9), 880-886.

[67] Shimohama, S., Kihara, T. (2001). Nicotinic receptor-mediated protection against beta-amyloid neurotoxicity. *Biol. Psychiatry,* 49 (3), 233-239.

[68] Utsuki, T., Shoaib, M., Holloway, H.W., Ingram, D.K., Wallace, W.C., Haroutunian, V., et al. (2002). Nicotine lowers the secretion of the Alzheimer's amyloid beta-protein precursor that contains amyloid beta-peptide in rat. *J. Alzheimers Dis.,* 4 (5), 405-415.

[69] Zhang, J., Liu, Q., Chen, Q., Liu, N.Q., Li, F.L., Lu, Z.B., et al. (2006). Nicotine attenuates beta-amyloid-induced neurotoxicity by regulating metal homeostasis. *FASEB J.,* 20 (8), 1212-1214.

[70] Belluardo, N., Mudò, G., Blum, M., Fuxe, K. (2000). Central nicotinic receptors, neurotrophic factors and neuroprotection. *Behav. Brain Res.,* 113 (1-2), 21-34.

[71] Linert, W., Bridge, M.H., Huber, M., Bjugstad, K.B., Grossman, S., Arendash, G.W. (1999). In vitro and in vivo studies investigating possible antioxidant actions of nicotine: relevance to Parkinson's and Alzheimer's diseases. *Biochim. Biophys. Acta,* 1454 (2), 143-152.

[72] Zamani, M.R., Allen, Y.S., Owen, G.P., Gray, J.A. (1997). Nicotine modulates the neurotoxic effect of beta-amyloid protein(25-35) in hippocampal cultures. *Neuroreport,* 8 (2), 513-517.

[73] Kihara, T., Shimohama, S., Sawada, H., Kimura, J., Kume, T., Kochiyama, H., et al. (1997). Nicotinic receptor stimulation protects neurons against beta-amyloid toxicity. *Ann. Neurol.,* 42 (2), 159-163.

[74] Kihara, T., Shimohama, S., Urushitani, M., Sawada, H., Kimura, J., Kume, T., et al. (1998). Stimulation of alpha4beta2 nicotinic acetylcholine receptors inhibits beta-amyloid toxicity *Brain Res.,* 792 (2), 331-334.

[75] Warpman, U., Nordberg, A. (1995). Epibatidine and ABT 418 reveal selective losses of alpha 4 beta 2 nicotinic receptors in Alzheimer's brains. *Neuroreport,* 6 (17), 2419-2423.

[76] Boess, F.G., De Vry, J., Erb, C., Flessner, T., Hendrix, M., Luithle, J., et al. (2007). The novel alpha7 nicotinic acetylcholine receptor agonist N-[(3R)-1-azabicyclo[2.2.2]oct-3-yl]-7-[2-(methoxy)phenyl]-1-benzofuran-2-carboxamide improves working and recognition memory in rodents. *J. Pharmacol. Exp. Ther.,* 321 (2), 716-725.

[77] Sapronov, N.S., Fedotoca, Y.O., Kuznetsova, N.N. (2006). Antiamnestic effect of alpha7-nicotinic receptor agonist RJR-2403 in middle-age ovariectomized rats with Alzheimer type dementia. *Bull. Exp. Biol. Med.,* 142 (6), 700-702.

[78] Potter, A., Corwin, J., Lang, J., Piasecki, M., Lenox, R., Newhouse, P.A. (1999). Acute effects of the selective cholinergic channel activator (nicotinic agonist) ABT-418 in Alzheimer's disease. *Psychopharmacology,* 142 (4), 334-342.

[79] Frölich, L., Ashwood, T., Nilsson, J., Eckerwall, G., Sirocco Investigators. (2011). Effects of AZD3480 on cognition in patients with mild-to-moderate Alzheimer's disease: a phase IIb dose-finding study. *J. Alzheimers Dis.,* 24 (2), 363-374.

[80] Dziewczapolski, G., Glogowski, C.M., Masliah, E., Heinemann, S.F. (2009). Deletion of the alpha 7 nicotinic acetylcholine receptor gene improves cognitive deficits and synaptic pathology in a mouse model of Alzheimer's disease. *J. Neurosci.,* 29 (27), 8805-8815.

[81] Mousavi, M., Hellström-Lindahl, E. (2009). Nicotinic receptor agonists and antagonists increase sAPPα and decrease Aβ levels in vitro. *Neurochem. Int.,* 54, 237-244.

[82] Prendergast, M.A., Jackson, W.J., Terry, A.V. Jr., Decker, M.W., Arneric, S.P., Buccafusco, J.J. (1998). Central nicotinic receptor agonists ABT-418, ABT-089, and (-)-nicotine reduce distractibility in adult monkeys. *Psychopharmacology,* 136 (1), 50-58.

[83] Baron, J.A. (1986). Cigarette smoking and Parkinson's disease. *Neurology,* 36 (11), 1490-1496.

[84] Baumann, R.J., Jameson, H.D., McKean, H.E., Haack, D.G., Weisberg, L.M. (1980). Cigarette smoking and Parkinson's disease: 1. Comparison of cases with matched neighbors. *Neurology,* 30 (8), 839-843.

[85] Perry, E.K., Curtis, M., Dick, D.J., Candy, J.M., Atack, J.R., Bloxham, C.A., et al. (1985). Cholinergic correlates of cognitive impairment in Parkinson's disease: comparisons with Alzheimer's disease. *J. Neurol. Neurosurg. Psychiatry,* 48 (5), 413-421.

[86] Kelton, M.C., Kahn, H.J., Conrath, C.L., Newhouse, P.A. (2000). The effects of nicotine on Parkinson's disease. *Brain Cogn.,* 43 (1-3), 274-282.

[87] Lester, D.B., Roger, T.D., Blaha, C.D. (2010). Acetylcholine-dopamine interactions in the pathophysiology and treatment of CNS disorders. *CNS Neurosci. Ther.,* 16, 137-162.

[88] Holmes, A.D., Copland, D.A., Silburn, P.A., Chenery, H.J. (2011). Acute nicotine enhances strategy-based semantic processing in Parkinson's disease. *Int. J. Neuro-psychopharmacology,* 1, 1-9.

[89] Holmes, A.D., Copland, D.A., Silburn, P.A., Chenery, H.J. (2011). Nicotine effects on general sematic priming in Parkinson's disease. *Exp. Clin. Psychopharmacol., 19*(3), 215-223.

[90] Sershen, H., Hashim, A., Lajtha, A. (1987). Behavioral and biochemical effects of nicotine in an MPTP-induced mouse model of Parkinson's disease. *Pharmacol. Biochem. Behav.,* 28 (2), 299-303.

[91] Takeuchi, H., Yanagida, T., Inden, M., Takata, K., Kitamura, Y., Yamakawa, K., et al. (2009). Nicotine receptor stimulation protects nigral dopaminergic neurons in rotenone-induced Parkinson's disease models. *J. Neurosci. Res.,* 87 (2), 576-585.

[92] Decamp, E., Schneider, J.S. (2006). Effects of nicotinic therapies on attention and executive functions in chronic low-dose MPTP-treated monkeys. *Eur. J. Neurosci.,* 24 (7), 2098-2104.

[93] Levin, E.D. (1997). Chronic haloperidol administration does not block acute nicotine-induced improvements in radial-arm maze performance in the rat. *Pharmacol. Biochem. Behav.,* 58 (4), 899-902.

[94] Perry, E.K., Morris, C.M., Court, J.A., Cheng, A., Fairbairn, A.F., McKeith, I.G., et al. (1995). Alteration in nicotine binding sites in Parkinson's disease, Lewy body dementia and Alzheimer's disease: possible index of early neuropathology. *Neuroscience,* 64 *(2),* 385-395.

[95] Quik, M., Huang, L.Z., Parameswaran, N., Bordia, T., Campos, C., Perez, X.A. (2009). Multiple roles for nicotine in Parkinson's disease. *Biochem. Pharmacol.,* 78(7), 677-685.

[96] Bordia, T., Parameswaran, N., Fan, H., Langston, J.W., McIntosh, J.M., Quik, M. (2006). Partial recovery of striatal nicotinic receptors in 1-methyl-4-phenyl-1,2,3,6-tetrahydropyridine (MPTP)-lesioned monkeys with chronic oral nicotine. *J. Pharmacol. Exp. Ther.,* 319 (1), 285-292.

[97] Janson, A.M., Fuxe, K., Goldstein, M. (1992). Differential effects of acute and chronic nicotine treatment of MPTP-(1-methyl-4-phenyl-1,2,3,6-tetrahydropyridine) induced degeneration of nigrostriatal dopamine neurons in the black mouse. *Clin. Investig,* 70 (3-4), 232-238.

[98] Janson, A.M., Moller, A. (1993). Chronic nicotine treatments counteracts nigral cell loss induced by a partial mesodiencephalic hemitransection: an analysis of the total number and mean volume of neurons and glia in substantia nigra of the male rat. *Neuroscience,* 57 (4), 931-941.

[99] Parain, K., Marchand, V., Dumery, B., Hirsch, E. (2001). Nicotine, but not continine, partially protects dopaminergic neurons against MPTP-induced degeneration in mice. *Brain Res.,* 890 (2), 347-350.

[100] Quik, M., Jeyarasasingam, G. (2000). Nicotinic receptors and Parkinson's disease. *Eur. J. Pharmacol.,* 393 (1-3), 223-230.

[101] Singh, S., Singh, K., Patel, D.K., Singh, C., Nath, C., Singh, V.K., Sing, R.K., Singh, M.P. (2009). The expression of CYP2D22, an ortholog of human CYP2D6, in mouse striatum and its modulation in 1-methyl 4-phenyl-1,2,3,6-tetrahydropyridine-induced Parkinson's disease phenotype and nicotine-mediated neuroprotection. *Rejuvenation Res.,* 12 (3), 185-197.

[102] Quik, M., Kulak, J.M. (2002), Nicotine and nicotinic receptors; relevance to Parkinson's disease. *Neurotoxicology,* 23 (4-5), 581-584.

[103] Xiao, C., Nashmi, R., McKinney, S., Cai, H., McIntosh, J.M., Lester, H.A. (2009). Chronic nicotine selectively enhances alph J Neurosci a4beta2* nicotinic acetylcholine receptors in the nigrostriatal dopamine pathway. *J. Neurosci.,* 29 (40), 12428-12439.

[104] Chapman, M.A. (2009). Does smoking reduce the risk of Parkinson's disease through stimulation of the ubiquitin-proteasome system? *Med. Hypotheses,* 73 (6), 887-891.

[105] Cromier, A., Morin, C., Zini, R., Tillement, J.P., Lagrue, G. (2003). Nicotine protects rat brain mitochondria against experimental injuries. *Neuropharmacology,* 44 (5), 642-652.

[106] Maggio, R., Riva, M., Vaglini, F., Fornai, F., Molteni, R., Armogida, M., Racagni, G., Corsini, G.U. (1998). Nicotine prevents experimental parkinsonism in rodents and induces striatal increase in neurotrophic factors. *J. Neurochem.,* 71 (6), 2439-2446.

[107] Singh, K., Singh, S., Singhal, N.K., Sharma, A., Parmar, D., Singh, M.P. (2010). Nicotine- and caffeine-mediated changes in gene expression patterns of MPTP-lesioned mouse striatum: Implications in neuroptection mechanism. *Chem. Biol. Interact.,* 185 (2), 81-93.

[108] Miksys, S., Tyndale, R.F. (2006). Nicotine induces brain CYP enzymes: relevance to Parkinson's disease. *J. Neural. Transm. Suppl.,* 70, 177-180.

[109] Hong, D.P., Fink, A.L., Uversky, V.N. (2009). Smoking and Parkinson's disease: does nicotine affect alpha-synuclein fibrillation? *Biochim. Biophys. Acta,* 1794 (2), 282-290.

[110] Smith, R.D., Kistler, M.K., Cohen-Williams, M., Coffin, V. (1996). Cholinergic improvement of a naturally-occurring memory deficits in the young rat. *Brain Res.,* 707, 13-21.

[111] Paul, R.H., Brickman, A.M., Cohen, R.A., Williams, L.M., Niaura, R., Pogun, S., et al. (2006). Cognitive status of young and older cigarette smokers: Data from the international brain database. *J. Clin. Neurosci.,* 13, 457-465.

[112] Ahmadi, S., Zarrindast, M.R., Haeri-Rohani, A., Rezayof, A., Nouri, M. (2007). Nicotine improves morphine-induced impairment of memory: possible involvement of N-methyl-D-aspartate receptors in the nucleus accumbens. *Dev. Neurobiol.*, 67(8), 1118-1127.

[113] Hiramatsu, M., Satoh, H., Kameyama, T., Nabeshima, T. (1994). Nootrophic effect of nicotine on carbon monoxide (CO)-induced delayed amnesia in mice. *Psychopharmacology,* 116 (1), 33-39.

[114] Rezayof, A., Shirazi-Zand, Z., Zarrindast, M.R., Nayer-Nouri, T. (2009). Nicotine improves ethanol-induced memory impairment: the role of dorsal hippocampal NMDA receptors. *Life Sci.*, 86 (7-8), 260-266.

[115] Zarraindast, M.R., Farahmandfar, M., Rostami, P., Rezayof, A. (2006). The influence of central administration of dopaminergic and cholinergic agents on morphine-induced amnesia in morphine-sensitized mice. *J. Psychopharmacol.,* 20 (1), 59-66.

[116] Taylor, G.T., Maloney, S., Dearborn, J., Weiss, J. (2009). Hormones in the mentally disturbed brain: Steroids and peptides in the development and treatment of psychopathology. *Cent. Nerv. Syst. Agents Med. Chem.*, 9 (4), 331-360.

[117] Povlishock, J.T., Katz, D.I. (2005). Update of neuropathology and neurological recovery after traumatic brain injury. *J. Head Trauma Rehabil.,* 20 (1), 76-94.

[118] Harris, B.T. (2008). Topics in Neuropathology. In M. Levin, G.L. Holmes, J.A. Cohen (Eds), *Educational Review Manual in Neurology* (Second Edition, 211-244) New York, NY: Castle Connolly Graduate Medical Publishing, Ltd.

[119] Globus, M.Y., Alonso, O., Dietrich, W.D., Busto, R., Ginsberg, M.D. (1995). Glutamate release and free radical production following brain injury: effects of posttraumatic hypothermia. *J. Neurochem.,* 64 (4), 1704-1711.

[120] Olney, J.W. (1974). Toxic effects of glutamate and related amino acids on the developing central nervous system. In W.L. Nyhan (Ed.) *Heritable Disorders of Amino Acid Metabolism* (501-512), New York: Wiley.

[121] Arciniegas, D.B. (2003). The cholinergic hypothesis of cognitive impairment caused by traumatic brain injury. *Curr. Psychiatry Rep.,* 5, 391-399.

[122] Lillie, R.A., Kowalski, K., Patry, B.N., Sira, C., Tuokko, H., Mateer, C.A. (2010). Everyday impact of traumatic brain injury. In T.D. Marcotte I. Grant. (302-330) New York, NYL The Guilford Press.

[123] Kraus, M.F., Little, D.M., Wojtowicz, S.M., Sweeney, J.A. (2010). Procedural learning impairments identified via predictive saccades in chronic traumatic brain injury. *Cogn. Behav. Neurol.,* 23 (4), 210-217.

[124] Murdoch, I., Perry, E.K., Court, J.A., Graham, D.I., Dewar, D. (1998). Cortical cholinergic dysfunction after human head injury. *J. Neurotrauma,* 15 (5), 295-305.

[125] Östberg, A., Virta, J., Rinne, J.O., Oikonen, V., Luoto, P., Någren, K., et al. (2011). Cholinergic dysfunction after traumatic brain injury: preliminary finding from a PET study. *Neurology,* 76 (12), 1046-1050.

[126] Verbois, S.L., Hopkins, D.M., Scheff, S.W., Pauly, J.R. (2003). Chronic intermittent nicotine administration attenuates traumatic brain injury-induced cognitive dysfunction. *Neuroscience,* 119 (4), 1199-1208.

[127] Verbois, S.L., Scheff, S.W., Pauly, J.R. (2003). Chronic nicotine treatment attenuates alpha 7 nicotinic receptor deficits following traumatic brain injury. *Neuropharmacology,* 44 (2), 224-233.

[128] Brown, R.W., Gonzalez, C.L., Kolb, B. (2000). Nicotine improves Morris water task performance in rats given medial frontal cortex. *Pharmacol. Biochem. Behav.,* 67 (3), 473-478.

[129] Akaike, A., Tamura, Y., Yokota, T., Shimohama, S., Kimura, J. (1994). Nicotine-induced protection of cultured cortical neurons against N-methyl-D-aspartate receptor-mediated glutamate cytotoxicity. *Brain Res.,* 644 (2), 181-187.

[130] Laudenbach, V., Medja, F., Zoli, M., Rossi, F.M., Evrard, P., Changeux, J.P., et al. (2002). Selective activation of central subtypes of the nicotinic acetylcholine receptor has opposite effects on neonatal excitotoxic brain injuries. *FASEB J.,* 16 (3), 423-425.

[131] Marin, P., Maus, M., Desagher, S., Glowinski, J., Prémont, J. (1994). Nicotine protects cultured striatal neurons against N-methyl-D-aspartate receptor-mediated neurotoxicity. *Neuroreport,* 5 (15), 1977-1980.

[132] Prendergast, M.A., Harris, B.R., Mayer, S., Holley, R.C., Pauly, J.R., Littleton, J.M. (2001). Nicotine exposure reduces N-methyl-D-aspartate toxicity in the hippocampus: relation to distribution of the alpha7 nicotinic acetylcholine receptor subunit. *Med. Sci. Monit.,* 7 (6), 1153-1160.

[133] Shin, E.J., Chae, J.S., Jung, M.E., Bing, G., Ko, K.H., Kim, W.K., et al. (2007). Repeated intracerebroventricular infusion of nicotine prevents kainite-induced neurotoxicity by activating the alpha7 nicotinic acetylcholine receptor. *Epilepsy Res.,* 73 (3), 292-298.

[134] Dajas-Bailador, F.A., Lima, P.A., Wonnacott, S. (2000). The alpha7 nicotinic acetylcholine receptor subtype mediates nicotine protection against NMDA excitotoxicity in primary hippocampal cultures though a Ca(2+) dependent mechanism. *Neuropharmacology,* 39 (13), 2799-2807.

[135] Stevens, T.R., Krueger, S.R., Fitzsimonds, R.M., Picciotto, M.R. (2003). Neuro-protection by nicotine in mouse primary cortical cultures involves activation of calcineurin L-type calcium channel inactivation. *J. Neurosci.,* 23 (31), 10093-10099.

[136] Saha, S., Chant, D., Welham, J., McGrath, J. (2005). A systematic review of the prevalence of schizophrenia. *PLoS Med.,* 2 (5), e141.

[137] Davis, K. L., Kahn, R. S., Ko, G., Davidson, M. (1991). Dopamine in schizophrenia: A review and reconceptualization. *Am. J. Psychiatr.,* 148, 1474-1486.

[138] Goff, D. C. Coyle, J. T. (2001). The emerging role of glutamate in the pathophysiology and treatment of schizophrenia. *Am. J. Psychiatr.,* 158, 1367-1377.

[139] Lisman, J. E., Coyle, J. T., Green, R. W., Javitt, D. C., Benes, F. M., Heckers, S., et al. (2008). Circuit-based framework for understanding neurotransmitter and risk gene interactions in schizophrenia. *Trends Neurosci.,* 31 (5), 234-242.

[140] Sumiyoshi, T., Matsui, M., Yamashita, I., Nohara, S., Kurachi, M., Uehara, T., et al. (2001). The effect of tandospirone, a serotonin-1A agonist, on memory function in schizophrenia. *Biol. Psychiatry,* 49, 861-868.

[141] Breese, C. R., Lee, M. J., Adams, C. E., Sullivan, B., Logel, J., Gillen, K. M., et al. (2000). Abnormal regulation of high affinity nicotinic receptors in subjects with schizophrenia. *Neuropsychopharmacology,* 23, 351-364.

[142] Chapman, S., Ragg, M. McGeechan, K. (2009). Citation bias in reported smoking prevalence in people with schizophrenia. *Aust. N. Z. J. Psychiatry,* 43, 277-282.

[143] De Leon, J. Diaz, F. J. (2005). A meta-analysis of worldwide studies demonstrates an association between schizophrenia and tobacco smoking behaviors. *Schizophr Res,* 76, 135-57.

[144] World Health Organization Tobacco Free Initiative. (2011). *WHO report on the global tobacco* epidemic, 2011: Warning about the dangers of tobacco. Geneva, Switzerland: Author.

[145] De Leon, J., Gurpegui, M., Diaz, F. J. (2007). Epidemiology of comorbid tobacco use and schizophrenia: Thinking about risks and protective factors. *J. Dual Diagn.,* 3 (3-4), 9-25.

[146] Dickens, G., Stubbs, J., Popham, R., Haw, C. (2005). Smoking in a forensic psychiatric service: A survey of inpatients' views. *J. Psychiatr. Ment. Health Nurs.*, 12, 672-678.

[147] Forchuk, C., Norman, R., Malla, A., Martin, M., McLean, T., Cheng, S., et al. (2002). Schizophrenia and the motivation for smoking. *Perspect. Psychiatr. Care,* 38 (2), 41-49.

[148] Leonard, S. Bertrand, D. (2001). Neuronal nicotinic receptors: From structure to function. *Nicotine Tob. Res.,* 3, 203-223.

[149] Freedman, R., Hall, M., Adler, L. E., Leonard, S. (1995). Evidence in postmortem brain tissue for decreased numbers of hippocampal nicotinic receptors in schizophrenia. *Biol. Psychiatry,* 38 (1), 22-33.

[150] Guan, Z.-Z., Zhang, X., Blennow, K., Nordberg, A. (1999). Decreased protein level of nicotinic receptor α7 subunit in the frontal cortex from schizophrenic brain. *NeuroReport,* 10, 1779-1782.

[151] Court, J., Spurden, D., Lloyd, S., McKeith, I., Ballard. C., Cairns, N., et al. (1999). Neuronal nicotinic receptors in dementia with Lewy bodies and schizophrenia: α-Bungarotoxin and nicotine binding in the thalamus. *J. Neurochem., 73,* 1590–1597.

[152] Fenster, C. P., Whitworth, T. L., Sheffield, E. B., Quick, M. W., Lester, R. A. J. (1999). Upregulation of surface α4β2 nicotinic receptors is initiated by receptor desensitization after chronic exposure to nicotine. *J. Neurosci.,* 19, 4804-4814.

[153] Adler, L.E., Pachtman, E., Franks, R.D. (1982). Neuropysiological evidence for a defect in neuronal mechanisms involved in sensory gating in schizophrenia. *Biol. Psychiatry,* 17, 639-654.

[154] Clementz, B. A., Geyer, M. A., Braff, D. L. (1998). Poor P50 suppression among schizophrenia patients and their first-degree biological relatives. *Am. J. Psychiatr.,* 155, 1691-1694.

[155] Freedman, R., Coon, H., Myles-Worsley, M., Orr-Urtreger, A., Olincy, A., Davis, A., et al. (1997). Linkage of a neurophysiological dificit in schizophrenia to a chromosome 15 locus. *Proc. Natl. Acad. Sci. U S A*, 94, 587-592.

[156] Freedman, R., Olincy, A., Ross, R. G., Waldo, M. C., Stevens, K. E., Adler, L. E., et al. (2003). The genetics of sensory gating deficits in schizophrenia. *Curr. Psychiatry Rep.,* 5, 155-161.

[157] Nagamoto, H. T., Adler, L. E., Hea, R. A., Griffith, J. M., McRae, K. A., Freedman, R. (1996). Gating of auditory P50 in schizophrenics: Unique effects of clozapine. *Biol. Psychiatry,* 40 (3), 181-188.

[158] Adler, L. E., Hoffer, L. J., Griffith, J., Waldo, M. C., Freedman, R. (1992). Normalization by nicotine of deficient auditory sensory gating in the relatives of schizophrenics. *Biol. Psychiatry,* 32, 607-616.

[159] Leonard, S., Gault, J., Hopkins, J., Logel, J., Vianzon, R., Short, M., et al. (2002). Association of promoter variants in the α7 nicotinic acetylcholine receptor subunit gene with an inhibitory deficit found in schizophrenia. *Arch. Gen. Psychiatry,* 59, 1085-1096.

[160] De Luca, V., Likhodi, O., Van Tol, H. H. M., Kennedy, J. L., Wong, A. H. C. (2006). Regulation of α7-nicotinic receptor subunit and α7-like gene expression in the prefrontal cortex of patients with bipolar disorder and schizophrenia. *Acta Psychiatr. Scand.,* 114, 211-215.

[161] Mexal, S., Berger, R., Logel, J., Ross, R. G., Freedman, R., Leonard, S. (2010). Differential regulation of α7 nicotinic receptor gene (CHRNA7) expression in schizophrenic smokers. *J. Mol. Neurosci.,* 40, 185-195.

[162] Luntz-Leybman, V., Bickford, P. C., Freedman, R. (1992). Cholinergic gating of response to auditory stimuli in rat hippocampus. *Brain Res.,* 587, 130-136.

[163] Stevens, K. E., Freedman, R., Collins, A. C., Hall, M., Leonard, S., Marks, M. J., et al. (1996). Genetic correlation of inhibitory gating of hippocampal auditory evoked response and α-bungarotoxin-binding nicotinic cholinergic receptors in inbred mouse strains. *Neuropsychopharmacology,* 15, 152-162.

[164] Stevens, K. E. Wear, K. D. (1997). Normalizing effects of nicotine and a novel nicotinic agonist on hippocampal auditory gating in two animal models. *Pharmacology Biochem. Behav.,* 57, 869-874.

[165] Stevens, K. E., Kem, W. R., Mahnir, V. M., Freedman, R. (1998). Selective a7-nicotinic agonists normalize inhibition of auditory response in DBA mice. *Psychopharmacology,* 136, 320-327.

[166] Holzman, P. S., Proctor, L. R., Levy, D. L., Yasillo, N. J., Meltzer, H. Y., Hurt, S. W. (1974). Eye-tracking dysfunctions in schizophrenic patients and their relatives. *Psychol. Monogr.,* 3, 143-151.

[167] Hong, L. E., Avila, M. T., Thaker, G. K. (2005). Response to unexpected target changes during sustained visual tracking in schizophrenic patients. *Exp. Brain Res.,* 165, 125-131.

[168] Avila, M. T., Sherr, J. D., Hong, E., Myers, C. S., Thaker, G. K. (2003). Effects of nicotine on leading saccades during smooth pursuit eye movements in smokers and nonsmokers with schizophrenia. *Neuropsychopharmacology,* 28, 2184-2191.

[169] Sherr, J. D., Myers, C., Avila, M. T., Elliott, A., Blaxton, T. A., Thaker, G. K. (2002). The effects of nicotine on specific eye tracking measures in schizophrenia. *Biol. Psychiatry,* 52, 721-728.

[170] Tanabe, J., Tregellas, J. R., Martin, L. F., Freedman, R. (2006). Effects of nicotine on hippocampal and cingulate activity during smooth pursuit eye movement in schizophrenia. *Biol. Psychiatry,* 59, 754-761.

[171] Dépatie, L., O'Driscoll, G. A., Holahan, A-L. V., Atkinson, V., Thavundayil, J. X., Kin, N. N. Y., et al. (2002). Nicotine and behavioral markers of risk for schizophrenia: A double-blind, placebo-controlled, cross-over study. *Neuropsychopharmacology,* 27, 1056-1070.

[172] Olincy, A., Johnson, L. L., Ross, R. G. (2003). Differential effects of cigarette smoking on performance of a smooth pursuit and a saccadic eye movement task in schizophrenia. *Psychiatr. Res.,* 117, 223-236.

[173] Olincy, A., Ross, R. G., Young, D. A., Roath, M., Freedman, R. (1998). Improvement in smooth pursuit eye movements after cigarette smoking in schizophrenic patients. *Neuropsychopharmacology,* 18, 175-185.

[174] Jacobsen, L. K., D'Souza, D. C., Mencl, W. E., Pugh, K. R., Skudlarski, P., Krystal, J. H. (2004). Nicotine effects on brain function and functional connectivity in schizophrenia. *Biol. Psychiatry,* 558, 850-858.

[175] Swerdlow, N. R. Geyer, M. A. (1998). Using an animal model of deficient sensorimotor gating to study the pathophysiology and new treatments of schizophrenia. *Schizophr. Bull.,* 24(2), 285-301.

[176] Braff, D. L. Geyer, M. A. (1990). Sensorimotor gating and schizophrenia. *Arch. Gen. Psychiatry,* 47, 181-188.

[177] Braff, D.L., Stone, C., Callaway, E., Geyer, M., Glick, I., Bali, L. (1978). Prestimulus effects on human startle reflex in normals and schizophrenics. *Psychophysiol.,* 15, 339-343.

[178] Grillon, C., Ameli, R., Charney, D. S., Krystal, J., Braff, D. (1992). Startle gating deficits occur across prepulse intensities in schizophrenic patients. *Biol. Psychiatry,* 32, 939-943.

[179] Parwani, A., Duncan, E. J., Bartlett, E., Madonick, S. H., Efferen, T. R., Rajan, R., et al. (2000). Impaired prepulse inhibition of acoustic startle in schizophrenia. *Biol. Psychiatry,* 7, 662-669.

[180] Kumari, V., Das, M., Zachariah, E., Ettinger, U., Sharma, T. (2005). Reduced prepulse inhibition in unaffected siblings of schizophrenia patients. *Psychophysiology,* 42, 588-594.

[181] Acri, J. B., Morse, D. E., Popke, E. J., Grunberg, N. E. (1994). Nicotine increases sensory gating measured as inhibition of the acoustic startle reflex in rats. *Psychopharmacology,* 114 (2), 369-374.

[182] Curzon, P., Kim, D. J. B., Decker, M. W. (1994). Effect of nicotine, lobeline, and mecamylamine on sensory gating in the rat. *Pharmacol. Biochem. Behav.,* 49, 877-882.

[183] Duncan, E., Madonick, S., Chakravorty, S., Parwani, A., Szilagyi, S., Efferen, T., et al. (2001). Effects of smoking on acoustic startle and prepulse inhibition in humans. *Psychopharmacology,* 156, 266-272.

[184] Kumari, V., Checkley, S. A., Gray, J. A. (1996). Effect of cigarette smoking on prepulse inhibition of the acoustic startle reflex in healthy male smokers. *Psychopharmacology,* 128, 54-60.

[185] Kumari, V., Cotter, P. A., Checkley, S. A., Gray, J. A. (1997). Effect of acute subcutaneous nicotine on prepulse inhibition of the acoustic startle reflex in healthy male non-smokers. *Psychopharmacology,* 132, 389-395.

[186] George, T. P., Termine, A., Sacco, K. A., Allen, T. M., Reutenauer, E., Vessicchio, J. C., et al. (2006). A preliminary study of the effects of cigarette smoking on prepulse inhibition in schizophrenia: Involvement of nicotinic receptor mechanisms. *Schizophr. Res.,* 87, 307-315.

[187] Kumari, V., Soni, W., Sharma, T. (2001). Influence of cigarette smoking on prepulse inhibition of the acoustic startle reflex in schizophrenia. *Human Psychopharmacol.,* 16, 321-326.

[188] Postma, P., Gray, J. A., Sharma, T., Geyer, M., Mehrotra, R., Das, M., et al. (2006). A behavioural and functional neuroimaging investigation into the effects of nicotine on sensorimotor gating in healthy subjects and persons with schizophrenia. *Psychopharmacology,* 184, 589-599.

[189] Zabala, A., Eguiluz, J. I., Segarra, R., Enjuto, S., Ezcurra, J., Pinto, A. G., et al. (2009). Cognitive performance and cigarette smoking in first-episode psychosis. *Eur. Arch. Psychiatry Clin. Neurosci.,* 259, 65-71.

[190] Harris, J. G., Kongs, S., Allensworth, D., Martin, L., Tregellas, J., Sullivan, B., et al. (2004). Effects of nicotine on cognitive deficits in schizophrenia. *Neuropsychopharmacology,* 29, 1378-1385.

[191] Sacco, K. A., Termine, A., Seyal, A., Dudas, M. M., Vessicchio, J. C., Krishnan-Sarin, S., et al. (2005). Effects of cigarette smoking on spatial working memory and attentional deficits in schizophrenia: Involvement of nicotinic receptor mechanisms. *Arch. Psychiatry Neurosci.,* 62, 649-659.

[192] Buchanan, R. W., Conley, R. R., Dickinson, D., Ball, M. P., Feldman, S., Gold, J. M., et al. (2008). Galantamine for the treatment of cognitive impairments in people with schizophrenia. *J. Am. Psychiatr.,* 165, 82-89.

[193] Dyer, M. A., Freudenreich, O., Culhane, M. A., Pachas, G. N., Deckersbach, T., Murphy, E., et al. (2008). High-dose galantamine augmentation inferior to placebo on attention, inhibitory control and working memory performance in nonsmokers with schizophrenia. *Schizophr. Res.,* 102, 88-95.

[194] Sharma, T., Reed, C., Aasen, I., Kumari, V. (2006). Cognitive effects of adjunctive 24-weeks Rivastigmine treatment to antipsychotics in schizophrenia: A randomized, placebo-controlled, double-blind investigation. *Schizophr. Res.,* 85, 73-83.

[195] Friedman, J. I., Adler, D. N., Howanitz, E., Harvey, P. D., Brenner, G., Temporini, H., et al. (2002). A double blind placebo controlled trial of donepezil adjunctive treatment to risperidone for the cognitive impairment of schizophrenia. *Biol. Psychiatry,* 51, 349-357.

[196] Gold, J. M. (2004). Cognitive deficits as treatment targets in schizophrenia. *Schizophr. Res.,* 72, 21-28.

[197] Harvey, P. D. Keefe, R. S. E. (2001). Studies of cognitive change in patients with schizophrenia following novel antipsychotic treatment. *Am. J. Psychiatr.,* 158, 176-184.

[198] Keefe, R. S. E., Bilder, R. M., Davis, S. M., Harvey, P. D., Palmer, B. W., Gold, J. M., et al. (2007). Neurocognitive effects of antipsychotic medications in patients with chronic schizophrenia in the CATIE trial. *Arch. Gen. Psychiatry,* 64, 633-647.

[199] Simosky, J. K., Stevens, K. E., Adler, L. E., Freedman, R. (2003). Clozapine improves deficient inhibitory auditory processing in DBA/2 mice, via a nicotinic cholinergic mechanism. *Psychopharmacology,* 165, 386-396.

[200] McEvoy, J., Freudenreich, O., McGee, M., VanderZwaag, C., Levin, E., Rose, J. (1995). Clozapine decreases smoking in patients with chronic schizophrenia. *Biol. Psychiatry,* 37, 550-552.

[201] Freedman, R., Olincy, A., Buchanan, R. W., Harris, J. G., Gold, J. M., Johnson, L., et al. (2008). Initial phase 2 trial of a nicotinic agonist in schizophrenia. *Am. J. Psychiatry,* 165, 1040–1047.

[202] Tregellas, J. R., Olincy, A., Johnson, L., Tanabe, J., Shatti, S., Martin, L. F., et al. (2010). Functional magnetic resonance imaging of effects of a nicotinic agonist in schizophrenia. *Neuropsychopharmacology,* 35, 938-942.

[203] Tregellas, J. R., Tanabe, J., Rojas, D. C., Shatti, S., Olincy, A., Johnson, L., et al. (2011). Effects of an alpha 7-nicotinic agonist on default network activity in schizophrenia. *Biol. Psychiatry,* 69, 7-11.

[204] Diaz, F. J., James, D., Botts, S., Maw, L., Susce, M. T., De Leon, J. (2009). Tobacco smoking behaviors in bipolar disorder: A comparison of the general population, schizophrenia, and major depression. *Bipolar. Disord.,* 11, 154-165.

[205] Lasser, K., Boyd, J. W., Woolhandler, S., Himmelstein, D. U., McCormick, D., Bor, D. H. (2000). Smoking and mental illness: A population-based prevalence study. *J. Am. Med. Assoc.,* 284, 2606-2610.

[206] Dagyté, G., Den Boer, J. A., Trentani, A. (2011). The cholinergic system and depression. *Behav. Brain Res.,* 221, 574-582.

[207] Salin-Pascual, R.J., De la Fuente, J.R., Galicia-Polo, L., Drucker-Colin, R. (1995). Effects of transderman [sic] nicotine on mood and sleep in nonsmoking major depressed patients. *Psychopharmacology,* 121, 476-479.

[208] Ostacher, M. J., Nierenberg, A. A., Perlis, R. H., Eidelman, P., Borrelli, D. J., Tran, T. B., et al. (2006). The relationship between smoking and suicidal behavior, comorbidity, and course of illness in bipolar disorder *J. Clin. Psychiatry,* 67, 1907-1911.

[209] Waxmonsky, J. A., Thomas, M. R., Miklowitz, D. J., Allen, M. H., Wisniewski, S. R., Zhang, H., et al. (2005). Prevalence and correlates of tobacco use in bipolar disorder: Data from the first 2000 participants in the Systematic Treatment Enhancement Program. *Gen. Hosp. Psychiatry,* 27, 321-328.

[210] Dodd, S., Brnabic, A. J. M., Berk, L., Fitzgerald, P. B., De Castella, A. R., Filia, S., et al. (2010). A prospective study of the impact of smoking on outcomes in bipolar and schizoaffective disorder. *Compr. Psychiatry,* 51, 504-509.

[211] Berk, M., Ng, F., Wang, W. V., Tohen, M., Lubman, D. I., Vieta, E., Dodd, S. (2008). Going up in smoke: Tobacco smoking is associated with worse treatment outcomes in mania. *J. Affect Disord.,* 110, 126-134.

[212] Ostacher, M. J., LeBeau, R. T., Perlis, R. H., Nierenberg, A. A., Lund, H. G., Moshier, S. J., et al. (2009). Cigarette smoking is associated with suicidality in bipolar disorder. *Bipolar. Disord.,* 11, 766-771.

[213] Hall, M-H., Schulze, K., Sham, P., Kalidindi, S., McDonald, C., Bramon, E., et al. (2008). Further evidence for shared genetic effects between psychotic bipolar disorder and P50 suppression: A combined twin and family study. *Am. J. Med. Genet. B Neuropsychiatr. Genet.,* 147*B*, 619-627.

[214] Olincy, A. Martin, L. (2005). Diminished suppression of the P50 auditory evoked potential in bipolar disorder subjects with a history of psychosis. *Am. J. Psychiatr.,* 162, 43-49.

[215] Martin, L. F., Leonard, S., Hall, M-H., Tregellas, J. R., Freedman, R., Olincy, A. (2007). Sensory gating and alpha-7 nicotinic receptor gene allelic variants in schizoaffective disorder, bipolar type. *Am. J. Med. Genet. B Neuropsychiatr. Genet.,* 144B, 611-614.

In: Nicotine Addiction
Editor: Giuseppe Di Giovanni

ISBN: 978-1-62081-290-7


*Chapter 5*

# STRESS AS A RISK FACTOR FOR TRANSITION TO HEIGHTENED NICOTINE INTAKE: EVIDENCE FROM A RAT MODEL OF NICOTINE SELF-ADMINISTRATION

*Xiu Liu*[*]
Department of Psychiatry and Human Behavior,
University of Mississippi Medical Center, Jackson, Mississippi, US

## ABSTRACT

Clinical literature indicates that stress is associated with high rates of cigarette smoking and that smokers use cigarette smoking to reduce their stress levels. However, the issue of whether acute stress exposure influences nicotine intake has received little experimental attention. The current study examined effects of pharmacological stress induced by yohimbine (a α2-selective adrenergic antagonist) on nicotine self-administration and compared these effects in rats that differed in their nicotine intake. Male Sprague-Dawley rats were trained in daily 1 h sessions to intravenously self-administer nicotine (0.03 mg/kg/infusion, free base) on an FR5 schedule. After self-administration behavior was stabilized in 20 sessions, rats were designated as low (≤6 infusions/session) and high (>6 infusions/session) nicotine-takers. In both the low nicotine-taking (LNT) and the high nicotine-taking (HNT) rats, yohimbine (0, 0.5, 1, 2 mg/kg) was intraperitoneally administered 30 min before test sessions in a within-subject, Latin Square design. A separate group of rats was included to test for nonspecific behavioral effect of yohimbine. The results showed that pretreatment with yohimbine dose-dependently increased active lever responses and corresponding nicotine infusions in the LNT but not the HNT rats. In addition, nicotine intake in the LNT rats remained high after yohimbine challenge. Yohimbine did not change lever responses in the control rats that received infusions of saline rather than nicotine. These results demonstrate that acute pharmacological stress induced by yohimbine administration selectively potentiates

[*] Correspondence: Xiu Liu, MD, PhD. Associate Professor, Department of Psychiatry and Human Behavior, University of Mississippi Medical Center, 2500 North State Street, Jackson, MS 39216. Tel: (601) 984-2875, Fax: (601) 984-5899. E-mail: xliu@umc.edu.

nicotine self-administration in the rats with previously low levels of nicotine intake. These data suggest that stressful life events may be effective in increasing tobacco smoking in light to moderate smokers and therefore increase the prevalence of nicotine dependence. As such, reducing stress levels in daily life may prove to be an effective approach to the prevention of nicotine addiction.

## INTRODUCTION

Clinical evidence indicates that stress contributes to initiation, maintenance and progression of tobacco smoking [33, 83]. For instance, college students increased smoking during periods of high stress such as the time leading up to final examination [94, 101]. In a sample of 2,961 adolescents, emotional distress in 10$^{th}$ grade was associated with increased smoking in these individuals once they were in 12$^{th}$ grade [67]. Smokers reportedly have more stressful situations and negative life events than do nonsmokers [24, 33, 66, 93] and stress increases craving for tobacco [27, 72, 73, 97]. Subjective accounts indicate that smokers use tobacco smoking to reduce their stress levels [48, 68] and expect smoking to decrease stress-induced negative affect [4, 45]. Indeed, numerous laboratory studies have found smoking produces reduction in negative affect associated with stress exposure [39, 44, 45, 73]. Taken together, these clinical data indicate stress as a facilitator of tobacco smoking and nicotine dependence.

Animal studies have shown that nicotine, the main addictive component of tobacco, attenuates stress-induced negative affect [32, 37, 96] and reduces stress-induced immobilezation and changes in corticomesolimbic dopamine levels [36, 64, 71]. Acute stress exposure in rodents effectively reinstates nicotine-seeking behavior in procedures modeling human smoking relapse [8, 12, 14, 78, 104]. To date, however, it remains unknown whether acute stress exposure influences nicotine intake in animal models of nicotine self-administration. The present study addressed this issue by challenging animals with a pharmacological stressor, yohimbine, after establishment of stable nicotine intake. Yohimbine is a α2 adrenergic receptor antagonist. It increases activity of noradrenergic systems including neural structures implicated in stress response [1, 3, 20, 98] and produces anxiety- and stress-like states in humans and laboratory animals [10, 11, 17, 25, 43, 49]. It has been increasingly used as a pharmacological stressor, especially in the field of drug addiction research [31, 35, 38, 51, 53, 65, 84, 88, 102]. Importantly, yohimbine-induced reinstatement of drug-seeking behavior in animal models of drug relapse appears to be more robust than that elicited by footshock stress [9, 50, 57, 85]. Therefore, this study employed yohimbine as an anxiogenic and stress-inducing agent to determine its effect on nicotine self-administration behavior.

Moreover, there are substantial individual differences in smoking behavior in humans and in nicotine self-administration in animals. Studies on individual differences in drug self-administration have usually focused on the effects of pre-existing behavioral profiles on drug intake. For instance, levels of locomotor response to novelty [2, 16, 74, 77, 95], anxiety-like behavior in the elevated plus-maze [15], and consumption of sucrose [26, 42] have been found to predict the propensity to self-administer psychostimulants including nicotine. However, in the operant nicotine self-administration literature animals that self-administer lower levels of nicotine are often excluded from experiments [e.g., 21, 54, 56, 69]. Consequently, no attempt has been made to examine the effect of smoking-predisposing factors such as stress in these low nicotine-taking subjects. Therefore, the second goal of this study was to compare the effects of stress on nicotine self-administration behavior in rats that differed in their nicotine intake prior to acute yohimbine challenge.

To get the most robust operant behavior for nicotine intake, this study used a nicotine unit dose of 0.03 mg/kg/infusion because it was the peak dose on dose-response curve for nicotine self-administration [23, 28, 89]. After establishment of stable nicotine self-administration, animals were designated as the low nicotine-taking (LNT) that self-administered ≤ 6 infusions/session and the high nicotine-taking (HNT) rats that self-administered > 6 infusions/session. Such a cut-off criterion was made based on two reasons. First, in adult smokers, it has been suggested that 5 cigarettes/day would be a reasonable threshold for establishing nicotine addiction [6] and that each cigarette has been estimated to deliver as much as 0.03 mg/kg to smokers [59]. Accordingly, six infusions/session at a unit dose of 0.03 mg/kg/infusion (free base) were comparable to the threshold for nicotine addiction. Therefore, the LNT rats could be taken as an equivalent to "social" or "light" human smokers, whereas the HNT rats could serve as the subjects with heavy smoking or addicted to nicotine. Second, as mentioned above, rats showing a lower nicotine intake have been usually excluded from experiments in order for the self-administration paradigm to serve as a valid model of nicotine addiction. For example, although the specific cut-off criteria reported in literature varied, rats self-administering ≤ 6 infusions/session at 0.03 mg/kg/infusion of nicotine are always excluded from experiments [21, 54, 56, 69].

## Materials and Methods

### Subjects

Male Sprague-Dawley rats (Charles River, Portage, MI, USA) weighing 200–225 g upon arrival were used. Animals were individually housed in a humidity- and temperature-controlled (21-22 °C) colony room on a reversed light/dark cycle (lights on 20:00; off 8:00) with unlimited access to water. After one week habituation, rats were placed on a food-restriction (20 g chow/day) regimen throughout the experiments. Training and experimental sessions were conducted during the dark phase at the same time each day (10:00-16:00). All experimental procedures were carried out in accordance with the *National Institutes of Health Guide for the Care and Use of Laboratory Animals* and approved (#1183) by the University of Mississippi Medical Center Institutional Animal Care and Use Committee.

### Self-Administration Apparatus

Experimental sessions were conducted in the standard operant conditioning chambers located inside sound-attenuating, ventilated cubicles (Med Associates, St. Albans, VT, USA). The chambers were equipped with two retractable response levers on one side panel and with a 28-V white light above each lever as well as a red house light on the top of the chambers. Between the two levers was a food pellet trough. Intravenous nicotine injections were delivered by a drug delivery system with a syringe pump (Med Associates, model PHM100-10 rpm). Experimental events and data collection were automatically controlled by an interfaced computer and software (Med Associetes, Med-PC® IV).

## Food Training

To facilitate learning of operant responding for nicotine self-administration (see below), rats began food training sessions on the day following the initiation of food-restriction regimen. Responses on the active lever were rewarded with delivery of a food pellet (45 mg). Sessions lasted 1-h with a maximum delivery of 45 food pellets on a fixed-ratio (FR) 1 schedule. Once the rats learned responding and earned 45 pellets total in a session, the reinforcement schedule was increased to FR5. Successful food training was achieved once rats earned in a single session the total 45 food pellets on the FR5 schedule. Food training was typically completed within 2-5 sessions.

## Surgery

After food training, the rats were anesthetized with an isoflurane-oxygen mixture (1–3% isoflurane) and implanted with jugular catheters. Catheters were constructed using a 15 cm piece of Silastic tubing (0.31 mm ID and 0.63 mm OD, Dow Corning Corporation, Midland, MI, USA) attached to a 22-gauge stainless-steel guide cannula. The latter was bent and molded onto a durable polyester mesh (Plastics One Inc., Roanoke, VA, USA) with dental cement and became the catheter base. Through an incision on the rat back, the base was anchored underneath the skin at the level of scapulae and the catheter passed subcutaneously to the ventral lower neck region and inserted into the right jugular vein (3.5 cm). Animals were allowed at least 7 days to recover from surgery. During the recovery period, the catheters were flushed daily with 0.1 ml of sterile saline containing heparin (30 U/ml) and timentin (66.7 mg/ml) to maintain catheter patency and prevent infection. Thereafter, the catheters were flushed with the heparinized saline before and after the experimental sessions throughout the experiments.

## Nicotine Self-Administration

After recovery from surgery, rats were trained to intravenously self-administer nicotine (0.03 mg/kg/infusion, free base). In the training sessions, animals were placed in the experimental chambers and connected to a drug delivery system. The daily 1-h sessions were initiated by extension of the two levers and illumination of the red house light. Once the rats reached the FR requirement on the active lever, an infusion of nicotine was dispensed by the drug delivery system in a volume of 0.1 ml in approximately 1 s depending on rat body weights. Each nicotine infusion was signaled with a presentation of a stimulus (5 s tone/20 s lever light on). The stimulus also signaled a 20 s timeout period, during which time responses were recorded but not reinforced. Responses on the inactivate lever had no consequence. An FR1 schedule was used for days 1-5, an FR2 for days 6-8 and an FR5 for remainder of the experiments. To test effect of pharmacological stress on nicotine self-administration during the maintenance phase, all rats received 20 daily training sessions. This procedure facilitated responding for nicotine self-administration before the start of drug treatment.

To control for possible nonspecific arousal and/or motor-activating effect of yohimbine stress, a separate set of rats was trained under similar conditions, except that saline rather than nicotine infusions were available.

## Effect of Pharmacological Stress on Nicotine Intake

Based on the number of nicotine infusions/session averaged across the final 5 sessions of the 20 daily training sessions, animals were divided into two groups. Rats that earned 1-6 nicotine infusions/session were designated as the LNT rats (n=12), whereas rats taking more than 6 nicotine infusions/session as the HNT rats (n=11). Following this, the yohimbine test sessions began. Thirty min before tests, yohimbine (0, 0.5, 1, 2 mg/kg) was intraperitoneally administered using a within-subject, Latin Square design in both the LNT and the HNT rats. The test sessions were performed under conditions exactly the same as described above and scheduled on every other day, i.e., sessions 21, 23, 25 27. Rats still received nicotine self-administration sessions without yohimbine pretreatment between the test sessions. The control group of animals that received saline rather than nicotine infusions (n=11) was subjected to the same yohimbine treatment arrangement.

## Statistical Analyses

Data were presented as the mean (±SEM) number of lever responses and nicotine infusions. A two-way ANOVA was used to analyze lever response data averaged across the final 5 sessions of the training phase with Group (LNT vs. HNT) as the between-subject factor and Lever (active vs. inactive) as the within-subject factor. The number of nicotine infusions in the final 5 training sessions was analyzed using a two-way ANOVA with repeated measures with Group (LNT vs. HNT) as the between-subject factor and Session as the within-subject factor. The data obtained from yohimbine tests were analyzed using one-way ANOVA. Differences among individual means were verified using the Fisher's PLSD *post hoc* tests.

# Results

## Nicotine Self-Administration in the LNT and HNT Rats

In the 20 daily 1-h training sessions, rats of both the LNT and the HNT groups readily acquired nicotine self-administration behavior. Since there was a small percentage of rats in each experiment that showed lower level of nicotine intake, the LNT rats (n=12) for this study were pooled across two experiments. Correspondingly, the HNT rats (n=11) were also allocated/matched from these experiments. As shown in Figure 1, there was a significant difference between the LNT and the HNT rats in the number of lever responses and corresponding nicotine infusions. A two-way ANOVA on the lever responses averaged across the final 5 self-administration sessions before yohimbine tests yielded significant effect of

Group [F(1,21) = 60.70, p < 0.0001] and Lever [F(1,21) = 142.66, p < 0.0001] as well as significant Group x Lever interaction [F(1,21) = 44.66, p < 0.0001. Furthermore, Fisher's PLSD *post hoc* tests revealed significant difference between the LNT and the HNT rats in the number of responses on both the active (p < 0.01) and inactive (p < 0.01) levers. Correspondingly, the LNT rats, compared to their HNT counterparts, earned significantly less nicotine injections per 1-h session, 4.6 ± 1.1 vs. 16.5 ± 1.2 averaged across the final 5 sessions. In both groups of rats, the number of responses on the active lever was significantly (p < 0.01) higher than on the inactive lever, indicating that both the LNT and the HNT rats successfully acquired nicotine self-administration behavior. The LNT and the HNT rats showed similar body weight gain during these experiments with 328 ± 7 g and 315± 10 g respectively as measured after completion of the 20 daily self-administration training.

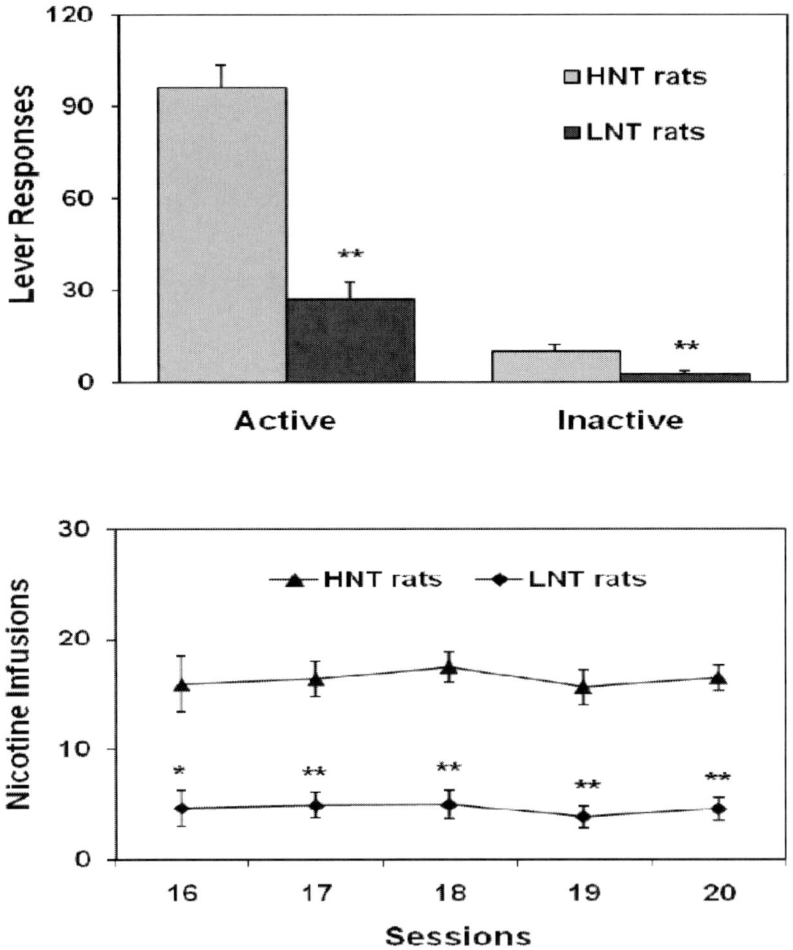


Figure 1. Profiles of nicotine self-administration in the LNT (n=12) and the HNT (n=11) rats. Top panel shows the number of lever responses averaged across the final 5 sessions of the 20 daily 1-h training phase; Bottom panel presents nicotine infusions earned in the final 5 sessions. Data are expressed as mean±SEM. * $p < 0.05$, ** $p < 0.01$ significant difference from the HNT rats.

## Effect of Yohimbine on Nicotine Self-Administration in the LNT Rats

As shown in Figure 2, yohimbine pretreatment significantly increased nicotine self-administration. One-way ANOVA on the number of responses on the active lever revealed a significant effect of Dose [$F(3,44) = 3.11$, $p < 0.05$]. Furthermore, Fisher's PLSD *post hoc* tests revealed significant difference between 2 mg/kg ($p < 0.01$) and 1 mg/kg ($p < 0.05$) vs. saline control condition. Correspondingly, yohimbine pretreatment dose-dependently increased the number of nicotine injections [$F(3,44) = 3.16$, $p < 0.05$]. However, responses on the inactive lever remained low and indistinguishable among different test conditions.

Moreover, in the subsequent 5 sessions conducted following the yohimbine test the active lever responses remained at a significantly higher level relative to the pre-test sessions, a level similar to that maintained by the HNT rats. Detailed information is shown in Figure 5.

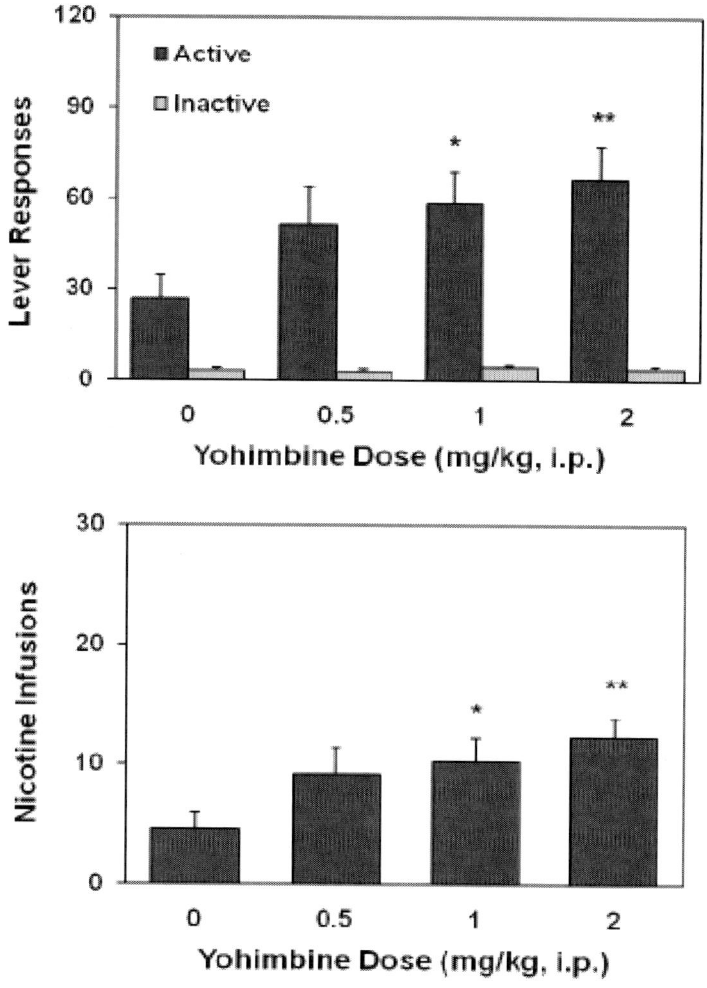


Figure 2. Effect of yohimbine on lever responses (top) and nicotine infusions earned (bottom) in the LNT rats (n=12). Thirty min before test, yohimbine was intraperitoneally administered in a within-subject, Latin Square design on every other day. Data are expressed as mean±SEM. * $p < 0.05$, ** $p < 0.01$ significant difference from saline control (0) condition.

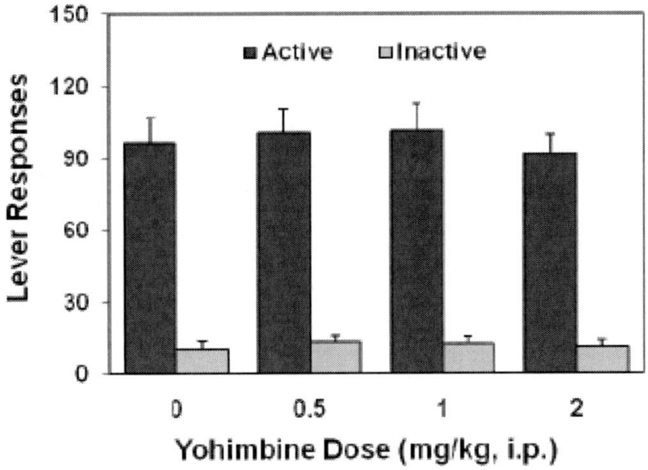


Figure 3. No effect of yohimbine pretreatment on nicotine self-administration behavior in the HNT rats (n=11). Thirty min before test, yohimbine was intraperitoneally administered in a within-subject, Latin Square design on every other day. Data are expressed as mean±SEM.

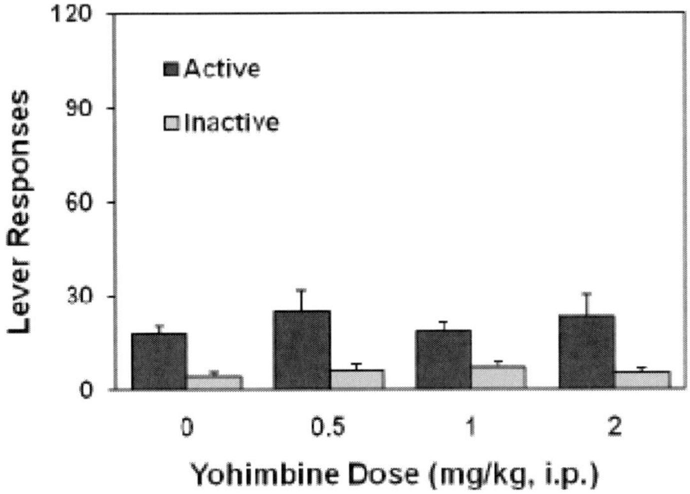


Figure 4. No effect of yohimbine pretreatment on lever responses in the rats (n=11) that had never self-administered nicotine. Responses on the active lever resulted in saline infusions and presentations of the stimulus. Data are expressed as mean±SEM.

## Effect of Yohimbine on Nicotine Self-Administration in the HNT Rats

Figure 3 shows the lever responses made by the HNT rats after yohimbine pretreatment. A one-way ANOVA on the number of responses on the active lever did not yield a significant effect of Dose [$F(3,40) = 0.49$, $p = 0.69$]. Similarly, there was no change observed on the inactive lever responses. Besides, the level of nicotine self-administration in the 5 sessions following yohimbine challenge remained comparable to the pre-test level (Figure 5).

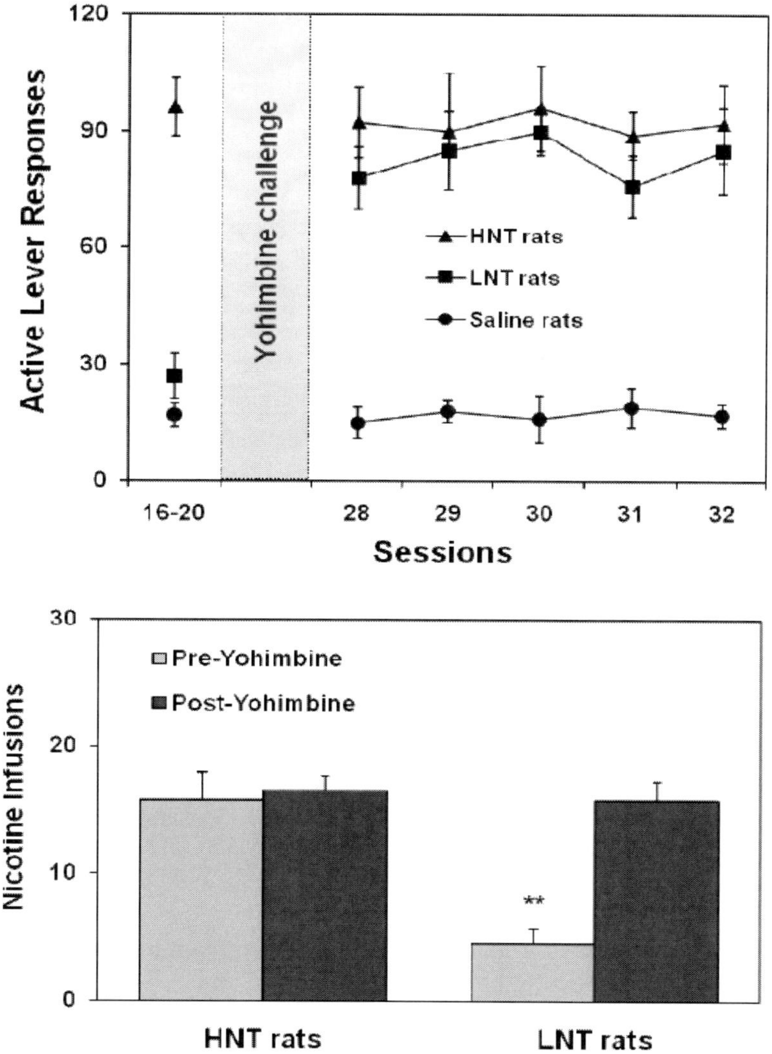


Figure 5. Top panel shows the sustained high level of nicotine self-administration behavior after exposure to yohimbine challenge in the LNT rats (N=12). For comparison, active lever responses emitted by the HNT rats (n=11) and the saline control counterparts (n=11) are shown. Bottom panel presents the number of nicotine infusions averaged across the 5 sessions following yohimbine challenge. Data are expressed as mean±SEM. ** $p < 0.01$ significant difference from both the pre-yohimbine condition of the HNT rats and the post-yohimbine condition in the LNT rats.

## Effect of Yohimbine in Saline-Trained Rats

During the 20 daily sessions, these rats showed low, but steady, levels of responses on the active lever that delivered presentation of the stimulus with saline rather than nicotine infusions. The mean±SEM number of responses averaged across the final 5 sessions before yohimbine tests were 15 ± 3 on the active and 4 ± 1 on the inactive levers. One-way ANOVA on the number of responses on the active lever obtained from yohimbine test sessions yielded no significant dose effect [$F(3,40) = 1.10$, $p = 0.36$], indicating that yohimbine did not change lever responding in these control rats (Figure 4). Further, after yohimbine tests lever responses in these animals remained at low levels comparable to pre-test sessions (Figure. 5).

## DISCUSSION

The current study shows that pharmacological stress induced by acute yohimbine administration significantly increases operant nicotine self-administration in rats that self-administer low levels of nicotine at baseline. Interestingly, under the same testing conditions, yohimbine challenge did not alter nicotine self-administration in rats that self-administered relatively high levels of nicotine at baseline. These results suggest that stress may prompt tobacco smoking in low to moderate smokers, which in turn could increase the prevalence of heavy smoking and nicotine dependence. Moreover, it is recommended that the low nicotine-taking animals may serve as good subjects for investigation on the risk factors precipitating tobacco smoking and the transition to nicotine addiction.

For proper interpretation of these behavioral data, there are two potential confounding factors that need to be addressed. One is the possible nonspecific arousal effect of yohimbine on locomotor activity. The other is that yohimbine might have produced an enhancing effect on the lever responses depending on the level of baseline responses, i.e., facilitating responses when the pre-test responses were low. The latter has been reported in literature. For example, a partial NMDA agonist D-cycloserine was found to decrease nicotine self-administration in rats with low but not high baseline levels of response [55]. To rule out these confounding factors, this study included a control group. For the rats of this control group, active lever responses on a FR5 schedule resulted in delivery of saline rather than nicotine, together with presentation of the stimulus that was used as nicotine cue in the nicotine-trained rats. As shown in figure 5, these rats emitted very low (lower than that maintained by the low nicotine-taking rats) but steady level of responses on the active lever. Pretreatment with yohimbine did not change lever responses in these rats as shown in figure 4. Together with the lack of effect of yohimbine in the rats that had already developed high level of nicotine self-administration as shown in figure 3, these control data negate any nonspecific action of yohimbine. Therefore, the pharmacological stress induced by yohimbine treatment selectively increased lever responses for nicotine self-administration in the LNT rats.

In drug self-administration literature, a lot attention has been paid to the predisposing traits such as response to novelty [2, 16, 74, 77, 95], anxiety levels [15], and consumption of sucrose [26, 42]. Differences in these traits have been found to co-vary with levels of self-administration of various drugs of abuse. For instance, rats showing relatively high levels of locomotor response to novel environments acquire nicotine self-administration more readily and have higher breaking points for nicotine under progressive-ratio schedules of reinforcement than do rats with lower locomotor responsiveness to novelty [95]. However, using such pre-existing traits as a drug intake predictor calls for debate because negative observations have been reported. For example, Abreu-Villaca et al. [2] did not find any influence of anxiety level on the preference and consumption of nicotine in mice in a free choice, home cage nicotine-drinking procedure. The degree of stress reactivity did not alter operant nicotine self-administration in a nose-poke procedure in mice selectively bred for different stress response [7]. Interestingly, in the latter study [7], reinstatement of nicotine-seeking behavior induced by footshock stress was observed only in the mice with highest stress reactivity. That finding was in line with human studies showing that acute psychological stress usually increased smoking desire [13, 19, 22, 30, 66] but not the amount of smoking if allowed to smoke [19]. The present study for the first time used the level of nicotine intake as a preexisting condition to test how acute stress changes nicotine self-administration in the maintenance phase. The results suggest that the level of nicotine consumption may present a new measurement that can be used to predict how stress changes drug intake. Obviously, more work on the issue will be warranted.

Acute pharmacological stress immediately increased nicotine self-administration in the LNT rats to a level comparabble to that maintained by the HNT rats. As such, stress seemed to eliminate the pre-existing difference in nicotine intake between the LNT and the HNT rats. This finding is in line with previous reports showing that systemic administration of corticosterone can eliminate difference in self-administration of cocaine and amphetamine between rats that differed in response to novelty [58, 76]. Taken together, these studies and the current data suggest that stress acts to equalize drug consumption across subjects that initially self-administered different amount of drugs of abuse. Even more significant is the find that after acute yohimbine challenge the LNT rats showed sustained high level of nicotine intake similar to that of the HNT counterparts. That means that exposure to stress has transformed the LNT into HNT rats. If the LNT rats are comparable to social smokers or light smoking whereas the HNT rats represent the heavy smokers, it is conceivable that exposure of stressful life events may prompt smoking in light smokers and thereby lead to heavy tobacco smoking. Therefore, stress may serve as an important risk factor for the transition from social smoking to heavy smokers or nicotine addiction.

One of the most prominent effects of stress is the activity of the hypothalamic-pituitary-adrenal (HPA) axis. The HPA axis has been implicated in the process of drug addiction including tobacco smoking [40, 52, 63, 92]. Nicotine has been shown to produce changes in the HPA axis functions. Acute nicotine self-administration activates the HPA axis [60, 61, 79, 86]. Effects of nicotine taken by operant self-administration procedures seem to be complex, from modest increase to suppression of the HPA functions [5, 18, 29, 34, 87]. It is postulated that the HNT rats compared to the LNT counterparts may have a blunted HPA response to stress, which might underlie the inability of yohimbine to facilitate nicotine intake in the HNT rats. In contrast, yohimbine may have substantially activated the HPA axis and thereby increased nicotine self-administration. Unfortunately, there was a limitation in the experimental design, which lacked measurement of HPA hormones in response to the yohimbine challenge. The role of HPA response to stress in nicotine intake between the LNT and HNT subjects deserves future investigation.

Increasing evidence suggests that both genetic and environmental factors, especially interactions between these factors contribute to individual vulnerability to drugs of abuse [81, 82, 99, 100]. The difference in nicotine consumption between the LNT and HNT rats may reside in genetic background of these animals. Such different genetic backgrounds may render the subjects to distinct profiles in terms of stress sensitization of the reinforcing properties of nicotine, a phenomenon reported from animal research [47, 70, 79, 80, 90] and indicated by studies in human smokers [62, 103]. In addition, our data showing a facilitating effect of acute pharmacological stress on nicotine self-administration only in the LNT rats may in fact represent an interaction between the genetic and environmental factors.

## CONCLUSION

The present study, using a rat model of nicotine self-administration, examined effect of acute pharmacological stress on nicotine intake with an emphasis on the comparison between rats that initially showed significantly different levels of nicotine self-administration. The results demonstrated that yohimbine challenge increased nicotine intake in the LNT rats but did not alter nicotine self-administration in the HNT rats. Importantly, after exposure to the yohimbine-induced stress, the heightened nicotine self-administration was sustained at a level comparable to that maintained by the HNT rats. These findings indicate that stress exposure transforms the LNT rats into the HNT subjects, suggesting that stressful life events may be particularly effective in prompting tobacco smoking in light to moderate smokers and therefore contribute to the high prevalence of heavy smokers and nicotine addiction. This is in line with previous reports that stressful life events contribute to the development of drug use and addiction [41, 46, 75, 90, 91]. As such, it is proposed that reducing stress levels in daily life may prove to be an effective approach to prevention of nicotine addiction.

## ACKNOWLEDGMENTS

This work was supported by NIH grant DA017288 from the National Institute on Drug Abuse. The author would like to thank Mrs. Maysa Gharib and Sheri Booth at the University of Pittsburgh and Mrs. Courtney Jernigan at the University of Mississippi Medical Center for their technical assistance.

## REFERENCES

[1] Abercrombie, E.D., Keller, R.W., Jr., Zigmond, M.J. (1988) Characterization of hippocampal norepinephrine release as measured by microdialysis perfusion: pharmacological and behavioral studies. *Neuroscience*, 27, 897-904.

[2] Abreu-Villaca, Y., Queiroz-Gomes Fdo, E., Dal Monte, A.P., Filgueiras, C.C., Manhaes, A.C. (2006) Individual differences in novelty-seeking behavior but not in anxiety response to a new environment can predict nicotine consumption in adolescent C57BL/6 mice. *Behav. Brain Res.*, 167, 175-182.

[3] Aghajanian, G.K., VanderMaelen, C.P. (1982) alpha 2-adrenoceptor-mediated hyperpolarization of locus coeruleus neurons: intracellular studies in vivo. *Science*, 215, 1394-1396.

[4] Baker, T.B., Brandon, T.H., Chassin, L. (2004) Motivational influences on cigarette smoking. *Annu. Rev. Psychol*, 55, 463-491.

[5] Baron, J.A., Comi, R.J., Cryns, V., Brinck-Johnsen, T., Mercer, N.G. (1995) The effect of cigarette smoking on adrenal cortical hormones. *J. Pharmacol. Exp. Ther.*, 272, 151-155.

[6] Benowitz, N.L., Henningfield, J.E. (1994) Establishing a nicotine threshold for addiction. The implications for tobacco regulation. *N. Engl. J. Med.*, 331, 123-125.

[7] Bilkei-Gorzo, A., Racz, I., Michel, K., Darvas, M., Maldonado, R., Zimmer, A. (2007) A Common Genetic Predisposition to Stress Sensitivity and Stress-Induced Nicotine Craving. *Biol. Psychiatry*.

[8] Bilkei-Gorzo, A., Racz, I., Michel, K., Darvas, M., Maldonado, R., Zimmer, A. (2008) A common genetic predisposition to stress sensitivity and stress-induced nicotine craving. *Biol. Psychiatry*, 63, 164-171.

[9] Bossert, J.M., Ghitza, U.E., Lu, L., Epstein, D.H., Shaham, Y. (2005) Neurobiology of relapse to heroin and cocaine seeking: an update and clinical implications. *Eur. J. Pharmacol.*, 526, 36-50.

[10] Bremner, J.D., Krystal, J.H., Southwick, S.M., Charney, D.S. (1996) Noradrenergic mechanisms in stress and anxiety: I. Preclinical studies. *Synapse*, 23, 28-38.

[11] Bremner, J.D., Krystal, J.H., Southwick, S.M., Charney, D.S. (1996) Noradrenergic mechanisms in stress and anxiety: II. Clinical studies. *Synapse*, 23, 39-51.

[12] Bruijnzeel, A.W., Prado, M., Isaac, S. (2009) Corticotropin-releasing factor-1 receptor activation mediates nicotine withdrawal-induced deficit in brain reward function and stress-induced relapse. *Biol. Psychiatry*, 66, 110-117.

[13] Buchmann, A.F., Laucht, M., Schmid, B., Wiedemann, K., Mann, K., Zimmermann, U.S. (2010) Cigarette craving increases after a psychosocial stress test and is related to cortisol stress response but not to dependence scores in daily smokers. *J. Psychopharmacol.*, 24, 247-255.

[14] Buczek, Y., Le, A.D., Stewart, J., Shaham, Y. (1999) Stress reinstates nicotine seeking but not sucrose solution seeking in rats. *Psychopharmacology (Berl)*, 144, 183-188.

[15] Bush, D.E., Vaccarino, F.J. (2007) Individual differences in elevated plus-maze exploration predicted progressive-ratio cocaine self-administration break points in Wistar rats. *Psychopharmacology (Berl)*. 194 (2), 211-219.

[16] Cain, M.E., Denehy, E.D., Bardo, M.T. (2008) Individual Differences in Amphetamine Self-Administration: The Role of the Central Nucleus of the Amygdala. *Neuro-psychopharmacology*. 33 (5), 1149-61.

[17] Charney, D.S., Heninger, G.R., Redmond, D.E., Jr. (1983) Yohimbine induced anxiety and increased noradrenergic function in humans: effects of diazepam and clonidine. *Life Sci.*, 33, 19-29.

[18] Chen, H., Fu, Y., Sharp, B.M. (2008) Chronic nicotine self-administration augments hypothalamic-pituitary-adrenal responses to mild acute stress. *Neuro-psychopharmacology*, 33, 721-730.

[19] Childs, E., de Wit, H. (2010) Effects of acute psychosocial stress on cigarette craving and smoking. *Nicotine Tob. Res.*, 12, 449-453.

[20] Chopin, P., Pellow, S., File, S.E. (1986) The effects of yohimbine on exploratory and locomotor behaviour are attributable to its effects at noradrenaline and not at benzodiazepine receptors. *Neuropharmacology*, 25, 53-57.

[21] Cohen, C., Perrault, G., Griebel, G., Soubrie, P. (2005) Nicotine-associated cues maintain nicotine-seeking behavior in rats several weeks after nicotine withdrawal: reversal by the cannabinoid (CB1) receptor antagonist, rimonabant (SR141716). *Neuropsychopharmacology*, 30, 145-155.

[22] Colamussi, L., Bovbjerg, D.H., Erblich, J. (2007) Stress- and cue-induced cigarette craving: effects of a family history of smoking. *Drug Alcohol. Depend.*, 88, 251-258.

[23] Corrigall, W.A. (1992) A rodent model of nicotine self-administration. In: Boulton, A., Baker, G., Wu, P.H. Eds, Animal models of drug addiction: Neuromethods., Humana Press. pp. 315-344.

[24] Croghan, I.T., Bronars, C., Patten, C.A., Schroeder, D.R., Nirelli, L.M., Thomas, J.L., Clark, M.M., Vickers, K.S., Foraker, R., Lane, K., Houlihan, D., Offord, K.P., Hurt, R.D. (2006) Is smoking related to body image satisfaction, stress, and self-esteem in young adults? *Am. J. Health Behav.*, 30, 322-333.

[25] Davis, M., Redmond, D.E., Jr., Baraban, J.M. (1979) Noradrenergic agonists and antagonists: effects on conditioned fear as measured by the potentiated startle paradigm. *Psychopharmacology (Berl)*, 65, 111-118.

[26] DeSousa, N.J., Bush, D.E., Vaccarino, F.J. (2000) Self-administration of intravenous amphetamine is predicted by individual differences in sucrose feeding in rats. *Psychopharmacology (Berl)*, 148, 52-58.

[27] Doherty, K., Kinnunen, T., Militello, F.S., Garvey, A.J. (1995) Urges to smoke during the first month of abstinence: relationship to relapse and predictors. *Psychopharmacology (Berl)*, 119, 171-178.

[28] Donny, E.C., Caggiula, A.R., Mielke, M.M., Jacobs, K.S., Rose, C., Sved, A.F. (1998) Acquisition of nicotine self-administration in rats: the effects of dose, feeding schedule, and drug contingency. *Psychopharmacology (Berl)*, 136, 83-90.

[29] Donny, E.C., Caggiula, A.R., Rose, C., Jacobs, K.S., Mielke, M.M., Sved, A.F. (2000) Differential effects of response-contingent and response-independent nicotine in rats. *Eur. J. Pharmacol.*, 402, 231-240.

[30] Erblich, J., Boyarsky, Y., Spring, B., Niaura, R., Bovbjerg, D.H. (2003) A family history of smoking predicts heightened levels of stress-induced cigarette craving. *Addiction*, 98, 657-664.

[31] Feltenstein, M.W., See, R.E. (2006) Potentiation of cue-induced reinstatement of cocaine-seeking in rats by the anxiogenic drug yohimbine. *Behav. Brain Res.*, 174, 1-8.

[32] File, S.E., Kenny, P.J., Ouagazzal, A.M. (1998) Bimodal modulation by nicotine of anxiety in the social interaction test: role of the dorsal hippocampus. *Behav. Neurosci.*, 112, 1423-1429.

[33] Finkelstein, D.M., Kubzansky, L.D., Goodman, E. (2006) Social status, stress, and adolescent smoking. *J. Adolesc. Health*, 39, 678-685.

[34] Frederick, S.L., Reus, V.I., Ginsberg, D., Hall, S.M., Munoz, R.F., Ellman, G. (1998) Cortisol and response to dexamethasone as predictors of withdrawal distress and abstinence success in smokers. *Biol. Psychiatry*, 43, 525-530.

[35] Funk, D., Li, Z., Le, A.D. (2006) Effects of environmental and pharmacological stressors on c-fos and corticotropin-releasing factor mRNA in rat brain: Relationship to the reinstatement of alcohol seeking. *Neuroscience*, 138, 235-243.

[36] George, T.P., Verrico, C.D., Roth, R.H. (1998) Effects of repeated nicotine pretreatment on mesoprefrontal dopaminergic and behavioral responses to acute footshock stress. *Brain Res.*, 801, 36-49.

[37] George, T.P., Verrico, C.D., Xu, L., Roth, R.H. (2000) Effects of repeated nicotine administration and footshock stress on rat mesoprefrontal dopamine systems: Evidence for opioid mechanisms. *Neuropsychopharmacology*, 23, 79-88.

[38] Ghitza, U.E., Gray, S.M., Epstein, D.H., Rice, K.C., Shaham, Y. (2006) The anxiogenic drug yohimbine reinstates palatable food seeking in a rat relapse model: a role of CRF1 receptors. *Neuropsychopharmacology*, 31, 2188-2196.

[39] Gilbert, D.G., Robinson, J.H., Chamberlin, C.L., Spielberger, C.D. (1989) Effects of smoking/nicotine on anxiety, heart rate, and lateralization of EEG during a stressful movie. *Psychophysiology*, 26, 311-320.

[40] Goeders, N.E. (2002) The HPA axis and cocaine reinforcement. *Psychoneuroendocrinology*, 27, 13-33.

[41] Goeders, N.E. (2002) Stress and cocaine addiction. *J. Pharmacol. Exp. Ther.*, 301, 785-789.

[42] Gosnell, B.A. (2000) Sucrose intake predicts rate of acquisition of cocaine self-administration. *Psychopharmacology (Berl)*, 149, 286-292.

[43] Holmberg, G., Gershon, S. (1961) Autonomic and psychic effects of yohimbine hydrochloride. *Psychopharmacologia*, 2, 93-106.

[44] Jarvik, M.E., Caskey, N.H., Rose, J.E., Herskovic, J.E., Sadeghpour, M. (1989) Anxiolytic effects of smoking associated with four stressors. *Addict. Behav.*, 14, 379-386.

[45] Juliano, L.M., Brandon, T.H. (2002) Effects of nicotine dose, instructional set, and outcome expectancies on the subjective effects of smoking in the presence of a stressor. *J. Abnorm. Psychol.*, 111, 88-97.

[46] Koob, G.F. (1999) Stress, corticotropin-releasing factor, and drug addiction. *Ann. N. Y. Acad. Sci.*, 897, 27-45.

[47] Koob, G.F., Le Moal, M. (1997) Drug abuse: hedonic homeostatic dysregulation. *Science*, 278, 52-58.

[48] Koval, J.J., Pederson, L.L., Chan, S.S. (2004) Psychosocial variables in a cohort of students in grades 8 and 11: a comparison of current and never smokers. *Prev. Med.*, 39, 1017-1025.

[49] Lang, W.J., Gershon, S. (1963) Effects of psychoactive drugs on yohimbine induced responses in conscious dogs. A proposed screening procedure for anti-anxiety agents. *Arch. Int. Pharmacodyn. Ther*, 142, 457-472.

[50] Le, A., Shaham, Y. (2002) Neurobiology of relapse to alcohol in rats. *Pharmacol. Ther.*, 94, 137-156.

[51] Le, A.D., Harding, S., Juzytsch, W., Funk, D., Shaham, Y. (2005) Role of alpha-2 adrenoceptors in stress-induced reinstatement of alcohol seeking and alcohol self-administration in rats. *Psychopharmacology (Berl)*, 179, 366-373.

[52] Lee, B., Tiefenbacher, S., Platt, D.M., Spealman, R.D. (2003) Role of the hypothalamic-pituitary-adrenal axis in reinstatement of cocaine-seeking behavior in squirrel monkeys. *Psychopharmacology (Berl)*, 168, 177-183.

[53] Lee, B., Tiefenbacher, S., Platt, D.M., Spealman, R.D. (2004) Pharmacological blockade of alpha2-adrenoceptors induces reinstatement of cocaine-seeking behavior in squirrel monkeys. *Neuropsychopharmacology*, 29, 686-693.

[54] LeSage, M.G., Burroughs, D., Dufek, M., Keyler, D.E., Pentel, P.R. (2004) Reinstatement of nicotine self-administration in rats by presentation of nicotine-paired stimuli, but not nicotine priming. *Pharmacol. Biochem. Behav.*, 79, 507-513.

[55] Levin, E.D., Slade, S., Wells, C., Petro, A., Rose, J.E. (2011) D-cycloserine selectively decreases nicotine self-administration in rats with low baseline levels of response. *Pharmacol. Biochem. Behav.*, 98, 210-214.

[56] Liu, X., Caggiula, A.R., Yee, S.K., Nobuta, H., Sved, A.F., Pechnick, R.N., Poland, R.E. (2007) Mecamylamine attenuates cue-induced reinstatement of nicotine-seeking behavior in rats. *Neuropsychopharmacology*, 32, 710-718.

[57] Lu, L., Shepard, J.D., Hall, F.S., Shaham, Y. (2003) Effect of environmental stressors on opiate and psychostimulant reinforcement, reinstatement and discrimination in rats: a review. *Neurosci. Biobehav. Rev.*, 27, 457-491.

[58] Mantsch, J.R., Saphier, D., Goeders, N.E. (1998) Corticosterone facilitates the acquisition of cocaine self-administration in rats: opposite effects of the type II glucocorticoid receptor agonist dexamethasone. *J. Pharmacol. Exp. Ther.*, 287, 72-80.

[59] Matta, S.G., Balfour, D.J., Benowitz, N.L., Boyd, R.T., Buccafusco, J.J., Caggiula, A.R., Craig, C.R., Collins, A.C., Damaj, M.I., Donny, E.C., Gardiner, P.S., Grady, S.R., Heberlein, U., Leonard, S.S., Levin, E.D., Lukas, R.J., Markou, A., Marks, M.J., McCallum, S.E., Parameswaran, N., Perkins, K.A., Picciotto, M.R., Quik, M., Rose, J.E., Rothenfluh, A., Schafer, W.R., Stolerman, I.P., Tyndale, R.F., Wehner, J.M., Zirger, J.M. (2007) Guidelines on nicotine dose selection for in vivo research. *Psychopharmacology (Berl)*, 190, 269-319.

[60] Matta, S.G., Foster, C.A., Sharp, B.M. (1993) Nicotine stimulates the expression of cFos protein in the parvocellular paraventricular nucleus and brainstem catecholaminergic regions. *Endocrinology*, 132, 2149-2156.

[61] Matta, S.G., Fu, Y., Valentine, J.D., Sharp, B.M. (1998) Response of the hypothalamo-pituitary-adrenal axis to nicotine. *Psychoneuroendocrinology*, 23, 103-113.

[62] McKee, S.A., Sinha, R., Weinberger, A.H., Sofuoglu, M., Harrison, E.L., Lavery, M., Wanzer, J. (2011) Stress decreases the ability to resist smoking and potentiates smoking intensity and reward. *J. Psychopharmacol.*, 25, 490-502.

[63] Mello, N.K. (2010) Hormones, nicotine, and cocaine: clinical studies. *Horm. Behav.*, 58, 57-71.

[64] Minowa, K., Pawlak, R., Takada, Y., Takada, A. (2000) Nicotine attenuates stress-induced changes in plasma amino acid concentrations and locomotor activity in rats. *Brain Res. Bull.*, 51, 83-88.

[65] Nair, S.G., Gray, S.M., Ghitza, U.E. (2006) Role of food type in yohimbine- and pellet-priming-induced reinstatement of food seeking. *Physiol. Behav.*, 88, 559-566.

[66] Niaura, R., Shadel, W.G., Britt, D.M., Abrams, D.B. (2002) Response to social stress, urge to smoke, and smoking cessation. *Addict. Behav.*, 27, 241-250.

[67] Orlando, M., Ellickson, P.L., Jinnett, K. (2001) The temporal relationship between emotional distress and cigarette smoking during adolescence and young adulthood. *J. Consult Clin. Psychol.*, 69, 959-970.

[68] Parrott, A.C. (1995) Stress modulation over the day in cigarette smokers. *Addiction*, 90, 233-244.

[69] Paterson, N.E., Froestl, W., Markou, A. (2005) Repeated administration of the GABAB receptor agonist CGP44532 decreased nicotine self-administration, and acute administration decreased cue-induced reinstatement of nicotine-seeking in rats. *Neuropsychopharmacology*, 30, 119-128.

[70] Pauly, J.R., Grun, E.U., Collins, A.C. (1992) Tolerance to nicotine following chronic treatment by injections: a potential role for corticosterone. *Psychopharmacology (Berl)*, 108, 33-39.

[71] Pawlak, R., Takada, Y., Takahashi, H., Urano, T., Ihara, H., Nagai, N., Takada, A. (2000) Differential effects of nicotine against stress-induced changes in dopaminergic system in rat striatum and hippocampus. *Eur. J. Pharmacol*, 387, 171-177.

[72] Payne, T.J., Schare, M.L., Levis, D.J., Colletti, G. (1991) Exposure to smoking-relevant cues: effects on desire to smoke and topographical components of smoking behavior. *Addict. Behav.*, 16, 467-479.

[73] Perkins, K.A., Grobe, J.E. (1992) Increased desire to smoke during acute stress. *Br. J. Addict.*, 87, 1037-1040.

[74] Piazza, P.V., Deminiere, J.M., Le Moal, M., Simon, H. (1989) Factors that predict individual vulnerability to amphetamine self-administration. *Science*, 245, 1511-1513.

[75] Piazza, P.V., LeMoal, M. (1996) Pathophysiological basis of vulnerability to drug abuse: Role of an interaction between stress, glucocorticoids, and dopaminergic neurons. *Annu. Rev. Pharmacol. Toxicol.*, 36, 359-378.

[76] Piazza, P.V., Maccari, S., Deminiere, J.M., Le Moal, M., Mormede, P., Simon, H. (1991) Corticosterone levels determine individual vulnerability to amphetamine self-administration. *Proc. Natl. Acad. Sci. U. S. A.*, 88, 2088-2092.

[77] Pierre, P.J., Vezina, P. (1997) Predisposition to self-administer amphetamine: the contribution of response to novelty and prior exposure to the drug. *Psychopharmacology (Berl)*, 129, 277-284.

[78] Plaza-Zabala, A., Martin-Garcia, E., de Lecea, L., Maldonado, R., Berrendero, F. (2010) Hypocretins regulate the anxiogenic-like effects of nicotine and induce reinstatement of nicotine-seeking behavior. *J. Neurosci.*, 30, 2300-2310.

[79] Pomerleau, O.F., Pomerleau, C.S. (1990) Cortisol response to a psychological stressor and/or nicotine. *Pharmacol. Biochem. Behav.*, 36, 211-213.

[80] Pomerleau, O.F., Pomerleau, C.S. (1991) Research on stress and smoking: progress and problems. *Br. J. Addict.*, 86, 599-603.

[81] Reich, T., Hinrichs, A., Culverhouse, R., Bierut, L. (1999) Genetic studies of alcoholism and substance dependence. *Am. J. Hum. Genet.*, 65, 599-605.

[82] Rhee, S.H., Hewitt, J.K., Young, S.E., Corley, R.P., Crowley, T.J., Stallings, M.C. (2003) Genetic and environmental influences on substance initiation, use, and problem use in adolescents. *Arch. Gen. Psychiatry*, 60, 1256-1264.

[83] Schepis, T.S., Rao, U. (2005) Epidemiology and etiology of adolescent smoking. *Curr. Opin. Pediatr.*, 17, 607-612.

[84] Schroeder, B.E., Schiltz, C.A., Kelley, A.E. (2003) Neural activation profile elicited by cues associated with the anxiogenic drug yohimbine differs from that observed for reward-paired cues. *Neuropsychopharmacology*, 28, 14-21.

[85] Shaham, Y., Erb, S., Stewart, J. (2000) Stress-induced relapse to heroin and cocaine seeking in rats: a review. *Brain Res. Brain Res. Rev.*, 33, 13-33.

[86] Sharp, B.M., Beyer, H.S. (1986) Rapid desensitization of the acute stimulatory effects of nicotine on rat plasma adrenocorticotropin and prolactin. *J. Pharmacol. Exp. Ther.*, 238, 486-491.

[87] Sharp, B.M., Matta, S.G. (1993) Detection by in vivo microdialysis of nicotine-induced norepinephrine secretion from the hypothalamic paraventricular nucleus of freely moving rats: dose-dependency and desensitization. *Endocrinology*, 133, 11-19.

[88] Shepard, J.D., Bossert, J.M., Liu, S.Y., Shaham, Y. (2004) The anxiogenic drug yohimbine reinstates methamphetamine seeking in a rat model of drug relapse. *Biol. Psychiatry*, 55, 1082-1089.

[89] Shoaib, M., Schindler, C.W., Goldberg, S.R. (1997) Nicotine self-administration in rats: strain and nicotine pre-exposure effects on acquisition. *Psychopharmacology (Berl)*, 129, 35-43.

[90] Sinha, R. (2001) How does stress increase risk of drug abuse and relapse? *Psychopharmacology (Berl)*, 158, 343-359.

[91] Sinha, R. (2008) Chronic stress, drug use, and vulnerability to addiction. *Ann. N. Y. Acad. Sci.*, 1141, 105-130.

[92] Sinha, R., Garcia, M., Paliwal, P., Kreek, M.J., Rounsaville, B.J. (2006) Stress-induced cocaine craving and hypothalamic-pituitary-adrenal responses are predictive of cocaine relapse outcomes. *Arch. Gen. Psychiatry*, 63, 324-331.

[93] Siqueira, L., Diab, M., Bodian, C., Rolnitzky, L. (2000) Adolescents becoming smokers: the roles of stress and coping methods. *J. Adolesc. Health*, 27, 399-408.

[94] Steptoe, A., Wardle, J., Pollard, T.M., Canaan, L., Davies, G.J. (1996) Stress, social support and health-related behavior: a study of smoking, alcohol consumption and physical exercise. *J. Psychosom. Res.*, 41, 171-180.

[95] Suto, N., Austin, J.D., Vezina, P. (2001) Locomotor response to novelty predicts a rat's propensity to self-administer nicotine. *Psychopharmacology (Berl)*, 158, 175-180.

[96] Szyndler, J., Sienkiewicz-Jarosz, H., Maciejak, P., Siemiatkowski, M., Rokicki, D., Czlonkowska, A.I., Plaznik, A. (2001) The anxiolytic-like effect of nicotine undergoes rapid tolerance in a model of contextual fear conditioning in rats. *Pharmacol. Biochem. Behav.*, 69, 511-518.

[97] Todd, M. (2004) Daily processes in stress and smoking: effects of negative events, nicotine dependence, and gender. *Psychol. Addict. Behav.*, 18, 31-39.

[98] Uhde, T.W., Boulenger, J.P., Post, R.M., Siever, L.J., Vittone, B.J., Jimerson, D.C., Roy-Byrne, P.P. (1984) Fear and anxiety: relationship to noradrenergic function. *Psychopathology*, 17 Suppl 3, 8-23.

[99] Uhl, G.R., Liu, Q.R., Naiman, D. (2002) Substance abuse vulnerability loci: converging genome scanning data. *Trends Genet.*, 18, 420-425.

[100] Vanyukov, M.M., Tarter, R.E. (2000) Genetic studies of substance abuse. *Drug Alcohol. Depend.*, 59, 101-123.

[101] West, R., Lennox, S. (1992) Function of cigarette smoking in relation to examinations. *Psychopharmacology (Berl)*, 108, 456-459.

[102] Zarrindast, M.R., Homayoun, H., Babaie, A., Etminani, A., Gharib, B. (2000) Involvement of adrenergic and cholinergic systems in nicotine-induced anxiogenesis in mice. *Eur. J. Pharmacol.*, 407, 145-158.

[103] Zinser, M.C., Baker, T.B., Sherman, J.E., Cannon, D.S. (1992) Relation between self-reported affect and drug urges and cravings in continuing and withdrawing smokers. *J. Abnorm. Psychol.*, 101, 617-629.

[104] Zislis, G., Desai, T.V., Prado, M., Shah, H.P., Bruijnzeel, A.W. (2007) Effects of the CRF receptor antagonist D-Phe CRF(12-41) and the alpha2-adrenergic receptor agonist clonidine on stress-induced reinstatement of nicotine-seeking behavior in rats. *Neuropharmacology*, 53, 958-966.

In: Nicotine Addiction
Editor: Giuseppe Di Giovanni

ISBN: 978-1-62081-290-7


*Chapter 6*

# SMOKING, NICOTINE AND DEPRESSION: A REVIEW

***Gonzalo Vázquez-Palacios[1,*] and Herlinda Bonilla-Jaime[2]***
[1]College of Science and Technology,
Universidad Autónoma de la Ciudad de México-San Lorenzo Tezonco,
Mexico City, Mexico
[2]Department of Reproductive Biology,
Universidad Autónoma Metropolitana-Iztapalapa,
Mexico City, Mexico

## ABSTRACT

Depression is a complex and heterogeneous mental disorder that manifests itself in chronic changes in mood and sleep patterns. According to the World Health Organization, the type called major depression is already a serious public health problem associated with an increased risk of disability and mortality, and will be the second most important cause of disability worldwide in 2020. Epidemiological studies clearly suggest an elevated risk of smoking in people with mood disorders. Depressed individuals tend to smoke more than non-depressed people, and interrupting this habit produces major depression that is reversed through the use of antidepressants or nicotine replacement therapies. Three explanations have been advanced for this association. The first, the ''self-medication theory'', supposes that depression leads to smoking because nicotine has antidepressant effects; while the second holds that smoking and depression share common environmental or genetic risk factors; and the third argues that depression is a sequela of brain dysfunction-induced smoking. Studies of the role of nicotine (NIC) and neuronal nicotinic acetylcholine receptors (nAChRs) in the pathophysiology of depression have found contradictory results, as both nAChR agonists and antagonists have been shown to exert antidepressant effects in animals and humans. These apparent contradictions may be due to the complexity of the nicotinic cholinergic system, its

[*] Correspondence concerning this article should be addressed to: Gonzalo Vázquez-Palacios, Academia de Biología, Colegio de Ciencia y Tecnología, Universidad Autónoma de la Ciudad de México-San Lorenzo Tezonco, Av. Prolongación San Isidro 151, Col. San Lorenzo Tezonco, Deleg., Iztapalapa, México, D.F., C.P. 09790, Phone: +52 525 8501901 Ext. 14510; e-Mail: gvp@ xanum. uam.mx.

structural intricacy, neuroanatomical distribution and peculiar functional antagonist effect on nAChRs. Also important is that several members of different antidepressant families have shown a marked antagonist activity on nAChRs. Though the neurobiological bases of this "nicotine-depression" association are unclear, the mechanism proposed to explain the antidepressant activity of nicotine involves direct action on two key neurotransmitter systems: serotonin and dopamine, or indirectly as a possible neuroprotective action that improves depressive symptoms. This chapter first summarizes the neurochemical aspects of nicotine and nicotinic receptors, before discussing the findings that show the close relationship between smoking and depression, and the evidence suggesting that nicotine has antidepressant properties in both animal models of depression and depressed subjects. Finally, we propose a possible mechanism to explain how nicotine acts on depression.

## Introduction

Depression is a complex mental disorder associated with an increase in the risk of disability and mortality (according to World Health Organization estimates, it will be the second-leading cause of disability worldwide in 2020). This psychiatric disorder affects from 5-17% of the world's population [1, 2] and is considered a public health problem [3]. Manifestations include feelings of despair and guilt, the inability to experience pleasure (anhedonia), and pessimism that can lead to suicide [4]. Depressed patients also present sleep alterations: a short latency to rapid eye movements (REM sleep) at the onset of the first sleep period is the principal characteristic of this disorder [5, 6]. At the neurochemical level, reductions in noradrenergic and serotoninergic activity have been detected, as has an increase in the plasma cortisol level that correlates with the presence of stress in depressed subjects. While the connection between smoking and substance abuse has a long history, the association between smoking and mental disorders has only been recognized since *ca.* 1990. Patients with some mental disorder consume nearly 44.3% of the total number of cigarettes smoked by the entire U.S. population [7]. The results of epidemiological studies in different populations suggest a powerful bi-directional relation between smoking and major depression, and pioneering studies suggest that nicotine (NIC) may play an important role as an antidepressant [8, 9]. NIC is an alkaloid and the main psychoactive agent in tobacco. Its effect on the central nervous system results from interaction with nicotinic receptors in the acetylcholine, complex receptors that are distributed widely in the brain and participate in multiple physiological and functional activities.

## General Aspects of Nicotine

### Pharmacology

When tobacco is smoked, nicotine is absorbed rapidly, though the amount depends on the volume and intensity of suction, dilution in air, and the profundity of inhalation. With each puff, high levels of NIC reach the brain within 10-20 seconds, more quickly even than via intravenous administration [10]. NIC concentrations in the arterial blood after smoking one cigarette usually range from 20-60 ng/mL, while concentrations after the first puff are 7 ng/mL [11]. Absorption of NIC through biological membranes depends on pH. It is very fast in the lungs, presumably because of the broad surface area that the alveoli present and the pH of pulmonary tissue (7.4). Almost 1 mg (0.3-2 mg) of nicotine is absorbed when smoking occurs [12, 13] and, once absorbed, it enters the bloodstream: at a pH of 7.4, 65% is ionized, 30% is deionized, and 5% bonds to plasma proteins [14]. Autopsies of smokers and studies conducted with animals show that the tissues with the greatest affinity for NIC are the kidney, liver, lung, brain, and heart; while skeletal muscle has a moderate affinity, and adipose tissue only a low level [15]. In addition, NIC accumulates in breast milk and readily crosses the placental barrier [12].

## Metabolism

The highest blood levels of NIC occur when the person stops smoking a cigarette, then decline quickly in the following 20 minutes as it spreads broadly into several body tissues. Distribution volume in humans is 2.6 times body weight [16]. The liver metabolizes NIC and six primary metabolites have been identified, of which the most important in quantitative terms is cotinine [17]. NIC is excreted through the kidneys via glomerular and tubular filtration with variable reabsorption, depending on the pH of the urine. In acidic urine, NIC is ionized and tubular reabsorption is minimized; while in alkaline urine, a larger amount of NIC is deionized, followed by tubular reabsorption. Excretion of cotinine is little affected by urinary pH, as it is more basic and, moreover, dependent on the rate of urinary flow [18]. Using radioactively marked NIC, a study showed that at least 1% of the NIC consumed is excreted in the feces [19]. Also, it has been reported that larger quantities of NIC than cotinine are excreted in the sweat of smokers, though amounts have not been tabulated [20]. Some have speculated that continuing to consume cigarettes while also taking a replacement therapy (such as transdermal patches, aerosol or chewing gum) can produce an overdose that manifests itself in nauseas, vomiting and the possibility of death; though there is no evidence of serious toxic effects when two or more replacement therapies are combined (eg., using multiple patches) [21].

## Nicotinic Receptors

Most of the nicotinic receptors are presynaptic, but some are postsynaptic. They are of the canal type, cationic in nature ($Na^+$ or $Ca^{++}$) [22] and pentameric in form, with at least two ligand-binding sites on the interface between subunits [23]. When acetylcholine or NIC bonds to those sites, they produce a structural change in the constituent subunits such that the canal opens to allow the flow of ions and the later depolarization and release of neurotransmitters. It has been reported that the nicotine-receptor bond induces the release of dopamine [24], γ-aminobutyric acid [25, 26], glutamate [27], serotonin (5-HT) [28, 29], orexin [30] and opioid peptides [31-33]. The genes that codify for the different subunits that make up the nicotinic receptor have been identified and cloned. Nicotinic cholinergic receptors consist of five sub-units [34, 35]. Mammal brains express nine α subunits (α2- α10) and three β sub-units (β2-β4). The most abundant receptors are α4β2, α3β4 and α7; the latter is homomeric [36-38] (Table 1).

**Table 1. Localization of different types of nicotinic receptors in the central nervous system**

| Localization | Subtype receptor |
|---|---|
| Cortex | $\alpha4\beta2$, $\alpha4\alpha5\beta2$, $\alpha7$ |
| Hippocampus | $\alpha4\beta2$, $\alpha4\alpha5\beta2$, $\alpha3\beta4$, $\alpha7$ |
| Thalamus | $\alpha4\beta2$, $\alpha7$ |
| Medial habenula | $\alpha4\beta2$, $\alpha3\beta4$, $\alpha3\beta3\beta4$, $\alpha7$ |
| Pineal gland | $\alpha3\beta4$, $\alpha7$ |
| Cerebellum | $\alpha4\beta2$, $\alpha3\beta4$, $\alpha7$, $\alpha3\beta2$ |
| Locus coeruleus | $\alpha3\beta4$, $\alpha6\beta2\beta3$ |
| Spinal cord | $\alpha4\beta2$, $\alpha3\beta2$, $\alpha7$ |
| Raphe nuclei | $\alpha4\beta2$ |
| Interpeduncular nucleus | $\alpha4\beta2$, $\alpha2\beta2$, $\alpha3\beta3\beta4$, $\alpha7$ |
| Substantia nigra<br>Ventral tegmental area | $\alpha4\beta2$, $\alpha4\alpha5\beta2$, $\alpha3\beta4$, $\alpha6\beta2\beta3$, $\alpha7$ |
| Hypothalamus | $\alpha4\beta2$, $\alpha7$ |
| Amygdala | $\alpha4\beta2$, $\alpha7$ |
| Striatum | $\alpha4\beta2$, $\alpha4\alpha5\beta2$, $\alpha6\beta2\beta3$, $\alpha6\alpha4\beta2\beta3$, $\alpha7$ |
| Olfactory bulb | $\alpha4\beta2$, $\alpha7$ |
| Basal pontine nucleus | $\alpha7$ |
| Broca´s diagonal band | $\alpha7$ |
| Meynert´s basal nucleus | $\alpha4\beta2$, $\alpha7$ |
| Inferior olivary nucleus | $\alpha7$ |

The assemblage of the subunits determines the different subtypes of nicotinic receptors (heteropentamers), which vary in terms of their pharmacological and biophysical properties [36-38]. Activation of the $\alpha4\beta2$ receptor has been related to the presence of depression and addictive behaviors such as tobacco consumption [39, 40]. The subtypes with $\alpha4\beta2\alpha5$ regulate the release of dopamine [41-42].

## General Characteristics of Depression

The American Psychiatric Association [4] defines major depression as a chronic heterogeneous disorder that often manifests itself in psychological, behavioral and physiological symptoms that include despondent moods that last for more than a day (irritability in children and adolescents may also indicate a depressed mood), an inability to experience pleasure in activities that once generated that sensation (anhedonia), increased or decreased appetite, insomnia or excessive sleepiness, psychomotor alterations (lack of energy or agitation), fatigue, lack of concentration, feelings of guilt or worthlessness, recurring thoughts of death or suicide, reduced libido, and poor personal hygiene [4]. Depression is twice as common in women as men [4, 43], and epidemiological studies show that approximately 40-50% of the risk of suffering depression is genetic [44, 45], indicating that it is a highly heritable disorder. However, the genes linked to depression have not been identified completely [46, 47]. Non-genetic factors such as stress, emotional trauma, infections, pharmacological treatments, etc., during brain development have also been implicated in the etiology of depression [43]. Findings from depressed patients who were victims of suicide show that they had a reduced volume in the prefrontal and orbitofrontal cortex, ventral striatum, amygdala and hippocampus [see details in 48]. Neurochemically, a reduction in the activity of the noradrenergic and serotoninergic systems has been observed, as have alterations in the rhythm of secretion and increases in plasma cortisol levels [49, 50].

## Smoking, Nicotine and Depression

### *Epidemiology*

The results of epidemiological studies in both general and clinical populations suggest a positive bidirectional relation between smoking and major depression. For example, in the National Comorbidity Survey, nearly 60% of participants with clinical histories of depression were smokers or ex-smokers, while the corresponding figure for the general population was just 39% [51, 52]. Moreover, 16.5% of the NIC-dependent people in the NESARC's study had suffered an current episode of major depression, a percentage several times higher than the rate for the population as a whole (2-7% in studies in different places in the world) [53, 54]. Additional reports show that depressed people tend to smoke more cigarettes, compared to non-depressed subjects [55-57]. In clinical studies of treatments for smoking, the prevalence of major depression during a person's lifetime was much greater in smokers than in the general population [56, 57]. In most longitudinal and retrospective studies, smoking at the beginning of the research was associated with a high rate of the onset of depression during the follow-up period, findings that suggest that smoking may be a risk factor for depression [52]. Most of those results also indicate that this relation is accentuated in women, even during adolescence [52, 58-62] though a study conducted in Finland found that this relation holds only for males [63, 64]. Also, depression may be a risk factor for increasing the smoking habit [52, 60, 61]. According to recent results from Leventhal et al. [65, 66], some of the symptoms of depression are more strongly linked to NIC-dependence than others [65, 66]; *i.e.*, symptoms of the melancholic subtype of major depression are more strongly associated with NIC dependence than are those of atypical depression (melancholic and atypical depression are subtypes of major depression based on DSM-IV, differentiated by certain symptoms) [65, 66]. However, data on the effects of depression on the index of success in smoking cessation vary. In one recent article, Ziedonis et al. [52], reached the conclusion – based on data from studies of subjects who attempted to quit smoking published between 1988 and 2006– that smokers with antecedents of depression have a similar probability of achieving abstinence in the short term (less than 3 months), but a lower possibility in the long term (over 6 months), though only in non-medicated patients. An earlier meta-analysis carried out by Hitsman et al. [67], processed the data from studies on smoking cessation published from 1988 to 2000, and concluded that a clinical history of depression was not a risk factor for relapses. Later, those same authors re-analyzed the data, but restricted the meta-analysis to the participants assigned randomly to the condition of having undergone at least one intensive treatment. Once again, they could detect no relation between a clinical history of depression and relapses [52, 67, 68]. However, data on the effects of episodes of depression in relation to success in smoking cessation are very scarce. Based on the results of three studies, Ziedonis et al. [52] concluded that efforts to quit smoking among patients with ongoing episodes of depression resulted in a similar percentage of abstinence as among depressed non-smokers [52]. In contrast, in the study by Japuntich et al. [68], current depression was a stronger predictor than previous episodes of depression for failed attempts to quit smoking in the short term (1 week) but not in the long term (3 months, 6 months). On the other hand, in a comparative study of NIC-replacement therapies against a placebo, subjects in the group treated with the placebo who had a current episode of depression at the onset of the study were significantly more prone to smoking at 12 months after treatment, compared to the non-depressed individuals in NIC-replacement therapies or the placebo, or to depressed subjects undergoing replacement therapy [68, 69] In contrast, patients with a current episode of major depression who succeeded in quitting smoking seem to have a higher possibility of improving their mood, compared to depressed patients who were unable to achieve abstinence [70, 71]. In another recent study, the authors found that smokers who had unsuccessfully attempted to quit smoking in the previous year experienced episodes of depression at a higher rate than smokers who had not tried to quit during that period, and former smokers (*i.e.*, those who had succeeded). Recurring depression seems to be more closely related to the failure to stop smoking than one sole episode of major depression [52]. Depressive episodes after dropping the smoking habit are more frequent in people with one or earlier episodes of depression than among those with no such episodes in their medical histories. Some results also suggest that an increase in the symptoms of depression while trying to quit smoking is more closely related to relapses than to a basal level of depression. In their recent review, however, Ziedonis et al. [52] conclude that it is not clear whether episodes of depression during treatment contribute to relapses among smokers that are vulnerable to bouts of depression [52, 69, 72-74]. Findings also indicate that a past or recent episode of depression while attempting to quit smoking is related to high levels of symptoms of abstinence and/or a prolonged period of abstinence [75-80]. In addition, in special populations (eg., patients hospitalized for acute cardiovascular events), depression at the onset of the study was a predictor of failure to quit smoking [79, 81, 82]. . The high mortality rates seen in patients with major depression are well-documented [53, 83-85]. Though some studies also suggest that depression could be an independent risk factor for cancer and cardiovascular disorders, it is easy to imagine that a high index of smoking in cases of major depression might reinforce the association between depression and the increased risk of mortality [83-86].

## Hypothesis on the Increase in Indexes of Smoking among Patients with Major Depression

As mentioned above, the results of epidemiological studies clearly suggest a high risk of smoking among people with mood disorders. Three explanations have been proposed for this association. The self-medication theory holds that depression leads to smoking because the NIC and/or other ingredients in tobacco smoke have antidepressant effects [80, 87], the second theory proposes that smoking and depression have common environmental and genetic risk factors; while the third argues that depression is a sequela of smoke consumption, such that smoking leads to brain dysfunction [88]. The physiopathological bases of depression are apparently quite complex. One of several theories in this field is the cholinergic hypothesis of depression [89-90], which is based on results obtained in recent decades indicating that physostigmine, an acetylcholinesterase inhibitor (AChE-I), might exacerbate depressed moods (though later research with other AChE-Is found the opposite effect), and that high levels of choline, the limiting precursor in acetylcholine synthesis, have been found in the brains of depressed patients [89, 91, 92]. A neurobiological link between depression and the cholinergic system is also supported by the potent antidepressant activity of the muscarinic antagonist scopolamine (some tricyclic antidepressants also show antimuscarínic action). In addition, research has found exaggerated neuroendocrine and pupillary responses in patients with mood disorders after administering cholinomimetic agents. Finally, ACh facilitates the release of several molecules related to hypothalamus-pituitary-adrenal axis of stress (eg., CRF, ACTH and corticosterone) [92, 93]. At first glance, the role of nAChR in the physiopathology of depression seems contradictory, as both nAChR agonists/partial agonists (eg., NIC, cytisine, ispronicline, and varenicline,) and antagonists (eg., mecamylamine, dihydro-beta-erythroidine, methyllycaconitine) show antidepressant properties in animal and human studies [94-106]. In the specific case of nicotine, several laboratories around the world have reported its antidepressant properties when administered by different means and varied doses, in both human [8, 9, 107] and animal models of depression [101-106, 108-113], and even in normal rats [100]. For example, pioneering studies found that the use of transdermal nicotine patches improves mood in depressed non-smoker patients, according to an assessment obtained using the Hamilton Depression Scale [8]. The antidepressant effect of 4 consecutive days of nicotine administration on depressed non-smoker patients has also been studied by the Salín-Pascual group [9], which observed an important clinical improvement after just two days of nicotine patch administration, though patients relapsed 4 days after applying the last patch. Similar results have been reported for chronic transdermal administration of nicotine (over one month) in non-smoker patients with depressive disorder [114]. It is important to emphasize this effect of rapid antidepressant action induced by nicotine because, as is well known, most of the antidepressants utilized in clinical practice produce their effects only in the long term –*i.e.*, 6-to-8 weeks after onset of treatment– and, as a consequence, may include a reduced adherence to therapy in some cases (eg., fluoxetine), the risk of suicide after initial motor improvement, and a delayed effect on mood. It is also important to stress that several members of different families of anti-depressants (eg. amitriptyline, imipramine, fluoxetine, bupropion, nefazodone) have shown a marked antagonist activity on nAChRs [92, 103]. The most probable and widely recognized explanation of this apparent contradiction is the hypothesis, which holds that inhibiting nAChRs frees the antidepressant effects of any given drug. Inhibition of the nAChRs can be induced either directly (as when nAChR antagonists are administered), or indirectly through functional antagonism (as when nAChRs are desensitized through the chronic administration of agonists; eg., NIC) [94, 96, 98, 104]. The importance of nAChRs in the physiopathology of depression is supported by results of research on knockout mice (KO). For example, α7 or β2 KO mice are insensitive to the antidepressant effects of mecamylamine [102]. Moreover, three animal models of depression (the tail-suspension, forced swim and learned helplessness tests) have shown that β2 KO mice are resistant to the effects of the tricyclic antidepressant amitriptyline [105]. In addition, KO β2 mice were resistant to the hippocampal cell proliferation induced by amitriptyline (another common marker of antidepressant action). These results strongly suggest that the β2 subunit is involved in the antidepressant response induced by amitriptyline [94, 96, 105] The role of nAChRs in depression is even more strongly supported by results from studies of different types of strains of rodents (eg., Flinders-Sensitive rats or Fawn-Hooded rats) with depressive characteristics, and in rodents after olfactory bulbectomies (an animal model of depression), a surgical procedure that modifies the neuronal density of nAChR [110-112]. It is also important to note that some antidepressants, such as bupropion and amitriptyline, are efficacious agents in individuals who attempt to drop the smoking habit, suggesting that nicotine dependence may share some common neuronal substrates with depression [94]. Various neurobiological theories have attempted to explain the antidepressive impact of nicotine and other nAChR agonists. For example, activation of nAChRs in the hippocampus (probably the α4β2 isoform) causes an increase in neurogenesis in the hippocampus, which is also considered a common action of antidepressants. Consonant with this is the fact that chronic stress and depression have been linked to a reduction in the volume of the hippocampus [115-117]. The antidepressant effect of NIC may also be related to the monoaminergic theory of depression, as the activity of the monoaminergic systems in the brain is deeply influenced by nAChRs [115, 118]. In this view, the role of the dopaminergic reward system appears to be of great importance, as the alteration of its function has been related to depression and, consistent with this, smokers with depression may feel that consumption of NIC is more gratifying than non-depressed smokers [119-121].

Though results are not totally consistent, exposure of animals to stressful environments seems to be associated with an increased activation of the amygdala, while the chronic administration of antidepressants is linked to a reduced activation (measured by immunorreactivity to c-fos). Both mecamylamine, a non-selective nAChR antagonist, and cytisine, a partial nAChR agonist have antidepressant activity, and their administration leads to a reduced expression of c-fos in the amygdala, which is consistent with the above mentioned conclusions [94, 106, 122-124]. In addition, it has been shown that chronic administration of NIC to Wistar rats results in a down-regulation of the beta-adrenergic receptors in the cortex, another common finding after treatments for depression, such as chronic antidepressant therapy, electroconvulsive therapy and sleep deprivation [115, 125]. As mentioned above, smoking is not equivalent to administering pure NIC, because tobacco smoke contains other psychoactive compounds, some of which are from the family of the β-carbolines and have inhibiting properties on monoamine oxidases (MAO, a family of enzymes that catalyze the oxidation of monoamines) and antidepressant properties [eg., the so-called norharman (β-carboline) and harman (1-methyl-β-carboline)] [126-128]. As stated earlier, one hypothesis suggests that the depressogenic effect of some ingredients of tobacco is responsible for the frequent co-occurrence of depression and smoking; indeed, several reports support this view. For example, it has been reported that smoking affects the function of serotonin (measured by the levels of 5-HIAA in CSF and the fenfluramine test) in depressed patients [129]. Acute tryptophan depletion (ATD) has a mood-lowering effect in euthymic individuals with mood disorder in their personal medical history or family history (*i.e.*, maintaining mood within the "normal" range, which entails the absence of depressed or agitated moods) [130]. Recently, the trigger effect of ATD-induced depression has been shown to be more pronounced in smokers with antecedents of major depression, compared to their non-smoking counterparts [130]. Chronic stress and depression have been associated with deregulation of the hypothalamus-pituitary-adrenal axis (HPA) [131]. As smoking does exert a strong influence on the activity of this axis, its effect could constitute another link between smoking and depression [132-134]. Oxidative stress induced by smoking may also be responsible for the frequent co-occurrence of depression and smoking, while it seems clear that an increase in oxidative stress occurs in major depression [60, 135]. Another possible mechanism in smoking-induced depression is related to chronic obstructive pulmonary disease (COPD). Smoking is a proven risk factor for COPD, and the incidence of depression among people who suffer COPD is high when compared to the general population [136, 137]. The permanent state of systemic inflammation and/or chronic hypoxia that are distinctive characteristics of COPD could explain the high rate of mood disorders in COPD patients [136]. Another hypothesis holds that smoking can cause mood changes in smokers due to the appearance of acute periods of NIC deprivation several times during the day. Consistent with this, several studies have found that is associated with lower levels of stress and anxiety in the long term [138-139]. One recent study has strengthened this theory by finding that in contrast to the experiences of smokers, high rates of smoking are associated with greater negative effects, and that this association is more marked on stressful days [139].

As mentioned above, a second theory holds that a genetic vulnerability, or one related to an environment that is common to both the smoking habit and depression, is responsible for high co-occurrence [52], an idea that has found support in different studies [52, 140-143]. Some research found that certain genetic variations in the genes in the dopaminergic route on the gene of the μ receptor for opioids are linked to effects on tobacco-induced mood swings. Data on the associations between susceptibility to major depression and the polymorphisms of the genes of the subunits of the nicotinic receptor are scarce [52, 144, 145]. Yet another interesting connection between smoking and depression is the association of NIC administration (through smoking) during pregnancy and the high vulnerability to mood disorders among children, according to the results of epidemiological studies and animal models. This association might be a result of the dramatic changes in the development of the nervous system that NIC induces [146-148].

Finally, the third proposal suggests that depression is a sequela of tobacco consumption, such that smoking leads to cerebral dysfunction. Various studies indicate that most of the adverse neurobiological and neurocognitive effects of chronic cigarette consumption are a function of the direct and indirect consequences of continuous exposure by the cardiopulmonary system, the cerebrovascular system and the cerebral parenchyma to the combination of products contained in the combustion of cigarette smoke [149-151]. Many potentially cytotoxic compounds in smoke (eg., carbon monoxide, aldehydes, ketones, nitrosamines, dihydroxybenzenes) can directly compromise the function of the cell membranes of brain tissue including, of course, the neuronal membrane [152]. As a result, chronic smoking is related to neurocognitive alterations, global cerebral atrophy and structural and biochemical anomalies in the anterior frontal regions, the subcortical nuclei and the commissural white matter [153-154].

Although the antidepressant effect of NIC has been demonstrated clearly from the behavioral perspective, the cellular mechanism through which NIC produces these effects of mood improvement in depressed patients is not yet well understood. There are indications that

NIC might act as a neuroprotector against the development of neurodegenerative diseases, such as Parkinson's and Alzheimer's [155]. In non-human primates and rodents, an improved ability to perform cognitive activities has been demonstrated [156]; reason for which it has been suggested that NIC and its agonists may favor the synthesis or release of neurotrophic factors, such as neural growth factor, fibroblastic growth factor and brain-derived neurotrophic factor (BDNF)[157]. These trophic factors play a role as neuroprotectors that has been fully demonstrated. However, at this time no work has yet elucidated the neurotrophic or neuroprotective action of NIC in depressed subjects. Thus, the objective of this review is to discuss the principal findings related to NIC and its action on the serotoninergic and dopaminergic systems, which are potential action candidates for this substance and its antidepressant properties.

## Interaction Mechanisms of Nicotine in Depressive Disorders

As mentioned earlier, several laboratories in the world have reported the antidepressant properties of NIC (and some agonists and antagonists), when administered through different vias and in distinct doses, in humans [9, 107], animal models of depression [101, 108, 158], and even normal rats [100]. Also, studies have demonstrated the antidepressant effect of both agonists [113, 159-163] and antagonists [104, 164-167]. In our own laboratory we have found that the subcutaneous administration of NIC (0.4 mg/kg of weight) in the modified forced swim test [168] reduces immobility behavior while increasing swimming behavior, a response pattern similar to that produced by drugs whose mechanism of action is mediated by the serotoninergic system, such as the selective inhibitors of the recapture of serotonin like fluoxetine [100, 101]. This suggests that the antidepressant effect of nicotine, at least at the dose utilized, may be mediated in part by the serotoninergic system through nicotinic receptors in the raphe nuclei . There is ample evidence of the bidirectional relation in the interaction between the nicotinic and serotoninergic systems [for a review see 169]. For example, nicotinic receptors are expressed in neurons of the raphe and researchers have seen that one of the immediate effects of NIC administration is that it induces a significant increase of serotonin in various regions of the brain, including the cortex, hippocampus, striatum, lateral septum of the nucleus dorsal raphe (NDR) and hypothalamus [169-173]. The physiological effect of the 5-HT released by NIC depends on the type of serotoninergic receptor that is stimulated and the region of the brain where it is released [112, 174-175]. In the case of depression, the 5-HT1A and 5-HT2 subtype receptors are directly involved [176, 177]. *In vitro* studies have reported that when stimulated by NIC, the neurons in the NDR reduce their firing frequency; though the simultaneous release of serotonin rises in the extracellular medium [178]. This result has led to the suggestion that NIC induces the release of 5-HT from the presynaptic terminals of the NDR, just like tricyclic antidepressants. This release mechanism of 5-HT may be mediated not only by the action of NIC when administered exogenously, but also endogenously, due to stimulation of the cholinergic fibers of the laterodorsal nucleus (LDT) and the pedunculopontine tegmental nucleus (PPT) in the brain stem. In addition, it has been suggested that NIC acts on the serotoninergic neurons of the NDR in two ways: first, by utilizing a direct mechanism of the excitatory type that would trigger the release of 5-HT; and, second, through an indirect mechanism of an inhibitory nature that would cause the hyperpolarization of NDR neurons [178, 179]. Also documented are physiological and pharmacological relations between 5-HT1A receptors and the serotonin transporter (5-HTT) in regulating the neurotransmission of 5-HT [180]. Moreover, it has been suggested that there is a relation between the 5-HT1A and 5-HTT receptors that would explain both the physiopathology of depression and the mechanism of action of antidepressants [181]. We have suggested that acute and chronic nicotine administration may modulate the expression of the 5-HT1A receptors localized not only in the nucleus of the raphe, but also in certain cortical regions and the limbic system [182], that participate in the etiology of depression [180]. All these effects lead us to postulate that nicotine-induced release of 5-HT could alter post-synaptic sensitivity to 5-HT [182, 184], by desensitizing the 5-HT1A autoreceptors [185-187], and that this mechanism could be mediated by the effects on mood associated with NIC. It is well known that today's most commonly used antidepressant treatments improve serotoninergic transmission (eg., fluoxetine) [188, 189]. We know that both fluoxetine and NIC increase activity in the serotoninergic system [178, 190, 191], but also that they do so through distinct mechanisms. In addition, we have demonstrated that there are no synergetic effects when NIC and fluoxetine are administered simultaneously to depressed rats following the model of neonatal clomipramine [101]. These effects could suggest that administering NIC and fluoxetine can induce rapid antidepressant effects and increase adherence to treatment in acute moments of antidepressant therapy. We have also reported that the antidepressant effect of NIC is immediate upon first administration, a result that is not seen with fluoxetine, the effect of which is not felt unless it is taken chronically [101]. This is another advantage of activating the serotoninergic system through the nicotinic system, and suggests that this mechanism could induce rapid-effect antidepressant results.

A second hypothesis –that does not preclude the first– suggests that the antidepressant effect of NIC could take place by releasing dopamine. Dopaminergic neurons from the ventral tegmental area and the *pars compacta* substance nigra express a wide variety of nicotinic receptors [192]. Inhibitors of the recapture of 5-HT increase the postsynaptic response to dopamine in the terminals of the mesolimbic system [193-194], just as NIC administration does in that region [195, 196]. Additional evidence indicates that the nicotinic receptors expressed in the neurons of the ventral tegmental area are desensitized by chronic exposure to NIC, even when doses similar to those found in the plasma of smokers are used [197]. Similar results have been reported when dopamine levels are measured in the nucleus accumbens, or upon recording the firing frequency in rats that received a NIC injection at a dosage similar to that found in the plasma of smokers [198]. Turning to the administration of nicotinic receptor antagonists such as mecamylamine in animals chronically exposed to NIC, studies have found that it induces the abstinence syndrome and reduces the release of dopamine by the nucleus accumbens [199]. This decline in the release of dopamine has been interpreted as the neuronal correlate of the anhedonia or dysphoria that smokers experience when they attempt to quit their habit [200]. On another point, a wide variety of treatments designed to end NIC dependence are commercially available, though only two general foci have gained empirical validation: behavioral intervention and pharmacotherapy. With regards to the latter, three types of medication have been available in the market to treat smoking: NIC replacement therapy (eg., transdermal patches, chewing gum, inhalers, nasal spray, etc.), slow-release bupropion, and varenicline. As stated earlier, bupropion is another antidepressant drug whose mechanism of action is mediated by dopamine. Also discussed above was the fact that the α4β2 nicotinic receptor is an ionic canal with a high affinity for NIC [201]. High concentrations of NIC bond to the α4β2 receptor, causing the aperture of the ionic canals and the flow of Na+, which then depolarizes the dopaminergic neurons. One-third of those receptors are found in the dopaminergic cells of the dopaminergic mesolimbic system [202, 203]. Some researchers have thought that the α4β2 receptor subtype performs a fundamental role in mediating the rewards of NIC [204], and this is supported, among many other findings, by the fact that blocking the α4β2 receptor with dihydro-β-erythroidine (DHβE) inhibits self-administration of NIC in rats [205]. These data suggest that nicotine's effects on behavior and the release of dopamine are predominantly mediated by activation of the α4β2 nicotinic receptor in the mesolimbic dopaminergic system [206]. Varenicline is a partial agonist of the α4β2 nicotinic receptor that is efficacious in treating tobacco dependence; however, the safety instructions for its use warn that it produces agitation, depression and suicide [207]. No causal connection between using varenicline and these symptoms has yet been established, though it has been reported that –like bupropion– it may have antidepressant properties that raise the antidepressant effect of selective serotonin reuptake inhibitors, such as sertraline [208].

Another hypothesis as to nicotine's possible mechanism in depressive disorders is that its effects may be mediated by neurotrophic or neuroprotective processes. A growing body of results demonstrates that nicotinic agonists are potential candidates for treating neurodegenerative diseases such as Alzheimer's or Parkinson's, and for attending cognitive disorders associated with schizophrenia [209], as the activation of nicotinic receptors shows neuroprotective and neurotrophic effects [210]. For example, it has been reported that prenatal exposure to NIC in rats induces the premature development of cholinergic projections in midbrain, brain stem and cortex [211]. Also, observations show that the α7 nicotinic receptors, which are expressed in the early stages of development and are important for the growth of neurites, participate in phenomena of synaptic remodeling [212]. Those receptors are expressed more in the hippocampus than in other regions of the brain. The hippocampus is an important area for the formation of memory, which is directly related to the induction of neuronal plasticity [213], and it is well known that antidepressant treatments promote various forms of plasticity, including neurogenesis, synaptogenesis and neuronal maturation in the hippocampus [214]. Specifically, it has been reported that brain-derived neurotrophic factor (BDNF) synthesis increases in the hippocampus and prefrontal cortex in depressed patients when treated with antidepressants [214]. Acute or chronic stress reduces the levels of BDNF in the dentate gyrus and the layer of pyramidal cells of the hippocampus in rodents [215], a decrease that seems to be partially mediated by glucocorticoids and possibly by an increase in serotoninergic transmission [215]. This in turn suggests that antidepressants promote the synthesis of trophic factors that then significantly impact the mood improvement seen in depressed subjects. Also, administering NIC enhances the performance of cognitive tasks in non-human primates and rodents [216], as does the administration of nicotinic agonist receptors, such as epibatidine [217], GTS-21 (a selective agonist for α7) [218], SIB-1508Y (selective for α4β2) and SIB-1553A (selective for β4) [219]. In contrast, blocking the nicotinic acetylcholine receptors deteriorates memory [220].

*In vitro*, NIC has also shown protective effects in neurons exposed to cytotoxic doses of glutamate, β-amyloid or 6-(OHDA)[221]; in the cytotoxicity induced by activating the NMDA and AMPA receptors [222]; in the neurotoxicity induced by kainic acid [223]; and in dopaminergic neurodegeneration in the nigrostriatal pathway induced by MPTP [224]. Taken together, this evidence supports the hypothesis that NIC could exert its antidepressant effect by releasing trophic factors [225]. Though there is evidence to support all these hypotheses, none excludes any of the others; but we must first clarify in detail the mechanisms through which NIC exerts its antidepressant effects.

## Conclusion

In conclusion, the results described herein suggest that NIC does indeed have antidepressant properties, though some of them are not yet clearly understood. However, it is evident that the possible mechanism of action operates by releasing serotonin from the cells in the NDR, releasing dopamine in the mesolimbic system, and exerting a neuroprotective effect. Thus, the potential therapeutic properties of NIC for treating depression must still be explored in greater detail.

## Acknowledgments

The preparation of this chapter was partially supported by the ICyT (PI-2010-14) and CONACyT (APOY-COMPL-2009, No. Proyecto: 119633).

## References

[1] Ebmeier, K.P., Donaghey, C., and Steele, J.D. (2006). Recent developments and current controversies in depression. *Lancet, 367,* 153–167.

[2] Rihmer, Z. and Angst, J. (2005). Mood disorders: epidemiology. In: Sadock, B.J. and Sadock, V.A. (Eds.), *Kaplan and Sadock's Comprehensive Textbook of Psychiatry 8th ed.* (pp. 1576–1582). Philadelphia: Lippincott Williams and Wilkins.

[3] Wong, M.L. and Licinio J. (2001). Research and treatment approaches to depression. *Nat. Rev. Neurosci., 2,* 343-351.

[4] American Psychiatric Association (2000). Major depressive Disorder. In: *Diagnostic and Statistical Manual of Mental Disorders DSM-IV-TR 4 Ed. (Text Revision) 4 ed.* (pp. 349-376). Washington: American Psychiatric Press.

[5] Adrien, J. (2002). Neurobiological bases for the relation between sleep and depression. *Sleep Med. Rev., 6(5),* 341–351.

[6] Wilson S. and Argyropoulos S. (2005). Antidepressants and sleep: a qualitative review of the literature. *Drugs, 65(7),* 927–947.

[7] Lasser, K., Boyd, J.W., Woolhandler, S., Himmelstein, D.U., McCormick, D., and Bor, D.H. (2000). Smoking and mental illness: A population-based prevalence study. *JAMA, 284(20),* 2606-2610.

[8] Salin-Pascual, R.J., Rosas, M., Jiménez-Genchi, A., Rivera-Meza, B.L. and Delgado-Parra, V. (1996). Antidepressant effect of transdermal nicotine patches in nonsmoking patients with major depression. *J. Clin. Psychiatry*, *57*, 387-389.

[9] Salin-Pascual, R.J., De la Fuente, J.R., Galicia-Polo, L., and Drucker-Colín, R. (1995). Effects of transdermal nicotine on mood and sleep in nonsmoking major depressed patients. *Psychopharmacology (Berl)*, *121,* 476-479.

[10] Benowitz, N.L. (2010). Nicotine addiction. *N. Engl. J. Med.*, *362(24),* 2295-2303.

[11] Lunell, E., Molander, L., Ekberg, K., and Wahren, J. (2000). Site of nicotine absorption from a vapour inhaler –comparison with cigarette smoking. *Eur. J. Clin. Pharmacol.*, *55,* 737-741.

[12] Gori, G.B., and Lynch, C.J. (1985). Analytical cigarette yields as predictors of smoke bioavailability. *Regul. Toxicol. Pharmacol.*, *5*, 314-326.

[13] Lee, E.M., Malson, J.L., Moolchan, E.T., and Pickworth, W.B. (2004). Quantitative comparisons between a nicotine delivery device (Eclipse) and conventional cigarette smoking. *Nicotine Tob. Res.*, *6,* 95-102.

[14] Benowitz, N.L., Jacob, P. III, Jones, R.T., and Rosenberg, J. (1982). Interindividual variability in the metabolism and cardiovascular effects of nicotine in man. *J. Pharmacol. Exp. Ther.*, *221,* 368-372.

[15] Benowitz, N.L. (1990). Clinical pharmacology of inhaled drugs of abuse: implications in understanding nicotine dependence. *NIDA Res. Monogr.*, *99,* 12-29.

[16] Rose, J.E., Behm, F.M., Westman, E.C., and Coleman RE. (1999). Arterial nicotine kinetics during cigarette smoking and intravenous nicotine administration: implications for addiction. *Drug Alcohol. Depend.*, *56,* 99-107.

[17] Benowitz, N.L., and Jacob, P. III. (1994). Metabolism of nicotine to cotinine studied by a dual stable isotope method. *Clin. Pharmacol. Ther.*, *56,* 483-493.

[18] Benowitz, N.L., and Jacob, P. III. (2001). Trans-3'-hydroxycotinine: disposition kinetics, effects and plasma levels during cigarette smoking. *Br. J. Clin. Pharmacol.*, *51*, 53-59.

[19] Armitage, A.K., Dollery, C.T., George, C.F., Houseman, T.H., Lewis, P.J., and Turner DM. (1975). Absorption and metabolism of nicotine from cigarettes. *Br. Med. J.*, *4*, 313-316.

[20] Kintz, P., Henrich, A., Cirimele, V., and Ludes, B. (1998). Nicotine monitoring in sweat with a sweat patch. *J. Chromatogr. B. Biomed. Sci. Appl.*, *705*, 357-361.

[21] Benowitz, N.L. (1988). Toxicity of nicotine: implications with regard to nicotine replacement therapy. *Prog. Clin. Biol. Res.*, *261*, 187-217.

[22] Dani, J.A., and Bertrand, D. (2007). Nicotinic acetylcholine receptors and nicotinic cholinergic mechanisms of the central nervous system. *Annu. Rev. Pharmacol. Toxicol.*, *47*, 699-729.

[23] Arias, H.R. (2000). Localization of agonist and competitive antagonist binding sites on nicotinic acetylcholine receptors. *Neurochem. Int.*, *36(7),* 595-645.

[24] Maskos, U. (2010). Role of endogenous acetylcholine in the control of the dopaminergic system via nicotinic receptors. *J. Neurochem.*, *114(3),* 641-646.

[25] Kalivas, P.W., Churchill, L., and Klitenick, M.A. (1993). GABA and enkephalin projection from the nucleus accumbens and ventral pallidum to the ventral tegmental area. *Neuroscience*, *57*, 1047-1060.

[26] Vlachou, S., and Markou, A. (2010). GABAB receptors in reward processes. *Adv. Pharmacol., 58*, 315-371.

[27] Olive, M.F., Cleva, R.M., Kalivas, P.W., and Malcolm, R.J. (2011). Glutamatergic medications for the treatment of drug and behavioral addictions. *Pharmacol. Biochem. Behav., 29(27),* 4512-4520.

[28] Ribeiro, E.B., Bettiker, R.L., Bogdanov, M., and Wurtman, R.J. (1993). Effects of systemic nicotine on serotonin release in rat brain. *Brain Res., 621*, 311-318.

[29] Watanabe, M.A., Nunes, S.O., Amarante, M.K., Guembarovski, R.L., Oda, J.M., Lima, K.W., and Fungaro, M.H. (2011). Genetic polymorphism of serotonin transporter 5-HTTLPR: involvement in smoking behaviour. *J. Genet., 90(1),* 179-185.

[30] Kane, J.K., Parker, S.L., Matta, S.G., Fu, Y., Sharp, B.M., and Li, M.D. (2000). Nicotine up-regulates expression of orexin and its receptors in rat brain. *Endocrinology, 141(10),* 3623-3629.

[31] Boyadjieva, N.I., and Sarkar, D.K. (1997). The secretory response of hypothalamic beta-endorphin neurons to acute and chronic nicotine treatments and following nicotine withdrawal. *Life Sci., 61,* 59-66.

[32] Pierzchala, K., Houdi, A.A., and Van Loon, G.R. (1987). Nicotine-induced alterations in brain regional concentrations of native and cryptic Met- and Leu-enkephalin. *Peptides*, 8, 1035-1043.

[33] Berrendero, F., Robledo, P., Trigo, J.M., Martín-García, E., and Maldonado, R. (2010). Neurobiological mechanisms involved in nicotine dependence and reward: participation of the endogenous opioid system. *Neurosci. Biobehav. Rev., 35(2)*, 220-231.

[34] Dani, J.A., and De Biasi, M. (2001). Cellular mechanisms of nicotine addiction. *Pharmacol. Biochem. Behav., 70*, 439-446.

[35] Barik, J., and Wonnacott, S. (2009). Molecular and cellular mechanisms of action of nicotine in the CNS. *Handb. Exp. Pharmacol., 192*, 173-207.

[36] Russo, P., Nastrucci, C., Alzetta, G., and Szalai, C. (2011). Tobacco habit: historical, cultural, neurobiological, and genetic features of people's relationship with an addictive drug. *Perspect. Biol. Med., 54(4),* 557-577.

[37] Picciotto, M.R., Caldarone, B.J., King, S.L., and Zachariou, V. (2000). Nicotinic receptors in the brain. Links between molecular biology and behavior. *Neuropsych-opharmacology, 22*, 451-465.

[38] Le Novere, N., Corringer, P.J., and Changeux, J.P. (2002). The diversity of subunit composition in nAChRs: evolutionary origins, physiologic and pharmacologic consequences. *J. Neurobiol., 53*, 447-456.

[39] Mineur, Y.S., and Picciotto, M.R. (2008). Genetics of nicotinic acetylcholine receptors: relevance to nicotine addiction. *Biochem. Pharmacol., 75*, 323–333.

[40] Philip, N.S., Carpenter, L.L., Tyrka, A.R., and Price, L.H. (2010). Nicotinic acetylcholine receptors and depression: a review of the preclinical and clinical literature. *Psychopharmacology (Berl), 212(1),* 1-12.

[41] Salminen, O., Murphy, K.L., McIntosh, J.M., Drago, J., Marks, M.J., Collins, A.C., and Grady, S.R. (2004). Subunit composition and pharmacology of two classes of striatal presynaptic nicotinic acetylcholine receptors mediating dopamine release in mice. *Mol. Pharmacol., 65(6),* 1526–1535.

[42] Zoli, M., Moretti, M., Zanardi, A., McIntosh, J.M., Clementi, F., and Gotti, C. (2002). Identification of the nicotinic receptor subtypes expressed on dopaminergic terminals in the rat striatum. *J. Neurosci., 22(20),* 8785–8789.

[43] Nestler, E.J., Barrot, M., DiLeone, R.J., Eisch, A.J., Gold, S.J., Monteggia, L.M. (2002). Neurobiology of depression. *Neuron*, 34, 13-25.

[44] Detera-Wadleigh, S.D., Badner, J.A., Berrettini, W.H., Yoshikawa, T., Goldin, L.R., and Turner, G., (1999). A high-density genome scan detects evidence for a bipolar-disorder susceptibility locus on 13q32 and other potential loci on 1q32 and 18p11.2. *Proc. Natl. Acad. Sci. USA*, *96*, 5604-5609.

[45] Porcelli, S., Drago, A., Fabbri, C., Gibiino, S., Calati, R., and Serretti, A. (2011). Pharmacogenetics of antidepressant response. *J. Psychiatry Neurosci., 36(2),* 87-113.

[46] Goltser-Dubner, T., Galili-Weisstub, E., and Segman, R.H. (2010). Genetics of unipolar major depressive disorder. *Isr. J. Psychiatry Relat. Sci., 47(1),* 72-82.

[47] Kato, M., and Serretti, A. (2010). Review and meta-analysis of antidepressant pharmacogenetic findings in major depressive disorder. *Mol. Psychiatry*, *15*(5), 473-500.

[48] Aan Het Rot, M., Mathew, S.J., and Charney, D.S. (2009). Neurobiological mechanisms in major depressive disorder. *CMAJ*, *180*, 305-313.

[49] Parker, K.J., Schatzberg, A.F., and Lyons, D.M. (2003). Neuroendocrine aspects of hypercortisolism in major depression. *Horm. Behav., 43*, 60–66.

[50] Raison, C.L., and Miller, A.H. (2003). When not enough is too much: the role of insufficient glucocorticoid signaling in the pathophysiology of stress-related disorders. *Am. J. Psychiatry*, *160*, 1554–1565.

[51] Lasser, K., Boyd, J.W., Woolhandler, S., Himmelstein, D.U., McCormick, D., and Bor, D.H. (2000). Smoking and mental illness: a population-based prevalence study. *JAMA*, *284*, 2606–2610.

[52] Ziedonis, D., Hitsman, B., Beckham, J.C., Zvolensky, M., Adler, L.E., Audrain-McGovern, J., Breslau, N., Brown, R.A., George, T.P., Williams, J., Calhoun, P.S., and Riley, W.T. (2008). Tobacco use and cessation in psychiatric disorders: National Institute of Mental Health report. *Nicotine Tob. Res., 10*, 1691–1715.

[53] Rihmer, Z., Angst, J. (2005). Mood disorders: epidemiology. In: Sadock, B.J., Sadock, V.A. (Eds.), *Kaplan and Sadock's Comprehensive Textbook of Psychiatry.* 8th ed. Lippincott Williams and Wilkins, pp. 1576–1582.

[54] Grant, B.F., Hasin, D.S., Chou, S.P., Stinson, F.S., and Dawson, D.A. (2004). Nicotine dependence and psychiatric disorders in the United States: results from the national epidemiologic survey on alcohol and related conditions. *Arch. Gen. Psychiatry, 61*, 1107–1115.

[55] Breslau, N., Peterson, E.L., Schultz, L.R., Chilcoat, H.D., and Andreski, P. (1998). Major depression and stages of smoking. A longitudinal investigation. *Arch. Gen. Psychiatry*, *55*, 161-166.

[56] Aubin, H.J., Rollema, H., Svensson, T.H., and Winterer, G. (2011). Smoking, quitting, and psychiatric disease: A review. *Neurosci. Biobehav. Rev., 36(1),* 271-284.

[57] Klungsøyr, O., Nygard, J.F., Sørensen, T., and Sandanger, I. (2006). Cigarette smoking and incidence of first depressive episode: an 11-year, population-based follow-up study. *Am. J. Epidemiol.*, *163*, 421–432.

[58] Steuber, T.L., and Danner, F. (2006). Adolescent smoking and depression: which comes first? *Addict. Behav.*, *31*, 133–136.

[59] Pasco, J.A., Williams, L.J., Jacka, F.N., Ng, F., Henry, M.J., Nicholson, G.C., Kotowicz, M.A., and Berk, M. (2008). Tobacco smoking as a risk factor for major depressive disorder: population-based study. *Br. J. Psychiatry*, *193*, 322–326.

[60] Pedersen, W., and Von Soest, T. (2009). Smoking, nicotine dependence and mental health among young adults: a 13-year population-based longitudinal study. *Addiction*, *104*, 129–137.

[61] Munafó, M.R., Hitsman, B., Rende, R., Metcalfe, C., and Niaura, R. (2008). Effects of progression to cigarette smoking on depressed mood in adolescents: evidence from the National Longitudinal Study of Adolescent Health. *Addiction*, *103*, 162–171.

[62] Korhonen, T., Broms, U., Varjonen, J., Romanov, K., Koskenvuo, M., Kinnunen, T., and Kaprio, J. (2007). Smoking behaviour as a predictor of depression among Finnish men and women: a prospective cohort study of adult twins. *Psychol. Med.*, *37*, 705–715.

[63] Husky, M.M., Mazure, C.M., Paliwal, P., and McKee, S.A. (2008). Gender differences in the comorbidity of smoking behavior and major depression. *Drug Alcohol. Depend.*, *93*, 176–179.

[64] Leventhal, A.M., Francione Witt, C., and Zimmerman, M. (2008). Associations between depression subtypes and substance use disorders. *Psychiatry Res.*, *161*, 43–50.

[65] Leventhal, A.M., Kahler, C.W., Ray, L.A., and Zimmerman, M. (2009). Refining the depression-nicotine dependence link: patterns of depressive symptoms in psychiatric outpatients with current, past, and no history of nicotine dependence. *Addict. Behav.*, *34*, 297–303.

[66] Hitsman, B., Borrelli, B., McChargue, D.E., Spring, B., and Niaura, R. (2003). History of depression and smoking cessation outcome: a meta-analysis. *J. Consult. Clin. Psychol.*, *71*, 657–663.

[67] Japuntich, S.J., Smith, S.S., Jorenby, D.E., Piper, M.E., Fiore, M.C., and Baker, T.B. (2007). Depression predicts smoking early but not late in a quit attempt. *Nicotine Tob. Res.*, *9*, 677–686.

[68] Kinnunen, T., Korhonen, T., and Garvey, A.J. (2008). Role of nicotine gum and pretreatment depressive symptoms in smoking cessation: twelve-month results of a randomized placebo controlled trial. *Int. J. Psychiatry Med.*, *38*, 373–389.

[69] Blalock, J.A., Robinson, J.D., Wetter, D.W., Schreindorfer, L.S., and Cinciripini, P.M. (2008). Nicotine withdrawal in smokers with current depressive disorders undergoing intensive smoking cessation treatment. *Psychol. Addict. Behav.*, *22*, 122–128.

[70] Prochaska, J.J., Hall, S.M., Tsoh, J.Y., Eisendrath, S., Rossi, J.S., Redding, C.A., Rosen, A.B., Meisner, M., Humfleet, G.L., and Gorecki, J.A. (2008). Treating tobacco dependence in clinically depressed smokers: effect of smoking cessation on mental health functioning. *Am. J. Public Health*, *98*, 446–448.

[71] Hughes, J.R., 2007. Depression during tobacco abstinence. *Nicotine Tob. Res.*, *9*, 443–446.

[72] Catley, D., Harris, K.J., Okuyemi, K.S., Mayo, M.S., Pankey, E., and Ahluwalia, J.S. (2005). The influence of depressive symptoms on smoking cessation among African Americans in a randomized trial of bupropion. *Nicotine Tob. Res*, *7*, 859–870.

[73] Killen, J.D., Fortmann, S.P., Schatzberg, A., Hayward, C., and Varady, A. (2003). Onset of major depression during treatment for nicotine dependence. *Addict. Behav.*, *28*, 461–470.

[74] Strong, D.R., Kahler, C.W., Ramsey, S.E., Abrantes, A., and Brown, R.A. (2004). Nicotine withdrawal among adolescents with acute psychopathology: an item response analysis. *Nicotine Tob. Res.*, *6*, 547–557.

[75] Covey, L.S., Glassman, A.H., and Stetner, F. (1990). Depression and depressive symptoms in smoking cessation. *Compr. Psychiatry*, *31*, 350–354.

[76] Covey, L., Glassman, A., and Stetner, F. (1997). Major depression following smoking cessation. *Am. J. Psychiatry*, *154*, 263–265.

[77] Covey, L.S., Glassman, A.H., and Stetner, F. (1998). Cigarette smoking and major depression. *J. Addict. Dis.*, *17*, 35–46.

[78] Thorndike, A.N., Regan, S., McKool, K., Pasternak, R.C., Swartz, S., Torres-Finnerty, N., and Rigotti, N.A. (2008). Depressive symptoms and smoking cessation after hospitalization for cardiovascular disease. *Arch. Intern. Med.*, *168*, 186–191.

[79] Breslau N, Peterson EL, Schultz LR, Chilcoat HD, Andreski P. (1998). Major depression and stages of smoking. A longitudinal investigation. *Arch. Gen. Psychiatry*, *55*, 161-166.

[80] Perez, G.H., Nicolau, J.C., Romano, B.W., and Laranjeira, R. (2008). Depression: a predictor of smoking relapse in a 6-month follow-up after hospitalization for acute coronary syndrome. *Eur. J. Cardiovasc. Prev. Rehabil.*, *15*, 89-94.

[81] Perez, X.A., Bordia, T., McIntosh, J.M., Grady, S.R., and Quik, M. (2008). Long-term nicotine treatment differentially regulates striatal alpha6alpha4beta2* and alpha6(nonalpha4)beta2* nAChR expression and function. *Mol. Pharmacol.*, *74*, 844–853.

[82] Surtees, P.G., Wainwright, N.W., Luben, R.N., Wareham, N.J., Bingham, S.A., and Khaw, K.T. (2008). Depression and ischemic heart disease mortality: evidence from the EPIC-Norfolk United Kingdom prospective cohort study. *Am. J. Psychiatry*, *165*, 515–523.

[83] Cuijpers, P., and Schoevers, R.A. (2004). Increased mortality in depressive disorders: a review. *Curr. Psychiatry Rep.*, *6*, 430–437.

[84] Pozuelo, L., Tesar, G., Zhang, J., Penn, M., Franco, K., and Jiang, W. (2009). Depression and heart disease: what do we know, and where are we headed? *Cleve. Clin. J. Med.*, *76*, 59–70.

[85] Oerlemans, M.E., van den Akker, M., Schuurman, A.G., Kellen, E., and Buntinx, F. (2007). A metaanalysis on depression and subsequent cancer risk. *Clin. Pract. Epidemol. Ment. Health, 3*, 29-40.

[86] Markou, A., Kosten, T.R., and Koob, G.F. (1998). Neurobiological similarities in depression and drug dependence: a self-medication hypothesis. *Neuropsychopharmacology*, *18*, 135-174.

[87] Duncan, B., and Rees, D.I. (2005). Effect of smoking on depressive symptomatology: a reexamination of data from the National Longitudinal Study of Adolescent. *Health Am. J. Epidemiol.*, *162*, 461–470.

[88] Picciotto, M.R. (2003). Nicotine as a modulator of behavior: beyond the inverted U. *Trends Pharmacol. Sci.*, *24*, 493–499.

[89] Mineur, Y.S., and Picciotto, M.R. (2010). Nicotine receptors and depression: revisiting and revising the cholinergic hypothesis. *Trends Pharmacol. Sci., 31(12),* 580-586.
[90] Elgamal, S., and MacQueen, G. (2008). Galantamine as an adjunctive treatment in major depression. *J. Clin. Psychopharmacol.*, *28*, 357–359.
[91] Shytle, R.D., Silver, A.A., Lukas, R.J., Newman, M.B., Sheehan, D.V., and Sanberg, P.R. (2002). Nicotinic acetylcholine receptors as targets for antidepressants. *Mol. Psychiatry*, *7*, 525–535.
[92] Furey, M.L., and Drevets, W.C. (2006). Antidepressant efficacy of the antimuscarinic drug scopolamine: a randomized, placebo-controlled clinical trial. *Arch. Gen. Psychiatry*, *63*, 1121–1129.
[93] Picciotto, M.R., Addy, N.A., Mineur, Y.S., and Brunzell, D.H. (2008). It is not ''either/or'': activation and desensitization of nicotinic acetylcholine receptors both contribute to behaviors related to nicotine addiction and mood. *Prog. Neurobiol.*, *84*, 329–342.
[94] Philip, N.S., Carpenter, L.L., Tyrka, A.R., Whiteley, L.B., and Price, L.H. (2009). Varenicline augmentation in depressed smokers: an 8-week, open-label study. *J. Clin. Psychiatry*, *70(7),* 1026-1031.
[95] Lodge, N.J., Li, Y.W., 2008. Ion channels as potential targets for the treatment of depression. *Curr. Opin. Drug Discov. Devel*, *11*, 633-641.
[96] Patterson, F., Jepson, C., Strasser, A.A., Loughead, J., Perkins, K.A., Gur, R.C., Frey, J.M., Siegel, S., and Lerman, C. (2009). Varenicline improves mood and cognition during smoking abstinence. *Biol. Psychiatry*, *65*, 144–149.
[97] George, T.P., Sacco, K.A., Vessicchio, J.C., Weinberger, A.H., and Shytle, R.D. (2008). Nicotinic antagonist augmentation of selective serotonin reuptake inhibitor refractory major depressive disorder: a preliminary study. *J. Clin. Psychopharmacol.*, *28*, 340–344.
[98] Popik, P., Kozela, E., and Krawczyk, M. (2003). Nicotine and nicotinic receptor antagonists potentiate the antidepressant-like effects of imipramine and citalopram. *Br. J. Pharmacol.*, *139*, 1196–1202.
[99] Vázquez-Palacios, G., Bonilla-Jaime, H., and Velázquez-Moctezuma, J. (2004). Antidepressant-like effects of the acute and chronic administration of nicotine in the rat forced swimming test and its interaction with fluoxetine. *Pharmacol. Biochem. Behav.*, *78*, 165–169.
[100] Vázquez-Palacios, G., Bonilla-Jaime, H., Velázquez-Moctezuma, J. (2005). Antidepressant effects of nicotine and fluoxetine in an animal model of depression induced by neonatal treatment with clomipramine. *J. Prog. Neuropsychopharmacol. Biol. Psychiatry*, *29(1*), 39-46.
[101] Rabenstein, R.L., Caldarone, B.J., and Picciotto, M.R. (2006). The nicotinic antagonist mecamylamine has antidepressant-like effects in wild-type but not beta2- or alpha7-nicotinic acetylcholine receptor subunit knockout mice. *Psychopharmacology (Berl)*, *189*, 395–401.
[102] Pacher, P., and Kecskemeti, V. (2004). Trends in the development of new antidepressants. Is there a light at the end of the tunnel? *Curr. Med. Chem.*, *11*, 925–943.

[103] Andreasen, J.T., and Redrobe, J.P. (2009). Antidepressant-like effects of nicotine and mecamylamine in the mouse forced swim and tail suspension tests: role of strain, test and sex. *Behav. Pharmacol.*, 20(3), 286-295.

[104] Caldarone, B.J., Harrist, A., Cleary, M.A., Beech, R.D., King, S.L., and Picciotto, M.R. (2004). High-affinity nicotinic acetylcholine receptors are required for antidepressant effects of amitriptyline on behavior and hippocampal cell proliferation. *Biol. Psychiatry, 56*, 657–664.

[105] Roche, M., Harkin, A., and Kelly, J.P. (2007). Chronic fluoxetine treatment attenuates stressor-induced changes in temperature, heart rate, and neuronal activation in the olfactory bulbectomized rat. *Neuropsychopharmacology*, *32*, 1312–1320.

[106] Moreno-Coutino, A., Calderón-Ezquerro, C., and Drucker-Colín, R. (2007). Long term changes in sleep and depressive symptoms of smokers in abstinence. *Nicotine Tob. Res.*, *9*, 389-396.

[107] Semba, J., Mataki, C., Yamada, S., Nankai, M., and Toru, M. (1998). Anti-depressantlike effects of chronic nicotine on learned helplessness paradigm in rats. *Biol. Psychiatry, 43*, 389-391.

[108] Djurić, V.J., Dunn, E., Overstreet, D.H., Dragomir, A., and Steiner, M. (1999). Antidepressant effect of ingested nicotine in female rats of Flinders resistant and sensitive lines. *Physiol Behav*, *67(4),* 533-537.

[109] Tizabi, Y., Rezvani, A.H., Russell, L.T., Tyler, K.Y., and Overstreet, D.H. (2000). Depressive characteristics of FSL rats: involvement of central nicotinic receptors. *Pharmacol. Biochem. Behav.*, *66*, 73–77.

[110] Tizabi, Y., Getachew, B., Rezvani, A.H., Hauser, S.R., and Overstreet, D.H. (2009). Antidepressant-like effects of nicotine and reduced nicotinic receptor binding in the Fawn-Hooded rat, an animal model of co-morbid depression and alcoholism. *Prog. Neuropsychopharmacol. Biol. Psychiatry, 33*, 398–402.

[111] Slotkin, T.A., Tate, C.A., Cousins, M.M., and Seidler, F.J. (2006). Prenatal nicotine exposure alters the responses to subsequent nicotine administration and withdrawal in adolescence: serotonin receptors and cell signaling. *Neuropsychopharmacology*, *31*, 2462-2475.

[112] Ferguson, S.M., Brodkin, J.D., Lloyd, G.K., and Menzaghi, F. (2000). Antidepressant-like effects of the subtype-selective nicotinic acetylcholine receptor agonist, SIB-1508Y, in the learned helplessness rat model of depression. *Psychopharmacology* (*Berl*), *152(3),* 295–303.

[113] Haro, R., and Drucker-Colín, R. A two-year study on the effects of nicotine and its withdrawal on mood and sleep. *Pharmacopsychiatry*. *37(5),* 221-227.

[114] Millan, M.J. (2006). Multi-target strategies for the improved treatment of depressive states: conceptual foundations and neuronal substrates, drug discovery and therapeutic application. *Pharmacol. Ther.*, *110*, 135–370.

[115] Banasr, M., and Duman, R.S. (2007). Regulation of neurogenesis and gliogenesis by stress and antidepressant treatment. *CNS Neurol. Disord. Drug Targets*, *6,* 311–320.

[116] Lucassen, P.J., Meerlo, P., Naylor, A.S., Van Dam, A.M., Dayer, A.G., Fuchs, E., Oomen, C.A., and Czéh, B. (2010). Regulation of adult neurogenesis by stress, sleep disruption, exercise and inflammation: Implications for depression and antidepressant action. *Eur. Neuropsychopharmacol.*, *20(1),* 1-17.

[117] Andreasen, J.T., and Redrobe, J.P. (2009). Nicotine, but not mecamylamine, enhances antidepressant-like effects of citalopram and reboxetine in the mouse forced swim and tail suspension tests. *Behav. Brain Res., 197(1),* 150-156.

[118] Spring, B., Pingitore, R., and McChargue, D.E. (2003). Reward value of cigarette smoking for comparably heavy smoking schizophrenic, depressed, and nonpatient smokers. *Am. J. Psychiatry, 160*, 316–322.

[119] Cardenas, L., Tremblay, L.K., Naranjo, C.A., Herrmann, N., Zack, M., and Busto, U.E. (2002). Brain reward system activity in major depression and comorbid nicotine dependence. *J. Pharmacol. Exp. Ther., 302*, 1265–1271.

[120] Martin-Soelch, C. (2009). Is depression associated with dysfunction of the central reward system? *Biochem. Soc. Trans, 37(1),* 313–317.

[121] Mineur, Y.S., Somenzi, O., and Picciotto, M.R. (2007). Cytisine, a partial agonist of high affinity nicotinic acetylcholine receptors, has antidepressant-like properties in male C57BL/6J mice. *Neuropharmacology, 52*, 1256–1262.

[122] Cunningham, J.T., Mifflin, S.W., Gould, G.G., and Frazer, A. (2008). Induction of c-Fos and DeltaFosB immunoreactivity in rat brain by vagal nerve stimulation. *Neuropsychopharmacology, 33*, 1884–1895.

[123] Andreasen, J.T., Olsen, G.M., Wiborg, O., and Redrobe, J.P. (2009). Antidepressant-like effects of nicotinic acetylcholine receptor antagonists, but not agonists, in the mouse forced swim and mouse tail suspension tests. *J. Psychopharmacol. 23(7),* 797-804.

[124] Popik, P., Krawczyk, M., Kos, T., Nalepa, I., Kowalska, M., Witarski, T., Antkiewicz-Michaluk, L., and Vetulani, J. (2005). Nicotine produces antidepressant-like actions: behavioral and neurochemical evidence. *Eur. J. Pharmacol., 515*, 128–133.

[125] Fortunato, J.J., Réus, G.Z., Kirsch, T.R., Stringari, R.B., Fries, G.R., Kapczinski, F., Hallak, J.E., Zuardi, A.W., Crippa, J.A., and Quevedo, J. (2010). Effects of beta-carboline harmine on behavioral and physiological parameters observed in the chronic mild stress model: further evidence of antidepressant properties. *Brain Res. Bull., 81(4-5),* 491-496.

[126] Fortunato, J.J., Réus, G.Z., Kirsch, T.R., Stringari, R.B., Fries, G.R., Kapczinski, F., Hallak, J.E., Zuardi, A.W., Crippa, J.A., and Quevedo, J. (2010). Chronic administration of harmine elicits antidepressant-like effects and increases BDNF levels in rat hippocampus. *J. Neural Transm., 117(10),* 1131-1137.

[127] Herraiz, T., and Chaparro, C. (2005). Human monoamine oxidase is inhibited by tobacco smoke: beta-carboline alkaloids act as potent and reversible inhibitors. *Biochem Biophys. Res. Comm., 326(2),* 378-386.

[128] Malone, K.M., Waternaux, C., Haas, G.L., Cooper, T.B., Li, S., and Mann, J.J. (2003). Cigarette smoking, suicidal behavior, and serotonin function in major psychiatric disorders. *Am. J. Psychiatry, 160*, 773–779.

[129] Spring, B., Hitsman, B., Pingitore, R., McChargue, D.E., Gunnarsdottir, D., Corsica, J., Pergadia, M., Doran, N., Crayton, J.W., Baruah, S., and Hedeker, D. (2007). Effect of tryptophan depletion on smokers and nonsmokers with and without history of major depression. *Biol. Psychiatry, 61*, 70–77.

[130] Carroll, B.J., Cassidy, F., Naftolowitz, D., Tatham, N.E., Wilson, W.H., Iranmanesh, A., Liu, P.Y., and Veldhuis, J.D. (2007). Pathophysiology of hypercortisolism in depression. *Acta Psychiatr. Scand., 433*, 90-103.

[131] Badrick, E., Kirschbaum, C., and Kumari, M. (2007). The relationship between smoking status and cortisol secretion. *J. Clin. Endocrinol. Metab., 92(3),* 819-824.

[132] Mendelson, J.H., Goletiani, N., Sholar, M.B., Siegel, A.J., and Mello, N.K. (2008). Effects of smoking successive low- and high-nicotine cigarettes on hypothalamic-pituitary-adrenal axis hormones and mood in men. *Neuropsychopharmacology, 33(4),* 749-760.

[133] Richards, J.M., Stipelman, B.A., Bornovalova, M.A., Daughters, S.B., Sinha, R., and Lejuez, C.W. (2011). Biological mechanisms underlying the relationship between stress and smoking: state of the science and directions for future work. *Biol. Psychol., 88(1),* 1-12.

[134] Zafir, A., Ara, A., and Banu, N. (2009). In vivo antioxidant status: a putative target of antidepressant action. *Prog. Neuropsychopharmacol. Biol. Psychiatry*, 33(2), 220-228.

[135] Decramer, M. (2008). Pulmonary rehabilitation 2007: from bench to practice and back. *Clin. Invest. Med., 31(5),* E312-318.

[136] Agusti, A., and Soriano, J.B. (2008). COPD as a systemic disease. *COPD*, 5(3-2):138.

[137] Parrott, A.C. (2006). Nicotine psychobiology: how chronic-dose prospective studies can illuminate some of the theoretical issues from acute-dose research. *Psychopharmacology* (*Berl*), *184(3-4),* 567-576.

[138] Aronson, K.R., Almeida, D.M., Stawski, R.S., Klein, L.C., and Kozlowski, L.T. (2008). Smoking is associated with worse mood on stressful days: results from a national diary study. *Ann Behav Med, 36(3),* 259-269.

[139] McCaffery, J.M., Papandonatos, G.D., Stanton, C., Lloyd-Richardson, E.E., and Niaura, R. (2008). Depressive symptoms and cigarette smoking in twins from the National Longitudinal. Study of Adolescent Health. *Health Psychol., 27(3),* S207-215.

[140] Kodl, M.M., Fu, S.S., Willenbring, M.L., Gravely, A., Nelson, D.B., and Joseph, A.M. (2008). The impact of depressive symptoms on alcohol and cigarette consumption following treatment for alcohol and nicotine dependence. *Alcohol. Clin. Exp. Res., 32(1),* 92-99.

[141] Lyons, M., Hitsman, B., Xian, H., Panizzon, M.S., Jerskey, B.A., Santangelo, S., Grant, M.D., Rende, R., Eisen, S., Eaves, L., and Tsuang, M.T. A twin study of smoking, nicotine dependence, and major depression in men. *Nicotine Tob. Res., 10(1),* 97-108.

[142] Korhonen, T., Broms, U., Varjonen, J., Romanov, K., Koskenvuo, M., Kinnunen, T., and Kaprio, J. (2007). Smoking behaviour as a predictor of depression among Finnish men and women: a prospective cohort study of adult twins. *Psychol. Med., 37(5),* 705-715.

[143] Perkins, K.A., Lerman, C., Grottenthaler, A., Ciccocioppo, M.M., Milanak, M., Conklin, C.A., Bergen, A.W., and Benowitz, N.L. (2008). Dopamine and opioid gene variants are associated with increased smoking reward and reinforcement owing to negative mood. *Behav. Pharmacol., S19(5-6),* 641-649.

[144] Ray. R., Ruparel, K., Newberg, A., Wileyto, E.P., Loughead, J.W., Divgi, C., Blendy, J.A., Logan, J., Zubieta, J.K., and Lerman, C. (2011). Human Mu Opioid Receptor (OPRM1 A118G) polymorphism is associated with brain mu-opioid receptor binding potential in smokers. *Proc. Natl. Acad. Sci. USA*, *108(22),* 9268-9273.

[145] Fergusson, D.M., Woodward, L.J., and Horwood, L.J. (1998). Maternal smoking during pregnancy and psychiatric adjustment in late adolescence. *Arch. Gen. Psychiatry*, *55(8),* 721-727.

[146] Dwyer, J.B., Broide, R.S., and Leslie, F.M. (2008). Nicotine and brain development. *Birth Defects Res. C. Embryo Today, 84(1),* 30-44.

[147] Heath, C.J., and Picciotto, M.R.(2009). Nicotine-induced plasticity during development: modulation of the cholinergic system and long-term consequences for circuits involved in attention and sensory processing. *Neuropharmacology, 56(1),* 254-262.

[148] Durazzo, T.C., Meyerhoff, D.J., and Nixon, S.J. (2010). Chronic cigarette smoking: implications for neurocognition and brain neurobiology. *Int. J. Environ. Res. Public Health, 7(10),* 3760-91.

[149] Swan, G.E., and Lessov-Schlaggar, C.N. (2007). The effects of tobacco smoke and nicotine on cognition and the brain. *Neuropsychol. Rev., 17*, 259–273.

[150] Haustein, K.O. (1999). Smoking tobacco, microcirculatory changes and the role of nicotine. *Int. J. Clin. Pharmacol. Ther., 37*, 76–85.

[151] Fowles, J., Bates, M., and Noiton, D. (2000). The chemical constituents in cigarettes and cigarette smoke: priorities for harm reduction. Epidemiology and toxicology group; Porirua, New Zealand, pp. 1–65.

[152] Brody, A.L., Mandelkern, M.A., Jarvik, M.E., Lee, G.S., Smith, E.C., Huang, J.C., Bota, R.G., Bartzokis, G., and London, E.D. (2004). Differences between smokers and nonsmokers in regional gray matter volumes and densities. *Biol. Psychiatry, 55*, 77–84.

[153] Ross, B., and Bluml, S. (2001). Magnetic resonance spectroscopy of the human brain. *Anat. Rec., 265*, 54–84.

[154] Ferrea, S., and Winterer, G. (2009). Neuroprotective and neurotoxic effects of nicotine. *Pharmacopsychiatry. 42(6),* 255-265.

[155] Buccafusco, J.J., Letchworth, S.R., Bencherif, M., and Lippiello, P.M. (2005). Long-lasting cognitive improvement with nicotinic receptor agonists: mechanisms of pharmacokinetic-pharmacodynamic discordance. *Trends Pharmacol. Sci., 26*, 352-360.

[156] Rattray, M. (2001). Is there nicotinic modulation of nerve growth factor? Implications for cholinergic therapies in Alzheimer's disease. *Biol. Psychiatry, 49*, 185-193.

[157] Tizabi, Y., Overstreet, D.H., Rezvani, A.H., Louis, V.A., Clark, E. Jr, and Janowsky, D.S. (1999). Antidepressant effects of nicotine in an animal model of depression. *Psychopharmacology (Berl), 142*, 193-199.

[158] Buckley, M.J., Surowy, C., Meyer, M., and Curzon, P. (2004). Mechanism of action of A-85380 in an animal model of depression. *Prog. Neuropsychopharmacol. Biol. Psychiatry, 28*, 723–730.

[159] Nakamura, K., andTanaka, Y. (2001). Antidepressant-like effects of aniracetam in aged rats and its mode of action. *Psychopharmacology, 158*, 205–212.

[160] Shioda, N., Yamamoto, Y., Han, F., Moriguchi, S., Yamaguchi, Y., Hino, M., and Fukunaga, K. (2010). A novel cognitive enhancer, ZSET1446/ST101, promotes hippocampal neurogenesis and ameliorates depressive behavior in olfactory bulbectomized mice. *J. Pharmacol. Exp. Ther., 333*(1), 43-50.

[161] Caldarone, B.J., Wang, D., Paterson, N.E., Manzano, M., Fedolak, A., Cavino, K., Kwan, M., Hanania, T., Chellappan, S.K., Kozikowski, A.P., Olivier, B., Picciotto, M.R., and Ghavami, A. (2011). Dissociation between duration of action in the forced swim test in mice and nicotinic acetylcholine receptor occupancy with sazetidine, varenicline, and 5-I-A85380. *Psychopharmacology (Berl), 217(2),* 199-210.

[162] Mineur, Y.S., Somenzi, O., and Picciotto, M.R. (2007). Cytisine, a partial agonist of high-affinity nicotinic acetylcholine receptors, has antidepressant-like properties in male C57BL/6J mice. *Neuropharmacology, 52(5),* 1256-1262.

[163] Andreasen, J.T., Olsen, G.M., Wiborg, O., and Redrobe, J.P. (2009). Antidepressant-like effects of nicotinic acetylcholine receptor antagonists, but not agonists, in the mouse forced swim and mouse tail suspension tests. *J. Psychopharmacol., 23(7),* 797-804.

[164] Lippiello, P.M., Beaver, J.S., Gatto, G.J., James, J.W., Jordan, K.G., Traina, V.M., Xie, J., and Bencherif, M. (2008). TC-5214 (S-(+)-mecamylamine): a neuronal nicotinic receptor modulator with antidepressant activity. *CNS Neurosci. Ther., 14(4),* 266-277.

[165] Rabenstein, R.L., Caldarone, B.J., and Picciotto, M.R. (2006). The nicotinic antagonist mecamylamine has antidepressant-like effects in wild-type but not beta2- or alpha7-nicotinic acetylcholine receptor subunit knockout mice. *Psychopharmacology (Berl), 189(3),* 395-401.

[166] Hall, B.J., Pearson, L.S., and Buccafusco, J.J. (2010). Effect of the use-dependent, nicotinic receptor antagonist BTMPS in the forced swim test and elevated plus maze after cocaine discontinuation in rats. *Neurosci. Lett., 474(2),* 84-87.

[167] Page, M.E., Detke, M.J., Dalvi, A., Kirby, L.G., and Lucki, I. (1999). Serotonergic mediation of the effects of fluoxetine, but not desipramine, in the rat forced swimming test. *Psychopharmacology (Berl), 147(2),* 162-167.

[168] Seth, P., Cheeta, S., Tucci, S., and File, S.E. (2002). Nicotinic–serotonergic interactions in brain and behavior. *Pharmacol. Biochem. Behav., 71,* 795–805.

[169] Guzmán-Marín, R., Alam, M.N., Mihailescu, S., Szymusiak, R., McGinty, D., and Drucker-Colin, R. (2001). Subcutaneous administration of nicotine changes dorsal raphe serotonergic neurons discharge rate during REM sleep. *Brain Res., 888*, 321-325.

[170] Ribeiro, E.B., Bettiker, R.L., Bogdanov, M., and Wurtman, R.J. (1993). Effects of systemic nicotine on serotonin release in rat brain. *Brain Res., 621,* 311-318.

[171] Mihailescu, S., Guzmán-Marín, R., and Drucker-Colin, R. (2001). Nicotine stimulation of dorsal raphe neurons: effects on laterodorsal and pedunculopontine neurons. *Eur. Neuropsychopharmacol., 11*, 359-366.

[172] Chang, B., Daniele, C., Gallagher, K., Madonia, M., Mitchum, R.D., Barrett, L., Vezina, P., and McGehee, D.S. (2011). Nicotinic excitation of serotonergic projections from dorsal raphe to the nucleus accumbens. *J. Neurophysiol., 106*, 801–808.

[173] Mannucci, C., Tedesco, M., Bellomo, M., Caputi, A.P., and Calapai, G. (2006). Long term effects of nicotine on the forced swimming test in mice: an experimental model for the study of depression caused by smoke. *Neurochem. Int.*, 49, 481-486.

[174] Cheeta, S., Irvine, E.E., Tucci, S., Sandhu, J., and File, S.E. (2001). In adolescence, female rats are more sensitive to the anxiolytic effect of nicotine than are male rats. *Neuropsychopharmacology*, *25*, 601-607.

[175] Arango, V., Underwood, M.D., Boldrini, M., Tamir, H., Kassir, S.A., and Hsiung, S. (2001). Serotonin-1A receptors, serotonin transporter binding and serotonin transporter mRNA expression in the brainstem of depressed suicide victims. *Neuropsychopharmacology, 25*, 892–903.

[176] Carr, G.V., and Lucki, I. (2011). The role of serotonin receptor subtypes in treating depression: a review of animal studies. *Psychopharmacology (Berl), 213(2-3),* 265-287.

[177] Mihailescu, S., Palomero-Rivero, M., Meade-Huerta, P., Maza-Flores, A., and Drucker-Colín, R. (1998). Effects of nicotine and mecamylamine on rat dorsal raphe neurons. *Eur. J. Pharmacol., 360,* 31-36.

[178] Li, X., Rainnie, D.G., McCarley, R.W., and Greene, R.W. Presynaptic nicotinic receptors facilitate monoaminergic transmission. *J. Neurosci., 18,* 1904-1912.

[179] Savitz, J., Lucki, I., and Drevets, W.C. (2009). 5-HT(1A) receptor function in major depressive disorder. *Prog. Neurobiol., 88(1),* 17-31.

[180] Bose, S.K., Mehta, M.A., Selvaraj, S., Howes, O.D., Hinz, R., Rabiner, E.A., Grasby, P.M., Turkheimer, F.E., and Murthy, V. (2011). Presynaptic 5-HT1A is related to 5-HTT receptor density in the human brain. *Neuropsychopharmacology, 36(11),* 2258-2265.

[181] Kenny, P.J., File, S.E., and Rattray, M. (2001). Nicotine regulates 5-HT(1A) receptor gene expression in the cerebral cortex and dorsal hippocampus. *Eur. J. Neurosci., 13(6),* 1267–1271.

[182] Savitz. J., Lucki, I., and Drevets, W.C. (2009). 5-HT(1A) receptor function in major depressive disorder. *Prog. Neurobiol., 88(1),* 17–31.

[183] Rasmussen, K., and Czachura, J.F. (1997). Nicotine withdrawal leads to increased sensitivity of serotonergic neurons to the 5-HT1A agonist 8-OH-DPAT. *Psychopharmacology (Berl), 133(4),* 343–346.

[184] Chaput, Y., Araneda, R.C., and Andrade, R. (1990). Pharmacological and functional analysis of a novel serotonin receptor in the rat hippocampus. *Eur. J. Pharmacol., 182(3),* 441–456.

[185] Le Poul, E., Laaris, N., Doucet, E., Laporte, A.M., Hamon, M., and Lanfumey, L. (1995). Early desensitization of somato-dendritic 5-HT1A autoreceptors in rats treated with fluoxetine or paroxetine. *Naunyn-Schmiedeberg's Arch. Pharmacol., 352(2),* 141–148.

[186] Le Poul, E., Boni, C., Hanoun, N., Laporte, A.M., Laaris, N., and Chauveau, J. (2000). Differential adaptation of brain 5-HT1A and 5-HT1B receptors and 5-HT transporter in rats treated chronically with fluoxetine. *Neuropharmacology, 39(1),* 110–122.

[187] Blier, P., and de Montigny, C. (1999). Serotonin and drug-induced therapeutic responses in major depression, obsessive–compulsive and panic disorders. *Neuropsychopharmacology, 21,* 91S–98S.

[188] Lesch, K.P., and Heils, A. Serotonergic gene transcriptional control regions: targets for antidepressant drug development? *Int. J. Neuropsychopharmacol., 3(1),* 67–79.

[189] Kreiss, D.S., and Lucki, I. (1995). Effects of acute and repeated administration of antidepressant drugs on extracellular levels of 5-hydroxytryptamine measured in vivo. *J. Pharmacol. Exp. Ther., 1274,* 866–876.

[190] Rutter, J.J., Gundlah, C., and Auerbach, S.B. (1994). Increase in extracellular serotonin produced by uptake inhibitors is enhanced after chronic treatment with fluoxetine. *Neurosci. Lett., 171,* 183–186.

[191] Livingstone, P.D., and Wonnacott, S. (2009). Nicotinic acetylcholine receptors and the ascending dopamine pathways. *Biochem. Pharmacol., 78,* 744-755.

[192] Ainsworth, K., Smith, S.E., Zetterstrom, T.S., Pei, Q., Franklin, M., and Sharp, T. (1998). Effect of antidepressant drugs on dopamine D1 and D2 receptor expression and dopamine release in the nucleus accumbens of the rat. *Psychopharmacology (Berl), 140,* 470-477.

[193] Collu. M., Poggiu, A.S., Devoto, P., and Serra, G. (1997). Behavioural sensitization of mesolimbic dopamine D2 receptors in chronic fluoxetine-treated rats. *Eur. J. Pharmacol., 322,* 123-127.

[194] Imperato, A., Mulas, A., and Di Chiara, G. (1986). Nicotine preferentially stimulates dopamine release in the limbic system of freely moving rats. *Eur. J. Pharmacol. 132,* 337-338.

[195] Nomikos, G.G., Damsma, G., Wenkstern, D., and Fibiger, H.C. Chronic desipramine enhances amphetamine-induced increases in interstitial concentrations of dopamine in the nucleus accumbens. *Eur. J. Pharmacol., 195*, 63-73.

[196] Pidoplichko, V.I., DeBiasi, M., Williams, J.T., and Dani, J.A. (1997). Nicotine activates and desensitizes midbrain dopamine neurons. *Nature, 390,* 401-404.

[197] Benwell, M.E., Balfour, D.J., and Birrell, C.E. (1995). Desensitization of the nicotine induced mesolimbic dopamine responses during constant infusion with nicotine. *Br. J. Pharmacol., 114,* 454-460.

[198] Hildebrand, B.E., Nomikos, G.G., Hertel, P., Schilstrom, B., and Svensson, T.H. (1998). Reduced dopamine output in the nucleus accumbens but not in the medial prefrontal cortex in rats displaying a mecamylamine-precipitated nicotine withdrawal syndrome. *Brain Res., 779,* 214-225.

[199] Epping-Jordan, M.P., Watkins, S.S., Koob, G.F., and Markou, A. (1998). Dramatic decreases in brain reward function during nicotine withdrawal. *Nature, 393*, 76-79.

[200] Dani, J.A., and Bertrand, D. (1998). Nicotinic acetylcholine receptors and nicotinic cholinergic mechanisms of the central nervous system. *Annu. Rev. Pharmacol. Toxicol., 47*, 699-729.

[201] Clarke, P.B., and Pert, A. (1985). Autoradiographic evidence for nicotine receptors on nigrostriatal and mesolimbic dopaminergic neurons. *Brain Res., 348(2),* 355-358.

[202] Zhou, F.M., Wilson, C., and Dani, J.A. (2003). Muscarinic and nicotinic cholinergic mechanisms in the mesostriatal dopamine systems. *Neuroscientist, 9,* 3609-3614.

[203] Le Novère, N., Corringer, P.J., and Changeux, J.P. (2002). The diversity of subunit composition in nAChRs: evolutionary origins, physiologic, and pharmacologic consequences. *J. Neurobiol., 53*, 447–456.

[204] Watkins, S.S., Epping-Jordan, M.P., Koob, G.F., and Markou, A. Blockade of nicotine self-administration with nicotinic antagonists in rats. *Pharmacol. Biochem. Behav., 62(4),* 743-751.

[205] Jones, S., Sudweeks, S., and Yakel, J.L. Nicotinic receptors in the brain: correlating physiology with function. *Trends Neurosci., 22(12),* 555-561.

[206] Zheng-Xiong, Xi. (2010). Preclinical pharmacology, efficacy, and safety of varenicline in smoking cessation and clinical utility in high-risk patients. *Drug Health Patient Saf., 2,* 39-48.

[207] Rollema, H., Guanowsky, V., Mineur, Y.S., Shrikhande, A., Coe, J.W., Seymour, P.A., Picciotto, M.R. (2009). Varenicline has antidepressant-like activity in the forced swim test and augments sertraline's effect. *Eur. J. Pharmacol., 605(1-3),* 114-116.

[208] Ferrea, S., and Winterer, G. (2009). Neuroprotective and neurotoxic effects of nicotine. *Pharmacopsychiatry, 42(6),* 255-265.

[209] Mudo G, , Belluardo, N., and Fuxe, K. (2007). Nicotinic receptor agonists as neuroprotective/neurotrophic drugs. Progress in molecular mechanisms. *J. Neural. Transm., 114,* 135-147.

[210] Navarro, H.A., Seidler, F.J., Eylers, J.P., Baker, F.E., Dobbins, S.S., Lappi, S.E. (1989). Effects of prenatal nicotine exposure on development of central and peripheral cholinergic neurotransmitter systems. Evidence for cholinergic trophic influences in developing brain. *J. Pharmacol. Exp. Ther., 251,* 894-900.

[211] Pugh, P.C., and Berg, D.K. Neuronal acetylcholine receptors that bind alpha-bungarotoxin mediate neurite retraction in a calcium-dependent manner. *J. Neurosci., 14,* 889-896.

[212] Huerta, P.T., and Lisman, J.E. (1993). Heightened synaptic plasticity of hippocampal CA1 neurons during a cholinergically induced rhythmic state. *Nature, 364,* 723-725.

[213] Castren, E., Voikar, V., and Rantamaki, T. Role of neurotrophic factors in depression. *Curr. Opin. Pharmacol., 7,* 18-21.

[214] Smith, M.A., Makino, S., Kvetnansky, R., and Post, R.M. (1995). Stress and glucocorticoids affect the expression of brain-derived neurotrophic factor and neurotrophin-3 mRNAs in the hippocampus. *J. Neurosci., 15,* 1768-1777.

[215] Buccafusco, J.J., Letchworth, S.R., Bencherif, M., and Lippiello, P.M. Long-lasting cognitive improvement with nicotinic receptor agonists: mechanisms of pharmacokinetic-pharmacodynamic discordance. *Trends Pharmacol. Sci., 26,* 352-360.

[216] Jonnala, R.R., and Buccafusco, J.J. (2001). Relationship between the increased cell surface alpha7 nicotinic receptor expression and neuroprotection induced by several nicotinic receptor agonists. *J. Neurosci. Res., 66,* 565-572.

[217] Arendash, G.W., Sengstock, G.J., Sanberg, P.R., and Kem, W.R. (1995). Improved learning and memory in aged rats with chronic administration of the nicotinic receptor agonist GTS-21. *Brain Res., 674,* 252-259.

[218] Schneider, J.S., Tinker, J.P., Van Velson, M., Menzaghi, F., and Lloyd, G.K. (1999). Nicotinic acetylcholine receptor agonist SIB-1508Y improves cognitive functioning in chronic low-dose MPTP-treated monkeys. *J. Pharmacol. Exp. Ther., 290,* 731-739.

[219] Rezvani, A.H., Bushnell, P.J., and Levin, E.D. (2002). Effects of nicotine and mecamylamine on choice accuracy in an operant visual signal detection task in female rats. *Psychopharmacology* (*Berl*), *164,* 369-375.

[220] Ryan, R.E., Ross, S.A., Drago, J., and Loiacono, R.E. (2001). Dose-related neuroprotective effects of chronic nicotine in 6-hydroxydopamine treated rats, and loss of neuroprotection in alpha4 nicotinic receptor subunit knockout mice. *Br. J. Pharmacol., 132,* 1650-1656.

[221] Kaneko, S., Maeda, T., Kume, T., Kochiyama, H., Akaike, A, and Shimohama, S. (1997). Nicotine protects cultured cortical neurons against glutamate-induced cytotoxicity via alpha7-neuronal receptors and neuronal CNS receptors. *Brain Res., 765*: 135-140.

[222] Semba, J., Miyoshi, R., and Kito, S. (1996). Nicotine protects against the dexamethasone potentiation of kainic acid-induced neurotoxicity in cultured hippocampal neurons. *Brain Res., 735,* 335-338.

[223] Singh, K., Singh, S., Singhal, N.K., Sharma, A., Parmar, D., and Singh, M.P. (2010). Nicotine- and caffeine-mediated changes in gene expression patterns of MPTP-lesioned mouse striatum: Implications in neuroprotection mechanism. *Chem. Biol. Interact., 185(2),* 81-93.

[224] Belluardo, N., Mudo, G., Blum, M., Amato, G., and Fuxe, K. (2000). Neurotrophic effects of central nicotinic receptor activation. *J. Neural. Transm., 60,* 227-245.

In: Nicotine Addiction
Editor: Giuseppe Di Giovanni

ISBN: 978-1-62081-290-7


*Chapter 7*

# NEW PSYCHOLOGICAL APPROACHES IN NICOTINE ADDICTION

***Clare Austen****
Attard, Malta

## ABSTRACT

Nicotine addiction shares with other forms of addiction the main features of a compulsion to use the drug, together with high levels of craving, with relapse as a common occurrence. Given copious, widely published research, it is evident that nicotine addiction presents one of the greatest preventable threats to health worldwide [1, 2]. Psychological research has therefore focused largely on three main areas: prevention, cessation and relapse prevention. Research into prevention has sought to understand the factors underlying smoking initiation, whilst cessation research has aimed to increase our understanding of how to encourage smokers to quit and how they can be assisted in this process. Relapse prevention has looked at the factors that influence abstinent smokers to continue and how to avoid relapse. Current research into these three areas will be reviewed and discussed.

## INTRODUCTION

The psychological approach to nicotine addiction is based on the premise that it is necessary to understand the processes involved, from the potential smoker, to the fully addicted. This understanding is required to allow the development of strategies to discourage initiation into smoking, motivate smokers to quit, and finally to avoid relapse Research into nicotine addiction has therefore focused on the three main area of prevention, cessation and relapse prevention. Current research into these three areas will be reviewed and discussed.

* Correspondence author: Dr Clare Austen, C.Psychol., Silver Stone, Mixtla St, Attard, Malta,E-mail: ccaugustine@tiscali.co.uk.

## Prevention

The adolescent years have been identified as having critical importance as regards smoking initiation. In the UK, only 1-3% of pupils were found to be smokers on beginning secondary school at 11-12 years; this figure rose to 10% by 13 years and increased to 30% by the age of 15 [3]. Research in the USA reveals a similar pattern [4]. Progressive stages between non smokers and the tobacco dependent have been identified, starting with susceptibility towards smoking, initiation, and a gradual evolution towards regular tobacco use and dependence [5]. Research has therefore focused on attempting to understand and explain these trends. Explanations have been usefully based within the theoretical framework of the Theory of Planned Behaviour (TPB) [6, 7] which has been shown to be a good predictor of smoking behaviour [8]. In TPB, behaviour is posited to be influenced both by the intention to engage in a given behaviour and Perceived Behavioural Control, or the perception that the performance of such behaviour is within one's control. Attitudes, (how we view a behaviour) subjective norms (how we think significant others view a behaviour) and PBC are all implicated in the evolution of intent. All of these factors have been shown to influence future behaviour [9]. Particularly, intention to smoke in the future and the perception of self efficacy have both been shown to be good predictors of future smoking behaviour [10]. Thus, intention to smoke has been suggested to be a major factor in both predicting and preventing smoking susceptibility and initiation [11].

However, the influence of additional variables on the TPB model has also been considered. Conner et al [12] found that anticipated regret and intention stability were also implicated in smoking behaviour. As might be expected, consistent stable intentions not to smoke resulted in less smoking uptake. Anticipated regret, or the expectation of negative emotion, moderated intentions' predictive power: intentions were predictive only when anticipated regret was not a factor. Thus, weak intention to avoid smoking and little anticipated regret were both found to be indicators of future smoking behaviour. The authors suggest that future smoking prevention programmes could therefore focus not only on changing attitudes, subjective norms and self efficacy but also on increasing the awareness of anticipated regret and helping to increase the temporal stability of intentions.

The influence of social factors in smoking initiation has also been identified. Vitoria et al [13] found that parents' norms were the main, most consistent factor in smoking initiation, whilst peers exerted an inconsistent influence. Further work by Vitoria, Salgueiro, Silva and de Vries [14] found that social influence influenced smoking behaviour both directly and indirectly. Their research found that social influence, operationalized as subjective norms and descriptive norms (the behaviour carried out by significant others) were both important factors in smoking behaviour. Behaviour was influenced more by descriptive norms, which appear to operate automatically, without conscious intent-for instance engaging in group behaviour without rationalizing the process and is often relevant to risky behaviour. On the other hand, intentions were more influenced by subjective norms. Unsurprisingly, the two most influential groups with regard to smoking intention and behaviour were parents and peers. Interestingly, the peer group's influence was chiefly through descriptive norms (what adolescents see their peers doing). However, Mercken et al [15] found that adolescents tend to choose, and aspire to friendships with, peers with similar smoking behaviour. This may indicate that rather than being influenced to smoke by their peers, adolescents choose friends with similar attitudes to smoking. Smoking prevention could therefore focus on the behaviour itself, by banning smoking in venues frequented by adolescents as well as using cognitive approaches to bring the subtleties involved in attitudes and decisions to smoke into conscious awareness. Parents' influence was found [14] to be through both descriptive and subjective norms. Parents may thus helpfully both model non smoking behaviour as well as promote anti smoking attitudes and should be made aware of the deleterious effects of their smoking behaviour on their offspring.

## CESSATION

Cessation may be usefully described in two phases: preparation and intervention. Preparation involves motivating the smoker to begin the intervention process. Given the craving and compulsive drug intake involved in nicotine addiction, encouraging cessation is problematic. This is also complicated by the fact that the addiction itself appears to affect smokers' brains so that the influence of the potential consequence of their smoking behaviour is diminished [16]. Research has focused on how smokers maintain their smoking behaviour in the face of mounting evidence of its pernicious effects, and how these beliefs may be challenged.

Risk perception was found to be minimised in smokers in a cross cultural study ~~by~~ [17]. Further, societal attitudes, in terms of the moral disapproval expressed also appeared to affect smokers' behaviour. In this study smokers in Denmark, where moralization is less apparent, minimized risk more vigorously than smokers in the USA, where an anti-smoking culture prevails. Risk perception appears, therefore, to be culturally based and may be influenced by societal norms. Thus, when a strong anti-smoking moralization culture is present, it is harder for smokers to engage in risk minimization.

Compensatory health beliefs have also been shown to be a factor in cessation avoidance. Smokers may rationalize their behaviour with the belief that the negative consequences of smoking may be compensated for by other, more healthy, behaviour, such as eating more healthily, or taking more exercise. These beliefs have been found to provide an impediment to smoking cessation [18] and the authors therefore suggest that such beliefs should be targeted in smoking cessation programmes.

Further, smoking behaviour is also maintained by the role cigarettes play in the social interactions of young people [19]. This research found that smoking cessation was impeded by the need to explain this decision to peers, and that smoking also served both as a social prop and status indicator. This complex social function of smoking behaviour will therefore also need to be addressed in smoking cessation programmes.

Personalization of the message in smoking cessation has been found to be effective, but only when the information was felt to be of high personal relevance: its persuasive power decreased, and may be counterproductive where it was viewed as having low personal relevance. [20] This approach must therefore be used with care, but was found to be effective, for instance, when used with cardiovascular patients [21]. In this trial, patients with smoking related vascular disease were shown images of their arteries, an image with high personal relevance. Thus, written or verbal methods of persuasion should contain similarly tailored messages.

Interventions for smoking cessation largely focus on psychoeducational techniques, which are targeted at motivation and goals, self efficacy, knowledge and skills, in order to bring about behavioural change. A systematic review by Huttunen-Lenz, Song and Poland [22] found these methods to be effective with coronary heart disease patients and that intense interventions were associated with increased effectiveness. Effectiveness may also be increased with the use of ecological momentary interventions delivering messages related to smoking cessation utilizing either a laptop or mobile phone [23] These measures were found to be more effective than psychoeducational techniques alone and were viewed positively by participants.

## Relapse Prevention

Although 70% of smokers worldwide would like to quit the habit, of the 45% who try each year, 80-90% fail in the first 3 months [24]. This research found evidence for the importance of both self efficacy, or the belief in oneself to change behaviour, and planning for quitting, in smoking cessation. Further, one method which has shown some success is motivational interviewing, which steers quitters towards a change in behaviour and helps to develop the experience of self efficacy [25, 26].

Smokers in Cessation Programmes, with group support, were also found less likely to relapse. Other psychological approaches have shown mixed results: self-forgiveness, whilst demonstrating considerable benefits in some aspects of self harming behaviour, health and well being [27] may have detrimental effects in relapse prevention [28]. These authors concluded that forgiving the self for negative habits may well help maintain the negative behaviour by sabotaging the motivation to change. Further, thought suppression, a frequently used intervention, has been demonstrated to cause a behavioural rebound, increasing both smoking behaviour and the need for repeated quit attempts [29]. Another often used treatment method includes behaviours and strategies aimed at avoiding the temptation to smoke, but these again have shown little success, apart from planning interventions aimed at identifying and resolving situations where the temptation to smoke was anticipated. [30]. This research also found some evidence of the benefits of the antidepressant varenicline, which worked in a similar way to nicotine replacement therapy, rather than in any action as an anti-depressant. Similarly, specific coping planning interventions in which strategies were formulated to respond to specific situations when smoking may occur, were found to be effective [31]. Also, this intervention was in the context of a national 'Quit and Win' campaign, when quitters had the added impetus of group action. Generally, however, further research into relapse prevention is required to identify the relevant factors that need to be targeted in helping ex-smokers avoid relapse.

## Conclusion

Research indicates that prevention of the smoking habit in adolescents is of paramount importance. The influence of parents in this has been demonstrated, both in developing attitudes towards smoking and in behaviour modelling. The influence of peers, whilst important, may be moderated not only by parental mores, but also by national campaigns inculcating positive attitudes towards abstention. As regards smoking cessation, risk minimisation and compensatory health beliefs hinder cessation motivation and this is further complicated by the role played by smoking as a social tool. Psychoeducational models encouraging cessation have been used with some success, and there is increasing evidence for technology based support in cessation programmes, as well as pharmacological interventions. National cessation campaigns have proved effective in both encouraging and maintaining cessation behaviour. Motivational interviewing has shown some success in relapse prevention, by encouraging self efficacy in ex-smokers. Further research is required in models for relapse prevention, including further techniques to develop self efficacy, together with coping planning.

## REFERENCES


[1] Callum, C, (1998). The UK smoking epidemic; deaths in 1995. London Health Education Authority.

[2] Doll, R., Peto, R., Boreham,J., Sutherland, I., (2004). Mortality in relation to smoking; 50 years' observations on male British doctors. *BMJ*, 328, 1519.

[3] Jarvis, L. (1997). Smoking among secondary children in England in 1996. HMSO, London.

[4] Pallonen, V.E., Prochaska, J.O., Velicher, W.F., Prokhorov, A.V., Smith, N.F. (1998). Stages of acquisition and cessation in adolescent smoking. *Addict. Behav.*, 23, 3, 303-324.

[5] Kremers, S. P., Mudde, A.N., De Vries, H. (2004). Model of unplanned smoking initiation of children and adolescents: An integrated stage model of smoking behaviour. *Prev. Med.*, 38, 642-650.

[6] Ajzen, I. (1988). Attitudes, Personality and Behaviour. Open University Press, Milton Keynes.

[7] Ajzen, I. (1991). The theory of planned behaviour. *Organ. Behav. Hum. Decis. Process*, 50, 179-211.

[8] Smith, B.N., Bean, M.K., Mitchell,, K.S., Speizer, I.S., Fries, E.A. (2007). Psychosocial factors associated with non-smoking adolescents' intentions to smoke. *Health Educ. Res*, 22 (2), 238-247.

[9] Armitage, C.J., Conner, M. (2001). Efficacy of the theory of planned behaviour: A meta-analytic review. *Br. J. Soc. Psychol.*, 40, 471-499.

[10] Sussman,S., Dent, C. W, Flay, B.R., Hansen, W.B., Johnson, C.A. (1987). Psychosocial predictors of cigarette smoking onset by white, black, Hispanic and Asian adolescents in Southern California. *Morb. Mortal. Wkly Rep.*, 36, 11S-16S.

[11] Choi, W.S., Gilpin, E.A, Farkas, A.J., Pierce, J.P. (2001). Determining the probability of future smoking among adolescents. *Addiction*, 96, 313-323.

[12] Conner, M., Sandberg, T. McMillan, B. Higgins, A. (2006). Role of anticipated regret, intention and intention stability in adolescent smoking intention. *Br. J. Health Psychol.*, 11, 85-101.

[13] Vitoria, P.D.,Salgueiro, M.F., Silva, S.A., de Vries, H. (2009). The impact of social influence on adolescent intention to smoke: Combining types and referents of influence. *Br. J. Health Psychol.*, 14, 4, 681-699.

[14] Vitoria, P.D., Salgueiro, M.F., Silva, S.A., de Vries, H. (2011) Social influence, intention to smoke, and adolescent smoking behaviour longitudinal relations. *Br. J. Health Psychol.*, 16, 4, 779-798.

[15] Mercken, L., Candel, M., van Osch, L. de Vries, H. (2011) No smoke without fire: The impact of future friends on smoking behaviour. *Br. J. Health Psychol.*, 16, 170-188.

[16] Chiu, P.H., Lohrenz, T.M., Montague, P. R. (2008). Smokers' brains compute, but ignore a fictive error signal in a sequential investment task. *Nature Neurosci.*, 11, 514-520.

[17] Helweg-Larsen, M., Tobias, M., Cerban, B. (2010). Risk perception and moralization among smokers in USA and Denmark: A qualitative approach. *Br. J. Health Psychol.*, 15, 4, 871-886.

[18] Radtke, T., Scholz, U., Keller, R., Knauper, B., Hornung, R. (2010). Smoking-specific compensatory health beliefs and the readiness to stop smoking in adolescents. *Br. J. Health Psychol.*, 16, 3, 610-625.

[19] Fry, G., Grogan, S., Gough, B., Conner, M. (2008). Smoking in the lived world: How young people make sense of the social role cigarettes play in their lives. *Br. J. Soc. Psychol.*, 47, 763-780.

[20] Dijkstra, A., Ballast, K. (2011). Personalization and perceived personal relevance in computer- tailored persuasion in smoking cessation. *Br. J. Health Psychol.*, in press.

[21] Shahab, L. Hall, S., Matrteau, T. (2007) Showing smokers with vascular disease images of their arteries to motivate cessation: A pilot study. *Br. J. Health Psychol.*, 12, 275-283.

[22] Huttunen-Lenz, M, Song, F., Poland, F. (2010). Are psychoeducational smoking cessation interventions for coronary heart disease patients effective? Meta-ananlysis of interventions. *Br. J. Health Psychol.*, 15, 749-777.

[23] Heron, K.E., Smyth, J.M. (2010). Ecological momentary interventions: Incorporating mobile technology into psychosocial and health behaviour treatments. *Br. J. Health Psychol.*, 15, 1-9.

[24] Elfeddali, I., Bolman, C., Candel, M.J., Wiers, De Vries, H. (2011). The role of self efficacy, recovery self efficacy and preparatory planning in predicting short term smoking relapse. *Br. J. Health Psychol.*, in press.

[25] Lai, D.T.C., Cahill, K., Qin, Y., Tang, J.L. (2010). Motivational interviewing for smoking cessation. Cochrane Library, DOI: 10.1002/14651858.CD003999.pub3

[26] Soria, R., Legido,A., Escolano, C., Yeste A.L. (2006). A randomized controlled trial of motivational interviewing for smoking cessation. *Br. J. Gen. Pract.*, 56 (531) 768-774.

[27] Wohl, M.J.A, Pychl, T.A., Bennett, S.H. (2010). I forgive myself, now I study: How self-forgiveness for procrastinating can reduce future procrastination. *Pers. Individ. Dif.*, 48, 803-808.

[28] Wohl, M.J.A., Thompson, A. (2011). A dark side to self forgiveness: Forgiving the self and its association with chronic unhealthy behaviour. *Br. J. Soc. Psychol.*, 50 (2), 354-364.

[29] Erskine, J.A.,Georgiou, G.J., Kvavlasvili, L. (2010). I suppress, therefore I smoke: effects of thought suppression on smoking behaviour. *Psychol. Sci.*, 21 (9), 1225-30.

[30] Hajek, P., Stead, L.F., West, R., Jarvis, M. Lancaster, T. (2009). Relapse prevention interventions for smoking cessation. Cochrane Library, DOI: 10.1002/14651858. CD003999.pub3

[31] Van Osch, L., Lechner, L., Reubsaet, A., Wigger, S. de Vries, H. (2008). Relapse prevention in a national smoking cessation contest: Effects of coping planning. *Br. J. Health Psychol.*, 13, 525-535.

In: Nicotine Addiction
Editor: Giuseppe Di Giovanni

ISBN: 978-1-62081-290-7


*Chapter 8*

# Cognitive Consequences of Adolescent and Adult Nicotine Exposure: Utility of Animal Models

***Robert C. Barnet*, Pamela S. Hunt, and Joshua A. Burk***
Department of Psychology, College of William and Mary,
Williamsburg, Virginia, US

## Abstract

Smoking and the use of other tobacco products create an enormous financial and health burden on the world. Given that prevention efforts have had only a modest effect on smoking rates, efforts to promote smoking cessation must continue to be an important area of study. A more complete understanding about the underlying processes that contribute to nicotine use is critical to improving approaches that intend to limit the use of tobacco products. Nicotine-induced alterations in cognitive processing have been proposed to contribute to continued nicotine administration. Due to the number of compounds in nicotine products, it is difficult to definitively associate specific cognitive changes with nicotine in smokers. Animal models offer an opportunity to more directly examine the effects of nicotine while also controlling numerous important factors including dose, timing, and age of administration. We will review recent findings from animal models and provide examples from experiments conducted in our laboratories emphasizing the cognitive effects of adolescent nicotine exposure. This review will also integrate findings from our laboratories with the existing literature to demonstrate that the effects of nicotine critically depend on age of administration. In adults, chronic nicotine administration can enhance attention and learning in several paradigms. However, in adolescents, nicotine produces detectable long-term impairments in attention and learning. Collectively, these data afford a novel idea that, for individuals who begin administering nicotine during adolescence, nicotine use may continue in order to alleviate cognitive deficits associated with exposure at this age.

* Please address correspondence to: Robert C. Barnet, Department of Psychology, College of William and Mary, Williamsburg, VA 23187. Tel: 757-221-3874, FAX: 757-221-3896. E-mail: rcbarn@wm.edu.

## INTRODUCTION

According to the Centers for Disease Control and Prevention, the health-related costs of smoking from 2000-2004, including lost productivity and direct medical costs, was $197 billion per year in the United States [1]. Numerous efforts have been undertaken to prevent smoking cigarettes, with relatively modest success. Thus, there remains a substantial need to continue to develop treatments that promote smoking cessation. The success of maintaining abstinence from smoking and use of other tobacco products critically depends on understanding the cognitive and behavioral effects of the major psychoactive ingredient, nicotine, in order to target any nicotine-related changes in cognitive processing and choice behavior that promote continued tobacco use.

There is particular interest in studying adolescents with respect to smoking and nicotine exposure. The adolescent period is viewed as one of enhanced vulnerability for smoking initiation [2, 3]. Of adults who smoke, the majority began smoking during adolescence [4]. Adolescent dispositions toward risk-taking and sensation-seeking may result in experimentation with drugs [5, 6]. In terms of nicotine, adolescents exhibit positive, rather than negative, affective mood with self-administration [7]. It has further been noted that adolescents who smoke develop dependence more rapidly than those who initiate as adults, and experience more difficulty quitting [8, 9]. As reviewed below, exposure to nicotine during adolescence may also produce long-term changes in the brain that contribute to these behavioral patterns.

Studies with humans are useful for examining the totality of the effects of smoking, including all of the substances in cigarettes, the behaviors associated with smoking as well as a range of social and other environmental factors that play an important role in maintaining smoking behavior [7]. However, one challenge with these studies is specifically examining the effects of nicotine through routes of administration that lead to rapid increases in nicotine levels within the brain. Moreover, some nicotine-induced cognitive effects (reviewed below) appear to be dependent upon numerous variables. Studies that examine the effects of protracted nicotine exposure in previously naïve humans are rare yet have critical implications for understanding the changes in cognitive processes and choice behavior of long-term smokers. Efforts to understand the complex relationships between these variables benefit from precise experimental control of numerous variables, such as the life history of the individual, something that can be difficult to achieve with humans. Thus, animal models offer an opportunity to examine the effects of rapidly elevated nicotine levels while maintaining control over the variables that impact the effects of nicotine on cognition.

## BENEFITS OF RAT MODELS FOR STUDYING DEVELOPMENTAL PROCESSES IN DRUG ADDICTION

Much information about neural substrates and hormonal factors modulating drug self-administration and the long-term consequences of drug exposure has been obtained from studies employing rodent species. The rat provides several advantages for such research, although there are certainly barriers to its use. For example, forebrain systems of rodents are substantially less prominent, their development is relatively short, and their social organization is less complicated than in humans and other primates. Human drug-taking behavior and drug addiction are complex behaviors with a multitude of determinants [7], many of which are inaccessible to animal researchers. It is impossible at present, for example, to study in rodents the influence of parenting style, social belonging, peer pressure or self-esteem in the decision-making processes involved in drug initiation and maintenance. Nevertheless, one of the major benefits of the use of animal models is the ability to study in detail brain regions and neurochemical systems involved in drug taking behavior and the effects of exposure to certain drugs in a manner that is technically impossible to do currently with humans. Although human brain imaging technology has seen remarkable advances in the past three decades, it is still not possible to determine molecular changes that cause or are a consequence of drug exposure in humans. The ability to alter brain activity directly, to investigate neurochemical systems via administration of receptor-specific agonists and antagonists, and the ability to exactly determine the dose, timing, and pattern of drug intake during particular stages of development are some of the reasons why rodents are used so extensively in drug research.

Rodents are also a multiparous species, giving birth to multiple offspring at a time. This provides certain advantages for research designs, including the ability to assign genetically similar littermates across all experimental conditions. Depending upon strain, parental age, and parity of the dam, litter sizes can range from 8-15 offspring. Because growth and development are dependent in large part on nutritional and other maternal resources, it is typical to standardize litter size to about 10 pups. By having this many offspring within each litter available for group assignment, rather unique control across experimental conditions is afforded.

Development of the rat proceeds quite rapidly, relative to that of primates. Pronounced developmental changes occur within the first few weeks after birth. Maturational changes that take years in humans can take only days or weeks in the rat, making this species particularly attractive for developmental research. While the brevity of development may be viewed by some as a limitation, it can also be extremely advantageous in terms of high throughput research. Rodents are particularly attractive for longitudinal analyses where intervals between drug exposure and changes in brain and/or behavior can be conducted within a relatively short period of time.

Inbred rodent strains are valuable in that they share very similar genetic background, and are important in studies in which the research goal is best achieved by minimizing genetic variation. There are a variety of rodent lines selected for particular behavioral traits, such as those selected for high or low alcohol drinking (e.g. P vs. NP, AA vs. ANA, see [10, 11, 12, 13]). These models are useful for examining the genetic determinants and gene-environment interactions contributing to drug sensitivity and self-administration, not only for alcohol but also other abused substances including nicotine (e.g. [14])

In the laboratory, rodents afford knowledge of life history and environmental experience of the individual, which can also be directly manipulated. Obviously, human development is greatly influenced by early experience and environmental factors, many of which are known to influence drug intake, maintenance and dependence [7]. Such factors are usually assessed in human research through complex statistical analyses and large sample sizes, and even then it is difficult to parse the influence of the individual variables. Analyses of the effects of certain experiential variables (e.g. social environment, stress, timing and pattern of drug exposure) in determining drug initiation or maintenance of drug taking behavior can therefore be more directly inferred from animal research.

## The Utility of the Rat as an Experimental Model of Adolescent Nicotine Exposure

Rodents are the most widely used animal models of human conditions and disease, and are useful in providing an interface between basic and clinical research. The mouse has gained considerable importance in recent years, primarily because of its sequenced genome and the potential for development of genetically modified animals that can be used to study mechanisms of disease [15]. Rats, however, continue to be used more than any other species in behavioral studies of development, drug effects, and cognitive processes related to the onset of drug taking and addiction. In the sections that follow we briefly review adolescent development. The primary focus is on the laboratory rat, *Rattus norvegicus*, since that is the animal model that we have used in our laboratories. Our intention is to highlight aspects of adolescent brain and behavioral development in the rat that appear to closely parallel those in humans.

## Hallmarks of Adolescence in the Rat

Given the intense interest in adolescent exposure to nicotine, rodents provide a unique opportunity to study cause-and-effect relationships that are difficult, if not impossible, to study in humans. It barely warrants mention that there are insurmountable ethical barriers that preclude direct administration of nicotine to human adolescents. Also, many questions about the adolescent brain in relation to drug taking behavior require experimental manipulations that necessitate the use of animals in research. One of the primary hurdles in animal research, however, is to define the period of adolescence, something that is also a struggle to define precisely in humans.

Because the events of adolescence are not well characterized, it is difficult to expressly define this developmental period. Adolescence is not a discrete developmental stage, but is rather a period of transition from the dependence of childhood to the independence of adulthood. No one particular event defines the onset or offset of adolescence, and the transition through this period is lengthy and somewhat ill-defined. Human adolescence is generally considered to span the second decade of life and may, depending upon the specific feature under investigation, span into the third decade [16, 17]. One of the main events occurring during adolescence is puberty. However, there are other age-specific neural and behavioral characteristics that appear relatively unique to adolescence that may be ubiquitous across mammalian species.

Given the difficulty in defining the ages that span the adolescent period in humans, it is not surprising that there is vast disagreement among researchers working with rodents in how to define the onset and offset of this transitional stage [6]. There are similarities between human adolescents and rodent models of adolescence in terms of age-specific behaviors and neural and hormonal characteristics. These resemblances provide some measure of construct validity that are sufficiently promising to promote the further development of these animal models as tools for the study of adolescence. The specific feature of adolescence a researcher identifies will determine the appropriateness of the particular animal species and age range that defines the adolescent period. Thus, the animal model chosen will, perhaps, only emulate a few of the specific characteristics of human adolescence.

Adolescence can be viewed as the entire period from weaning to sexual maturation of both sexes (see [6, 18] for reviews and definitional considerations). This period spans the earliest signs of puberty in females (approximately postnatal day [PD] 20) to the termination of changes in the later maturing males (up to PD 60). However, some researchers have attempted to more narrowly define the period of adolescence in rats on the basis of a set of specific behavioral and neural characteristics. Spear and Brake [19] reviewed data consistent with the peak period of adolescence as between PD 28 and 42 occasioned, for example, by a hyporesponsive catecholamine system, behavioral hyperactivity, and reduced sensitivity to appetitive reinforcement contingencies (see also [5, 20]). In our research that examines the long-term effects of adolescent nicotine exposure in rats, we primarily use Spear and Brake's [19] definition and consider adolescent rats to be between the ages of 28 and 42 days postnatal. This age range is also used in other aspects of our laboratory work (e.g. [21, 22, 23])

There are a number of age-specific characteristics that can be examined in rodents that parallel those of human adolescence. These include, but are certainly not limited to, an adolescent growth spurt, an increase in peer-directed social interactions, lack of impulse control, and an increase in risk-taking and sensation-seeking behaviors. There are also particular patterns of neural changes, including alterations in dopamine balance in frontal cortex and the nucleus accumbens that seem universal in adolescence. Some of these are briefly reviewed in the next section. We also review information on some of the effects of nicotine exposure on behavioral and neural development.

*Neural development.* Changes in the nervous system continue through adolescence in many species. Reorganization, synaptogenesis and myelination in the hippocampus, frontal cortex, and other areas continue through adolescence into young adulthood. Another hallmark feature of this developmental period is the extensive remodeling of neurochemical systems, in particular dopaminergic systems in the reward pathway (nucleus accumbens) and frontal cortical regions. In this section, we highlight some of the maturational changes that occur in the brain during adolescence, but this is not intended as an exhaustive review. Research on the effects of adolescent exposure to nicotine on learning and memory, which we review below, has principally focused on tasks involving the hippocampal or frontal cortex, and those are the regions on which we focus here.

*Structural changes*: Both the hippocampus and the frontal cortex undergo extensive growth during adolescence. Hippocampal volume is increased [24], there is an age-dependent enhancement in cell proliferation of dentate gyrus granule neurons [25], and substantial structural remodeling of these cells [26]. Frontal regions of the cortex also exhibit changes during adolescence, and these areas are considered to be the last to mature [27, 28]. Frontal white matter increases, while gray matter decreases [29]. There is a significant loss of synapses on frontal cortical neurons [30, 31] together with an overall decrease in volume of the frontal cortex [32, 33].

*Neurochemical changes:* There is increasing evidence that there are significant changes in neurotransmitter activity that begin during adolescence [34]. Cholinergic innervation to both the hippocampus and frontal cortex increase during this developmental stage [35, 36], accompanied by increases in functionality [21, 26, 37]. Glutamatergic systems also change, with significant reductions in glutamate receptors in both hippocampal and frontal regions during adolescence [38, 39]. A major area of research has focused on alterations in dopaminergic systems that occur during adolescence. There is a reasonably well-characterized shift in dopamine balance in limbic areas involved in reward (e.g. nucleus accumbens) and prefrontal cortex [6]. During adolescence dopamine activity in the nucleus accumbens decreases [40] while that in the frontal cortex increases [41, 42]. It has been suggested that these changes may underlie the development of impulse control and more adult-like patterns of impulsivity, tolerance to delayed reward, and reductions in risk-taking and sensation-seeking behavior that develop into adulthood [5, 43, 44, 45].

*Increased risk taking and sensation seeking.* Similar to humans, adolescent-age rodents show behaviors that reflect enhanced risk-taking and sensation-seeking [46, 47] that include enhanced preference for novelty and exploration [48, 49]. As indicated above, these characteristics are associated with experimentation with drugs in humans. Likewise, adolescent rodents seem particularly sensitive to the rewarding effects of nicotine, with nicotine supporting place preference conditioning under circumstances in which there is no learning in adults [50, 51, 52, 53]. Adolescent mice and rats will both self-administer nicotine at a greater rate than adults of those species ([50, 54, 55]; but see [56]). And, adolescent exposure to nicotine induces a long-lasting increase in motivation to work for nicotine self-administration later in life [50, 57].

*Peer-directed social behaviors.* Integral to the period of adolescence is an increase in peer-directed social behaviors and a waning of interactions with parents. Peer-directed social behaviors in rats are at their highest during adolescence [58]. In particular, behaviors collectively regarded as social play are at their peak during adolescence. These include pinning, biting at the nape of the neck and pouncing [59]. Social interactions with peers have high incentive value [60]. This is most evident in what is referred to as a "rebound" effect [61, 62]. Following a period of social deprivation adolescent animals engage in much higher levels of interaction, including play, when the deprivation period ends. Access to play partners can also serve as a reward that supports learning [63, 64].

Not only is the opportunity to interact with peers motivationally significant, it also appears necessary for proper development of the brain and the appropriate adult behavioral repertoire. Depriving adolescent rodents of the opportunity for social interaction and play can produce profound negative effects on behavioral and brain development. Several studies have examined adult rat behavior following social isolation during adolescence. Some of the major changes that are seen include persistent hyperactivity [65], an increase in defensive response to social threat [66], overall reductions in social interactions with conspecifics [67], altered sexual behavior in males [67, 68, 69], and increased aggression [70]. There are also marked changes in hormonal response to aversive social situations [67, 71]. Social isolation during adolescence may also lead to long-term impairments in spatial memory and reversal learning [72, 73], which may reflect changes in hippocampal and frontal cortical function, respectively. In fact, Bell et al. [60] reported that adolescent rats deprived of social interactions exhibit altered morphology in frontal cortical regions, a finding that was not observed in animals that were deprived at younger or older ages. This finding suggests that opportunities for physical interactions with similar-age members of the species are necessary for proper cortical remodeling and that adolescence is a critical period for this effect. Even minimal durations of social isolation (1 h/day) can decrease hippocampal cell proliferation and reduce survival of hippocampal neurons [74].

The effects of nicotine on social interactions and play in adolescent rats have not been studied extensively. Thiel et al. [52] reported that acute nicotine reduced play behavior in adolescent rats. Similarly, Panksepp et al. [59] reported a dose-dependent reduction in play following nicotine administration. It is possible that chronic nicotine administration would change social behavior during adolescence to the point where it might induce an "isolation syndrome" [65], although this has not been investigated. Given that depriving animals of social interactions can lead to neural and hormonal changes and produce long-lasting cognitive impairments, it is possible that some of the long-term deficits in learning and memory observed following chronic adolescent nicotine administration may be exacerbated by nicotine-induced changes in social interactions. Further research is needed to fully examine this speculation.

## EFFECTS OF ADULT NICOTINE EXPOSURE ON COGNITION IN ANIMALS

The focus of this chapter largely concerns the effects of nicotine administration during adolescence on cognition. However, we will also compare the effects of nicotine during adolescence and adulthood. Thus, the literature regarding some of the well-studied effects of adult nicotine exposure will be briefly summarized in this section.

*Attention.* The effects of nicotine on attention can be dissociated into the effects of acute and chronic exposure. Acute nicotine administration in adult animals has generally been shown to enhance performance in attention-demanding tasks [75], although the effects appear to depend on several variables, including task parameters [76] and rat strain [77]. Further support that nicotinic receptors are involved in attention has come from the task-impairing effects of the general nicotinic receptor antagonist, mecamylamine [76, 78, 79, 80] and from the performance enhancing effects of nicotinic receptor agonists [81]. More recent experiments have employed choline-sensitive biosensors that allow measurement of acetylcholine levels with high temporal resolution [82, 83] to understand the mechanisms underlying nicotinic receptor-related attentional enhancement. These experiments have provided evidence that the rate of the rise and of the decay of prefrontal cortical cholinergic transients importantly contributes to beneficial cognitive effects mediated by nicotinic receptors [84].

The effects of chronic nicotine exposure on attention in adult animals have not been well-studied, but appear to support the conclusion that nicotine has beneficial effects. Hahn and Stolerman [85] found that initial exposure to nicotine did not affect accuracy (though failures to complete a trial were increased by nicotine) over the first week of administration in a five-choice serial reaction time task. However, continued nicotine exposure during weeks 2-6 enhanced attentional performance. Moreover, during weeks 9-10, chronic nicotine exposed rats performed significantly better than saline-treated rats when a visual distracter was presented. Thus, chronic nicotine appeared to robustly enhance attentional performance. Collectively, the available evidence supports the conclusion that nicotine administration in adults can facilitate attentional processing, an effect that may contribute to continued nicotine administration in humans.

*Learning and memory.* The effects of nicotine on learning and memory have been well-summarized in a previous review [75] and, thus, only a few keys findings will be highlighted here. The majority of the experimental work has involved testing animals in tasks that are known to rely on frontal cortical and/or hippocampal regions. For example, working memory, assessed in many spatial tasks, is known to be enhanced by acute nicotine exposure in adults [86, 87], although reference memory is unaffected [88]. Nicotine has also been shown to enhance performance in a variety of testing conditions assessing other forms of learning and memory in rats. Acute nicotine, for example, enhances object recognition memory in rats [89]. In mice, acute nicotine can enhance contextual fear conditioning [90] and trace fear conditioning [91]. Thus, numerous experiments have supported the conclusion that acute nicotine can enhance aspects of learning and memory in adults.

The effects of chronic nicotine exposure during adulthood are not as clear. Levin et al. [75] report that the increase in working memory observed following acute nicotine is maintained during a chronic dosing regimen. In contrast, Gould and colleagues [92, 93] have reported no change in context or trace conditioning in mice with chronic nicotine exposure, although impairments are observed in these tasks during acute withdrawal from nicotine. Thus, the conclusion seems to be that acute nicotine acts as a general cognitive enhancer, but that withdrawal from nicotine can impair aspects of learning and memory.

*Impulsivity.* Another nicotine-induced change that may promote continued tobacco use is increased impulsivity. There are several components of impulsivity. One component that has been studied with regard to nicotine in animal models is impulsive decision-making. Impulsive decision-making can be measured by offering two choices, a smaller reward that is available immediately or with less effort and a larger reward that is accessible after some delay or with greater effort. In rats, acute nicotine increases the likelihood of choosing the smaller, immediately accessible reward [94, 95]. Locey and Dallery [96] examined whether these nicotine-induced changes in choice behavior were due to differences in sensitivity to the reward magnitude or to the delay between the two choices. Acute nicotine increased preference for a smaller reward compared with vehicle administration but did not affect preference for choosing rewards associated with different delays (see also [97]). Thus, acute nicotine appears to alter sensitivity to reward, but not the sensitivity to delay. Few experiments have examined the effects of chronic nicotine on impulsive choice. In one, Dallery and Locey [94] exposed rats to nicotine for at least 65 days. Chronic nicotine exposure increased impulsive choice, an effect that persisted for 30 drug-free days after nicotine exposure was terminated. Thus, chronic nicotine produces impulsive behaviors that can persist even when nicotine is no longer administered. This long-term increase in impulsivity may importantly contribute to periods when the probability of smoking relapse is particularly high. In fact, in rats, the presence of impulsive choice behavior predicted a reduced ability to inhibit nicotine administration during abstinence and an increased vulnerability to relapse when nicotine-related cues were again presented [98].

Impulsive choice behavior is known to depend on the integrity of the nucleus accumbens core [99]. Moreover, lesions of the lateral orbitofrontal cortex increase preference for a small, immediate reward compared to a larger, delayed reward [100]. Finally, inactivation of the medial prefrontal cortex, basolateral amygdala or a disconnection between the two regions increased preference for a smaller, immediate reward [101]. The exact mechanisms through which nicotine influences these structures or others to affect impulsive choice behavior have not been extensively studied. However, one experiment employing receptor subtype selective compounds implicated the α4β2 subtype receptors in the infralimbic cortex as important for mediating some of the effects of nicotine on impulsive choice [102].

## Effects of Adolescent Nicotine Exposure on Neural Development and Cognition in Animals

*Effects of nicotine on neural development.* In general, nicotine-induced changes in cell structure and morphology, neurochemical activity and receptor densities have been reported in regions involved in reward and memory function [103] and many of these are specific to nicotine exposure during the adolescent period. Following chronic adolescent nicotine exposure, a number of neural alterations have been reported. These include cell damage and reduction in cell size in the hippocampus and changes in several neurotransmitter systems (for review, see [20]). Some of these effects were sex-specific, but all were typically evident following adolescent exposure to nicotine but not when exposure occurred at younger or older ages. Changes in neural protein levels in the hippocampus are also evident [104] and appear to be specific to nicotine exposure during adolescence. Within the hippocampus, adolescent nicotine produces an upregulation of nicotinic acetylcholine receptors [105] and a downregulation of AMPA glutamate receptors [106]. There is an overall increase in apoptosis within the dentate gyrus and area CA1 of hippocampus [107].

Morphology of cells in the medial prefrontal cortex (mPFC) is also changed by adolescent nicotine, in a way that is different from that observed following adult exposure [108]. Additionally, nicotine exposure during this period produces a cortical upregulation of nicotinic acetylcholine receptors, and the pattern of upregulation in the cortex compared to that of midbrain and hippocampus differs in adolescents and adults [109]. Among other effects, nicotine modulates glutamate release in prefrontal cortex [110] and, recently, has been discovered to reduce mGluR2 protein levels in the mPFC associated with attentional deficits in rats exposed to nicotine as adolescents [111]. These and other changes may be the basis for some of the cognitive deficits that have been reported and which we review below.

*Effects of adolescent nicotine on cognition.* The previous sections reveal that nicotine exposure not only affects behavior but that it can affect complex systems of behavior (social interaction and development) and behavioral regulation (impulsivity). Additionally, there is developing interest in how adolescent exposure to nicotine affects function in later adulthood, though this is among the least well delineated consequence of nicotine exposure and nicotine addiction. Analysis of how adolescent nicotine affects cognition reflects further interest in nicotine's impact on complex behavioral systems important to adaptive function. In this section we will focus on long-term effects of adolescent nicotine exposure on cognition, highlighting recent findings from our laboratories. Indicators from the literature reviewed are consistent with the long-term cognitive enhancing effects of nicotine exposure in adults, as implied by findings discussed earlier. Research from our own laboratories reveals a different profile for the long-term effects of nicotine exposure during adolescence, namely, one that highlights long-term cognitive impairing effects of nicotine.

In general, the effects of chronic nicotine on learning and memory have been less well-characterized than the effects of acute nicotine. In normal rats, chronic nicotine exposure in some cases does not appear to have strong effects on spatial memory [112]. However, adolescent treated rats sometimes display long lasting improvements in spatial memory. Levin [113] for example, exposed adolescent rats (PD 30-58) to chronic nicotine, then later to radial maze training when the rats were adults (PD 82). Nicotine treated rats where shown to perform significantly better than saline treated rats and this improvement persisted across training. Additionally, chronic nicotine exposure has been shown to attenuate learning and memory deficits in aged animals and in animal models of Alzheimer's disease [114, 115, 116]. The cognitive benefits of chronic nicotine on learning and memory deficits in these models appear to be reproduced by α7 receptor agonists [117, 118]. In summary, there is not an extensive literature regarding the effects of chronic nicotine on learning and memory, but the available evidence suggests that chronic nicotine may be beneficial, including the results of work in some models characterized by learning and memory deficits.

*Spontaneous Alternation.* Spontaneous alternation is a nonreinforced spatial task thought to involve novelty seeking and recognition memory. In this task, sequences of maze arm entries are scored as correct if the animal enters a sequence of arms without re-entry. Like other hippocampus-dependent tasks such as trace conditioning discussed later (e.g., [21, 119]), spontaneous alternation performance may be developmentally dissociated. Bronstein et al. [120] reported that very young rats (PD 15) do not alternate whereas by adolescence (PD 30) rats alternate at high levels similar to that of adults (see also [121]). A similar dissociation has been observed in humans in a modified alternation task in which infants' reach for an identical toy on the same versus alternate side of a midline. Vecera et al. [122] demonstrated that 6 month old infants reached for the toy on the same versus alternate side of the midline equally often but that 18 month old infants alternated significantly more. These findings are consistent with the late development of the hippocampus [37, 123, 124] and performance in spatial tasks is well recognized to rely on the hippocampus [125, 126]. Accordingly, lesions of the ventral hippocampus have been shown to impair spontaneous alternation [127] and may also impair social interactions, as previously discussed [128].

Few studies have investigated the effects of nicotine on spontaneous alternation. Similar to the enhancing effects of acute nicotine on radial maze performance [113] acute nicotine was shown to ameliorate the deficit in spontaneous alternation in adolescent (approximately PD 42) stroke-prone spontaneously hypertensive rats (SHRSP, an animal model of attention deficit hyperactivity disorder [129]). In rats, chronic nicotine exposure in adulthood does not impair reinforced alternation performance [130]. However, in guinea pigs, chronic prenatal exposure to nicotine produced deficits in alternation performance when tested as neonates or at puberty [131]. That we are aware, no previous study has examined the effects of chronic adolescent nicotine exposure on spontaneous alternation in rats.

In one experiment from our laboratory, Sprague-Dawley rats received two injections per day (saline vs. 0.40 mg/kg nicotine tartrate, i.p.) every other day during adolescence, from PD 28-42. Eighteen days later on PD 60 spontaneous alternation was assessed in a single session. Saline and nicotine exposed animals did not differ and alternation performance was 70.0% in the saline group and 77.1% in the nicotine group. However, in radial maze tasks access to extramaze cues can facilitate performance and restricting or manipulating cues can impair performance [132]. A subsequent experiment in our laboratory exposed adolescent rats to the same dosing protocol as described but with daily injections and tested animals in adolescence on PD 45 under "cue-rich" (salient extramaze cues present) and "cue-poor" (salient extramaze cues absent) conditions over three days. Figure 1 shows the overall mean from testing and reveals spontaneous alternation was impaired by adolescent nicotine exposure. A Cue Condition (Rich vs. Poor) X Drug (saline vs. 0.40 mg/kg) analysis revealed a significant effect of Drug ($F(1, 48)=5.27$, $p<.03$) and marginal effect of Cue Condition ($p=.06$). Patterns of alternation performance across days are shown in Figure 2 (Cue Rich) and Figure 3 (Cue Poor). In both conditions, nicotine treated animals show consistent impairment in spontaneous alternation with a slight tendency toward larger (Figure 1) and more consistent impairment in Cue Poor conditions (Figure 3). It is possible that the effects of nicotine withdrawal mediated these changes in alternation performance, although nicotine withdrawal after chronic treatment in adults has been shown to not impair performance in the radial maze even in sessions immediately following nicotine cessation [113].

*Trace conditioning*. Pavlovian fear conditioning is a widely-used model system for studies of the neurobiology of learning and memory. Delay fear conditioning in which a conditioned stimulus (CS) is presented in a contiguous manner with an unconditioned stimulus (US), requires the amygdala for both its acquisition and expression [133]. Trace conditioning, in which US presentation occurs some time after CS offset, additionally requires the hippocampus [134, 135] and lesions of the hippocampus impair trace conditioning [136, 137]. As with other memory phenomena described, acute nicotine enhances trace conditioning [91, 138], and also enhances performance in models that display memory impairment [114, 116].

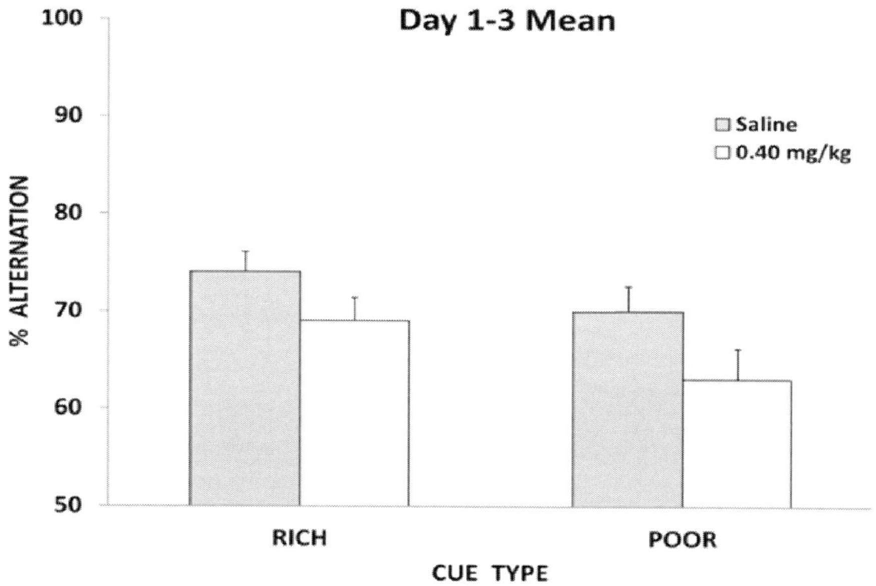


Figure 1. Mean spontaneous alternation performance averaged over the three days of testing which began PD 45, following adolescent PD 28-42 nicotine (0.40 mg/kg) versus saline exposure (i.p). Cue Rich = salient extra maze cues present; Cue Poor = salient extra maze cues absent. Error bars represent SEMs.

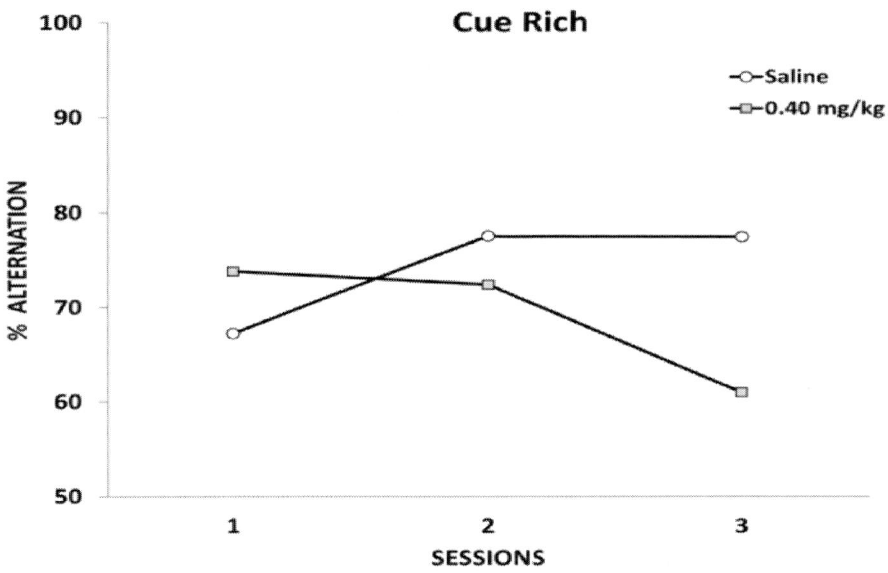


Figure 2. Mean spontaneous alternation performance on each of three test days beginning PD 45, following adolescent PD 28-42 nicotine (0.40 mg/kg) versus saline exposure (i.p.). Cue Rich = salient extra maze cues present.

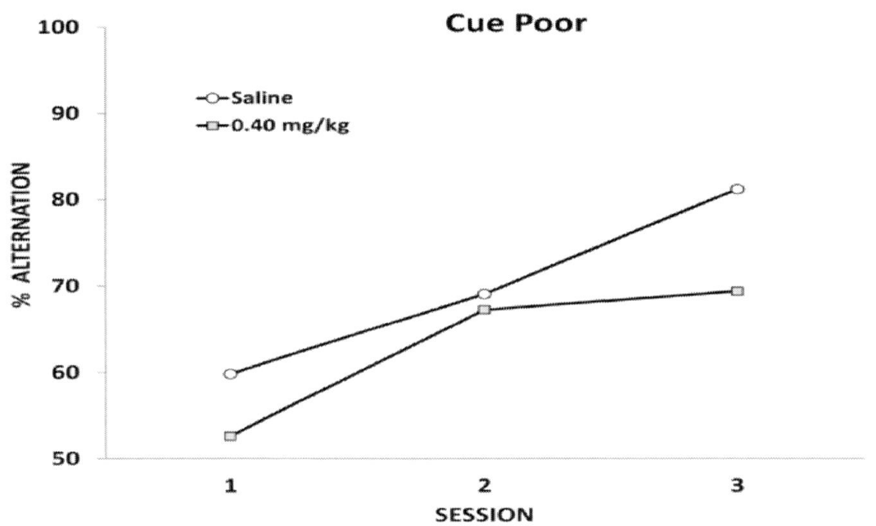


Figure 3. Mean spontaneous alternation performance on each of three test days beginning PD 45, following adolescent PD 28-42 nicotine (0.40 mg/kg) versus saline exposure (i.p.). Cue Poor = salient extra maze cues absent.

We [139] conducted experiments designed to examine the potential beneficial effects of adolescent exposure to nicotine on later hippocampal-dependent learning in an animal model of fetal alcohol spectrum disorders (FASD). It is recognized that nicotine is abused in populations with cognitive impairment, such as schizophrenia, attention-deficit disorder with and without hyperactivity, and FASD [140, 141, 142, 143].

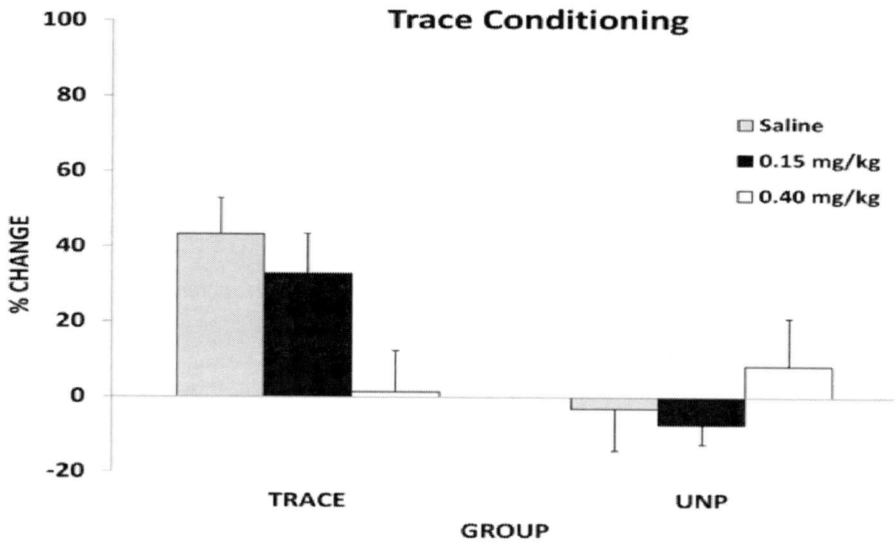


Figure 4. Mean % Change (fear-potentiated startle) in Trace and Unpaired groups following PD 28-42 nicotine (0.15 mg/kg, 0.40 mg/kg) versus saline exposure (i.p). Training and testing began in adulthood on PD 60. Trace groups received light-shock training with a 5-sec unfilled gap between light and shock; Unpaired groups received light and shock explicitly unpaired. Error bars represent SEMs.

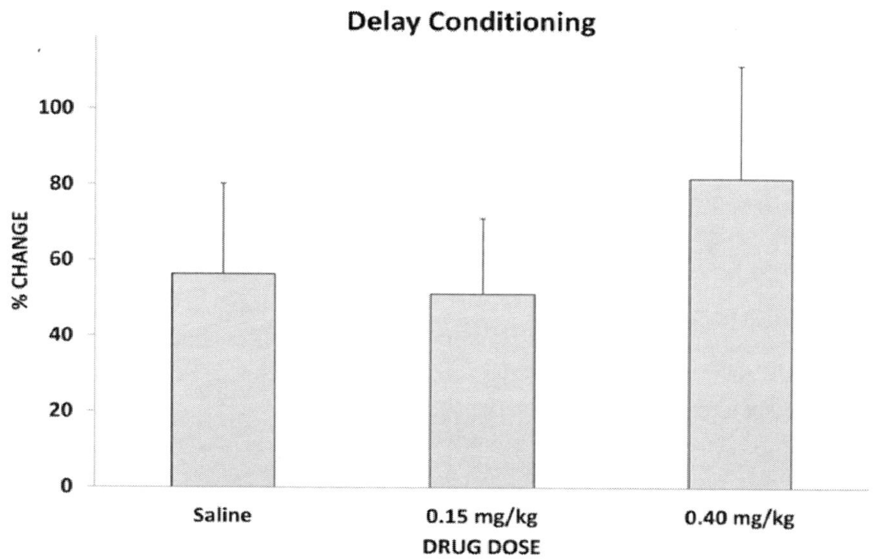


Figure 5. Mean % Change (fear-potentiated startle) in Delay groups following PD 28-42 nicotine (0.15 mg/kg, 0.40 mg/kg) versus saline exposure (i.p). Training and testing began in adulthood on PD 60. Delay groups received light-shock training in which shock immediately followed light. Error bars represent SEMs.

The self-medication hypothesis asserts that the drug nicotine is abused in such populations because its use can alleviate cognitive deficits, a suggestion we return to later. Levillain ([139], Experiment 1) first demonstrated a dose-response curve for nicotine's cognitive-enhancing effect in normal adolescent rats in the trace paradigm. Rats were administered nicotine (saline, 0.15 mg/kg or 0.30 mg/kg) via i.p. injection on PD 28, 30, 32 and 34. On PD 40 animals were trained with delay or trace conditioning. The CS was a light of 10 sec duration and the US was footshock. For Delay groups the offset of the light CS was coincident with US onset. For Trace groups, the offset of the CS and onset of the US were separated by a 10-sec trace interval. Approximately 24 hours later animals were placed into a novel context and tested for the species-typical behavior of freezing (immobility) to the light CS. The intermediate dose of nicotine (0.15 mg/kg) facilitated hippocampus-dependent trace conditioning as evidenced by significantly higher levels of CS freezing compared to freezing in the saline group, but had no effect on hippocampus-independent delay fear conditioning (none of the Delay groups differed statistically).

Our model of FASD [144, 145, 146] involves administration of high doses of ethanol to young rats, during a period of time that is comparable to the third-trimester of human gestation [147]. In the next experiment ([139], Experiment 2), young rats were administered 5.25 g/kg/day ethanol on PD 4-9. Control animals were given sham intubations during this time or were left undisturbed (unhandled) during the neonatal period. During adolescence, these animals were administered nicotine and trained according to the regimen described above. FASD animals showed very low levels of freezing to the trace CS, an effect we have reported previously [146]. The critical finding was that prior intermittent nicotine administration resulted in greater trace conditioning in the FASD subjects and this effect was dose-dependent; higher doses of nicotine produced a greater facilitation of trace conditioning. Indeed, the levels of CS elicited freezing evident in FASD animals previously given the highest dose of nicotine (0.30 mg/kg) were comparable to those seen in controls not exposed to fetal alcohol treatment. These findings support the hypothesis that hippocampus-dependent learning, which is severely impaired in FASD, can be facilitated by nicotine exposure in adolescence.

In a further study we examined the effects of protracted nicotine administration during adolescence on trace fear conditioning. On PD 28-42, Sprague-Dawley rats received one i.p. injection per day every other day with saline, 0.15 mg/kg, or 0.40 mg/kg nicotine. Animals were allowed to age and become adults before initiation of training. On PD 60 as adults, animals in the Trace condition (TRACE) were exposed to pairings of a 5-sec light CS with footshock US, separated by a 5-sec trace interval. Animals in the Unpaired condition (UNP) received equal exposure to light and shock but these events were explicitly unpaired. Twenty-four hours later subjects were tested for fear-potentiated startle (FPS; [148]) to the light CS. Data from the startle test are shown in Figure 4.

The data suggest that nicotine administered intermittently but for a protracted period of adolescence produced functional changes in the hippocampus that resulted in trace conditioning impairment when animals were tested as adults. A Condition (Trace vs. Unpaired) X Drug (saline, 0.15 mg/kg, 0.40 mg/kg) analysis revealed a Condition X Drug interaction ($F(2, 51)=3.84$, $p<.03$). For TRACE groups, significantly impaired FPS was observed in 0.40 mg/kg treated rats compared to either saline or 0.15 mg/kg treated animals ($ps<.05$). Performance in the saline and 0.15 mg/kg treated trace rats did not differ, nor did any of the unpaired groups. In this and the delay conditioning study reported next, nicotine similarly had no effect on baseline startle in either pre-test habituation trials or noise-alone test trials common to the FPS paradigm. A follow up study was conducted to evaluate the effect of otherwise identical adolescent nicotine exposure on delay conditioning which does not require the hippocampus. The drug and conditioning treatments were identical to those just described, except that footshock immediately followed CS presentation during light-shock training and no trace interval was imposed. Data from the test with delay conditioned animals are shown in Figure 5. Adolescent nicotine exposure failed to produce any evidence of impairment in delay conditioning. Saline and drug groups did not differ, and there was a tendency toward delay enhancement in the high-dose (0.40 mg/kg) group (cf. [149]).

Interestingly, Raybuck and Gould [138] reported no effect of chronic nicotine exposure on trace conditioning in mice when testing occurred during nicotine administration but that chronic nicotine induced a deficit in trace conditioning during a period of acute withdrawal. Our data suggest a longer time course for the impairing effect of nicotine exposure that is not due to immediate withdrawal effects. Adolescent nicotine exposure impaired hippocampus-dependent trace conditioning, even though animals were tested in adulthood and despite a long period of abstinence.

*Context Conditioning.* Contextual conditioning involves learning about situational cues and requires a functional hippocampus, and hippocampal damage is known to impair context conditioning in rodents [150, 151]. Our next study [152] investigated whether chronic nicotine exposure during adolescence in rats would produce long-term impairments in context conditioning. To the extent that adolescent nicotine impairs hippocampal function, impaired context conditioning may be predicted. However, the prediction for impaired context conditioning following nicotine exposure is not ubiquitous. Gould and colleagues [90, 153, 154] have shown that contextual fear conditioning in adult mice is facilitated if the mice are exposed to acute nicotine immediately prior to training. However, our hypothesis was that chronic (as opposed to acute) nicotine exposure during adolescence (as opposed to in adulthood) would produce long-term alterations in hippocampal function manifest as impaired learning about contextual cues. On PD 28 Sprague-Dawley rats were surgically implanted with osmotic minipumps that delivered saline, 3.0 mg/kg/d, or 6.0 mg/kg/d nicotine tartrate. The minipumps administered nicotine during an adolescent period from PD 28-42 at which time the pumps were removed. The adolescent rats were then allowed to age and become adults before training and testing. Training for context conditioning began on PD 65. Animals were exposed to the conditioning chambers during no-shock acclimation sessions, followed either by unsignaled shock training (context conditioning in shock groups) or no shock exposure in the context (no shock groups). Twenty-four hours after shock training all animals were tested on three consecutive no-shock test days for suppression of drinking from a lick tube in the presence of context cues. Day 1 of the test provided the critical measure to assess strength of context conditioning. Days 2 and 3 of the test were included to permit evaluation of differential extinction of context learning in drug and no drug controls. Rate of extinction is known to be affected by the prefrontal cortex [155, 156] and different rates of extinction in drug and no drug controls would imply alterations in this brain region. Spaeth et al. [152] observed higher suppression in all shock groups compared with no shock groups, which did not differ. Of critical interest, there was significantly lower suppression on the first test day in each of the two nicotine treated groups compared to the saline group. Each shock trained group had received identical shock training treatment but different adolescent drug treatments. Rates of extinction did not differ among drug conditions, and similar to the findings above concerning trace conditioning, Spaeth et al. [152] observed no impairing effect of adolescent nicotine on delay conditioning.

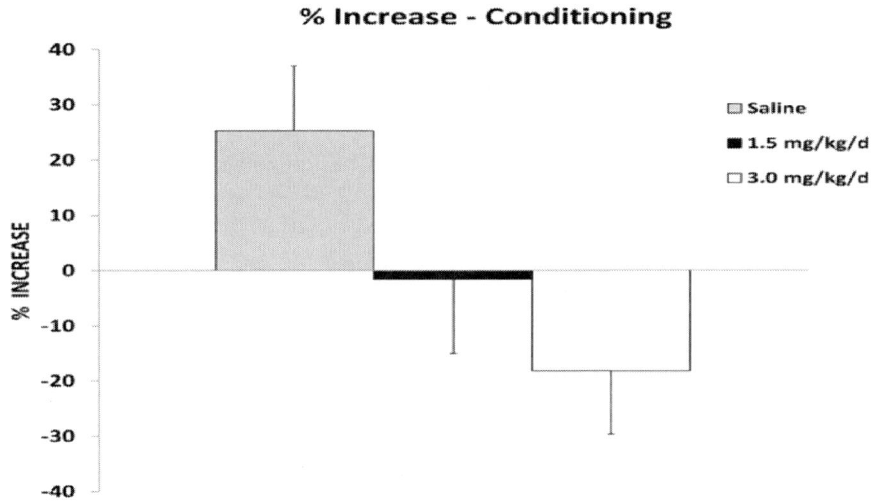


Figure 6. Mean % Increase (conditioned lick suppression) measuring the strength of context conditioning following adolescent PD 28-55 nicotine (1.5 mg/kg/d, 3.0 mg/kg/d) versus saline exposure (osmotic minipump). Training and testing began in adulthood on PD 77. % Increase scores computed from drink latencies (transformed, log10) on the test day relative to the baseline day immediately preceding shock training. Error bars represent SEMs.

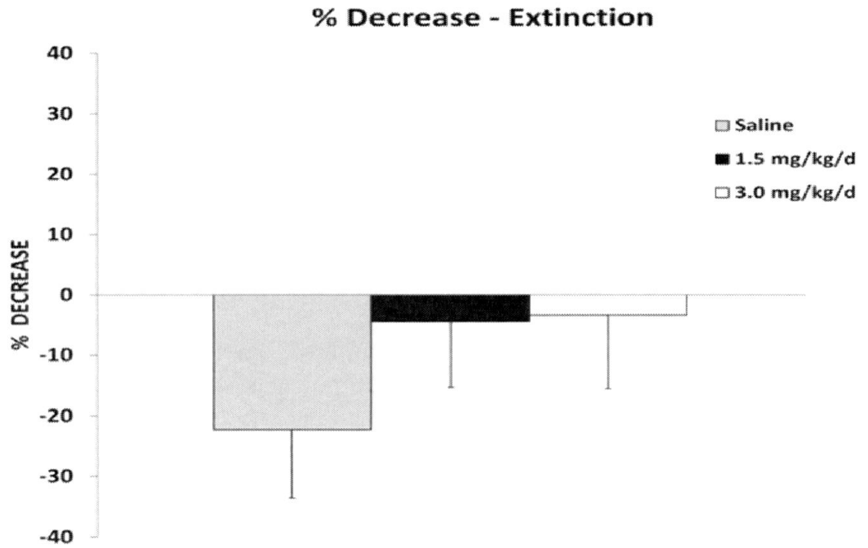


Figure 7. Mean % Decrease (conditioned lick suppression) measuring extinction of context conditioning following adolescent PD 28-55 nicotine (1.5 mg/kg/d, 3.0 mg/kg/d) versus saline exposure (osmotic minipump). Training and testing began in adulthood on PD 77. % Decrease scores computed from drink latencies (transformed, log10) on the first relative to second test day. Error bars represent SEMs.

Interestingly, Spaeth et al. [152] observed a stronger impairing effect of adolescent nicotine on context learning in the moderate dose group (3.0 mg/kg/d) and a follow up study was conducted using this dose as the dose of upper limit. Rats were exposed to saline, 1.5

mg/kg/d or 3.0 mg/kg/d nicotine from PD 28-55 via osmotic minipump and context conditioning began on PD 77 identical to that of the shock groups in Spaeth et al. [152]. Animals were first exposed to no shock acclimation (pre-shock baseline) sessions, followed by shock training and in this experiment two nonreinforced test sessions. As in Spaeth et al. [152], interest was in whether adolescent nicotine exposure would impair context conditioning, or extinction. Acquisition of context conditioning was expressed as a percentage increase in suppression that occurred from the last acclimation session to the first test session (Figure 6) and extinction was expressed as a percentage decrease in suppression that occurred from the first to the second test day (Figure 7).

No differences across drug conditions were observed during pre-shock acclimation sessions. Thus, nicotine did not affect baseline suppression. But, as suggested by Figure 6, nicotine exposure did impact the strength of context conditioning. Groups differed significantly in the strength of context conditioning (Drug effect: $F(2, 34)=3.64$, $p=.037$). Saline treated animals showed the largest increase in suppression and neither drug group showed any positive increase at all, though only the 3.0 mg/kg/d group had significantly lower scores than the saline group ($p<.05$). As discussed, Spaeth et al. [152] observed that adolescent nicotine exposure impaired context conditioning although all shock trained groups in that report did show some evidence of context learning. In the present experiment which employed a longer dosing period (PD 28-55), no evidence of context conditioning was seen in either drug exposed group. Although evaluation of extinction data in Figure 7 suggests nicotine treated animals had smaller decreases in suppression across extinction test days compared to saline treated animals, none of these groups differed statistically. Collectively, these findings from the effects of adolescent nicotine on context conditioning converge with our observations on the effects of adolescent nicotine on trace conditioning. Both tasks are known to be hippocampus dependent, and adult performance in both tasks was shown to be impaired when nicotine exposure occurred earlier in adolescence.

Context conditioning paradigms are often used to reveal the effect of drug or lesion manipulation on the magnitude of this type of learning. A final context conditioning experiment was conducted and results from that study suggest a somewhat novel possibility that chronic adolescent nicotine exposure may, qualitatively, affect the way in which the adult animal responds to environmental stress. This experiment was conceptually similar to the previous experiments from our laboratory described but permitted more detailed evaluation of nicotine's impact on fear expression within the context learning paradigm. On PD 28, Sprague-Dawley rats were surgically implanted with osmotic minipumps that delivered saline, 3.0 mg/kg/d, or 6.0 mg/kg/d nicotine tartrate. As in Spaeth et al. [152] the minipumps administered nicotine during an adolescent period from PD 28-42 at which time the pumps were removed. The adolescent rats were then allowed to age and become adults before training and testing. Training for context conditioning began on PD 60. In this experiment rats received either 10 unsignaled shocks in the context or context exposure only with no shock during a single session. On the shock training day, animals were placed in chambers and allowed to acclimate for 5 min before onset of the first shock. Twenty-four hours after shock training all animals were tested during a 10-min no-shock test for freezing in the presence of context cues. Freezing data for each minute of the test session were recorded, permitting minute-by-minute assessment of fear expression. Note that fear might generally be expected to be highest during that minute of the test session which had immediately preceded onset of the shock series on the prior shock training day. That is, fear might be highest whenever shock is most imminently expected to occur because of prior training, and research in fear learning supports the view that animals learn when in time shocks are delivered [148, 157]. In this view, during the shock-free test day, asymptotic fear should occur at minute 5 into the session because this is the minute at which the shock series had onset on the prior shock training day.

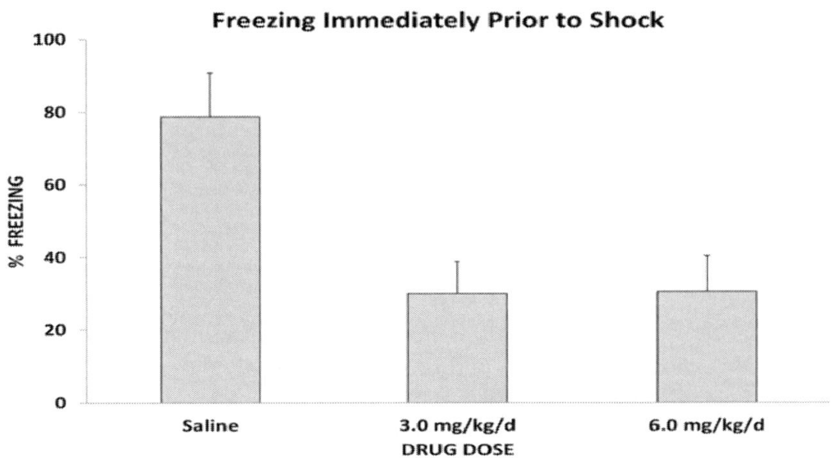


Figure 8. Mean % Freezing in the context during minute 5, the minute immediately prior to the "expected" time of shock delivery, based on prior shock training in shock groups. Animals received adolescent PD 28-42 nicotine (3.0 mg/kg/d, 6.0 mg/kg/d) versus saline exposure (osmotic minipump). Training and testing began in adulthood on PD 60. Control (no-shock) groups had very low levels of freezing and are not shown. Error bars represent SEMs.

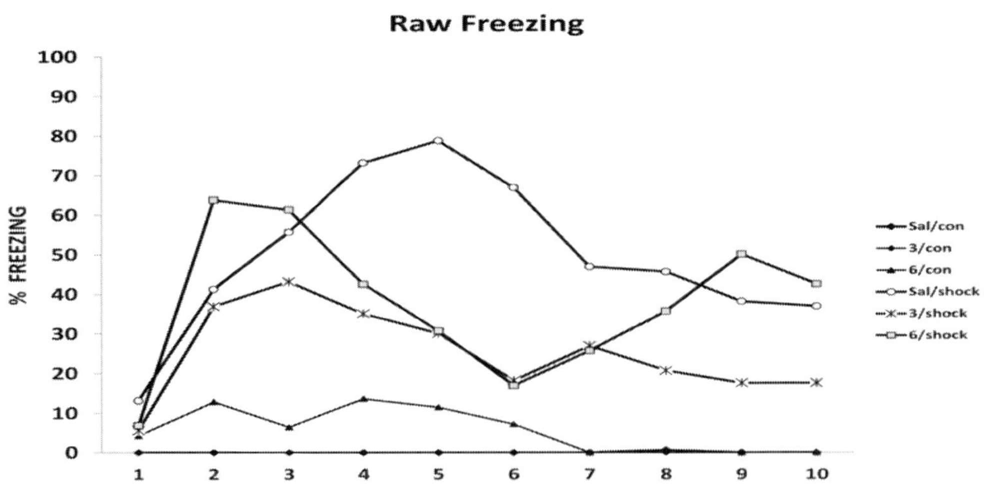


Figure 9. Mean % Freezing in the context during each minute of the shock free test. Shock had onset at the end of minute 5 on the prior shock day for all shock groups. Animals received adolescent PD 28-42 nicotine (3.0 mg/kg/d, 6.0 mg/kg/d) versus saline exposure (osmotic minipump). Training and testing began in adulthood on PD 60.

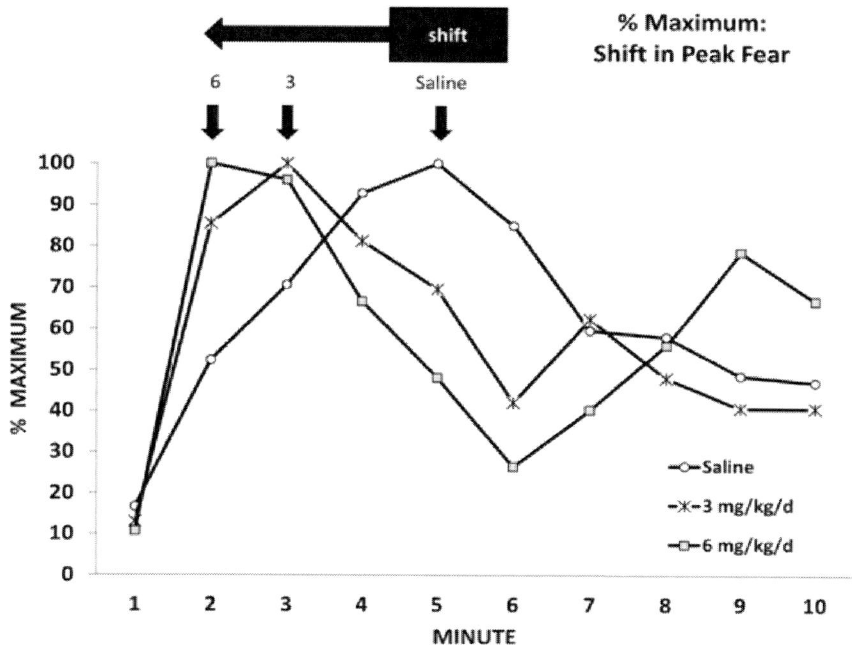


Figure 10. Freezing data in shock groups expressed as a % of Maximum in respective groups. Shock had onset at the end of minute 5 on the shock training day. Fear peaks at minute 5 in saline treated animals but peaks earlier in nicotine treated animals. Animals received adolescent PD 28-42 nicotine (3.0 mg/kg/d, 6.0 mg/kg/d) versus saline exposure (osmotic minipump). Training and testing began in adulthood on PD 60.

Data from minute 5 of the test are shown in Figure 8 for shock groups and provide an indicator of context conditioning when context fear should be strongest. Data for all minutes of the test for all groups are shown in Figure 9.

Analyses of data from this experiment revealed a significant Conditioning Treatment (shock vs. no shock) X Drug (saline, 3.0 mg/kg/d, 6.0 mg/kg/d) interaction ($F(2, 42)=7.16$, $p=.002$), and significant effects of Drug ($F(2, 42)=4.72$ $p<.01$) and Conditioning Treatment ($F(1, 42)=39.15$, $p<.001$). The data, some of which are depicted in Figure 8, replicate the context conditioning impairments observed in the previous experiment (see Figure 6) as well as Spaeth et al. [152]. Animals exposed to adolescent nicotine revealed significant impairments in hippocampus-dependent context conditioning, even though training and testing occurred in adulthood and a long period after initial nicotine exposure. Significantly lower levels of freezing were observed in each of the two drug treated shock groups compared to the saline shock group from Figure 8 ($p$s<.001). Each of these groups received identical shock training but different adolescent drug treatments. As already reported, these outcomes indicate that the effects of nicotine exposure during adolescence were long lasting and impaired context conditioning in later adulthood.

Data from Figure 9 display freezing means during all minutes of the test session for all groups. No shock groups showed little freezing (the 3.0 mg/kg/d and 6.0 mg/kg/d no shock groups are represented in Figure 9 but cannot be seen because of near zero freezing). What is immediately apparent is that the three shock groups all displayed some freezing throughout the test session but the patterns of freezing differed. A Minute (1-10) X Conditioning

Treatment (shock vs. no shock) x Drug (saline, 3.0 mg/kg/d, 6.0 mg/kg/d) analysis revealed significant effects of Minute ($F(9, 378)=5.68$, $p<.001$), Conditioning Treatment ($F(1, 42)= 64.98$, $p<.001$), a Minute X Conditioning Treatment interaction ($F(9, 378)= 4.17$, $p<.001$), and a Minute X Conditioning Treatment X Drug interaction ($F(18, 378)= 1.89$, $p=.016$). Interaction contrasts conducted separately for shock and no shock groups revealed a significant Minute x Drug interaction for shock groups ($F(18, 189)=1.81$, p=.027), but not for no shock groups. Data from Figure 9 also reveal that the impairment in context conditioning following adolescent drug exposure was not limited to only minute 5 of the test session. Both nicotine treated groups showed significantly lower freezing during minutes 4, 5, 6 and 7 compared to the saline group, and the 3.0 mg/kg/d group additionally had significantly lower freezing compared to the saline group during minutes 8 and 9 ($ps<.05$). No shock groups did not differ during any minute of the test. Alterations in the temporal distribution of freezing behavior during the test session may be informative. What is apparent from Figure 9 is that *peak* freezing responses are not the same in each of the three shock groups. Figure 10 illustrates the same data from Figure 9 but transformed so that means from each shock group are plotted to have the same maximum freezing value (100%). This permits ready comparison of the distribution of freezing behavior across the test session in the three groups.

Figure 10 illustrates data from the freezing test as a % of Maximum within each group ([$\text{Minute}_x$ within group/ $\text{Mean}_x$ Maximum Peak within group]*100). These data suggest that animals had differing profiles of fear responding during the test that varied as a function of adolescent drug condition. Peak freezing (maximal fear) seems adaptively timed in saline controls. Shock had onset at minute 5 on the shock training day and freezing peaked at minute 5 (the time at which shock would be expected) on the no-shock test day for these animals. For the remaining two nicotine groups, the peak freezing response shifts to earlier points in the test session and does so in a dose-dependent manner. Rats treated with 3.0 mg/kg/d during adolescence show peak freezing at min 3. Rats treated with the highest dose of nicotine, 6.0 mg/kg/d, show earlier and relatively immediate peak freezing at minute 2. Thus, there was a dose-dependent change in the character of fear expression upon exposure to the environmental stressor (context).

The mechanism for such an effect is not clear but nicotine is known to modulate dopamine release [158, 159, 160] which affects timing and time perception [161]. In several experiments, dopamine agonists have been suggested to speed the 'internal clock' and produce an overestimate of elapsed time [162, 163, 164]. Additionally, hippocampal damage can produce temporal foreshortening of the expected time of reinforcement [165] which could be related to the shift in peak freezing observed. Elucidation of specific mechanisms await further study but these data nonetheless suggest that adolescent nicotine may produce long-lasting changes in *how* vulnerability to environmental stressors is expressed. Adult rats exposed to nicotine as adolescents may not regulate fear as well as non-treated animals, and display a more 'immediate stress' response upon exposure to the stressor. To the extent that immediate stressors are more subjectively potent than delayed stressors, these outcomes may have implications for the role of adolescent nicotine on anxiety responses to stressors in adulthood which could modulate the reinforcing effectiveness of smoking behavior.

## CONCLUSION

Analysis of the effects of nicotine on different forms of hippocampal memory may prove to be a powerful and sophisticated analytical tool because *there are* different forms of hippocampal memory. Rodent models provide a range of such tasks including spatial memory tasks (standard radial maze, Morris water maze, T-maze, spontaneous alternation), trace conditioning, and context conditioning. Kenny and Gould [166] recently emphasized that comparing the effects of nicotine in different hippocampus-dependent learning tasks may be a valuable tactic in more precisely clarifying the effect of nicotine on separate brain regions, neurotransmitter receptor types, and genetic regulation *because* the neural substrates are different in these different tasks.

Acute, and in some cases chronic nicotine are known to have cognitive enhancing effects in a wide array of rodent models reviewed, including spatial navigation in the radial maze, context conditioning, and trace conditioning. In humans, memory and other functional deficits produced by nicotine cessation can be ameliorated by smoking or transdermal nicotine [167] and in some cases the likelihood of relapse during abstinence is even positively correlated with the magnitude of such deficits [168].

Adolescence is a critical period of vulnerability for the neurodegenerative effects of nicotine and for nicotine dependence [6, 18, 20, 169]. As an interesting caveat, some researchers have suggested a period of insensitivity of hippocampal LTP and Fos immunoreactivity to environmental input that precedes PD 30 [121]. If the hippocampus is insulated from environmentally induced plasticity during this early period, teratogenic agents such as nicotine may have a more devastating impact on the developmental cascade. In the present context, we suggest this as a novel reason for why the early adolescent or immature hippocampus may be especially sensitive to pharmacological insult.

Findings from our laboratories suggest chronic nicotine exposure, particularly if that exposure occurs in adolescence, may produce significant and long-lasting impairments in brain systems that underlie memory. There is also evidence that the effects of chronic nicotine exposure, including cognitive impairments, may be delayed to periods after nicotine cessation. Counotte et al. [170] reported impairments in an attention task in adult rats that was produced by earlier chronic adolescent nicotine exposure. Importantly, deficits did not emerge in early training but only after multiple sessions (see also [138, 171]). Examples of delayed cognitive and neural impairment are also not limited to early phase withdrawal or even those produced by nicotine exposure. In rats, early post-natal stress on PD 2 produced by restricting access to nesting material of the dam, which induces aberrant maternal behavior, results in a deficit in Morris water maze performance that is strongly manifest at 12 months of age but not earlier [172]. Thus, there is some basis to hypothesize a neuro-degenerative incubation period whereby cognitive deficits produced by earlier experience are not expressed until later adulthood.

This raises the possibility that brain-induced changes which enhance dependence potential may begin with adolescent drug exposure but dependence and addictive behavior continues in order to alleviate cognitive impairments that either begin in adolescence, or, that emerge later. Taken together with data indicative of memory impairments present in adulthood, produced much earlier by adolescent nicotine exposure, a potential for sustained nicotine dependence that extends beyond the window of adolescence becomes evident.

The experiments described in this chapter demonstrate the value of animal research in order to examine, across numerous well-controlled points in development, the impact of nicotine on cognition. Nicotine appears to have beneficial effects on attention, learning and memory in adults, at least under some conditions. Nicotinic receptors continue to be potential targets for pharmacotherapies for several disorders, including Alzheimer's disease and schizophrenia and may have therapeutic potential for FASD. However, our data suggest there may be cognitive deficits that emerge following adolescent nicotine exposure. These data suggest a complicated profile for targeting nicotinic receptors to treat disorders, particularly during adolescence. While modification of nicotinic receptors may be able to produce initial benefits, it remains to be studied whether and when deficits emerge when nicotine (or more specific nicotinic receptor agonists) treatment is stopped. Our data most clearly suggest that, in "normal" organisms, adolescent nicotine can produce deficits that last into adulthood. A continuing goal and value of animal models is that they not only inform clinical practice on substance abuse but also progress our capacity to isolate and explain different levels of function.

## Acknowledgments

This research was supported by a grant from the Virginia Tobacco Settlement Foundation. We thank Caity Smyth for assistance in data collection.

## References

[1] Centers for Disease Control and Prevention. (2008). Smoking-attributable mortality, years of potential life lost, and productivity losses – United States, 2000-2004. *MMWR*, 57, 1226-1228.

[2] Chambers, R.A., Taylor, J.R. Potenza, M.N. (2003). Developmental neurocircuitry of motivation in adolescence: A critical period of addiction vulnerability. *Am. J. Psychiatry*, 160, 1041-1052.

[3] Taioli, E., Wynder, E.L. (1991). Effect of the age at which smoking begins on frequency of smoking in adulthood. *N. Engl. J. Med. Overseas*, 325, 968-969.

[4] Eisenberg, T., Balster, R. (2000). Initial tobacco use in adolescents: Current knowledge, future directions. *Drug Alcohol. Depend.*, 59, 41-60.

[5] Dahl, R.E., Spear, L.P. (2004). Adolescent brain development. *Ann. N. Y. Acad. Sci.*, 1021, 1–22.

[6] Spear L.P. (2000). The adolescent brain and age-related behavioral manifestations. *Neurosci. Biobehav. Rev.*, 24, 417-463.

[7] Turner, L., Mermelstein, R., Flay, B. (2004). Individual and contextual influences on adolescent smoking. *Ann. N. Y. Acad. Sci.*, 1021, 175-197.

[8] Breslau, N., Peterson, E.L. (1996). Smoking cessation in young adults: Age at initiation of cigarette smoking and other suspected influences. *Am. J. Public Health*, 86, 214-220.

[9] Chen, J., Millar, W.J. (1998). Age of smoking initiation: *Implications for quitting. Health Report*, 9, 39-46.

[10] Bell, R.L., Rodd, Z.A., Lumeng, L., Murphy, J.M., McBride, W.J. (2006). The alcohol-preferring P rat and animal models of excessive alcohol drinking. *Addict. Biol.,* 11, 270–288.

[11] Eriksson, C.J (1981) Finnish selection studies on alcohol-related behaviors: factors regulating voluntary alcohol consumption. In McClearn, G.E., Deitrich, R.A., Erwin G., eds. Development of Animal Models as Pharmacogenetic Tools, pp. 119–145. Rockville, MD: US Government Printing Office.

[12] Li, T.K., Lumeng L., Doolittle, D.P. (1993). Selective breeding for alcohol preference and associated responses. *Behav. Genet.*, 23, 163–170.

[13] Sinclair, J.D., Le, A.D., Kiianmaa, K. (1989). The AA and ANA rat lines, selected for differences in voluntary alcohol consumption. *Experientia*, 45, 798–805.

[14] Kemppainen, H., Hyytia, P. Kiianmaa, K. (2009). Behavioral consequences of repeated nicotine during adolescence in alcohol-preferring AA and alcohol-avoiding ANA rats. Alcoholism: *Clinical and Experimental Research*, 33, 340-349.

[15] Bedell, M.A, Largaespada, D.A., Jenkins, N.A., Copeland, N.G. (1997). Mouse models of human disease. Part II: recent progress and future directions. *Genes. Dev.*, 11, 11-43.

[16] Baumrind, D. (1987). A developmental perspective on adolescent risk taking in contemporary America. In Irwin Jr. C.E., ed. Adolescent social behavior and health. San Francisco, CA: *Jossey-Bass*, pp. 93-125.

[17] Peterson, A.C., Silbereisen, R.K., Sorensen, S. (1996). Adolescent development: a global perspective. In Hurrelmann, K., Hamilton, S.F., eds. Social problems and social contexts in adolescence. New York: NY: *Aldine de Gruyter*, pp.3-37.

[18] Smith, R.F. (2003). Animal models of periadolescent substance abuse. *Neurotoxicol. Teratol.,* 25, 291-301.

[19] Spear L.P., Brake S.C. (1983). Periadolescence: age-dependent behavior and psychopharmacological responsivity in rats. *Dev. Psychobiol.,* 16, 83–109.

[20] Slotkin, T.A. (2002). Nicotine and the adolescent brain: Insights from an animal model. *Neurotoxicol. Teratol.*, 24, 369-384.

[21] Barnet, R.C., Hunt, P.S. (2005). Parallel ontogeny of trace and long delay fear conditioning in the rat. *Learn Behav.*, 33, 437-443.

[22] Hunt, P.S., Holloway, J.L., Scordalakes, E.M. (2001). Social interaction with an intoxicated sibling can result in a preference for ethanol in periadolescent rats. *Dev. Psychobiol.*, 38, 101-109.

[23] Yttri, E.A., Burk, J.A. Hunt, P.S. (2004). Intermittent ethanol exposure in adolescent rats: Dose-dependent impairment in trace conditioning. *Alcohol. Clin. Exp. Res.*, 28, 1433-1436.

[24] Suzuki, M., Hagino, H., Nohara, S., Zhou, S.-Y., Kawasaki, Y., Takahashi, T., Matsui, M., Seto, H., Ono, T., Kurachi, M. (2005). Male-specific volume expansion of the human hippocampus during adolescence. *Cereb. Cortex,* 15, 187-193.

[25] He, J., Crews, F.T. (2007). Neurogenesis decreases during brain maturation from adolescence to adulthood. *Pharmacol. Biochem. Behav.*, 86, 327-333.

[26] Zehr, J.L., Nichols, L.R., Schulz, K.M., Sisk, C.L. (2008). Adolescent development of neuron structure in dentate gyrus granule cells of male Syrian hamsters. *Dev. Neurobiol.,* 68, 1517-1526.

[27] Crews, F., He, J., Hodge, C. (2007). Adolescent cortical development: A critical period of vulnerability for addiction. *Pharmacol. Biochem. Behav.*, 86, 189-199.

[28] Giedd, J.N. (2004). Structural magnetic resonance imaging of the adolescent brain. In R.E. Dahl, L.P. Spear (Eds.), Adolescent brain development: Vulnerabilities and opportunities. *Ann. N. Y. Acad. Sci.*, 1021, 77-85.

[29] Sowell, E.R., Thompson, P.M., Tessner, K.D., Toga, A.W. (2001). Mapping continued brain growth and gray matter density reduction in dorsal frontal cortex: Inverse relationships during postadolescent brain maturation. *J. Neurosci.*, 21, 8819-8829.

[30] Huttenlocher, P.R. (1984). Synapse elimination and plasticity in developing human cerebral cortex. *Am. J. Ment. Defic.*, 88, 488-496.

[31] Rakic, P., Bourgeois, J.-P. Goldman-Rakic, P.S. (1994). Synaptic development of the cerebral cortex: Implications for learning, memory, and mental illness. In J. van Pelt, M.A. Corner, H.B.M. Uylings, F.H., Lopes, da Silva (Eds.). Progress in brain research, The self-organizing brain: From growth cones to functional networks, Vol. 102 (pp. 227-243). Amsterdam, *Elsevier*.

[32] Jernigan. T.L., Trauner, D.A., Hesselink, J.R. Tallal, P.A. (1991). Maturation of human cerebrum observed in vivo during adolescence. *Brain*, 114, 2037-2049.

[33] van Eden, C.G., Kros, J.M., Uylings, H.B.M. (1990). The development of the rat prefrontal cortex: Its size and development of connections with thalamus, spinal cord and other cortical areas. In H.B.M. Uylings, C.G., van Eden, J.P.C., De Bruin, M.A., Corner, M.G.P., Feenstra, (Eds.), Progress in brain research, The prefrontal cortex: It's structure, function and pathology, Vol. 85 (pp. 169-183). Amsterdam, *Elsevier*.

[34] Andersen, S.L. (2003). Trajectories of brain development: Point of vulnerability or window of opportunity? *Neurosci. Biobehav. Rev.*, 27, 3-18.

[35] Gould, E., Woolf, N.J., Butcher, L.L. (1991). Postnatal development of cholinergic neurons in the rat: I. Forebrain. *Brain Res. Bull.*, 27, 767-789.

[36] Matthews, D.A., Nadler, J.V., Lynch, G.S., Cotman, C.W. (1974). Development of cholinergic innervations in the hippocampal formation of the rat. *Dev. Biol.*, 36, 130-141.

[37] Rudy, J.W. (1993). Contextual conditioning and auditory cue conditioning dissociate during development. *Behav. Neurosci.*, 107, 887-891.

[38] Guilarte, T.R., McGlothan, J.L. (1998). Hippocampal NMDA receptor mRNA undergoes subunit specific changes during developmental lead exposure. *Brain Res.*, 790, 98-107.

[39] Insel, T.R., Miller, L.P. Gelhard, R.E. (1990). The ontogeny of excitatory amino acid receptors in rat forebrain: I. N-methyl-D-aspartate and quisqualate receptors. *Neuroscience*, 35, 31-43.

[40] Tarazi, F.I., Tomasini, E.C. Baldessarini, R.J. (1999). Postnatal development of dopamine D1-like receptors in rat cortical and striatolimbic brain regions: An autoradiographic study. *Dev. Neurosci.*, 21, 43-49.

[41] Kalsbeek, A., Voorn, P., Buijs, R.M., Pools, C.W., Uylings, H.B.M. (1988). Development of the dopaminergic innervations in the prefrontal cortex of the rat. *J. Comp. Neurol.*, 269, 58-72.

[42] Rosenberg, D.R. Lewis, D.A. (1994). Changes in the dopaminergic innervations of monkey prefrontal cortex during late postnatal development: A tyrosine hydroxylase immunohistochemical study. *Biol. Psychiatry*, 36, 272-277.

[43] Geier, C.F., Terwilliger, R., Teslovich, T., Velanova, K., Luna, B. (2010). Immaturities in reward processing and its influence on inhibitory control in adolescence. *Cereb. Cortex*, 20 (7), 1613–1629.

[44] Krain, A.L., Hefton, S., Pine, D.S., Ernst, M., Castellanos, F.X., Klein, R.G. Molham, M.P. (2006). An fMRI examination of developmental differences in the neural correlates of uncertainty and decision-making. *J. Child Psychol. Psychiatry*, 47, 1023-1030.

[45] Yurgelun-Todd, D. (2007). Emotional and cognitive changes during adolescence. *Curr. Opin. Neurobiol.,* 17, 251-257.

[46] Laviola, G.S., Macri, S., Morley-Fletcher, S., Adriani, W. (2003). Risk-taking behavior in adolescent mice: Psychobiological determinants and early epigenetic influence. *Neurosci. Biobehav. Rev.*, 27, 19-31.

[47] Toledo-Rodriguez, M., Sandi, C. (2011). Stress during adolescence increases novelty seeking and risk-taking behavior in male and female rats. *Front Behav. Neurosci.*, 5, 17.

[48] Adriani, W., Chiarotti, F.,, Laviola, G. (1998). Elevated novelty seeking and peculiar D-amphetamine sensitization in periadolescent mice compared with adult mice. *Behav. Neurosci.*, 112, 1152-1166.

[49] Spear, L.P., Shalaby, I.A., Brick, J. (1980). Chronic administration of haloperidol during development: behavioral and psychopharmacological effects. *Psychopharmacology*, 70, 47-58.

[50] Adriani W., Laviola G. (2004). Windows of vulnerability to psychopathology and therapeutic strategy in the adolescent rodent model. *Behav. Pharmacol.*, 15, 341–352.

[51] Belluzzi, J.D., Lee, A.G., Oliff, H.S., Leslie, F.M. (2004). Age-dependent effects of nicotine on locomotor activity and conditioned place preference in rats. *Psychopharmacology*, 174, 389-395.

[52] Thiel, K.J., Sanabria, F., Neisewander, J.L. (2009). Synergistic interaction between nicotine and social rewards in adolescent male rats. *Psychopharmacology*, 204, 391-402.

[53] Vastola, B.J., Douglas, L.A., Varlinskaya, E.I., Spear, L.P. (2002). Nicotine-induced conditioned place preference in adolescent and adult rats. *Physiol. Behav.*, 77, 107-114.

[54] Chen, H., Matta, S.G. Sharp, B.M. (2007). Acquisition of nicotine self-administration in adolescent rats given prolonged access to the drug. *Neuropsychopharmacology*, 32, 700-709.

[55] Levin, E.D., Lawrence, S.S., Petro, A., Horton, K., Rezvani, A.H., Seidler, F.J., Slotkin, T.A. (2007). Adolescent vs. adult-onset nicotine self-administration in male rats: Duration of effect and differential nicotinic receptor correlates. *Neurotoxicol. Teratol.*, 29, 458-465.

[56] Shram, M.J., Funk, D., Li, Z., Le, A.D. (2008). Nicotine self-administration, extinction responding and reinstatement in adolescent and adult male rats: Evidence against a biological vulnerability to nicotine addiction during adolescence. *Neuropsychopharmacology*, 33, 739-748.

[57] Levin, E.D., Rezvani, A.H., Montoya, D., Rose, J.E., Swartzwelder, S. (2003). Adolescent-onset nicotine self-administration modeled in female rats. *Psychopharmacology*, 169, 141-149.

[58] Thor, D.H., Holloway, W.R. (1984). Developmental analyses of social play-behavior in juvenile rats. *Bull. Psychon. Soc.*, 22, 587-590.
[59] Panksepp J., Siviy, S.,, Normansell L.A. (1984). The psychobiology of play: Theoretical and methodological perspectives. *Neurosci. Biobehav. Rev.* 8, 465–492.
[60] Bell, H.C., Pellis, S.M., Kolb, B. (2010). Juvenile peer play experience and the development of the orbitofrontal and medial prefrontal cortices. *Behav. Brain Res.*, 207, 7-13.
[61] Hole, G. (1991). The effects of social deprivation on levels of social play in the laboratory rat Rattus norvegicus. *Behav. Processes*, 25, 41-53.
[62] Walton, D., Latane, B. (1972). Visual vs. physical social deprivation and affiliation in rats. *Psychon. Sci.*, 26, 4-6.
[63] Calcagnetti, D.J. Schechter, M.D. (1992). Place conditioning reveals the rewarding aspect of social interaction in juvenile rats. *Physiol. Behav.*, 51, 667-672.
[64] Humphreys, A.P. Einon, D.F. (1981). Play as a reinforce for maze-learning in juvenile rats. *Anim. Behav.*, 29, 259-270.
[65] Robbins, T.W., Jones, G.H. Wilkinson, L.S. (1996). Behavioural and neurochemical effects of early social deprivation in the rat. *J. Psychopharmacol.*, 10, 39-47.
[66] Einon, D., Potegal, M. (1991). Enhanced defense in adult rats deprived of playfighting experience as juveniles. *Aggress Behav.*, 17, 27-40.
[67] van den Berg, C.L., Hol, T., Van Ree, J.M., Spruijt, B.M., Everts, H., Koolhaas, J.M. (1999). Play is indispensable for an adequate development of coping with social challenges in the rat. *Dev. Psychobiol*, 34, 129-138.
[68] Hole, G.J., Einon, D.F. Plotkin, H.C. (1986). The role of social experience in the development of sexual competence in Rattus norvegicus. *Behav. Processes*, 12, 187-202.
[69] Toth, M., Halasz, J., Mikics, E., Barsy, B. Haller, J. (2008). Early social deprivation induces disturbed social communication and violent aggression in adulthood. *Behav. Neurosci.*, 122, 849-854.
[70] Day, H.G., Seay, B.M., Hale, P., Hendricks, D. (1982). Early social deprivation and the ontogeny of unrestricted social behavior in the laboratory rat. *Dev. Psychobiol.*, 15, 47-59.
[71] Dessi-Fulgheri, F., di Prisco, C.L., Verdarelli, P. (1976). Effects of two kinds of social deprivation on testosterone and estradiol-17b plasma levels in the male rat. *Experimentia*, 32, 114-115.
[72] Einon, D.F. (1980). Spatial memory and response strategies in rats: Age, sex and rearing differences in performance. *Q. J. Exp. Psychol.*, 32, 473-489.
[73] Einon, D.F. Morgan, M.J. (1977). A critical period for social isolation in the rat. *Dev. Psychobiol.*, 10, 123-132.
[74] McCormick, C.M., Nixon, F., Thomas, C., Lowie, B. Dyck, J. (2010). Hippocampal cell proliferation and spatial memory performance after social instability stress in adolescence in female rats. *Behav. Brain Res.*, 208, 23-29.
[75] Levin, E.D., McClernon, F.J. Rezvani, A.H. (2006). Nicotinic effects on cognitive function: behavioral characterization, pharmacological specification, and anatomic localization. *Psychopharmacology*, 184, 523-539.
[76] Mirza, N.R. Stolerman, I.P. (1998). Nicotine enhances sustained attention in the rat under specific task conditions. *Psychopharmacology* (Berlin), 138, 266-274.

[77] Mirza, N.R. Bright, J.L. (2001). Nicotine-induced enhancements in the five-choice serial reaction time task in rats are strain-dependent. *Psychopharmacology*, 154, 8-12.

[78] Grottick, A.J. Higgins, G.A. (2000). Effect of subtype selective nicotinic compounds on attention as assessed by the five-choice serial reaction time task. *Behav. Brain Res.*, 117, 197-208.

[79] McQuail, J.A. Burk, J.A. (2006). Evaluation of muscarinic and nicotinic receptor antagonists on attention and working memory. *Pharmacol. Biochem. Behav.*, 85, 796-803.

[80] Turchi, J., Holley, L.A., Sarter, M. (1995). Effects of nicotinic acetylcholine receptor ligands on behavioral vigilance in rats. *Psychopharmacology*, 118, 195-205.

[81] McGaughy J, Decker, M.W. Sarter, M. (1999). Enhancement of sustained attention performance by the nicotinic acetylcholine receptor agonist ABT-418 in intact but not basal forebrain-lesioned rats. *Psychopharmacology*, 144, 175-182.

[82] Giuliano, C., Parikh, V., Ward, J.R., Chiamulera, C. Sarter, M. (2008). Increases in cholinergic neurotransmission measured by using choline-sensitive microelectrodes: enhanced detection by hydrolysis of acetylcholine on recording sites? *Neurochem. Int.*, 52, 1343-1350.

[83] Parikh, V., Kozak, R., Martinez, V. Sarter, M. (2007). Prefrontal acetylcholine release controls cue detection on multiple timescales. *Neuron*, 56, 141-154.

[84] Howe, W.M., Ji, J., Parikh, V., Williams, S., Mocaër, E., Trocmé-Thibierge, C. Sarter, M. (2010). Enhancement of attentional performance by selective stimulation of alpha4beta2(*) nAChRs: underlying cholinergic mechanisms. *Neuropsychopharmacology*, 35, 1391-1401.

[85] Hahn, B., Stolerman, I.P. (2002). Nicotine-induced attentional enhancement in rats: effects of chronic exposure to nicotine. *Neuropsychopharmacology*, 27, 712-722.

[86] Levin, E.D. (2002). Nicotinic receptor subtypes and cognitive function. *J. Neurobiol.*, 53, 633-640.

[87] Levin, E.D., Torry, D. (1996). Acute and chronic nicotine effects on working memory in aged rats. *Psychopharmacology*, 123, 88-97.

[88] Levin, E.D., Kim, P., Meray, R. (1996). Chronic nicotine effects on working and reference memory in the 16-arm radial maze: interactions with D1 agonist and antagonist drugs. *Psychopharmacology*, 127, 25-30.

[89] Puma, C., Deschaux, O., Molimard, R. Bizot, J.C. (1999). Nicotine improves memory in an object recognition task in rats. *Eur. Neuropsychopharmacol.*, 9, 323-327.

[90] Gould, T.J., Wehner, J.M. (1999). Nicotine enhancement of contextual fear conditioning. *Behav. Brain Res.*, 102, 31-39.

[91] Gould, T.J., Feiro, O., Moore, D. (2004). Nicotine enhances trace cued fear conditioning but not delay cued fear conditioning in C57BL/6 mice. *Behav. Brain Res.*, 155, 167-173.

[92] Davis, J.A. Gould, T.J. (2010). Hippocampal nAChRs mediate nicotine withdrawal-related learning deficits. *Eur. Neuropsychopharmacol.*, 19, 551-561.

[93] Portugal, G.S. Gould, T.J. (2009). Nicotine withdrawal disrupts new contextual learning. *Pharmacol. Biochem. Behav.*, 92, 117-123.

[94] Dallery, J. Locey M.L. (2005). Effects of acute and chronic nicotine on impulsive choice in rats. *Behav. Pharmacol.*, 16, 15-23.

[95] Kolokotroni, K.Z., Rodgers, R.J. Harrison, A.A. (2011). Acute nicotine increases both impulsive choice and behavioural disinhibition in rats. *Psychopharmacology*, 217 (4), 455-73.

[96] Locey, M.L. Dallery, J. (2009). Isolating behavioral mechanisms of intertemporal choice: nicotine effects on delay discounting and amount sensitivity. *J. Exp. Anal. Behav.*, 91, 213-223.

[97] Locey, M.L. Dallery, J. (2011). Nicotine and behavioral mechanisms of intertemporal choice. *Behav. Processes*, 87, 18-24.

[98] Diergaarde, L, Pattij, T., Poortvliet, I., Hogenboom, F., de Vries, W., Schoffelmeer, A.N.and De Vries, T.J. (2008). Impulsive choice and impulsive action predict vulnerability to distinct stages of nicotine seeking in rats. *Biol. Psychiatry*, 63, 301-308.

[99] Cardinal, R.N., Pennicott, D.R., Sugathapala, C.L., Robbins, T.W., Everitt, B.J. (2001). Impulsive choice induced in rats by lesions of the nucleus accumbens core. *Science*, 292, 2499-2501.

[100] Mar, A.C., Walker, A.L., Theobald, D.E., Eagle, D.M., Robbins, T.W. (2011). Dissociable effects of lesions to orbitofrontal cortex subregions on impulsive choice in the rat. *J. Neurosci.*, 31, 6398-6404.

[101] Churchwell, J.C., Morris, A.M., Heurtelou, N.M., Kesner, R.P. (2009). Interactions between the prefrontal cortex and amygdala during delay discounting and reversal. *Behav. Neurosci.*, 123, 1185-1196.

[102] Tsutsui-Kimura, I., Ohmura, Y., Izumi, T., Yamaguchi, T., Yoshida, T., Yoshioka, M. (2010). Nicotine provokes impulsive-like action by stimulating alpha4beta2 nicotinic acetylcholine receptors in the infralimbic, but not in the prelimbic cortex. *Psychopharmacology*, 209, 351-359.

[103] Soderstrom, K., Qui, W., Williams, H., Taylor, D.A., McMillen, B.A. (2007). Nicotine increases FosB expression within a subset of reward- and memory-related brain regions during both peri- and post-adolescence. *Psychopharmacology*, 19, 891-897.

[104] Xu, Z., Seidler, F.J., Tate, C.A., Garcia, S.J., Slikker, W., Jr., Slotkin, T.A. (2003). Sex-selective hippocampal alterations after adolescent nicotine administration: Effects on neurospecific proteins. *Nicotine Tob. Res.*, 5, 955-960.

[105] Abreu-Villaca, Y., Seidler, F.J., Qiao, D., Tate, C.A., Cousins, M.M., Thillai, I., Slotkin, T.A. (2003). Short-term adolescent nicotine exposure has immediate and persistent effects on cholinergic systems: Critical periods, patterns of exposure, dose thresholds. *Neuropsychopharmacology*, 28, 1935-1949.

[106] Adriani, W., Granstrem, O., Macri, S., Izykenova, D., Dambinova, S., Laviola, G. (2004). Behavioral and neurochemical vulnerability during adolescence in mice: Studies with nicotine. *Neuropsychopharmacology*, 29, 869-878.

[107] Oliveira-da-Silva, A., Vieira, F.B., Cristina-Rodrigues, F., Filgueiras, C.C., Manhaes, A.C., Abreu-Villaca, Y. (2009). Increased apoptosis and reduced neuronal and glial densities in the hippocampus due to nicotine and ethanol exposure in adolescent mice. *Int. J. Dev. Neurosci.*, 27, 539-548.

[108] Bergstrom, H.C., McDonald, C.G., French, H.T., Smith, R.F. (2008). Continuous nicotine administration produces selective, age-dependent structural alteration of pyramidal neurons from prelimbic cortex. *Synapse*, 62, 31-39.

[109] Trauth, J.A., Siedler, F.J., McCook, E.C., Slotkin, T.A. (1999). Adolescent nicotine exposure causes persistent upregulation of nicotinic cholinergic receptors in rat brain regions. *Brain Res.*, 851, 9-19.

[110] Lambe E.K., Picciotto M.R.,, Aghajanian, G.K. (2003). Nicotine induces glutamate release from thalamocortical terminals in prefrontal cortex. *Neuropsychopharmacology* 28, 216–225.

[111] Counotte, D.S., Goriounova, N.A., Li, W.K., Loos, M., van der Schors, R.C., Shetters, D., Schoffelmeer, A.N.M., Smit, A.B., Mansvelder, H.D., Pattij, T., Spijker, S. (2011). Lasting synaptic changes underlie attention deficits by nicotine exposure during adolescence. *Nature Neurosci.*, 14, 417-419.

[112] Bancroft, A., Levin E.D. (2000). Ventral hippocampal alpha4beta2 nicotinic receptors and chronic nicotine effects on memory. *Neuropharmacology*, 39, 2770-2778.

[113] Levin, E.D. (1999). Persisting effects of chronic adolescent nicotine administration on radial arm maze learning and response to nicotine challenges. *Neurotoxicol. Teratol.*, 21, 338.

[114] Alkadhi, K.A., Alzoubi, K.H., Srivareerat, M., Tran, T.T. (2011). Elevation of BACE in an Aβ rat model of Alzheimer's disease: exacerbation by chronic stress and prevention by nicotine. *Int. J. Neuropsychopharmacol.*, 28, 1-11.

[115] Fujii, S. and Sumikawa, K. (2001) Acute and chronic nicotine exposure reverse age-related declines in the induction of LTP in the hippocampus of aged rats. *Brain Res.* 894: 347-353.

[116] Srivareerat, M., Tran, T.T, Salim, S., Abdulaziz M., Aleisa, A.M.' Alkadhi, K.A. (2011). Chronic nicotine restores normal Aβ levels and prevents short-term memory and E-LTP impairment in Aβ rat model of Alzheimer's disease. *Neurobiol. Aging,* 32, 834-844.

[117] Ren, K., Thinschmidt, J., Liu, J., Ai, L., Papke, R.L, King, M.A., Hughes, J.A., Meyer, E.M. (2007). Alpha7 nicotinic receptor gene delivery into mouse hippocampal neurons leads to functional receptor expression, improved spatial memory-related performance, and tau hyperphosphorylation. *Neuroscience*, 145, 314-322.

[118] Sapronov, N.S., Fedotova, Y.O., Kuznetsova, N.N. (2006). Antiamnestic effects of alpha7-nicotinic receptor agonist RJR-2403 in middle-aged ovariectomized rats with Alzheimer type dementia. *Bull. Exp. Biol. Med.*, 142, 700-702.

[119] Moye, T.B., Rudy, J.W. (1987). Ontogenesis of trace conditioning in young rats: Dissociation of associative and memory processes. *Dev. Psychobiol.*, 20, 405-414.

[120] Bronstein, P.M., Dworkin, T., Bilder, B.H. (1974). Age-related differences in rats' spontaneous alternation. *Anim. Learn Behav.*, 2, 285-288.

[121] Waters N., Klintsova, A.Y., Foster, T.C. (1997). Insensitivity of the hippocampus to environmental stimulation during postnatal development. *J. Neurosci.*,17, 7967-79763.

[122] Vecera, S.P., Rothbart, M.K.,, Posner, M.I. (1991). Development of spontaneous alternation in infancy. *J. Cogn. Neurosci.*, 3, 351-354.

[123] Douglas, R.J. (1975). The development of hippocampal function: implications for theory and therapy. In The hippocampus: Vol 2, Neurophysiology and behavior (Isaacson R.L., Pribram, K.H., Eds), pp. 327-361. New York: Plenum.

[124] Rudy, J.W., Stadler-Morris, S., Albert, P. (1987). Ontogeny of spatial navigation in the rat: dissociation of "proximal" and "distal"-cue based behaviors. *Behav. Neurosci.*, 101, 62-73.

[125] O'Keefe, J., Nadel, L. (1978). The Hippocampus as a Cognitive Map. Oxford University Press.

[126] Olton, D.S., Becket, J.T., Handelmann, G.E. (1979). Hippocampus, space and memory. *Behav. Brain Sci.*, 2, 313-365.

[127] Marquis, J.P., Goulet, S., Doré, F.Y. (2008). Dissociable onset of cognitive and motivational dysfunctions following neonatal lesions of the ventral hippocampus in rats. *Behav. Neurosci.*, 122, 629-642.

[128] Sams-Dodd, F., Lipska, B.K., Weinberger, D.R. (1997). Neonatal lesions of the rat ventral hippocampus result in hyperlocomotion and deficits in social behaviour in adulthood. *Psychopharmacology*, 132, 303–310.

[129] Ueno, K., Togashi, H., Matsumoto, M., Ohashi, S., Saito, H., Yoshioka, M. (2002). $\alpha 4\beta 2$ nicotinic acetylcholine receptor activation ameliorates impairment of spontaneous alternation behavior in stroke-prone spontaneously hypertensive rats, an animal model of attention deficit hyperactivity disorder. *J. Pharmacol. Exp. Ther.*, 302, 95–100.

[130] Levin, E.D., Christopher N.C., Briggs, S.J. (1997). Chronic nicotinic agonist and antagonist effects on T-maze alternation. *Physiology, Behavior*, 61, 863–866.

[131] Johns, J.M., Walters, P.A., Zimmerman, L.I. (2001). The effects of chronic prenatal exposure to nicotine on the behavior of guinea pigs (Cavia porcellus). *J. Soc. Psychol.*, 120, 49-63.

[132] Suzuki S, Augerinos G, Black A.H. (1980). Stimulus control of spatial behavior on the eight-arm maze in rats. *Learn Motiv.*, 11, 1-18.

[133] LeDoux, J.E. (2000). Emotion circuits in the brain. *Annu. Rev. Neurosci.*, 23, 155-184.

[134] Burman, M.A., Starr, M.J., Gewirtz, J.C. (2006). Dissociable effects of hippocampus lesions on expression of fear and trace fear conditioning memories in rats. *Hippocampus* 16, 103-113.

[135] Chowdhury N., Quinn J.J, Fanselow M.S. (2005). Dorsal hippocampus involvement in trace fear conditioning with long, but not short, trace intervals in mice. *Behav. Neurosci.*, 119, 1396-1402.

[136] McEchron, M.D., Bouwmeester, H., Tseng, W., Weiss, C., Disterhoft, J.F. (1998). Hippocampectomy disrupts auditory trace fear conditioning and contextual fear conditioning in the rat. *Hippocampus*, 8, 638-646.

[137] Quinn, J.J., Oommen, S.S., Morrison, G.E., Fanselow, M.F. (2002). Post-training excitotoxic lesions of the dorsal hippocampus attenuate forward trace, backward trace, and delay fear conditioning in a temporally specific manner. *Hippocampus*, 12, 495-504.

[138] Raybuck, J.D., Gould, T.J. (2009). Nicotine withdrawal-induced deficits in trace fear conditioning in C57BL/6 mice – a role for high-affinity $\beta 2$ subunit-containing nicotinic acetylcholine receptors. *Eur. J. Neurosci.*, 29, 377-387.

[139] Levillain, M.E. (2003). Nicotine facilitates trace fear conditioning in normal and FASD rats tested as adolescents. Unpublished master's thesis, College of William, Mary.

[140] Burke, J.D., Loeber R., Lahey, B.B. (2001). Which aspects of ADHD are associated with tobacco use in early adolescence? *J. Child Psychol. Psychiatry*, 42, 93–502.

[141] Jones R.T., Benowitz N.L. (2002) Therapeutics for Nicotine Addiction. In Davis, K.L., Charney, D., Coyle, J.T., Nemeroff, C. (Eds.), Neuropsychopharmacology: The Fifth Generation of Progress (pp1533-1544). Nashville, TN: American College of Neuropsychopharmacology.

[142] Willins, T.E. (2007). The nature of the relationship between attention-deficit/hyperactivity disorder and substance use. *J. Clin. Psychiatry*, 68, 4-8.
[143] Yates, W.R., Cadoret, R.J., Troughton, E.P., Stewart, M., Giunta, T.S. (1998). Effect of fetal alcohol exposure on adult symptoms of nicotine, alcohol, and drug dependence. *Alcohol. Clin. Exp. Res.*, 22, 914-920.
[144] Hunt, P.S., Jacobson, S.E., Torok, E.J. (2009). A rat model of fetal alcohol exposure exhibits deficits in trace fear conditioning: Dose-response and timing effects. *Alcohol, 43*, 465-474.
[145] Hunt, P.S., Morasch, K.C. (2004). Modality-specific impairments in orienting response habituation following neonatal binge ethanol exposure. *Neurotoxicol. Teratol.,* 26, 451-459.
[146] Wagner, A.F., Hunt, P.S. (2006). Impaired trace fear conditioning following neonatal ethanol: Reversal by choline. *Behav. Neurosci.*, 120, 482-487.
[147] Dobbing, J., Sands, J. (1979). Comparative aspects of the brain growth spurt. *Early Hum. Dev.*, 3, 79-83.
[148] Davis, M., Scheslinger, L.S., Sorenson, C.A. (1989). Temporal specificity of fear conditioning: Effects of different conditioned stimulus-unconditioned stimulus intervals on the fear-potentiated startle effect. *J. Exp. Psychol. Anim. Behav. Process*, 14, 295-310.
[149] Smith. L.N., McDonald, C.G., Bergstrom, H.C., Brielmaier, J.M., Eppolito, A.K., Wheeler, T.L., Falco, A.M., Smith, R.F. (2006). Long-term changes in fear conditioning and anxiety-like behavior following nicotine exposure in adult versus adolescent rats. *Pharmacol. Biochem. Behav.*, 85, 91-97.
[150] Maren, S., Anagnostaras, S.G., Fanselow, M.S. (1998). The startled seahorse: Is the hippocampus necessary for contextual fear conditioning? *Trends Cogn. Neurosci.*, 2, 39-42.
[151] Phillips, R.G., LeDoux, J.E. (1992). Differential contribution of amygdala and hippocampus to cued and contextual fear conditioning. *Behav. Neurosci.*, 106, 274-285.
[152] Spaeth, A.M., Barnet, R.C., Hunt, P.S., Burk, J.A. (2010). Adolescent nicotine exposure disrupts context conditioning in adulthood in rats. *Pharmacol. Biochem. Behav.*, 96, 501-506.
[153] Davis, J.A., Kenney, J.W., Gould, T.J. (2007) Hippocampal alpha4beta2 nicotinic acetylcholine receptor involvement in the enhancing effect of acute nicotine on contextual fear conditioning. Journal of Neuroscience *J. Neurosci.*, 27, 10870–10877.
[154] Gould, T.J., Lommock, J.A. (2003). Nicotine enhances contextual fear conditioning and ameliorates ethanol-induced deficits in contextual fear conditioning. *Behav. Neurosci.,* 117, 1276-1282.
[155] Espejo, E. (2003). Prefrontocortical dopamine loss in rats delays long-term extinction of contextual conditioned fear, and reduces social interaction without affecting short-term social interaction memory. *Neuropsychopharmacology*, 28, 490-498.
[156] Milland, M.R., Quirk, G.J. (2002). Neurons in medial prefrontal cortex signal memory for fear extinction. *Nature*, 420, 70-74.
[157] Barnet, R.C., Cole, R.P., Miller, R.R. (1997). Temporal integration in second-order conditioning and sensory preconditioning. *Anim. Learn Behav.*, 25, 221-233.

[158] Di Chiara G., Imperato A (1988). Drugs abused by humans preferentially increase synaptic dopamine concentrations in the mesolimbic system of freely moving rats. *Proc. Natl. Acad. Sci. USA* 85, 5274–5278.

[159] Lichtensteiger, W. Hefti, F. Felix, D., Huwyler, T. Melamed, E., Schlumpf, M. (1982). Stimulation of nigrostriatal dopamine neurons by nicotine. *Neuropharmacology*, 21, 963-968.

[160] Pontieri, F.E., Tanda G., Orzi F., Di Chiara G. (1996). Effects of nicotine on the nucleus accumbens and similarity to those of addictive drugs. *Nature* 382: 255–257.

[161] Meck, W.H. (1996). Neuropharmacology of timing and time perception, *Brain Res. Cogn. Brain Res.* 3, 227–242.

[162] Cheng R.K., Hahak O., Meck W.H. (2007). Habit formation and the loss of control of an internal clock: inverse relationship between the level of baseline training and the clock-speed enhancing effects of methamphetamine. *Psychopharmacology* 193, 351–362.

[163] Maricq A.V., Roberts S., Church R.M. (1981). Methamphetamine and time estimation. *J. Exp. Psychol. Anim. Behav. Process*, 7, 18–30.

[164] Matell M.S., Bateson M., Meck W.H. (2006). Single-trials analyses demonstrate that increases in clock speed contribute to the methamphetamine-induced horizontal shifts in peak-interval timing functions. *Psychopharmacology*, 188, 201–212.

[165] Meck, W.H., Church, R.M., Olton, D.S. (1984). Hippocampus, time, and memory, *Behav. Neurosci.*, 98, 3-22.

[166] Kenny, J.W., Gould, T.J. (2008). Modulation of hippocampus-dependent learning and synaptic plasticity by nicotine. *Mol. Neurobiol.*, 2008, 38, 101-121.

[167] Kleykamp, B.A., Jennings, J.M., Eissenberg, T. (2011). Effects of transdermal nicotine and concurrent smoking on cognitive performance in tobacco-abstinent smokers. *Exp. Clin. Psychopharmacol.*, 19, 75-84.

[168] Patterson, F. Jepson, C., Loughead, J., Perkins, K., Strasser, A.A., Siegel, S. Frey, J. Gur, R., Lerman, C. (2010). Working memory deficits predict short-term smoking resumption following brief abstinence. *Drug Alcohol. Depend.*, 106, 61-64.

[169] Baron, S. White, A., Swartzwelder, H.S., Bell, R.L., Rodd, Z.A., Slawecki, C.J., Ehlers, C.L., Levin, E.D., Rezvani, A.H., Spear, L.P. (2005). Adolescent vulnerabilities to chronic alcohol or nicotine exposure: Findings from rodent models. *Alcohol. Clin. Exp. Res.*, 29, 1720-1725.

[170] Counotte, D.S., Spijker, S., Van de Burgwal, L.H., Hogenboom, F., Schoffelmeer, A.N., De Vries, T.J., Smit, AB., Pattij, T. (2009). Long-lasting cognitive deficits resulting from adolescent nicotine exposure in rats. *Neuropsychopharmacology*, 34, 29-306.

[171] Trauth, J.A., Seidler, F.J., Slotkin, T.A. (2000). Persistent and delayed behavioral changes after nicotine treatment in adolescent rats. *Brain Res.*, 880, 167– 172.

[172] Brunson, K.L., Krama, E., Lin, B., Chen, Y., Colgin, L.L., Yanagihara, T.K., Lynch, G., Baram, T.Z. (2005). Mechanisms of late-onset cognitive decline after early-life stress. *J. Neurosci.*, 25 (41), 9328 –9338.

In: Nicotine Addiction
Editor: Giuseppe Di Giovanni

ISBN: 978-1-62081-290-7


*Chapter 9*

# PSYCHOSOCIAL RISK FACTORS FOR SMOKING AND NICOTINE DEPENDENCE: IMPLICATIONS FOR PREVENTION AND TREATMENT

***Diane Burgermeister****
Madonna University, College of Nursing and Health, Livonia, Michigan, US

## ABSTRACT

Although cigarette smoking has declined in the United States between 2002 and 2009, one quarter of Americans continue to smoke despite the risks to health. Cigarette smoking slowly rises according to age, and reaches a peak for young adults between the ages of 21 and 25. These smokers are at risk for nicotine dependence since many began smoking during adolescence and continue throughout their lifetime. The aim of this study was to examine psychosocial risk factors contributing to smoking and nicotine dependence among young adults, in order to inform prevention and treatment strategies used by health care clinicians. A sample of 300 young adult smokers who attended two Midwestern universities in the United States were given five survey type questionnaires to measure smoking status, major depression, personality trait of neuroticism, adverse childhood experiences, and expectancies (cognitive beliefs) about the desired effects of smoking.

The results of the study indicated that the presence of all risk factors were highest among the daily nicotine dependent smokers compared to non-daily smokers. However, nicotine dependent smokers did not perceive the negative effects of smoking compared to non-dependent smokers. Female smokers were more likely to have experienced a major depression when compared to male smokers. Expectancies had greater impact upon nicotine dependent smoking than depression and level of education. The conclusions are that psychosocial factors need to be included when designing cessation programs. Cognitive beliefs of smokers can be assessed so that greater knowledge and awareness can be used to counter marketing efforts used by the tobacco industry. The assessment and treatment of depression among smokers, especially women would contribute toward cessation success by reducing distressing feelings.

* Correspondence author: Diane Burgermeister PhD, RN Madonna University, College of Nursing and Health, 36600 Schoolcraft Rd, Livonia, MI 48150, phone: 734-432-5472, dburgermeister@madonna.edu.

# INTRODUCTION

Although cigarette smoking has declined in the United States between 2002 and 2009, one quarter of Americans continue to smoke despite the risks to health. Cigarette smoking slowly rises according to age, and reaches a peak for young adults between the ages of 21 and 25 [1]. In the United States 36% of young adults are current smokers (DHHS). These smokers are at risk for nicotine dependence since many began smoking during adolescence and continue throughout their lifetime [2]. Although a high percentage of adolescents attempt to quit, few are successful.

Nicotine dependence is defined as a substance use disorder in the Diagnostic and Statistical Manual of Mental Disorders and characterized by compulsive use accompanied by tolerance and withdrawal [3]. The cigarette smoker uses more than intended despite health problems and attempts to cut down are not successful. Individual and environmental risk factors contribute to continued smoking and the transition to dependency or addiction.

# PURPOSE OF STUDY

The purpose of this cross-sectional, correlation design study was to examine psychosocial risk factors contributing to smoking and nicotine dependence in college students. The risk factors of depression, cognitive beliefs called expectancies, adverse childhood experiences and the personality trait of neuroticism were selected based upon a literature review of factors influencing continued smoking. No study has examined all of these factors to determine which have the greatest impact. Risk factors contribute to the reasons why some people are not able to control smoking behavior and continue to smoke despite the risk to health.

The results of the study have implications for prevention and treatment. Those smokers not yet dependent upon nicotine can identify their cognitive beliefs about the desired effects of smoking and learn to increase resistance to media messages. In addition, developing coping skills to address distressing emotions help identify situations for relapse. Assessment that begins with useful and quick screening instruments can guide the pharmacological and psychological approaches chosen by health care professionals.

# BACKGROUND

## Properties and Effects of Nicotine

Nicotine is quickly absorbed from the lungs, buccal and nasal mucosa, skin and gastrointestinal tract. Most cigarettes contain between 0.5 and 2.0 mgs of nicotine and 20% of nicotine in a cigarette is inhaled and absorbed into the bloodstream. Nicotine is rapidly metabolized by the hepatic enzyme CYP2A6. During cigarette smoking, high blood nicotine levels rise within 2-3 minutes of initiation and can be maintained for 10 minutes. Nicotine is quickly distributed throughout the body, penetrating the brain, crossing the placental barrier and appearing in all body fluids including breast milk. The liver metabolizes about 80-90% of the nicotine before it is excreted in the kidneys. The elimination half -life of nicotine in a chronic smoker is about 2 hours, so frequent administration is needed to maintain blood levels. Each cigarette produces a sharp increase in nicotine concentration within the brain to the desired plasma concentration, usually between 20-40 nanograms (ng) of nicotine per milliliter (mL) of plasma [4].

In the early stages of smoking, nicotine causes nausea and vomiting by stimulating the vomiting center in the brain stem and sensory receptors in the stomach. Tolerance to this effect develops quickly. Nicotine reduces the activity of the afferent nerve fibers coming from the muscles to create muscle relaxation. Nicotine also stimulates cognitive functioning, attention, and memory retrieval and reduces appetite which results in weight loss, but retention of fluid occurs due to the stimulation of the hypothalamus to release anti-diuretic hormone [4].

Because of nicotine's two hour half-life, there is low residual level of nicotine in the blood and brain after a night's sleep. The smoker wakes each morning in a state of drug withdrawal and the first cigarette brings relief and becomes a powerful reinforcement of smoking behavior. In cigarette smoking the user can control levels of blood nicotine by regulating the depth and rate of inhalation to achieve the desired effect (relaxation and increased concentration) and avoid unpleasant effects associated with too high levels (dizzy) or too low (desire to smoke or withdrawal). Higher peak levels of nicotine and more rapid absorption into the blood stream occur during cigarette smoking as compared to chewing tobacco or nicotine gum [4].

## Mechanism of Nicotine Dependence

Nicotine dependence leads to significant psychological and physical impairment or distress. An individual who smokes can be diagnosed as nicotine dependent according to specific criteria in Table 1 [3].

**Table 1. Symptoms of Nicotine Dependence**

| Three or more of the following symptoms occurring in the same 12 month period of time: |
|---|
| Tolerance, i.e. the number of cigarettes increase in order to obtain desired effect or there is diminished effect when smoking the same amount |
| Withdrawal, i.e. characteristic syndrome of low mood, irritability or anger, low heart rate, insomnia, anxiety or restlessness, difficulty concentrating, appetite and weight gain |
| Smoking more than intended or over longer period of time |
| Persistent desire or unsuccessful in cutting down or quitting |
| Great deal of time spent in activities to obtain cigarettes or chain smoking |
| Important social, occupational, or recreational activities are given up or reduced |
| Continued smoking despite recurrent physical or psychological problems caused or exacerbated by smoking |
| Persistence of the above symptoms for at least one month or the occurrence repeatedly over time. |

Two hallmark symptoms of dependence are tolerance and withdrawal. Tolerance occurs because nicotine is quickly metabolized and has a short half- life, therefore receptors in the brain can adapt to the drug after continued use by reducing the number of receptors or reducing sensitivity so that higher levels of nicotine are needed to obtain the desired effect [5]. Characteristic withdrawal symptoms such as irritability and anxiety occur when a nicotine dependent smoker tries to quit and then makes an effort to avoid the distressing symptoms by continuing to smoke.

## Theoretical Framework

Two models of nicotine dependence include the neurobiological model and associative learning model, both of which have important implications for understanding and selecting smoking cessation strategies. These models also help the practitioner to appreciate how difficult it is for a nicotine dependent smoker to quit smoking, therefore there is a need to use both pharmacological and psychological treatment approaches.

### Neurobiological Model

Neural mechanisms have evolved in the human being to increase the probability that behavior will promote species survival. One primary mechanism is the activation of neural systems that promote a sense of satisfaction and pleasure, referred to as the brain reward system. The administration of drugs can stimulate brain reward mechanisms and when repeated often enough, the drug becomes rewarding in its own right. There are two dopaminergic neuronal systems (DA) in the brain that are involved in psychomotor stimulant reward function. These include the mesolimbic dopamine system that projects from the ventral tegmentum (VTA) of the forebrain to the nucleus accumbens (NA), or the limbic striatum area; and the mesocortical dopamine system that projects from the VTA to the frontal lobe [6]. The 2-neuron system forms a dopaminergic loop between forebrain and the VTA. Nicotine, a psychomotor stimulant indirectly activates DA neurons projecting to the NA, a center for the experience of reward. The metabolism of nicotine occurs in the shell of the NA that has projections to the amydala and therefore is involved with both innate and acquired emotional response [7]. This is the basis for reinforcement of expectations or beliefs about nicotine use. Nicotinic acetylcholine receptors (nAChR) on dopaminergic cell bodies are necessary for DA release elicited by nicotine, enabling nicotine agonists to have a rewarding effect.

### Associative Learning Model

Expectations about the effects and outcome of a substance contribute to the continued use of a drug. The associative learning model explains that the repeating of events over time is associated with drug taking. When repeated often enough the events are rapidly encoded in memory and retrieved quickly, contributing to involuntary and habitual behavior characterized by loss of control. Associative learning involves an environmental cue for a drug (S), a drug stimulus ($S^*_d$), response to a drug ($R_d$), and an outcome (S*). Successive pairs of these events provide three expectancies that concern drug administration, type of response, and its consequence [8].

The first expectancy is represented by the statement ($S \rightarrow S^*_d$). A stimulus cue (S) such as an ashtray precedes the behavior of smoking, the drug stimulus ($S^*_d$); and therefore the expectation of taking the drug (nicotine) occurs when seeing the ashtray after these events are repeated over time. The second expectancy involves learning that a second pair of events relate the drug stimulus ($S^*_d$) to a particular type of response to the drug ($R_d$) and is represented by the statement ($S^*_d$) $\rightarrow$($R_d$). For example, one comes to expect that smoking will reduce distressing feelings and this becomes associated with a reduction in sad mood. A third type of expectancy involves the consequence of the drug represented by the statement ($R_d \rightarrow S^*$). The response to smoking brings an outcome such as feeling relaxed ($R_d$) but the outcome can change with the situation (S*). For example, a person may be motivated to smoke because of the expected positive consequence that smoking will help them to feel calm, yet if this individual has problems functioning because of poor breathing and associates smoking with a negative impact upon health, they may be motivated to quit smoking due to the associated negative consequences.

## Depression

Two lines of evidence will be discussed in an effort to understand how smoking has a rewarding effect for depressed smokers. The neurobiological mechanisms that contribute to the relationship between nicotine dependence and depression address the following: a) smoking has antidepressant effects, and b) smokers are sensitive to stress and depression. Symptoms of a major depression are stated in Table 2 from the Diagnostic Manual of Mental Disorders [3].

It has been suggested that a sense of euphoria occurs during cigarette smoking and that this can account for the use of smoking to self- medicate depressed mood [9]. The sense of well-being is reinforced by dopamine release in the mesolimbic system, involving the shell of the nucleus accumbens (NA) that is associated with the expression of emotion.

**Table 2. Symptoms of Major Depression**

| Depressed mood and/or loss of interest over the same two week period of time |
|---|
| In addition to the above, at least 4 of the following symptoms:<br>• Trouble falling or staying asleep, or sleeping too much<br>• Feeling tired or little energy<br>• Poor appetite or overeating<br>• Change in activity by moving too slowly or restlessness<br>• Difficulty making decisions<br>• Feelings of worthlessness or guilt<br>• Recurrent thoughts of death or suicide |

Nicotine also increases the release of norepinephrine into the neuronal synapse creating an anti-depressant effect. Another mechanism that may account for the anti-depressant like effect of nicotine is related to compounds in cigarette smoke that contribute to a lowering of monamine oxidase (MAO), an enzyme that metabolizes dopamine, serotonin, and norepinephrine. The inhibition of MAO from cigarette smoking is thought to contribute to increasing mood, given that more dopamine, serotonin, and norepinephrine become available. Inhibited levels of MAO type B enzyme have been found in smokers as compared to former smokers and non-smokers [10]. A review of the effects of nicotine on neural pathways suggest that people smoke because they are sensitive to stress and experience the reinforcing effects of dopamine associated with relief [11]. Stressful life events have been shown to contribute toward vulnerability to depression. As the exposure to threat increases, the likelihood of the onset of a major depression within two months of the stressful event increases, especially in individuals with a less efficient serotonin transporter genotype [12]. Nicotine has an inhibitory effect on serotonin release (5-HT) in some parts of the hippocampus and this effect may attenuate habituation to stress [11]. In addition, the 5-HT receptors that occupy the hippocampus also regulate the release of glucocorticoids during stress and over time a down-regulation of glucocorticoid receptors occur contributing to an increased sensitivity to the rewarding effects of drugs.

## Smoking Expectancies

Smoking outcome expectancies are social cognitive risk factors about the anticipated consequences of cigarette smoking. People develop expectancies about smoking either through direct experience with cigarettes or through observation of others who smoke [8]. Expectancies are conceptualized as a memory network in which beliefs are drawn from long term memory and are automatic in that little conscious attention and decision making are required. People are motivated to begin smoking, continue smoking, quit smoking, and relapse after quitting due to the strengths of these cognitive beliefs called expectancies, about the positive and negative consequences of smoking. The motivation to perform a given behavior at a given moment is a function of one's memory of the anticipated consequences of the behavior and can be affected by emotional states [8].

The activation of expectancies trigger processes that drive voluntary substance use decisions and involuntary addictive behavior. Smokers who are depressed have the expectation that cigarette smoking will relieve negative affect and this provides motivation to continue to smoke [13]. College students who are daily smokers have higher expectations than occasional smokers, ex-smokers, triers, and never smokers that smoking helps control weight, tastes good and helps deal with stress and tension [14]. Smokers who hold these cognitive beliefs about the effects of smoking that are considered positive or helpful have a more difficult time quitting. The maintenance of abstinence has been shown to be influenced by decreasing the strengths of these beliefs that the smoker holds. In contrast, smokers planning to quit smoking have higher expectancies about negative consequences of smoking, such as that "smoking takes years off my life or "cigarettes make my lungs hurt." [15]

Recent research has focused upon examining implicit or unconscious memory processes and the association with expectancy word statements. Single word adjectives used by smokers such as, "smoking makes a person feel *high*" vary according to the type of smoker (ever smoked versus never smoked), smoking history (current versus past smoker), and dependence (non-dependent versus dependent) [16]. The expectations that smokers have for the desired effects of smoking versus nicotine have been shown to be highly specific in that negative consequences of smoking such as health risks are more often associated with smoking, whereas addictive expectancies are associated with nicotine indicating that smokers have a realistic understanding of the role of nicotine in smoking [17].

## The Personality Trait of Neuroticism

Personality factors are individual characteristics that can predispose people to choose a lifestyle that contributes toward promoting health or increasing risk for disease. Neuroticism is a broadly defined domain of personality that encompasses various aspects of negative affect, such as depression and anxiety. The personality trait of neuroticism accounts for differences in behavior because of a biological basis located within the visceral brain or limbic system responsible for emotion. The limbic system interprets experiences in terms of feeling rather than in terms of intellectual, symbolized constructs. Individuals with low thresholds for limbic system activation are predisposed toward more intense, frequent and prolonged emotional reactions [18]. Regular smokers with vulnerability toward panic attacks also experience high levels of neurotic behavior [19].

Genetic differences are a basis for individual differences in neurobiological structures in the brain and therefore individuals have different psychological and biological responses to nicotine. Genetic studies have examined smoking status and neuroticism among combined samples of males and females. Genetically based differences have been found in the rewarding effects of nicotine among white male and female participants [20]. Neuroticism was positively correlated with being a current smoker in contrast to having never smoked and former smokers who were found to have the short form of the serotonin transporter. The dopamine circuit in the brain that is activated during the rewarding behavior of smoking is modulated by serotonin (5-HT) and the transporter determines how long serotonin will remain active before being taken back up into the neuron.

High levels of neuroticism in African American persons with the short form of the serotonin transporter have also been found to be associated with nicotine intake, nicotine dependence, and smoking to reduce negative mood and smoking for stimulation [21]. Smoking may be a psychological resource to cope with negative affect and individuals who experience vulnerability toward emotionality can also be expected to use smoking as a psychological resource to cope with chronic stress [22].

## Childhood Adversity

Stressful events in childhood impact adult development throughout life. One adversity, namely childhood sexual abuse has been associated with the development of later adult drug dependence and major depression [23]. However researchers caution that events in childhood do not occur in isolation. Results from the large National Comorbidity Survey (NCR) suggest that "clusters" of exposure to childhood abuse and household dysfunction are associated with multiple adult health behaviors rather than one type of adversity [24]. Multiple factors are associated with childhood sexual abuse and include exposure to high levels of parental conflict, poor parental bonding, and exposure to parents with alcohol problems or parents who use illicit drugs.

Multiple adverse childhood experiences such as exposure to psychological, physical, and sexual abuse and household dysfunction, such as household substance abuse, physical abuse of mother, mental illness, and criminal behavior have been found to be risk factors for smoking. The prevalence and odds ratio (risk) increase for smoking, severe obesity, physical inactivity, depressed mood, and suicide attempts as the number of childhood adverse experiences increase [25]. With regard to smoking, when persons with four categories of adverse childhood experiences were compared to those with none, the risk for current smoking more than doubled.

Prevalence rates in smoking status such as initiation before the age of 14 years and having ever smoked at least 100 cigarettes, increase as the number of childhood adverse experiences becomes higher [25]. There is an increased risk for heavy smoking, defined as consuming at least 20 cigarettes per day, when 5 or more adverse childhood experiences are reported. For any given number of adverse childhood experiences, the percentage of smokers reporting problems with depressed affect is higher than among nonsmokers [26].

## Methodology of the Study

### Sample

Participants were 300 students who reported having smoked at least one cigarette in their lives and who attended two mid-western universities. Women comprised 55% of the sample and the majority of participants (87%) were between the ages of 18-30 years with a modal age of 18 years (M=23, SD=7.2). Whites comprised 55% of the sample followed by Blacks (18%), Asian (15%), Arab-Chaldean 7% and 5 % were of other racial groups. Three participants did not answer the question. The average household income was < or equal to $39,000 reported by 65% of participants. The majority of participants were not married (86%). Convenience samples were obtained and participants categorized according to smoking status based upon history and frequency of cigarette use and having met criteria for nicotine dependence.

### Measures

Cigarette use and dependence was assessed by The Cigarette Use Questionnaire (CUQ), a paper and pencil adaptation of the National Institute of Mental Health Diagnostic Interview Schedule (NIMH-DIS) [27]. All participants in the study (N = 300) answered *yes* to the question on the CUQ, "have you ever smoked a cigarette?" The never smoked daily group (n = 132) further answered *no* to the question, "have you ever smoked a cigarette daily for a month or more?" The daily smokers (n = 168) answered *yes* to both of the above questions. The daily nicotine dependent smokers (n = 77) met criteria for nicotine dependence based upon the presence and duration of symptoms according to the NIMH-DIS criteria. The daily non-dependent smokers (n = 91) did not meet the criteria for dependence. Sensitivity (percentage of cases correctly identified and specificity (percentage of non-cases identified correctly) for the NIMH-DIS is between 89-90%. The kappa between interviewers which is the ability to provide a correct diagnosis is 78% for identification of positive cases using the NIMH-DIS.

A history of lifetime depression was assessed using two stem questions from the World Health Organization Composite International Diagnostic Interview Short Form (CIDI-SF) [28]. The two questions screen for the likelihood of having experienced a major depression any time in life. The two screen questions are, " in your lifetime, have you ever had two weeks or longer when nearly every day you felt, sad, blue, or depressed?" and "in your lifetime have you ever had two weeks or longer when you lost interest in most things like work or hobbies or things you usually do for fun?" The percentage of accuracy for a diagnosis of major depression using screen questions from the CIDI-SF is 93% [28]. Participants who responded affirmatively to at least one of the screen questions were asked to complete the Nine Symptom Checklist of Primary Care Evaluation for Mental Disorders Patient Health Questionnaire, depression module (PRIME-MD, PHQ) [29]. The PRIME-MD is based upon a 4-point scale that scores the duration of nine symptoms of major depression (1 = never, 4 = nearly every day). The number and duration of symptoms were counted to arrive at three categories: 0-1 counts = no depression, 2-4 counts = some symptoms of depression, 5-9 counts=major depression. Cohen's kappa is 0.65 for the PRIME-MD [30].

Smoking outcome expectancies were assessed by using the Smoking Consequences Questionnaire (SCQ) [15]. The instrument uses 55 items to identify 10 scales describing positive and negative smoking outcome expectancies: negative affect reduction (NAR), stimulation/state enhancement (SS), taste/sensorimotor manipulation (T/S), social facilitation (SF), weight control (WC), craving/addiction (C/A), health risk (HR), negative physical feeling (NPF), boredom reduction (BR), negative social impression (NSI). The likelihood of beliefs about the consequences of smoking was assessed by a 10-point scale (1=completely unlikely, 10=completely likely). Reliability ranged from $\alpha = 0.67$ for health risk expectancy scale to $\alpha = 0.97$ negative affect reduction scale.

Neuroticism was measured by the number of affirmative responses to the Eysenck Personality Questionnaire Short Form (EPQ-SF) neuroticism scale (range 0-12) [31]. The neuroticism scale reflects the dimensions of emotions such as nervousness and reactivity that predispose one to have unpleasant experiences described in the items. The alpha coefficient reliabilities on the neuroticism scale for males and females are 0.84 and 0.80 respectively [31]. Persons scoring high on the dimension of neuroticism are prone to worry, anxiety, and depression. The EPQ-R as a whole has a test-retest reliability of .86 and an internal consistency in the range of 0.80.

Adverse childhood experiences defined as childhood exposure to abuse and household dysfunction was assessed using questions adapted from The Adverse Childhood Experiences (ACE) Study Questionnaire [25]. Categories of exposure to abuse included the following six areas: psychological abuse, physical abuse, sexual abuse, parental alcohol abuse, parental mental illness, and maternal battering. Participants were asked to circle yes or no responses to questions that inquired as to psychological (2 questions), physical (2 questions), and sexual abuse (4 questions) that respondents remember occurring before the age of 18 years. Exposure to household dysfunction was measured by yes or no responses to questions that inquired as to parental alcohol abuse (2 questions), parental depression (2 questions), and maternal battering (4 questions) remembered as occurring before the age of 18 year. All questions are introduced with the phrase, "While you were growing up during your first 18 years of life...." Respondents were defined as exposed to a category if they answered yes to one or more of the questions in that category. Each category received a score of 1 if respondents replied *yes* and 0 if respondents responded *no* to the questions, with a range from 0-6 categories. The total number of possible questions answered ranged from 0-14. There was a 98-100% rate of response to questions on the Adverse Childhood Experiences Questionnaire (N = 300).

### Data Collection

Recruitment announcements were posted on campus. Students completed questionnaires that were arranged in counter balanced order and placed in envelopes. Students completed the forms either in groups on campus or at home and returned them to a designated campus mailbox. Informed consent was obtained and prior approved obtained by the respective university Human Subjects Committees. There was no identifying link between consent forms and questionnaires and questionnaire pages were number coded for identification.

## RESULTS

Descriptive statistics were used to analyze smoking groups according to risk factors and demographics. Smoking groups consisted of never smoked daily (NSD) (n =132); daily, non-dependent (DnD) (n = 91); and daily, nicotine dependent (DND) (n =77). Mean scores for age, educational level, depression, neuroticism, and adverse childhood experiences according to smoking status is given in Table 3. The chi-square test of independence indicated that smoking groups differed significantly according to age. Mean scores for smoking expectancy scales according to smoking status are given in Table 4.

A multinomial logistic regression model was used to analyze the data in comparing smokers as shown in Table 5. Correlations among expectancies were run. The expectancy for negative affect reduction (NAR) and social facilitation (SF) were removed because they were highly correlated with each other and could cancel each other out. The main effects of the variables were analyzed according to the odds ratio and confidence interval tests using the never smoked daily category as the reference group. A deviance test of goodness of fit was non-significant indicating that the model fit the data (p = 0.999). The Pseudo R Square Cox and Snell test indicated that 44.6% of variation in responses could be explained by the predictors. The least significant variables were removed after conducting a Likelihood Ratio Test using backwards selection. The variables removed were negative physical feeling expectancy, abuse, age of first cigarette, white race. The classification rate for this model was 64.2%. In the second backwards selection the variables gender, neuroticism, and health risk expectancy were removed which increased the prediction of classification of smokers to 66.7%. The classification table is shown in Table 6. Mean scores on MDD according to gender indicated significant differences between males (n = 134) *M* = 3.0, SD (0.27) and females (n = 166), *M*=3.9, SD (0.25), p=≤.05.

**Table 3. Baseline Description of Variables on Study Measures (N=300)**

| | Smoking Status | | |
|---|---|---|---|
| | NSD (n=132) | DnD (n=91) | DND (n=77) |
| *Age (years) | 21.5 ±5.5 | 23.3 ± 7.4 | 25.5 ± 8.7 |
| Educational Level (years) | 14.0 ±1.9 | 15.0 ± 2.3 | 14.7 ± 2.2 |
| Age began smoking (year) | 14.7± 3.3 | 14.9 ± 2.9 | 14.0 ± 3.5 |
| $*\chi^2/_2 = 16.25$, p=.000 | | | |
| PRIME-MD counts (0-9) | 3.0± 3.3 | 2.6± 2.9 | 4.8± 3.0 |
| EPQ, R-SF (0-12) | 5.3 ± 3.2 | 4.8 ± 3.4 | 6.2 ± 3.7 |
| ACE (0-6) | 1.2 ±1.4 | 1.3 ± 1.5 | 1.4 ± 1.5 |

Note. MDD= likelihood of major depression based upon range of counts (5-9) on Primary Care Evaluation of Mental Disorders Patient Health Questionnaire (PRIME-MD). EPQ, R-SF= Eysenck Personality Questionnaire, Revised, Short Form, ACE= Adverse Childhood Experiences Questionnaire. NSD=never smoked daily, Dnd=daily, non-dependent, DND=daily, nicotine dependent. Scores are means with standard deviations.

**Table 4. Mean Scores on Scales of the Smoking Consequences Questionnaire (SCQ-A) by Smoking Status (N=300)**

| | Smoking Status Group | | | | | |
|---|---|---|---|---|---|---|
| | NSD | | DnD | | DND | |
| Scale | *M* | *SD* | *M* | *SD* | *M* | *SD* |
| T/S | 2.61 | 1.96 | 4.37 | 2.30 | 5.58 | 2.07 |
| NAR | 3.40 | 2.61 | 5.39 | 2.81 | 7.03 | 2.47 |
| S/S | 2.48 | 1.87 | 3.49 | 2.04 | 4.07 | 2.25 |
| HR | 8.37 | 1.85 | 8.28 | 2.00 | 8.99 | 1.70 |
| SF | 2.84 | 2.84 | 4.09 | 2.26 | 5.21 | 2.31 |
| WC | 2.75 | 2.01 | 3.92 | 2.53 | 5.47 | 2.75 |
| NPF | 5.60 | 2.90 | 4.89 | 2.73 | 5.22 | 2.39 |
| BR | 2.92 | 2.32 | 4.35 | 2.62 | 6.36 | 2.44 |
| NSI | 6.97 | 2.44 | 5.61 | 2.69 | 5.95 | 2.56 |
| C/A | 4.01 | 2.36 | 5.58 | 2.49 | 7.40 | 2.07 |

Note. NSD = never smoked daily, DnD = daily, non-dependent, DND=daily, nicotine dependent. T/S = taste/sensorimotor manipulation, NAR = negative affect reduction, S/S = stimulation/state enhance ment, HR = health risk, SF = social facilitation, WC = weight control, NPF = negative physical feeling, BR = boredom reduction, NSI = negative social impression, C/A = craving/ Addiction.

**Table 5. Predictors of Daily Non-Dependent and Daily Nicotine Dependent Smokers**

| Predictor | Daily-Non Dependent OR (95% CI) | P value | Daily-Nicotine Dependent OR (95% CI) | P value |
|---|---|---|---|---|
| MDD | .615(0.32-1.17) | 0.141 | 1.85 (.87-3.93) | 0.108 |
| TS | 1.43(1.13-1.81) | 0.003 * | 1.49 (1.15-1.93) | 0.002 * |
| SS | 0.807(.62-1.04) | 0.100 | .637 (.48-.83) | 0.001 * |
| WC | 1.13 (.95-1.33) | 0.149 | 1.27 (1.05-1.52) | 0.011 * |
| BR | 0.980(.81-1.18) | 0.834 | 1.23 (1.00-1.52) | 0.042 * |
| NSI | 0.825 (.72-.94) | 0.004 * | 0.775 (0.65-.91) | 0.003 * |
| CA | 1.13 (.96-1.34) | 0.134 | 1.49 (1.20-1.84) | 0.000 * |
| Education | 1.26(1.08-1.46) | 0.002 * | 1.16 (0.97-1.38) | 0.093 |

Note. Reference group: never smoked daily smokers, asterisk indicates predictor is significant at $p < 0.05$. MDD = likelihood of major depression based upon range of counts (5-9) on Primary Care Evaluation of Mental Disorders Patient Health Questionnaire (PRIME-MD), Expectancy mean scores on Smoking Consequences Questionnaire-Adult (SCQ-A): T/S = taste/sensorimotor manipulation, S/S = stimulation/state enhancement, WC = weight control, BR = boredom reduction, NSI = negative social impression, C/A = craving/ Addiction, Educational level.

**Table 6. Summary Classification Table for Smoking Status**

| | | | Predicted Group Membership | | | |
|---|---|---|---|---|---|---|
| Observed Group Membership (N) | | | 1=NSD | 2=DnD | 3=DND | % correct |
| 1 | NSD | 132 | 106 | 15 | 11 | 80.3 |
| 2 | DnD | 91 | 31 | 40 | 20 | 44.0 |
| 3 | DND | 77 | 12 | 11 | 54 | 70.1 |
| Overall % | | | 49.7 | 22.0 | 28.3 | *66.7* |

# CONCLUSION

The results of the study indicate that all risk factors, namely depression, childhood adversity, neuroticism, and the cognitive beliefs about what smokers expect from cigarettes (expectancies), were higher among the daily nicotine dependent smokers compared to non-dependent smokers. Nicotine dependent smokers tended to be older due to more years in smoking. Female smokers were more likely to have experienced a major depression when compared to male smokers but all nicotine dependent smokers experienced a greater likelihood for depression than non-dependent smokers. The multinomial logistic regression model predicted which risk factors would contribute the most to the likelihood of becoming a daily nicotine dependent smoker. Expectancies have higher impact on the daily nicotine dependent smoker (DnD) than depression or level of education. For example, the belief that cigarettes taste good (TS), help control weight (WC), reduce boredom (BR), and satisfies the urge to smoke (CA), all contribute toward nicotine dependence. Negative social impression (NSI) such as the belief that one looks "ridiculous" while smoking or that one smokes for stimulation (SS), both reduce the odds of becoming nicotine dependent. Although the main limitation to this study is the correlational design versus a prospective one so that factors could be examined over time, still the implications for treatment are important. Psychosocial factors need to be included when designing cessation programs in addition to providing pharmacological treatment for smokers. This paper will now discuss the treatment of nicotine dependence using the results of this study as a basis for the development of a comprehensive set of strategies.

## Implications for Treatment: Assessment

Ruling out the presence or history of major depression in a smoker is important for the following reasons. First, major depression is prevalent among nicotine dependent smokers. Second, depressive symptoms can occur during quit attempts. Third, all smokers are at greater risk for progressing in smoking behavior from non-dependence to dependence when there has been a history of a major depression or if there is a current untreated major depression [32]. Smokers who are depressed may find that the rewarding effects of reducing mood is a more compelling reason to continue to smoke in contrast to quitting for health reasons.

Smokers who are seen by a health care professional can easily be screened using tools that are both efficient and effective in diagnosing the likelihood of nicotine dependence and major depression, as given in Table 7.

**Table 7. Quick Screening Tools**

| Condition | Screening Tool |
|---|---|
| Nicotine Dependence | Fagerstrom Test for Nicotine Dependence[33]<br>• Do you smoke within 30 minutes of waking?<br>• How many cigarettes do you consume in a day? |
| Major Depressive Episode | World Health Organization Composite International Diagnostic Interview Short Form (CIDI-SF)[28]<br>• Have you ever had two weeks or longer when nearly every day you felt sad, blue, or depressed?<br>• Have you ever had two weeks or longer when you lost interest in most things like work or hobbies or things you usually do for fun? |

Two questions found to reliability assess for nicotine dependence include asking if the person has smoked the first cigarette of the day within 30 minutes of waking *and* if more than 20 cigarettes are smoked per day [33]. Affirmative responses to both questions are needed to assess for withdrawal and tolerance; both hallmarks of dependence. The likelihood of a major depression having occurred can be assessed by using two stem questions from the CIDI-SF as previously stated and affirmative responses to both questions that address low mood and loss of interest for two weeks are necessary.

## Nicotine Replacement Therapy

Nicotine replacement therapy (NRT) consists of nicotine gum, transdermal nicotine (patch), inhaler, nicotine spray, and nicotine lozenge. Nicotine replacement therapy facilitates abstinence through two primary mechanisms: NRT provides the smoker with a lower dose of nicotine to attenuate withdrawal symptoms and ease in transition to non-smoking status; and NRT allows the smoker to develop coping strategies to address the behavioral aspects of addiction while physical components are treated [4].

All forms of NRT such as gum, patch, lozenge, nasal spray and oral inhalator have been found to be effective when compared to placebo [34]. Treatment with the transdermal patch results in the highest overall abstinent rate after both initial treatment and after six months [35-36] as shown in Table 8. Cost, patient preference, and side effects are considerations when choosing NRT. Common side effects of NRT include irritation of the buccal mucosa, skin or throat.

**Table 8. Dose, Quit Rates, and Side Effects by Type of Treatment**

| Type | Dose | Initial % Quit | 6 Month % Quit | Side Effects |
|---|---|---|---|---|
| Varencline | days1-3, 0.5mg daily, days 4-7 0.5mg twice daily, days 8-end of treatment 1mg twice daily. | 44% | 22%* | Headache, nausea, insomnia, dreams |
| Bupropion | 300 mg<br>3-10 weeks | 43-60% | 18-30% | Seizures, arrythmias, dry mouth, headache, agitation, constipation |
| Nicotine Gum | 2-4 mg<br>6-8 weeks | 30-81% | 19-44% | Mouth or throat irritation, jaw pain, dyspepsia |
| Patch | 21 mg 4-6 weeks, plus 14 mg 2 weeks | 15-62% | 10-54% | Local erythema, rash, headache, palpitations, dyspepsia, insomnia |
| Inhaler | 16 or less cartridges per day, 12 weeks | 28-46% | 17-35% | Mouth/ throat irritation, cough, headache, rhinitis, dyspepsia |
| Spray | 8-40 doses for 8 weeks | 43-66% | 24-44% | Throat irritation, watery eyes, Sneezing |
| Lozenge | 9 per day and taper for 6 weeks | 46-49% | not reported | Tingling, heartburn, nausea |

* 9 through 25 weeks.

## Anti-Depressant Therapy

The most widely used anti-depressant in treating nicotine dependence is the drug bupropion i.e. Wellbutrin or Zyban. Bupropion is a second generation antidepressant that inhibits the post synaptic reuptake of dopamine and norepinephrine. In a randomized controlled trial of over 800 smokers, cessation rate was highest when the nicotine transdermal patch was used in combination with bupropion compared to bupropion alone (35% versus 30%) at 12 months post treatment [37]. In this same study, these results also indicated that the combination therapy or bupropion alone was found to be more effective than either the nicotine patch alone or placebo.

Therapy with either slow release bupropion or nortiptyline (another anti-depressant) doubles the odds of successfully quitting smoking at 6 months post treatment [38]. A review of randomized clinical trials indicated that bupropion is effective in lessening the symptoms of depression during quit attempts in nicotine dependent smokers and is equally effective for smoking cessation in nicotine dependent smokers who are not depressed [38].

## Varencline

Varencline (Chantix) is an $a_4b_2$ nicotinic acetylcholine receptor subtype that works to reinforce the effects of nicotine as measured by dopamine turnover and release in the nucleus accumbens (NA). Varencline binds with the receptor subtype to simulate the release of dopamine to reduce craving and withdrawal while simultaneously blocking the binding and consequent reinforcement effects of smoked nicotine. Although, long term cessation rates after treatment with varencline were found to be higher than treatment with bupropion (21% versus 16%) over a period of 9 to 52 weeks, the clinician needs to review the latest information about varencline because there have been reports that some patients have developed neuropsychiatric symptoms such as agitation, depressed mood, and suicidal ideation [39-40]. Further information regarding treatment for nicotine dependence can be obtained online by locating the American Psychiatric Association Practice Guidelines [41].

## Strategies to Motivate Change and Prevent Relapse

The associative learning model of dependence helps to explain the powerful effect that expectations about smoking have in reinforcing habitual behavior. Changing the expectancies or beliefs about smoking is an important cognitive strategy to help create awareness about the consequences of smoking, an important step in the change process. For example, smokers who remain abstinent three months after participation in a smoking cessation program are more likely to express weaker beliefs about the desired effects of smoking than individuals who hold stronger beliefs in these effects [14]. A nicotine dependent smoker can be helped while quitting to be aware of specific expectations he or she may have about the consequences of smoking. This awareness helps to encourage conscious decision making. Smoking beliefs from The Smoking Consequences Questionnaire for Adults (SCQ-A) are given in Table 9 [15].

**Table 9. Smoking Consequences Questionnaire-Adult (SCQ-A)**

Instructions: We are interested in the beliefs that people have about the consequences of smoking a cigarette. We are interested in your expectations about the consequences of smoking a cigarette right now. Below is a list of statements that contain possible consequences of smoking. For each of the statements, please indicate how LIKELY or UNLIKELY you believe each consequence is for you if you smoked a cigarette right now. If the consequence seems LIKELY to you, circle a number from 6-10. If you believe that a consequence would never happen, circle 1 and if you believe that a consequence would be completely likely, circle 10.

Use the guide below to aid you further. For example, if a consequence seems somewhat likely, you would circle 7. If a consequence seems somewhat unlikely, you would circle 4.

| 1 | 2 | 3 | 4 | 5 | 6 | 7 | 8 | 9 | 10 |
|---|---|---|---|---|---|---|---|---|---|
| Completely Extremely | | Very | A little Somewhat | | A little | Somewhat | Very | | Completely Extremely |
| Unlikely | | | | x | | Unlikely | | | Likely Likely |

Cigarettes taste good.

Smoking controls my appetite.

My throat burns after smoking.

Cigarettes help me deal with anxiety or worry.

Nicotine "fits" can be controlled by smoking.

When I am angry a cigarette can calm me down

When I am alone, a cigarette can help me pass the day.

I become more addicted the more I smoke.

If I am tense, a cigarette helps me to relax.

Cigarettes keep me from overeating.

Smoking a cigarette energizes me.

Cigarettes help me deal with anger.

Smoking calms me down when I feel nervous.

Cigarettes make my lungs hurt.

I feel like I do a better job when I am smoking.

A cigarette can give me energy when I'm bored/tired

Cigarettes can really make me feel good.

When I'm feeling happy, smoking helps me keep that feeling.

I will enjoy the flavor of a cigarette.

If I have nothing to do, a smoke can help kill time.

I will enjoy feeling a cigarette on my tongue/lips

Smoking will satisfy my nicotine cravings.

I feel like part of the group when I'm around other smokers.

Smoking makes me seem less attractive.

By smoking I risk heart disease and lung cancer.

Smoking helps me enjoy people more.

Cigarettes help me reduce or handle tension.

I feel better physically after having a cigarette.

I enjoy parties more when I am smoking.

**Table 9. (Continued)**

| |
|---|
| People think less of me if they see me smoking. |
| A cigarette can satisfy my urge to smoke. |
| Just handling a cigarette is pleasurable. |
| If I'm feeling irritable, a smoke will help me relax. |
| Smoking irritates my mouth and throat. |
| When I feel bored and tired, a cigarette can really help. |
| I will become more dependent on nicotine if I continue smoking. |
| Smoking helps me control my weight. |
| When I'm upset with someone, a cigarette helps me cope. |
| The more I smoke, the more I risk my health. |
| Cigarettes keep me from eating more than I should. |
| I enjoy the steps I take to light up. |
| Conversations seem more special if we are all smoking. |
| I look ridiculous while smoking. |
| Smoking keeps my weight down. |
| I like the way a cigarette makes me feel physically. |
| Smoking is hazardous to my health. |

I enjoy feeling the smoke hit my mouth and back of my throat.

When I smoke, the taste is pleasant.

I like to watch the smoke from my cigarette.

When I am worrying about something, a cigarette is helpful.

Smoking temporarily reduces those repeated urges for cigarettes.

I enjoy the taste sensations while smoking

I feel more at ease with other people if I have a cigarette.

Cigarettes are good for dealing with boredom.

Smoking takes years off my life.

Note. Adapted from Smoking Consequences Questionnaire-Adult, permission for use by author.

Smokers can take this questionnaire home and circle the likelihood of belief in each consequence of smoking on a scale from 1 to 10 (1=completely unlikely and 10=completely likely). On a follow up visit the provider can discuss these beliefs and help to correct through education and counseling. Once individuals are aware of beliefs regarding the consequences of smoking they can then be helped to monitor situations in everyday life that may provoke reinforcement. A useful strategy is to suggest that the patient keep an expectancy chart or journal that documents beliefs, feelings, and coping strategies.

## Case Study

K is a 20 year old college student who works part time while attending classes in a large popular pizza restaurant. K lives off campus and shares an apartment with other college friends. On campus she can often be seen smoking outside campus offices, taking a break between classes. K has been smoking cigarettes since age 14 and currently smokes a pack per day and continues to smoke to avoid withdrawal symptoms. She has attempted to quit twice but each time lit up after experiencing a "lousy" feeling of irritation, anxiety and craving for a cigarette.

K comes to the college health care clinic seeking a prescription for antidepressant medication. She states she has been worrying about a lot of things and this has made her feel depressed. She has not shown up a few times for class or work lately and states she could fail out of college and lose her job. K told her department chairperson and employer that she was coming to the clinic today to get treatment for depression.

K is vague about her depression. She states she has a "bad attitude" and feels like "sliding through life". She describes her "bad attitude" as, "I get up in the morning, sit down at the table, and then that's as far as I get sometimes". K is aware that she also has a problem with smoking because she can't go a day without a cigarette. She admits to sometimes drinking too much beer in order to "feel good" and usually lights up while drinking with friends. K wants to quit smoking but feels that it would be too hard to quit both cigarettes and beer at the same time; in addition she would lose her friends. She has taken antidepressants before and states "they really helped me and I cut back on beer."

Treatment begins with assessment and from observation and a clinical interview the clinician obtains the following information then proceeds to screen K for signs of major depression and nicotine dependence. K has a 6 year history of cigarette use and is currently smoking, and experiences withdrawal symptoms, a strong indication of nicotine dependence. K smokes 20 or more cigarettes per day and states she also smokes within 30 minutes of waking indicating the likelihood of nicotine dependence. K states that she is depressed and her use of anti-depressants in the past indicate a possible recurrent depression. The two stem questions from The World Health Organization Composite International Diagnostic Interview Short Form (CIDI-SF) can be used to quickly assess for the likelihood of symptoms of major depression [28]. K is asked if in the past two weeks, she has experienced depressed mood and loss of interest in normal activities for most days. She responds yes, indicating the likelihood of a recurrent major depression.

Once the likelihood of concurrent nicotine dependence and major depression diagnosis has been made, next a plan for treatment is needed. A schematic for health workers that represents treatment, motivation, and prevention of relapse, based upon evidence based research can be referred to as an outline for care (see Figure 1) [42].

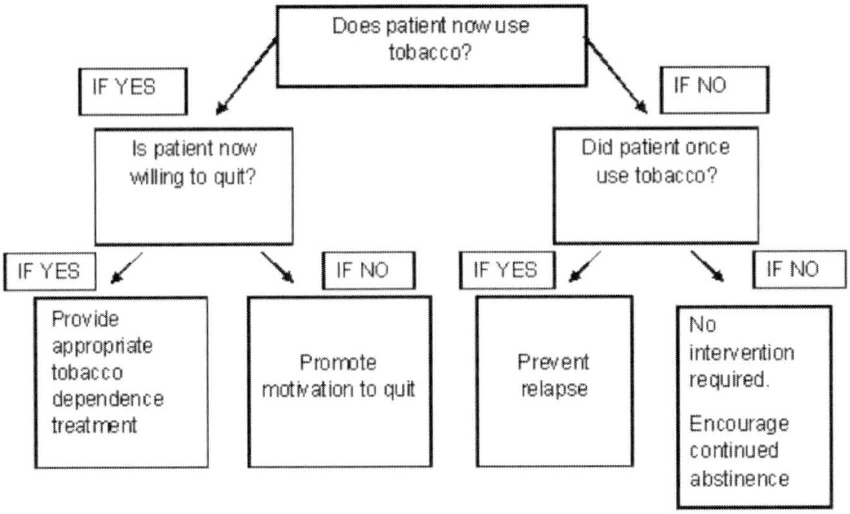


Figure 1. Screen for tobacco use status.

Tobacco dependence treatments appropriate for an individual experiencing both nicotine dependence and depression include the patch plus buproprion slow release (SR) or buproprion alone. Treatment with buproprion is 150 mg daily for 3 days, followed by 150 mg twice daily and continue for 7-12 weeks [34]. The patch dose can begin at 21 mg per day for 4-6 weeks, followed by a tampering of 14mg per day for 2 weeks, then 7mg per day for 2 weeks [34].

The keeping of an expectancy chart can be used to describe a particular triggering situation that serves as a smoking cue followed by writing down the specific belief about smoking (Table 10). There is a need to help the smoker develop and substitute skills such as learning how to regulate feelings in contrast to the use of cigarettes for "self-medicating" purposes.

**Table 10. Sample Expectancy Chart**

| Triggers to Lighting Up | Expectancy | Feeling | Alternative Coping |
|---|---|---|---|
| | | | |
| Demands of job | If I am tense, cigarettes help me to relax<br>Cigarettes help me deal with anger<br>I like to do a better job when smoking | Identify and accept feelings of tension or anger | Practice deep breathing exercises<br>Prioritize work tasks, communicate needs<br>Drink water, exercise at work |
| Going to parties with friends | Smoking helps me enjoy people more<br><br>I feel more at ease with other people if I have a cigarette<br><br>I enjoy the steps I take to light up | Identify and accept feelings of confidence, likeability, power | Converse in a manner and on a topic you enjoy and you are comfortable with.<br>Dress in your favorite outfit<br>Substitute water or soft drinks for alcohol<br>Do not sit near an ashtray |
| During class breaks, especially after an exam | When I feel bored and tired, a cigarette can really help<br><br>Cigarettes calm me down when I feel nervous<br><br>Smoking a cigarette energizes me | Identify that nicotine increases attention and memory<br>Accept the feeling of alertness and enjoyment | Set goal to study and prepare for exams and classes. Take satisfaction in accomplishment based upon self- efforts (drug free)<br>Take a walk |
| Depressed mood | When I am alone, a cigarette can help me pass the day<br><br>Cigarettes can really make me feel good | Identify and accept sadness, depression, boredom, guilt | Monitor triggering feelings and describe context in a journal. Seek the help of a mental health professional |

## Further Recommendations

In addition to examining smoking beliefs that serve as barriers to quitting, behavioral therapies such as brief bursts of advice using the Five A's , individual counseling, suggesting physical exercise, and providing telephone quit line resources increase cessation success when adding this to NRT and anti-depressant therapy [34]. The Five A's ( ask, advise, assess, assist, and arrange) are interventions developed from clinical guidelines by the United States Public Health Service to help clinicians guide smokers who are motivated to quit [43]. For example every person who presents at a clinic should be screened and asked about tobacco use followed by advice that is clear, strong and personalized. Next each person is assessed to determine willingness to quit and is assisted with recommended treatment and follow up arrangements. For those smokers not willing to quit, counseling interventions include discussion of risks, rewards and barriers or roadblocks to quitting. Benefits to quitting occur within the first few days and include: decreased blood pressure and pulse rate, improved circulation, improved ability to taste and smell, and easier breathing. Longer term smoking abstinence reduces the risk of a heart attack, stroke, cancer, and respiratory disease. These rewards along with the barriers to quitting need to be discussed and these can include a lack of social support, lack of self- confidence, concerns about weight gain, depression, and fear of failure.

Many barriers to quitting are based upon personal beliefs about the desired effects of smoking that are reinforced by actual smoking behaviors. If smokers can identify these beliefs that often are unconscious and result in involuntary smoking behavior, the progression from non-daily to nicotine dependent smoking can be interrupted. Smokers can be helped to analyze these beliefs and become critical thinkers about the effects of tobacco in order to resist media messages. Learning how to evaluate who is being targeted by the advertisement, the accuracy of the message, and the personal significance of the message creates strategies to prevent relapse.

## References


[1] Office of Applied Services, Department of Health and Human Services Substance Abuse and Mental Health Services Administration. 2009 National Survey on Drug Use and Health. Accessed 08/16/11. Available at: www. oas.samhsa.gov/NSDUH.

[2] US Department of Health and Human Services, Office of the Surgeon General. Preventing tobacco use among young people: a report of the Surgeon General. Atlanta, GA: US Department of Health and Human Services, CDC; 1994. Accessed July 1, 2011 Available from: http://www.cdc.gov/tobacco/data_statistics/sgr/1994/index.htm

[3] American Psychiatric Association. Diagnostic and statistical manual of mental disorders IV-TR, 4th ed. Washington, DC, *American Psychiatric Association*, 2000.

[4] Julien, R.M., Advokat., C.D, Comaty., J.E. (2011). A primer of drug action 12th edition. *New York,* NY: Worth.

[5] Sudhof, T.C. (2000).The synaptic vesicle revisited. *Neuron*, 28, 317-320.

[6] Wise, R.A. (2001).Theories of Addiction. *Addiction*, 96, 3-13.

[7] Pontieri, F.E., Tanda, G., Orzi, F., DiChiara, G. (1996). Effects of nicotine on the nucleus accumbens and similarity to those of addictive drugs. *Nature*, 382, 255-257.

[8] Vogel-Sprott, M., Fillmore, M.T. (1999). Expectancy and behavioral effects of socially used drugs. In Kirsch I, editor. How expectancies shape behavior. Washington, DC: *Am. Psychol. Assoc.*, 215-232.

[9] Quattrocki, E., Baird, A., Yurgelun-Todd D. (2000). Biological aspects of the link between smoking and depression. *Harv. Rev. Psychiatry*, 3, 99-110.

[10] Fowler, J.S.,Volkow, N.D., Wang, G.L., et al. (1996). Inhibition of monoamine oxidase B in the brains of smokers. *Nature*, 379 (22), 733-736.

[11] Balfour, D.J.K, Ridley, D L. (2000). The effects of nicotine on neural pathways implicated in depression: a factor in nicotine addiction? *Pharmacol. Biochem. Behav.* 66 (1), 79-85.

[12] Kendler, S., Kuhn, J.W., Vittum, J., Prescott, C.A., Riley, B., (2005). The interaction of stressful life events and a serotonin transporter Polymorphism in the prediction of episodes of major depression: A replication. *Archives of General Psychiatry*, 62, 529-535.

[13] Brandon, T.H., Baker, T B. (1991). The Smoking Consequences Questionnaire: The subjective expected utility of smoking in college students. *Psychol. Assess.*, 3 (3), 484-491.

[14] Brandon, T.H., Juliano, L.M., Copeland, A M. (1999). Expectancies for tobacco smoking. In Kirsch, I editor. How expectancies shape experience. Washington, DC: *American Psychological Association*, 263-299.

[15] Copeland, A.L., Brandon, T.H., Quinn. (1995). The Smoking Consequences Questionnaire-Adult: measurement of smoking outcome expectancies of experienced smokers. *Psychol. Assess.*, 7 (4), 484-494.

[16] Mullennix, J.W., Kilby, M.M., Fisicaro, S.A., Farnsworth, L.M., Torrento, R. (2003). The representation of smoking expectancies by single-work adjectives and their relationship to smoking characteristics. *Nicotine Tob. Res.*, 5 (5), 681-694.

[17] Hendricks, P.S., Brandon, T.H. (2008). Smoker's expectancies for smoking versus nicotine. *Psychol. Addict. Behav*, 22, 135-140.

[18] Eysenck, H. J. The biological basis of personality. Springfield, ILL: Carles C. Thomas, 1967.

[19] Goodwin, R., and Hamilton, SP. (2002). Cigarette smoking and panic: the role of neuroticism. *Am. J. Psychiatry*, 159, 1208-1213.

[20] Hu, S., Brody, C.L., Fisher, C., Gunzerath, L., Nelson, M.L., Sabol, S.Z., Sirota, L.A., Marcus, S.E., Greenburg, B.D., Murphy, D.L., Hamer, D.H. (2000). Interaction between the serotonin transporter gene and neuroticism in cigarette smoking behavior. *Mol. Psychiatry*, 5, 181-188.

[21] Lerman, C., Caporaso, N.E., Audrain, J., Main, D., Boyd, N.R., Shields, P.G. (2000). Interacting effects of serotonin transporter gene and neuroticism in smoking practices and nicotine dependence. *Mol. Psychiatry*, 5, 189-192.

[22] Gilbert, D.G. Smoking: Individual differences, psychopathology, and emotion. Washington, DC: Taylor and Francis, 1995.

[23] Kendler, K.S., Bulik, C.M., Silberg, J., Hettema, J.M., Myers, J., Prescott, C.A. (2000). Childhood sexual abuse and adult psychiatric substance use disorders in women: An epidemiological and co-twin control analysis. *Arch. Gen. Psychiatry*, 57, 953-959.

[24] Kessler, R.C., Davis, C.G. Kendler, K.S. (1997). Childhood adversity and adult psychiatric disorder in the US Cormorbidity Survey. *Psychol. Med.*, 27, 1101-1119.

[25] Felitti, V.J., Anda, R.F., Norenberg, D., Williamson, D.F., Spitz, A.M., Edwards, V., Koss, M. P., Marks, J.S. (1998). Relationship of childhood abuse and household dysfunction to many of the leading causes of death in adults: The Adverse Childhood Experiences (ACE) Study. *Am. J. Prev. Med.*, 14(4), 245-257.

[26] Anda, R.F., Croft, J.B., Felitti, V.J., Nordenberg, D., Giles, W.H.,Williamson, D.F., Giovin, G.A. (1999). Adverse childhood experiences and smoking during adolescence and adulthood. *J. Am. Med. Assoc.*, 282(17), 1652-1658.

[27] Robins, L.N Helzer, Cottler, J.E., Golding, E. NIMH Diagnostic Interview Schedule VersionIII Revised, St. Louis: Washington University, 1989.

[28] Kessler, R.C., Andrews, G., Mroczek, D., Ustun, B., Wittchen, H-U. (1998). The World Health Organization Composite International Diagnostic Interview Short-Form (CIDI-SF). *Int. J. Methods Psychiatr. Res.*, 7(4), 171-185.

[29] Spitzer, R.L., Kroenke, K., Williams, J.B.W. he Patient Health Questionnaire Primary Study Group, Validity and utility of a self- report version of the PRIME-MD: (1999). The Primary Care Study. *J. Am. Med. Assoc.*, 282 (18), 1737-1744.

[30] Spitzer, R.L., Williams, J.B W., Kroenke, K., Linzer, M., deGruy, F., Hahn, S.R., Brody, D., Johnson, J.G. Utility of a new procedure for diagnosing mental disorders in primary care: The Prime-MD 1000 Study. *J. Am. Med. Assoc.*, (1994). 272 (22), 1749-1756.

[31] Eysenck, S.B.G., Eysenck, H.J., Barrett, P.A. (1985). Revised version of the Psychoticism Scale. *J. Pers. Individ. Dif.*, 6 (1), 21-29.

[32] Breslau, N., Novak, S.P., Kessler, R.C. (2004). Psychiatric disorders and stages of smoking. *Biol. Psychiatry*, 55, 69-76.

[33] Tate, J.C., Schmitz, J.M. (1993). A proposed revision of the Fagerstrom Tolerance Questionnaire. *Addict. Behav.*, 18, 135-143.

[34] Brunnhuber, K., Cummings, M.K, Feit, S., Sherman, S., Woodcock, J., (2007). Putting evidence into practice: Smoking cessation. *The BMJ Publishing Group,* (suppl), 1-40.

[35] Lerman, C., Patterson, F., Berrettini, W. (2005).Treating tobacco dependence: state of the science and new directions. *J. Clin. Oncol.*, 23 (2), 311-323.

[36] Devereaux, T., Nativio, D.G. (2007). Smoking cessation: a protocol for adolescents. *Adv. Nurse Pract.*, 15 (2), 35-44

[37] Jorenby, DE., Leischow, SJ., Nides, M., Rennard, SI., Johnston, JA., Hughes, AR., Smith, SS., Muramoto, ML., Daughton, DM., Doan, K., Fiore, MC., Baker, TB.

[38] (1999). A controlled trial of sustained release bupropion, a nicotine patch, or both for smoking cessation. *N. Engl. J. Med.* 340, 685-691.

[39] Torrens, M., Fonseca, F., Mateu, G., Farre, M. (2005). Efficacy of antidepressants in substance use disorders with and without comorbid depression: a systematic review and meta-analysis. *Drug Alcohol Depend.*, 78, 1-22.

[40] Gonzales, D., Rennard, S.I Nides, et al and the Varencicline Phase 3 Study Group. (2006). Varenicline, an a4b2 Nicotine Acetylcholine Receptor partial agonist vs sustained- release bupropion and placebo for smoking cessation: a randomized controlled trial. *J. Am. Med. Assoc.* 296 (1), 47-55.

[41] Pfizer Labs, Highlights of Prescribing Information, Accessed August 6, 2011 Available from: http://labeling.pfizer.com/ShowLabeling.aspx?id=557

[42] American Psychiatric Association, Psychiatry Online: Practice Guidelines For the treatment of patients with substance use disorders. Accessed August 6, 2011. Available from: http://www.psychiatryonline.com/content.aspx?aID=141810

[43] US Public Health Service. Treating Tobacco Use and Dependence Clinician's Packet. A How-To Guide For Implementing the Public Health Service Clinical Practice Guidelines, 2000, accessed August 6, 2011. Available at: http://www. surgeon general. gov/tobacco/treating_tobacco_use.pdf

[44] Fiore, M.C., Jean, C.R., Baker, T.B., et al. (2008). A clinical practice guideline for treating tobacco use and dependence: 2008 update. A U.S. Public Health Service report. *Am. J. Prev. Med.*, 35 (2), 158-176.

In: Nicotine Addiction
Editor: Giuseppe Di Giovanni

ISBN: 978-1-62081-290-7


*Chapter 10*

# EFFECTS ASSOCIATED WITH THE STRUCTURE OF ADSORBENTS ON THE DEGREES TO WHICH NICOTINE, TAR AND CO ARE REDUCED IN TOBACCO SMOKE

***Borivoj Adnadjevic[2,*], Miroslava Nikolic[1], and Jelena Jovanovic[2]***
[1]Faculty of Physical Chemistry, University of Belgrade, Belgrade, R. Serbia
[2]Faculty of Agriculture, University of Belgrade, Belgrade-Zemun, R. Serbia

## ABSTRACT

The effects of different classes and types of adsorbents with different texture properties were investigated as they pertain to the degree of reduction of nicotine, tar and carbon monoxide (NTC) in tobacco smoke. The adsorbents of different classes of materials: hydrophilic zeolites (structural types: LTA, FAU and MFI), hydrophobic zeolites (structural types: MFI and FAU) and various amorphous materials were synthesized according to the original procedures. The basic physico-chemical proprieties of the synthesized materials were determined: chemical compositions, crystallinity degree, degree of hydrophobicity and texture properties (specific area, specific pore volume, and average pore diameter). An acetate filter was loaded with samples of synthesized materials in powder form by a novel procedure to create a composite filter. The amounts of NTC in mainstream smoke were determined by using standard ISO methods.

It was established that a remarkable reduction of NTC ( $\geq$50%) in tobacco smoke was achieved by using hydrophylic zeolites of structural types LTA and FAU, hydrophobic zeolites (structural type FAU) and each of the amorphous materials. It was found that hydrophilic zeolite type LTA had a maximal selectivity relative to the tar contained in tobacco smoke. Amorphous material type AM-2 is maximally selective to nicotine, whereas hydrophylic zeolite type Z-3 is maximally selective to CO.

[*] Corresponding author: Dr. Borivoj Adnadjevic, prof., Faculty of Physical Chemistry, University of Belgrade, Studentski trg 12-16, 11001 Belgrade, R. Serbia. Tel: ++381113336871, E-mail: bora@ ffh.bg.ac.rs

A novel, so called sorption mechanism of NTC reduction from tobacco smoke was suggested and experimentally proved. By means of that sorption mechanism, the selectivity found for reducing particular components in tobacco smoke was explained. The possibility of nearly completely and selectively reducing nicotine and tar from tobacco smoke by applying a new class of amorphous materials of type AM-4 was investigated.

# INTRODUCTION

For centuries people have enjoyed tobacco, as extract or as smoke, but have been admonished for its potential negative influences on health. Before the 1950s, general remarks about tobacco smoke's relationship to nicotine addiction, asthma, lung emphysema, and lower birth weights had already been established [1, 2]. Nonetheless, there were only a few precisely established relationships between particular smoke compounds and certain diseases [3, 4].

Due to the rapid development and advancement in separation sciences, tobacco smoke has been better defined than any other consumer product. Over 5,200 components have been identified in tobacco smoke [5], approximately 4,800 components in mainstream smoke (MSS), 500 components in sidestream smoke (SSS) and 100 components in environmental tobacco smoke (ETS) [6].

Development in toxicology and medicine enabled us to associate levels of specific components and exposure duration with certain health problems. Much research has been conducted in attempts to define specific "genicities", but there are no complete answers to all the questions as of yet [7].

Regarding health aspects, smoke components can be classified as: toxicants, tumorogenics, mutagens and compounds without any significant influence. Most often, tobacco smoke components act like all of these depending on their concentrations in the smoke and time of exposure. The classification of a single tobacco smoke compound or a group of compounds according to biological effect is very difficult because it is always present as a highly complex mixture such as mainstream smoke, sidestream smoke or environmental tobacco smoke.

**Table 1. Toxic and Carcinogenic effects of cigarette smoke components**

| Carcinogenic components | Provoke |
|---|---|
| Polycyclic aromatic hydrocarbons (PAHs) | lung cancer |
| N- Nitrosamines (TSNAs) | neoplastic diseases, liver cancer |
| Aza-Arenes and other polycyclic nitrogen compounds (Quinolines, Acridines, Carbazoles) | tumorogenics |
| Low molecular weight fenoles | promoters of cancerogens |
| Aldehydes and ketones (Propenal, Formaldehyde, Acetaldehyde, Propanal, Crotonaldehyde, 2-Butanone) | ciliastatic in vitro |
| Aromatic amines (Aniline, 2-Toluidine, Bnezenamine hydrazine, 2-Naphthalenamine) | promoters of cancerogens |
| Metalic items ($^{210}$Po, Ni) | |
| Ethyl urethan | promoters of cancerogens |

Many of the tobacco smoke constituents individually administered with high dosage levels can be considered as toxic substances, but this is not the case if the particular compound is in a low concentration in a highly complex mixture [5, 8, 9]. Due to this fact, only those components of tobacco smoke which have a maximum concentration per cigarette can cause acute toxicity and are assigned as toxicants. Chronic exposure to the lower concentrations of such components can lead to some other health problems. Made accordingly to this definition, the list of toxicants is rather short: PM, in general [10, 11]; nicotine [11, 12]; carbon monoxide [11, 13]; polycyclic aromatic hydrocarbons [5, 14]; and some nytro components (nitrobenzene, nitro-methane, 2-nytropropane) [15, 16].

The numerous publications during the past two decades on the identifications, quantization, and health hazards of various classes of smoke components identified most of them either as tumor initiators or promoters of carcinogens. [5, 17, 18, 19]. According to these findings, the following list of tumorogens can be made as presented in Table 1.

What has to be underlined after all of this is that all of the data has been obtained as a result of experiments on the animals which, according to many authors [17, 5], can not be considered as proof for the human experience. The evidence from *in vitro* studies indicates that exposure to tobacco smoke, either as mainstream smoke, sidestream smoke or their mixture, can cause: DNA single strain brakes, oxidative DNA damage, chromosome aberrations, and micronuclei [20]. The causes of these genotoxic or citotoxic effects come from many classes of substances in tobacco smoke, mostly from ones already mentioned: PAHs, azo-Arenes, N- nitrosamines, and N-heterocyclicamines [5].

The newest and very complete list of smoke constituents relevant to smoking–related diseases is presented in Rodgman and Perfetti's catalog [5] published in 2009.

The possibilities for reducing various toxic species and carcinogenic compounds contained in cigarette smoke have been investigated by many authors. Among the various methods, the application of various adsorbents presents an effective and inexpensive method that has been investigated in numerous scientific papers.

Gao et al. (2008) presented a strategy for reducing the harmful effects of smoking by using a NaA zeolite to reduce the level of N-nitrosamines in mainstream smoke. The latter strategy consists of dispersing zeolites into the tobacco rod of cigarettes. It was found that the zeolite additive in the tobacco rod neither changed the combustion of tobacco nor formed tiny particles in the mainstream. The efficiency of this strategy was checked by *in vitro* and *in vivo* tests. Lower mutagenic activity and higher cell livability were found for the test cigarette containing the zeolite in comparison with the control cigarettes, and no significant damage was detected in animal experiments when exposed to cigarette smoke with the NaA zeolite additive. [21]

Cao et al. presented novel amorphous functional materials as efficient adsorbents to trap both volatile nitrosamines and bulky tobacco specific nitrosamines in the environment. Novel amorphous functional materials are designed to modify amorphous silica with alumina. This new concept of designing a multifunctional trap for carcinogenic pollutants, which combines the amorphous silica's pore structure with the specific adsorbing/catalyzing features of metal ions, was presented and proved as feasible. Due to the special interaction between the N-NO group of nitrosamines and the aluminum ion in the composite, nitrosamines can be very easily trapped by the composite. Moreover, this cost-efficient material first shows a remarkable adsorptive capability and catalytic activity when reducing NNN (N-nitrosonornicotine) in the liquid phase [22].

Xu et al. investigated the effects of a porous structure and the acidity of zeolite types (NaA and KA, Na-ZSM, NaY, MCM-48 and SBA-15), based on the degree that they removed nitrosamines from mainstream cigarette smoke [23].

A new strategy to intercept the particles and trap the tobacco-specific nitrosamines (TSNA) in smoke by using a porous calcosilicate material with fiber-like morphology plus a two-dimensional eight-ring channel system is depicted and assessed in the recent work of Gaoa et al. They reported that a zeolite-like calcosilicate (CAS-1) can effectively intercept the particles and reduce the TSNA level of mainstream smoke in the range of 30–60% when it is added into the cigarette filter, owing to its specific fiber-like morphology and chemical composition. The importance associated with the morphology of zeolite-like porous materials, as it relates to the adsorption of nitrosamines in smoke, is discussed. It was established that the morphology of porous adsorbents seriously affects their actual performance in reducing the TSNA level of tobacco smoke. The CAS-1 with a fiber morphology exhibits a higher activity than the zeolite NaA with the cubic crystal with the same amount. No obvious impact of morphology was observed in the instantaneous adsorption of volatile nitrosamines over CAS-1 and zeolites, in which CAS-1 shows a weak ability similar to that of the KA zeolite, owing to its two-dimensional eight-ring channel system [24].

Nitrogen oxides (NO, NOx) in MS cigarette smoke may contribute to the formation of carcinogenic nitrosamine not only in smoke, but also upon endogenous smoke inhalation. Several of the amines present may also serve as precursors for volatile nitrosamines (VNA) in cigarette smoke. The possibility for the adsorption of nitrosamine, i.e. the binding of the –N-N=0 group onto the zeolite, was examined by Cvetkovic et al. [25]. Based on the obtained results, the authors concluded that adding the zeolite Cu-ZSM-5 to the cigarette filter is the most efficient means to eliminate NO from the mainstream smoke, whereas the proven best method to reduce other nitrogen oxides from cigarette smoke is by adding Cu-ZSM-5 to the cigarette tobacco blend.

M. Meier and K. Siegmann studied the use of zeolites in the removal of carcinogenic compounds from cigarette smoke, particularly of nitrosamines and polycyclic aromatics (PAHs). The zeolite catalysts placed directly on the tobacco were the most effective in reducing toxic compounds. In the case of polycyclic aromatics, shape selectivity could be observed when using Y-type zeolites. They reported that with these zeolites nicotine levels remained practically unaffected in the mainstream and were distinctly reduced in the sidestream [26].

Yong et al. established that MCM-48 mesoporous silica and cerium incorporated Ce-MCM-48 mesoporous silica, hydrothermally synthesized using a mixed templating method, act as the shape-selective adsorption/catalysts on the tobacco and provide a good means to reduce the bulky polycyclic aromatic hydrocarbons (PAHs) in mainstream cigarette smoke. The incorporation of cerium into the mesoporous silica host effectively improves its catalytic activity, and so, the reduction of PAHs by Ce-MCM-48 exceeds that by the MCM-48 mesoporous silica [27].

Radojicic et al. investigated the effects of cigarette pyrolitic temperatures on the PAHs' degree of reduction by using zeolites, types NaY and ZSM-5, and found that the addition of the zeolite powder into the tobacco blend led to a decreasing of the pyrolitic temperature and the amounts of PAHs in cigarette smoke [28].

Tobacco-catalyst mixtures for reducing the toxic compounds in tobacco smoke are presented in the patent application of Marcilla Gomis et al. (2009) [29]. The invention provides for the use of additives that could be admixed with the tobacco with aim to reduce the quantity of toxic and cancerous substances present in tobacco smoke. The following groups are selected as valuable additives: a) zeolites in their acid, sodium or interchanged with iron forms; b) mesoporous aluminosilicates in their acid, sodium or interchanged with iron forms; c) mixtures of the above mentioned materials with iron oxides, cerium or zirconium; and d) a mixture of the materials mentioned above. The invention provides a composition that consists of any form of tobacco. They also presented a use for the additives dry mixed with the tobacco [29].

The patent of Gomis et al. describes and makes special emphasis of the fact that a drastic reduction in very important certain toxic substances is produced, for example in CO [29].

Adnadjevic et al. investigated the possibility for reducing the amount of nicotine, tar and CO in cigarette smoke by applying the dual filter loaded with zeolites types NaA and KA, CaA, Na-X, Na-Y, Na-ZSM-5, and H-ZSM-5. They found that the maximal reduction associated with the amounts of nicotine and CO was achieved by using zeolite type Na-Y, whereas zeolite type CaA is best for the maximal reduction of tar [30].

Vultic et al. investigated the selective adsorption of tar and nicotine in tobacco smoke by adding various mineral additives and active alumo-silicate to the acetate filter. They found that tar reduced up to 5 times and nicotine reduced up to 7 times, but the selectivity of nicotine relative to tar was small. Also, they found that there was no significant difference between the using 3A and 10A types of adsorbent on the reduction of either nicotine or tar, but that the amount of added adsorbent influenced the degree of reduction [31].

Chen et al. (2006) studied and compared the adsorption of nicotine and tar from the mainstream smoke by the filter tips filled with oxidized carbon nanotubes (O-CNTs) and activated carbon and zeolite (NaY). It was shown that the adsorption capability of O-CNTs for nicotine and tar from MS is much higher than that of the activated carbon and zeolite (NaY) and that the O-CNTs show exceptional removal efficiency. Their adsorption mechanisms were investigated. Nicotine and tar may be adsorbed in the inner hole, at the interior of the tube wall, in the inter-layers and at the exterior of the tube wall of O-CNTs. Capillary condensation of some ingredients from mainstream smoke in the inner hole of OCNTs may be the primary reason for their superior removal efficiency [32].

The application of the natural zeolite type clinoptilolite in a mono and dual filter, to reduce nicotine and tar content in cigarette smoke, was discussed in the work of Mijajlovic [33].

With an intention to optimize nicotin-zeolite interactions, Lazarevic et al. [34] performed a detailed investigation of the mechanism and thermodynamics of nicotine adsorption onto hydrophobic zeolite type USY. It was established that the adsorption isotherm of nicotine could be modeled by the model of Freundlich's adsorption isotherms. Based on the experimentally found dependence of the heat and entropy of adsorption on the degree of adsorption, the density function associated with the probability of the heat's adsorption was calculated. The authors proved that the shape of the adsorption isotherm and density function associated with the probability of the heat's adsorption were direct consequences of the exponential decay of the heat of adsorption of nicotine with the increasing degree of adsorption.

Lazarevic et al. [35] investigated the kinetics associated with the adsorption of nicotine onto a zeolite type USY. By applying the model-fitting method, the kinetics model of nicotine adsorption and values of the kinetics parameters were determined ($E_a$ and lnA). A model for the chemisorption of nicotine on the active centers of a zeolite type USY was suggested and discussed.

Bearing in mind the above presented results, this Chapter will summarize the results obtained for reducing the amount of NTC in mainstream cigarette smoke obtained by applying a mono filter filled with different types of zeolites and highly structural types of amorphous materials.

## NOVEL MATERIALS EFFICIENT FOR REDUCING NICOTINE, TAR AND CO CONTENTS

Novel materials aimed to be efficient in reducing the contents of nicotine, tar and CO in tobacco smoke were synthesized at the Faculty of Physical Chemistry, Belgrade, R. Serbia, according to the procedure originally developed by Adnadjevic et al. [36, 37]

The basic physico-chemical properties of the used materials (chemical composition; degree of crystallinity; textural properties: specific area, specific volume pore, average diameter pore), as well as the methods used for their determination, are summarized in Tables 2-4. Basic physico-chemical properties of the hydrophilic zeolite are presented in Table 2.

**Table 2. Basic physico-chemical properties of the hydrophilic zeolites**

| Properties | Type of the hydrophilic zeolite | | | | Method |
|---|---|---|---|---|---|
| | Z-1 | Z-2 | Z-3 | Z-4 | |
| $SiO_2$ , % wt | 42.2 | 47.7 | 63.7 | 92.1 | Chemical analysis |
| $Al_2O_3$ , % wt | 35.9 | 32.5 | 22.6 | 5.22 | Chemical analysis |
| $Na_20$, % wt | | | | | Chemical analysis |
| Degree of crystallinity, % | 100 | 100 | 100 | 100 | X-ray |
| Nominal pore diameter, nm | 0.50 | 0.74 | 0.74 | 0.56 | Adsorption |
| Specific surface area, $m^2/g$ | 850 | 820 | 900 | 450 | Nitrogen adsorption, BET method |
| Specific pore volume, $cm^3/g$ | 0.297 | 0.350 | 0.333 | 0.126 | Nitrogen adsorption |
| Degree of hydrophobicity, % | 0 | 0 | 0 | 0 | Patent GB 2014970 |

**Table 3. Basic physico-chemical properties of the hydrophobic zeolites**

| Properties | Type of the hydrophobic zeolite | | | | Method |
|---|---|---|---|---|---|
| | HFZ-1 | HFZ-2 | HFZ-3 | HFZ-4 | |
| $SiO_2$ ,% wt | 98.1 | 99.1 | 99.4 | 94.6 | Chemical analysis |
| $Al_2O_3$ ,% wt | 1.85 | 0.84 | 0.56 | 8.05 | Chemical analysis |
| Degree of crystallinity, % | 100 | 100 | 100 | 100 | X-ray |
| Nominal pore diameter, nm | 0.56 | 0.56 | 0.56 | 2.0 | Adsorption |
| Specific surface area, $m^2/g$ | 350 | 400 | 420 | 400 | Nitrogen adsorption, BET method |
| Specific pore volume, $cm^3/g$ | 0.19 | 0.19 | 0.20 | 0.40 | Nitrogen adsorption |
| Degree of hydrophobicity, % | 28 | 92 | 98 | 100 | Patent GB 2014970 |

**Table 4. Basic physico-chemical properties of the amorphous materials**

| Properties | Type of the hydrophilic zeolite | | | | Method |
|---|---|---|---|---|---|
| | AM-1 | AM-2 | AM-3 | AM-4 | |
| $R_20$ , % wt | 56.0 | 42.9 | 0 | 99 | Chemical analysis |
| C, % wt) | 0 | 0 | 100 | 0 | Chemical analysis |
| Degree of crystallinity, % | 0 | 0 | 0 | 0 | X-ray |
| Specific surface area, $m^2/g$ | 60 | 200 | 1050 | 170 | Nitrogen adsorption, BET method |
| Specific pore volume, $cm^3/g$ | 0.35 | 0.40 | 0.60 | 0.35 | Nitrogen adsorption |
| Nominal pore diameter, nm | 10.2 | 4.6 | 1.52 | 4.9 | Adsorption |
| Degree of hydrophobicity, % | 0 | 0 | 100 | 0 | Patent GB 2014970 |

Basic physico-chemical properties of the hydrophobic zeolites are given in Table 3, whereas the basic physico-chemical properties of the amorphous materials are summarized in Table 4.

## Preparation of Cigarette Samples

To prepare the cigarettes, a tobacco blend (modified American blend), from the production program of the Tobacco Factory –Nis, R. Serbia, was used. The tobacco blend was put into the hopper of a "PROTOS" type cigarette making machine. The following manufacturing supplies were used for making the cigarettes: a filter rod 120 mm long, made of acetate tow, 2, 1Y/42000 with a nonporous plug wrap, produced by DIN NIS; acetate tow produced by Celanese; non-porous tipping paper, produced by Cartiera Rossi SpA, Italy; porous cigarette paper with a ventilation of 40±2.5 CORESTA (Cooperation Center for Scientific Research Relative to Tobacco) units, produced by Schoeller and Hoechst, Germany. The filter length of the cigarette was 20 mm, the tipping paper length was 24 mm, and the whole cigarette length was 84 mm.

## Composite Filter

The composite filter was produced by an original procedure by Adnadjevic et al. [37], on the modified machine HAANU, type AC-2, by adding zeolite powder in the free space of the acetate filter in the amount of 60mg/cigarette.

## Chemical Composition of the Mainstream Tobacco Smoke

The cigarettes with acetate and composite filters were smoked by an automatic smoking machine, Borgwaldt Model RM 20/CS, according to CORESTA No. 22. Twenty cigarettes were smoked at a time with a puff volume of 35±0.3 ml, a puff's duration of 2 ±0.03 s, and at a puff interval of 58 seconds to a 28 mm butt length. Particulate matter (TPM) from tobacco smoke was collected on a Cambridge filter in accordance with ISO 4387.

The gas phase was collected in bags. The quantity of raw and dry condensate was determined according to CORESTA standard No 10.

The contents of nicotine and tar in the tobacco smoke were determined according to standard methods ISO 3400 and ISO 4387. The quantity of CO in the tobacco smoke was determined according to ISO methods 8454.

The mainstream smoke of the cigarette with the acetate filter contained an average amount of nicotine (0.645 mg/cigarette), tar (14.42 mg/cigarette) and CO (9.43mg/cigarette).

## Efficiency of the Sorption Removal

The efficiency of nicotine, tar and CO sorption removal from the tobacco smoke was evaluated on the basis of the calculated degree of reduction associated with the amount of a particular compound in tobacco smoke ($R_i$) according to the Equation:

$$R_i = \frac{C_i - C_{o,i}}{Co,i} \cdot 100 \quad (1)$$

where, $C_{o,i}$ is the content of a particular "*i*" compound in the smoke of the cigarette with the acetate filter, and $C_i$ is the content of an "*i*" compound in the smoke of the cigarette with the composite filter.

## The Factor of Selectivity

The selectivity of the investigated material toward the "*i*" component of tobacco smoke in comparison to the "*j*" component of tobacco smoke was determined by calculating the so-called selectivity factor ($S_{i/j}$):

$$S_{i/j} = \frac{R_i}{R_j} \cdot 100 \quad . \quad (2)$$

## Specific Sorption Capacity of Investigated Material

The specific sorption capacity of the investigated material toward the "*i*" compound in tobacco smoke was calculated according to the Equation:

$$X_i = \frac{C_{o,i} - C_i}{60} \quad . \quad (3)$$

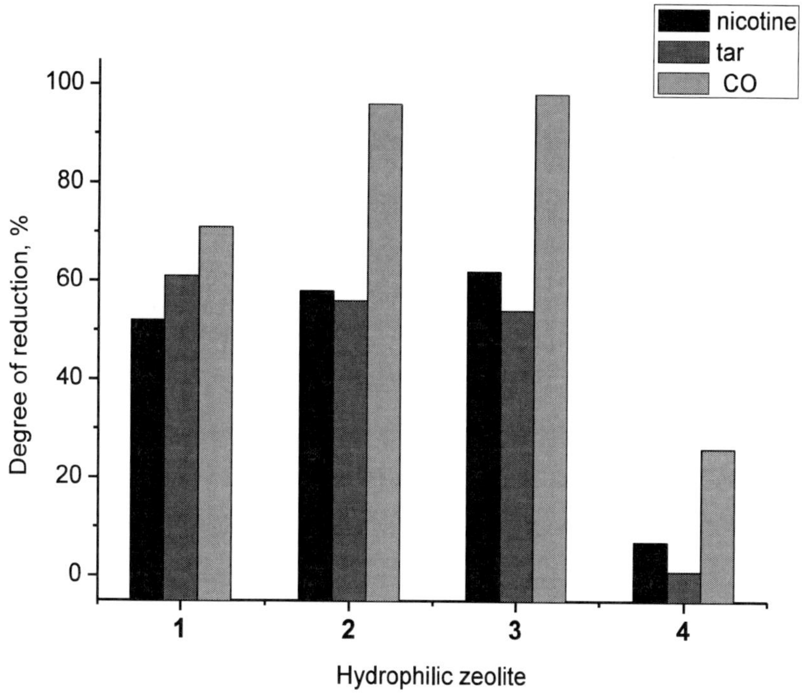


Figure 1. The degrees of reductions of tobacco smoke components by hydrophilic zeolites.

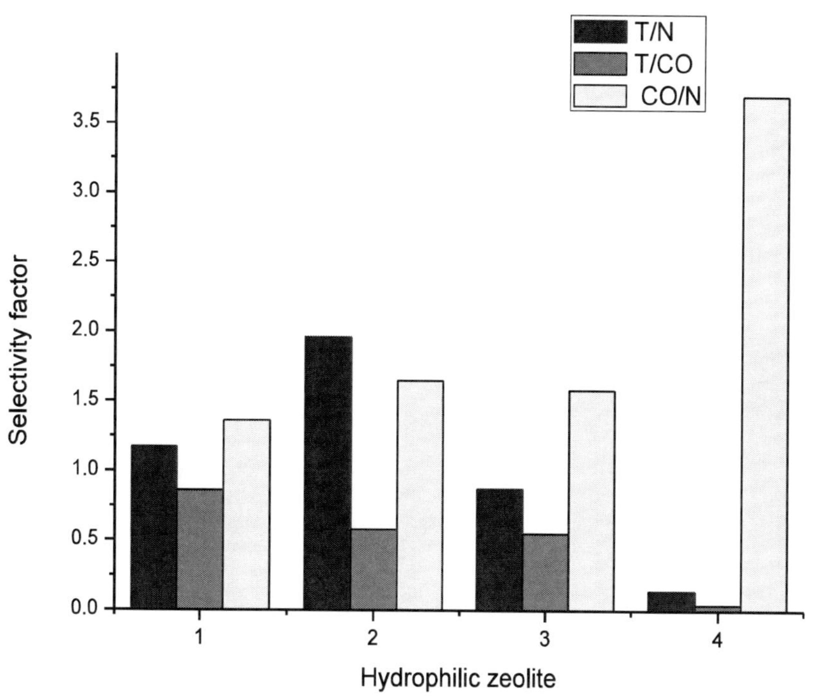


Figure 2. The selectivity factors for hydrophilic zeolites.

**Table 5. Specific sorption capacities of the hydrophilic zeolites**

| Hydrophilic Zeolite | $X_N$, % | $X_T$, % | $X_{CO}$, % | $X_{TOT}$, % |
|---|---|---|---|---|
| Z-1 | 0.5 | 14.7 | 11.0 | 26.2 |
| Z-2 | 0.56 | 13.7 | 15.0 | 29.3 |
| Z-3 | 0.68 | 15.4 | 15.4 | 29.1 |
| Z-4 | 0.08 | 0.23 | 4.0 | 4.5 |

## THE EFFECTS OF A HYDROPHILIC TYPE ZEOLITE ON THE DEGREE OF REDUCTION OF NICOTINE, TAR AND CO IN TOBACCO SMOKE

The degrees of reduction of nicotine ($R_N$), tar ($R_T$) and CO ($R_{CO}$), and the selectivity factors of tar and nicotine related to CO ($S_{T/N}$ and $S_{T/CO}$), as well as the selectivity factor of CO related to nicotine ($S_{CO/N}$), in tobacco smoke that were obtained by introducing hydrophilic types of zeolites into an acetate filter, are presented in Figures 1 and 2, respectively.

The specific sorption capacities of the hydrophilic zeolites are presented in Table 5.

It is clear from the results presented above (in Figures 1 and 2 and Table 5) that the degrees of reduction, the selectivity factors and the sorption capacities toward a particular component in tobacco smoke are dependent on the type of applied hydrophilic zeolite. All the applied hydrophilic zeolites manifested a maximal degree of reduction for CO in tobacco smoke. The zeolite of structural type LTA (Z-1) has a higher degree of reduction associated with tar than with nicotine, whereas for all the other types of hydrophilic zeolites, the degree of reduction for nicotine is higher than for tar. All of the investigated hydrophilic zeolites are selectively toward CO. Zeolite Z-1 is more selective to tar in comparison to nicotine, whereas the other zeolites are more selective to nicotine in comparison to tar. The determined changes in the degrees of reduction and factors of selectivity when hydrophilic zeolites were applied may be attributed to their specific sorption capacities toward a particular component in tobacco smoke.

Exceptionally small values of specific sorption capacities of all of the investigated hydrophilic zeolites related to nicotine are a consequence of their lack of ability of nicotine sorption, as the diameter of a molecule of nicotine (d=0.78nm) is larger than the pore size of the entrance hole in the structure of zeolite [32]. Due to this fact, molecules of nicotine may be adsorbed at the outer surface of a zeolite particle and in the free space between zeolite particles.

Maximal values of specific sorption capacities for CO were found for all types of applied zeolites in accordance with their abilities to selectively adsorb CO from the mixture with other components [25]. The maximal value associated with the specific sorption capacity of the hydrophilic zeolite of FAU structural types (Z-2 and Z-3) to tar implies that the tar of the investigated tobacco smoke contains significant portions of substances which have molecular dimensions lower than d=0.74 nm. This is the case, for example, with naphthalene, acenaphthylene, antracene, etc. In contrast, the maximal value associated with specific sorption capacities of the hydrophilic zeolites of LTA structural types relative to tar implies that there is a different mechanism for removing tar from tobacco smoke, confirming

Ebbesen's hypothesis [38]. The latter hypothesis states that the reason for tar reduction from tobacco smoke is due to its capillary condensation at a crystal of zeolite Z-1.

## The Effects Associated with the Degree of Hydrophobicity of the Zeolite on the Degree of Reduction of Tobacco Smoke Components

The degrees of reduction of nicotine, tar and CO in tobacco smoke is presented in Figure 3, whereas Figure 4 shows the selectivity factors of tar and nicotine related to CO ($S_{T/N}$ and $S_{T/CO}$) and the selectivity factor of CO related to nicotine ($S_{CO/N}$).

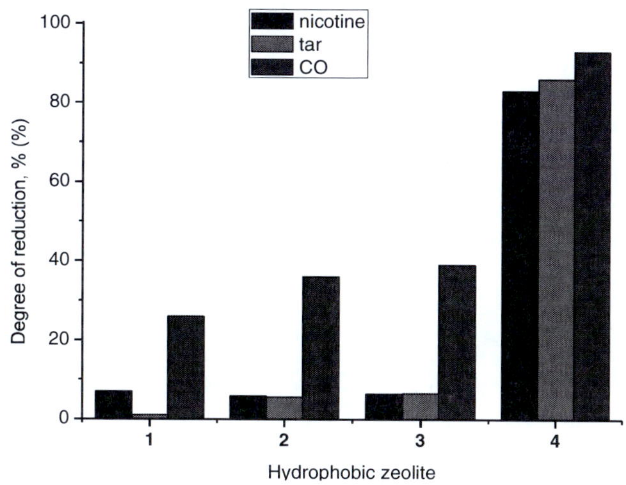


Figure 3. The degrees of reductions of tobacco smoke components by hydrophobic zeolites.

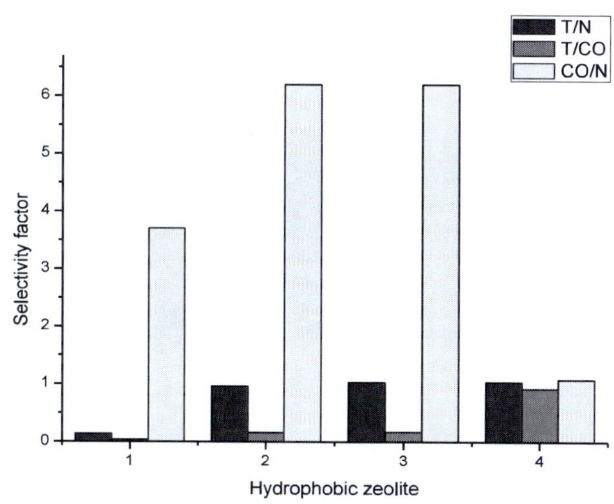


Figure 4. The selectivity factors for hydrophobic zeolites.

**Table 6. Specific sorption capacities of hydrophilic zeolites**

| Hydrophobic Zeolite | $X_N$, % | $X_T$, % | $X_{CO}$, % | $X_{TOTALt}$, % |
|---|---|---|---|---|
| HFZ-1 | 0.08 | 0.23 | 4.0 | 4.31 |
| HFZ-2 | 0.08 | 1.37 | 5.7 | 7.10 |
| HFZ-3 | 1.07 | 1.57 | 6.13 | 7.77 |
| HFZ-4 | 0.09 | 20.7 | 14.7 | 35.4 |

Specific sorption capacities of hydrophilic zeolites are given in Table 6.

As in the case of hydrophilic zeolites, the degrees of reduction of tobacco smoke components, their selectivity factors and specific sorption capacities depend on the type and structure of the zeolite and their textural properties.

In the case of hydrophobic zeolites, the increase in the degree of hydrophobicity of zeolite structural type MFI leads to an increase in the degree of reduction of tar and CO, as well as the selectivity factors of tar relative to nicotine and CO relative to nicotine. The found changes in the degree of reductivity and selectivity factors are consequences of the increase in the specific sorption capacities of zeolite type MFI related to tar and CO. The increased specific sorption capacities may be attributed to the increased hydrophobicity of their sorption interaction interface.

The established higher values of the degrees of reduction and specific sorption capacities of hydrophilic zeolites than their corresponding values obtained for the hydrophobic zeolites, may be explained with the higher sorption capacities of hydrophilic zeolites related to particular components of tobacco smoke than of hydrophobic zeolites.

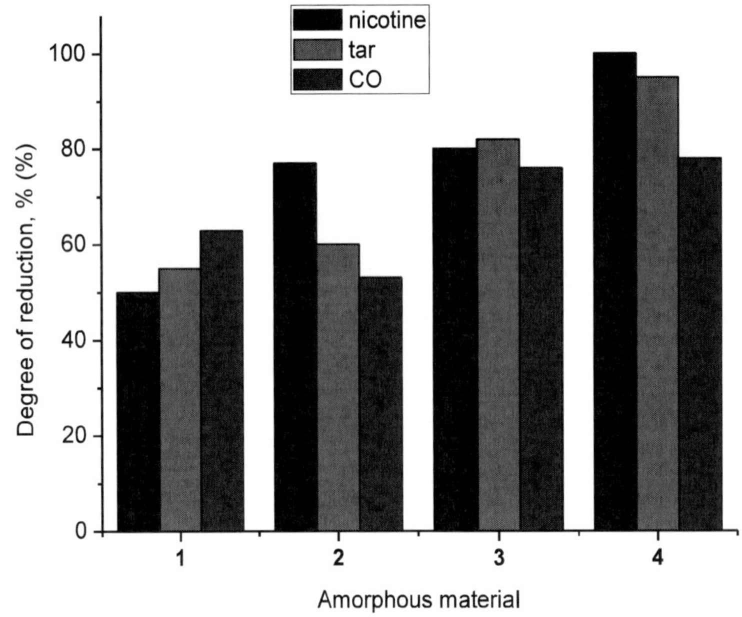


Figure 5. The degrees of reductions of tobacco smoke components by amorphous materials.

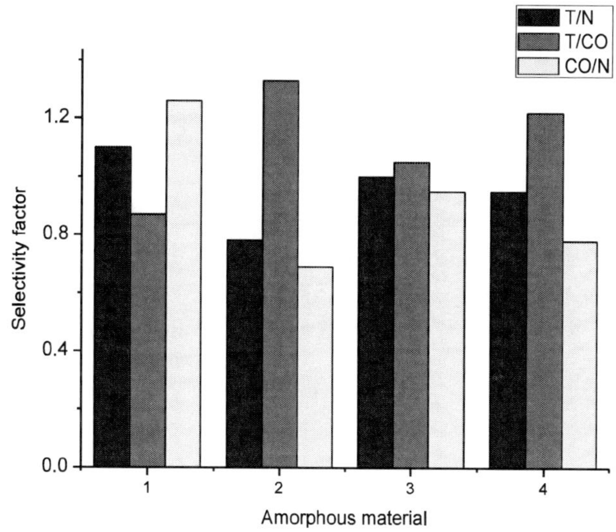


Figure 6. The selectivity factors for amorphous materials

**Table 7. Specific sorption capacities of the amorphous material**

| Amorphous Material | $X_N$, % | $X_T$, % | $X_{CO}$, % | $X_{TOTALt}$, % |
|---|---|---|---|---|
| AM-1 | 0.5 | 13.21 | 9.90 | 23.61 |
| AM -2 | 0.82 | 14.42 | 8.30 | 23.54 |
| AM -3 | 0.86 | 19.22 | 11.94 | 32.02 |
| AM -4 | 1.08 | 22.83 | 12.26 | 36.17 |

However, in contrast, the hydrophobic zeolite of structural type FAU (USY-zeolite) more significantly reduces the content of nicotine and tar in tobacco smoke than does the hydrophilic zeolite.

Considerable increases in the degrees of reduction of nicotine and tar, in the case of HFZ 4, is a consequence of its specific porous structure (mean pore diameter d = 2.0 nm). That structure makes the maximal sorption of nicotine and of almost the all components contained in tar possible.

## The Effects Associated With the Type of Amorphous Material on the Degree of Reduction of Tobacco Smoke Components

The effects associated with the type of amorphous material on the degrees of reduction of nicotine, tar and CO in tobacco smoke are presented in Figure 5 and their selectivity factors in Figure 6.

Table 7 presents specific sorption capacities of the amorphous material.

The ability to reduce nicotine, tar and CO in tobacco smoke, and the selectivity of the investigated amorphous material, depends on the type of amorphous material and its texture properties. Amorphous material manifested a higher capability to reduce nicotine, tar and CO content in tobacco smoke than both a hydrophilic zeolite and a hydrophobic zeolite type MFI. Amorphous material AM-4 has a maximal degree of reduction of nicotine, tar and CO in tobacco smoke. Amorphous materials AM-4 and AM-2 have the highest degree of reduction of nicotine. In contrast to this, the amorphous material AM-3 has a maximal degree of reduction of tar, whereas the AM-13 has maximal degree of reduction of CO. The extremely high reduction capacity of these materials may be attributed to their specifically porous structures and to their specific energetic distribution of adsorption centers, two reasons for the extraordinarily high selective sorption of nicotine molecules and different molecules contained in tar. Amorphous materials of AM-4 type are capable to completely remove the nicotine content and almost completely reduce the tar content, and so they present unique materials that exhibit such sorption properties known up to-date.

## CONCLUSION

The considerable reduction of nicotine, tar and CO ($\geq$50% ) in tobacco smoke was achieved with hydrophilic zeolites types Z-1, 2, 3, hydrophobic zeolite type HFZ-4 and with all of the used amorphous materials. The maximal degree of nicotine and tar reduction was found for amorphous material type AM-4, whereas the maximal reduction of CO was found for zeolite type Z-3. Hydrophobic zeolite type Z-1 has significant selectivity relative to the molecules contained in tar.

It was found that amorphous material type AM-2 is maximally selective relative to nicotine, whereas hydrophilic zeolite type Z-3 is maximally selective relative to CO.

It is concluded that the achieved degrees of reduction of nicotine, tar and CO by applying the different classes of materials was dependent on the type of applied material and on their textural properties.

The reduction of nicotine, tar and CO from tobacco smoke by using hydrophilic and hydrophobic zeolites, or amorphous materials is attained by a sorption mechanism.

The reduction of tar by using hydrophilic zeolite type Z-1 is achieved by a mechanism of condensation.

The novel synthesized material type AM-4 enable the maximal reduction of nicotine, tar and CO from tobacco smoke.

## ACKNOWLEDGMENT

This investigation was supported by the Ministry of Science and Technical Development of the Republic of Serbia, through Project No.172015 OI.

## REFERENCES


[1] Shear, M.J., Leiter J. (1941). Studies in carcinogenesis. XVI. Production of subcutaneous tumors in mice by miscellaneous polycyclic compounds. *J. Natl. Cancer Inst.*, 2, 241–258.

[2] Wynder, L.E., Little, E. (1955). Biologic effects of tobacco. In *Brown and Company*, Boston, MA.

[3] Kosak, A.I. (1954). The composition of tobacco smoke. *Experientia*, 10, 69–71.

[4] Stedman, R.L. (1968). The chemical composition of tobacco and tobacco smoke; *Chem. Rev.*, 68, 153–207.

[5] Rodgman, A., Perfetti, A.T. (2009). The Chemical components of tobacco and tobacco smoke, *CRC Press*, Boca Raton, FL.

[6] Rodgman, A. (1992). Environmental tobacco smoke. *Regul. Toxicol. Pharmacol.*, 16, 223–244.

[7] Rodgman, A. (2003). The composition of cigarette smoke: Problems with lists of tumorigens. *Beitr. Tabakforsch. Int.*, 402–437.

[8] Gold, L.S., Slone, T.H., Ames, B.N. (1997). Overview of the carcinogenic potency database; In *Handbook of carcinogenic potency and genotoxicity databases* (pp. 661–685). edited by Gold L.S. Seiger E. CRC Press, Boca Raton, FL.

[9] Hoffmann, D., Schmeltz I., Hecht, S.S., Wynder, E.L. (1978) Tobacco carcinogenesis; Chapter 5 (p.p.119–130) In Gelboin H.V. Ts'o P.O. *Polycyclic hydrocarbons and cancer*, Vol. 1, *Chemistry molecular biology and environment*, Academic Press, New York, NY.

[10] Richard, R., Baker, E., Massey D., Smith G. (*2004*). An overview of the effects of tobacco ingredients on smoke chemistry and toxicity. *Food Chem. Toxicol.*, 42 (1), *53-83.*

[11] Hoffmann, D., Hoffmann, I. (2001). The changing cigarette: Chemical studies and bioassays; Chapter 5 In *Risks associated with smoking cigarettes with low machine-measured yields of tar and nicotine, NCI Smoking and tobacco control*, (pp 159–191). Monograph 13, edited by Burns D.M., Benowitz N.L., Bethesda, MD.

[12] Hoffmann, D., LaVoie, E.J., Hecht, S.S. (1985). Nicotine: A precursor for carcinogens. *Cancer Lett.*, 26, 67–75.

[13] Henderson, A.J. (2008). The effects of tobacco smoke exposure on respiratory health in school-aged children *Paediatr. Respir. Rev.*, 9(1), *21-28.*

[14] Rodgman, A. Perfetti, T.A. (2006). The composition of cigarette smoke: A catalogue of the polycyclic aromatic hydrocarbons. *Beitr. Tabakforsch. Int.*, 22, 13–69.

[15] Hoffmann, D., Hoffmann, I., El-Bayoumy K. (2001). The less harmful cigarette: A controversial issue. Atribute to Ernst L. Wynder; *Chem. Res. Toxicol.*, 14 767–790.

[16] Occupational Safety and Health Administration (OSHA) (1994). Indoor air quality; *Fed. Reg.*, 5 *(65)*, 15968–16039.

[17] Wynder, E.L., Hoffmann, D. (1969). A study of tobacco carcinogenesis. X. Tumor promoting activity; *Cancer*, 24, 289–301.

[18] Tsuchiya, K., Hayashi, Y., Onodera, M., Hasegawa, T. (1975). Toxicity of formaldehyde in experimental animals: Concentrations of the chemical in the elution from dishes of formaldehyde resin in some vegetables. *Keio J. Med.*, 24, 19–37.

[19] USPHS: Reducing the health consequences of smoking. 25 Years of progress. (1989). A report of the Surgeon General, (pp 89–8411) DHHS Publ. No. (PHS).

[20] Hoffmann, D., Hecht, S.S. (1990). Advances in tobacco carcinogenesis. In Chemical carcinogenesis and mutagenesis. (pp 64–102). *Edited by Cooper C.S. and Grover, P., Springer- Verlag*, London, UK.

[21] Gao, L., Wang, Y., Xu, Y., Zhou, S.L., Zhuang, T.T., Wu, Z. Y., Zhu J.H., (2008). New Strategy to Reduce the Harmful Effects of Smoking: Reducing the Level of N-nitrosamines in Mainstream Smoke by NaA Zeolite and In vitro and In vivo Investigations, *Clean,* 36(3), 270 – 278.

[22] C a o , Y., S h i , L. Y., Z h o u , C. F., Y u n , Z. Y., W a n g , Y., Z h u, J. H . (2005). Novel Amorphous Functional Materials for Trapping Nitrosamines. *Environ. Sci. Technol.,* 39, 7254-7259.

[23] Yang, X., Zhu, J.H., Ma, L.L., Ji, A., We, Y.L., Shang, X.Y. (2003). Removing nitrosamines from mainsteamsmoke of cigarettes by zeolites. *Microporous Mesoporous Mater.,* 60, 125-138.

[24] Gao, L., Cao, Y., Zhou, S.L., Zhuang, T.T., Wang, Y., Zhua, J. H. (2009). Eliminating carcinogenic pollutants in environment: Reducing the tobacco specific nitrosamines level of smoke by zeolite-like calcosilicate. *J. Hazard Mater.,* 169, 1034–1039.

[25] Cvetkovic, N., Adnadjevic, B., Nikolic, M. (2002). Catalytic Reduction of NO and NOx Content in Tobacco Smoke. *Beitråge zur Tabakforsung International Contributions to Tobacco Research,* 20 (1), 43-48.

[26] Meier, W.M., Siegmann, K. (1999). Significant reduction of carcinogenic compounds in tobacco smoke by the use of zeolite catalysts. *Microporous. Mesoporous. Mater.,* 33, 307–310.

[27] Yong, G-p., Jin, Z-x., Tong , H-w., Yan, X-y., Li, G-s., and Liu, S-m., (2006). Selective reduction of bulky polycyclic aromatic hydrocarbons from mainstream smoke of cigarettes by mesoporous materials. *Microporous Mesoporous Mater.,* 91, 238-243.

[28] Radojicic, V., Nikolic, M., Adnadjevic, B., (2009). The influence of zeolite type added to cigarette blend on the changes of pyrolitic temperature. *Chem. Industry,* 63(5a), 579-583.

[29] Marcilla Gomis, A., Beltran Rico, M.I., Gomez Siurana, A., Navarro Martinez, R., Berenguer Muñoz, D., Martinez Castellanos, I. (2009). Tobacco/Catalyst Mixtures For Reducing Toxic Compounds In Tobacco Smoke. EP 2 092 838 A1, *Bulletin,* 2009/35.

[30] Adnadjevic, B., Nikolic, M. (1998). New filtration materials for nicotine, tar and carbon monoxide reduction in cigarette smoke. Proceedings of III Yugoslavien symposia on food technology. (pp. 63-67). Vol III, Belgarde.

[31] Vuletic, N., Tomic, L., Svecnjak, N. (1995). Selective reduction of only nicotine in cigarette smoke In *JAZU,* (*Proceedings from scientific and professional work in 1995*) (pp.153-156) Vol. 21, Zagreb.

[32] Chen Z., Zhang, L., Tang, Y., Jia, Z. (2006). Adsorption of nicotine and tar from the mainstream smoke of cigarettes by oxidized carbon nanotubes. *Applied Surface Science*, 252, 2933–2937.

[33] Mijajlovic S., (2002). The influence of type and structure of materials on manufacturing filter and on filtration of cigarette smoke. *Ms. Thesis*, Faculty of Agriculture, Belgrade, R. Serbia.

[34] Lazarevic N., Adnadjevic B., Jovanovic J., (2011). Adsorption of nicotine from Aqueous Solution onto hydrophobic zeolite type USY. *Appl. Surf. Sci.,* 257, 8017-8023.

[35] Lazarevic, N., Jovanovic, J., Jevremovic, M., Nikolic, M., Adnadjevic, B. (2010) Kinetics of Isothermal Nicotine Adsorption from the Aqueous Solution onto the USY Zeolite, *Ind. Eng. Chem. Res.,* 49 (14), 6302-6308.

[36] Adnadjevic, B.K. (1997). Review of basic achievements in the development of zeolite catalysts and novel catalytic processes. In Monograph In *New Challenges in Catalysis I,* (p.p 71-94). Serbian Academy of Science and Arts, Branch in Novi Sad.

[37] Adnadjevic, B., Popovic A., Jovanovic J. (2002). Summary of achieved results in application of new catalytic processes in environmental protection, In *New Challenges in Catalysis III,* (p.p.119-135), Serbian Academy of Science and Arts, Branch in Novi Sad.

[38] Ebbesen, T.W. (2000), Production and Purifuication of Carbon Nanotubes. In Carbon Nanotubes, preparation and properties. Ebbesen, T.W. Ed. *CRC Inc Press*, Boca Raton.

In: Nicotine Addiction
Editor: Giuseppe Di Giovanni
ISBN: 978-1-62081-290-7


*Chapter 11*

# KINETICS OF NICOTINE BONDING ONTO AND RELEASE FROM POLY (ACRYLIC -*CO*-METHACRYLIC ACID) HYDROGEL

***Borivoj Adnadjevic[1,*], Natasa Lazarevic[2], and Jelena Jovanovic[1]***
[1]Faculty of Physical Chemistry, University of Belgrade, Belgrade, R. Serbia
[2]Nuclear Facilities of Serbia", Belgrade, Vinca, R. Serbia

## ABSTRACT

The isothermal kinetics of nicotine bonding from aqueous solutions onto poly(acrylic-*co*-methacrylic acid) xerogel/hydrogel and the release of binded nicotine from the same xerogel in distilled water were investigated.

The isothermal kinetic curve of nicotine bonding and the release to/or from PAM hydrogel were determined at a temperature range of 294- 314 K.

By applying the method of model fitting, it was established that the isothermal kinetics of nicotine bonding at xerogel/hydrogel can be described by the kinetics model of two dimensional diffusion (D-2), whereas the kinetics of nicotine release is best described by the kinetics model of tridimensional contracting area (R-3). The values of kinetic parameters ($Ea$ and $\ln A$) of nicotine bonding ($E_a$ = 10 kJmol$^{-1}$ ; ln[A/min$^{-1}$] =1.62) and nicotine release ($Ea$ = 28 kJmol$^{-1}$ ; ln[A/min$^{-1}$] = 8.0 ) were determined.

By applying the differential isoconversional method, it was established that both nicotine bonding and release are kinetically complex processes.

The new models for the mechanism of nicotine bonding and release were proposed and suggested.

The functions of density distribution $E_{a,\alpha}$. of nicotine bonding and release were calculated and are presented here.

The established kinetics model of bonding and release and their kinetic parameters are explained with the suggested models of the mechanism of nicotine bonding and release, and with the specific shapes of the density distribution functions.

---

* Corresponding author: Dr. Borivoj Adnadjevic, prof., Faculty of Physical Chemistry, Studentski trg 12-16, 11001 Belgrade, R. Serbia. Tel: ++381113336871, E-mail: bora@ffh.bg.ac.rs.

## INTRODUCTION

Three-dimensional slightly crosslinked hydrophilic material which are capable of absorbing large amounts of water and aqueous fluids in a short time and retaining water under pressure are named hydrogels.

Due to their characteristic properties (ability of swelling, intoxicity, biocompatibility etc.), hydrogels have a wide range of application such as in agriculture and horticulture [1], drilling fluid additives [2], soil additives [3], water-swellable rubbers [4] water-blocking tapes [5] sanitary goods such as disposable diapers and hygienic napkins [6], sealing composites [ 7 ], artificial snow [8], coal dewatering [9], fire fighting [10], enhanced oil recovery [11], biosensors [12], bioactive components like proteins [13], , dyalisis membrane [14], medicine for biomedical and tissue engineering [15], and drug delivery systems [16].

With aims to optimize novel sorption procedures for nicotine removal from underground and municipal waters, it is of great importance to know and understand the kinetics of nicotine bonding into the hydrogel and the kinetics of the bonded nicotine release into the surrounding medium.

The incorporation of any substance or drug into hydrogel delivery matrices can be achieved via one of the following ways: 1) post-loading: absorption of drugs after hydrogel network are formed; (2) in situ loading: drugs or drug-polymer conjugates are mixed with polymer precursor solution and hydrogel network formation and drug encapsulation are accomplished simultaneously.

In the case of "post-loading", if an inert hydrogel system is in use, diffusion is the major driving force for drug uptake and release will be determined by diffusion and/or gel swelling.

In the systems where ""in situ loading"" is in use , release of drugs can be controlled by diffusion , hydrogel swelling, reversible drug-polymer interaction, or degradation of labile covalent bonds.

The kinetics of "post-loading" are most commonly described by:

(1) The rate Equation (1) of Langergren [17]:

$$\ln\left(x_{\max} - x_t\right) = \ln x_{\max} - k_L t \tag{1}$$

where $x_{max}$ are equilibrium adsorption capacities , $x_t$ is adsorption capacity in time $t$, and $k_L$ is the rate constant of pseudo-first order adsorption reactions.

(2) The pseudo-second order Equation [18]:

$$\frac{t}{x_t} = \frac{1}{k_2 x_{\max}^2} + \frac{t}{x_{\max}} \tag{2}$$

where $k_2$ is the rate constant for the pseudo–second order adsorption reactions.

(3) The Equation of Elovich [19] :

$$x_t = \beta \ln\left(\alpha\beta\right) + \frac{1}{\beta} \ln t \tag{3}$$

where α is the initial chemisorption rate and β is the desorption constant.

(4) The Equation (4) for inter-particle (pore) diffusion [20]:

$$x_t = k_{id} t^{1/2} \tag{4}$$

where $k_{id}$ is the inter-particle (pore) diffusion rate constant.

The mechanism of substance–drug release offers a convenient way to categorize controlled release systems into (1) diffusion-controlled, (2) swelling-controlled, and (3) chemical controlled [21] groups.

Diffusion–controlled is the most widely applicable mechanism for describing drug release from hydrogel, dividing it into two major types: reservoir devices and matrix devices [22].

Reservoir systems consist of a polymer membrane surrounding a core consisting of the drug. In matrix devices, the drug is dispersed throughout the three-dimensional structure of hydrogel.

Higuchi T. developed a mathematical model to describe drug release from a matrix system [23]. This model is based on several hypotheses, as: (1) initial drug concentration in the matrix is much higher than drug solubility; (2) drug diffusion takes place only in one dimension; (3) drug particles are much smaller than system thickness; (4) matrix swelling and dissolution is negligible; (5) drug diffusivity is constant; and (6) perfect sink conditions are always attained in the release environment.

Accordingly, model expression is given by:

$$x_R = A\sqrt{D(2c_o - c_s)c_s t} \tag{5}$$

where $x_R$ is the amount of drug released until time $t$, $A$ is the release area, D is the drug diffusion coefficient, $c_o$ is the initial drug concentration in the matrix, while $c_s$ is drug solubility.

In the investigations of the diffusion controlled kinetics of substance release from the hydrogel , the so called empirical Equation of Peppas [24] is commonly used, which is the power law equation:

$$\frac{x_R}{x_{R,\infty}} = kt^n \tag{6}$$

where $x_{R,\infty}$ is the amount of drug released in infinite time, and $k$ and $n$ are constants characteristic of the drug polymer system. The diffusion exponent, $n$, is dependent on the geometry of the device as well as the physical mechanism for release.

Based on the diffusion exponent, the drug transports in slab geometry are classified as Fickian diffusion, Case II transports, non-Fickian or anomalous transports, and Super Case II transports.

For the case of anomalous transports, Peppas and Sahlin [25] showed a new equation for describing the kinetics of release:

$$\frac{x_R}{x_{R,\infty}} = k_q t^n + k_2 t^{1/2} \tag{7}$$

where $k_I$ is the constant of relaxation rate for the controlled transport process and $k_2$ is the constant of relaxation rate for the diffusion controlled process.

Another mechanism for drug delivery is swelling controlled delivery.

Swelling controlled release occurs when diffusion of a drug is faster than hydrogel swelling. The modeling of this mechanism usually involves moving boundary conditions where molecules are released at the interface of rubbery and glassy phases of swollen hydrogels.

The rate of drug release is controlled by the rate and position of the front dividing the glassy (dry) and rubbery (swelled) portions of the polymer.

In order to describe the kinetics of drug release controlled with the rate of hydrogel swelling, the empirical Equation of Peppas (6) or its modified form are frequently used:

$$\frac{x_R}{x_{R,\infty}} = k_1 t^n + k_2 t^{2n} \tag{8}$$

where $k_I$ and $k_2$ are the constants.

Two major types of chemically controlled release systems are erodible drug delivery systems and pendant chain systems. In erodible systems, drug release occurs due to degradation or dissolution of the hydrogel. In pendant chain systems, the drug is affixed to the polymer backbone through degradable linkages. As these linkages degrade, the drug is released.

For the case of erodible drug delivery systems, Hoffenberg [26] presented an equation which describes the kinetics of drug release:

$$\frac{x_R}{x_{R,\infty}} = 1 - \left(1 - \frac{k_{R,t}}{c_o a_o}\right) \tag{9}$$

where $a_o$ is the radius of a spherical or cylindrical geometry or a half-thickness , $c_o$ is the drug concentration in the surface of the eroding device, $n$ is 1, 2, or 3 for the slab, cylinder, or sphere, respectively, and $k_R$ is radial degradation constant.

In order to optimize the technological parameters for sorption removal of nicotine from waters flows and for the possible application of nicotine loaded hydrogel, the kinetics of post-loading nicotine from water solution into the poly(acrylic *-co-*methacrylic acid) xerogel / hydrogel and the kinetics of the loaded-nicotine release into distilled water were investigated.

**Table 1. Basic physicochemical properties of the used PAM xerogel**

| Propertry | $SD_{eq}$, g/g | $\rho_x$ , $g/cm^3$ | $M_c \cdot 10^{-5}$, g/mol | $\rho_c . 10^3$, $mol/m^3$ | d, nm |
|---|---|---|---|---|---|
| Value | 180 | 1.317 | 2.14 | 6.15 | 123 |

# POLY(ACRYLIC ACID-CCO-METHACRYLIC ACID) HYDROGEL SYNTHESIS; NICOTINE BONDING AND RELEASE

## Poly(Acrylic Acid-*co*-methacrylic Acid) Hydrogel Synthesis

Poly(acrylic acid-comethacrylic acid) hydrogel (PAM) have been synthesized by a procedure based on crosslinking radical polymerization of acrylic acid and methacrylic acid (4:1 mol ratio), using the procedure which we described in detail in our prevous work [27].

In reference to the equilibrium swelling degree (SDeq), xerogel density ($\rho_x$), and the primary structural parameters (PSP) of the synthesized poly(acrylic acid) xerogels: average molar mass between the network crosslinks ($M_c$), crosslinking degree ($\rho_c$) and the distance between the macromolecular chains (*d*) were calculated by application of the Flory and Rehner Equation [28]. Table 1 presents the basic macroscopic properties of the primary structural parameters of the xerogel used in this investigation.

Based on the determined values of the macroscopic properties and the primary structural parameters, it may be concluded that the applied sample of xerogel was slightly crosslinked, macroporous, and highly absorbing.

## Nicotine Bonding

Nicotine loading was carried out by immersing the known weight of the xerogel sample (0.2 g) in an excess of nicotine solution (250 ml of 5% solution) at temperatures ranging from 294 K to 314 K. The sample nicotine solutions (2mL) were undertaken in predetermined time intervals. The residual nicotine was detrmined spectrometrically by using the method ISO 2881. The spectars were recorded on a Cintra 10e, UV-Visible Spectrometer, Serial No. V 3163. The absorbancy was measured at 259 nm.

The specific amount of nicotine bonded was determined using Eq. (10):

$$x = \frac{(c_o - c)V}{m} \tag{10}$$

where $c_o$ is initial nicotine concentration, $c$ is residual nicotine concentration in time $t$, $m$ is the weight of xerogel, and $V$ is the volume of the solution.

The degree of bonded nicotine ($\alpha_B$) was calculated using Eq. (11):

$$\alpha_B = \frac{x}{x_{max}} \tag{11}$$

where $x_{max}$ is the equilibrium nicotine concentration at a certain temperature.

### Nicotine Release

The nicotine release was carried out by immersing the xerogel – nicotine loaded sample in distilled water at temperatures of 26 °C, 30 °C, 36 °C, 41 °C, and 45 °C. A xerogel – nicotine loaded sample (0.2 g) was added to 100 mL of distilled water and the vessel was placed in the thermostat at a pre-determined temperature. Samples were taken from this system at regular time intervals. The released nicotine concentration ($c_R$) in the water solution was determined as previously described.

The degree of nicotine released ($\alpha_R$) is calculated as a ratio of nicotine concentration in the water solution released at time ($t$), ($c_R$) and equilibrium released nicotine concentrations in the water solution released ($c_{R,max}$) using Eq. (12):

$$\alpha_R = \frac{c_R}{c_{\max}} \tag{12}$$

## Isothermal Kinetics of Nicotine Bonding and Release

The isothermal kinetic curves of bonding nicotine from water solution at PAM xerogel/hydrogel and the release of the nicotine bonded from PAM xerogel in distilled water are presented in Figures 1 and 2, respectively.

The results, as depicted in the above Figures, revealed that the isothermal kinetic curves were similar in shape for both nicotine bonding at xerogel/hydrogel and the release from hydrogel for all the investigated temperatures. Three characteristic regions of the changes of the specific amount of nicotine bonding and concentration of nicotine release with time can be clearly observed from the kinetic curves, and time can be distinguished in all of the kinetics and conversional curves (linear, non-linear, and the saturation part or plateau). The curves show that the amount of nicotine either bonded or released increases significantly with time, then slows down gradually until equilibrium is reached. Increasing the temperature resulted in an increase of the slope of the linear part of the dependence of the specific amount of the nicotine bond to the hydrogel and the concentration of nicotine released from the hydrogel *vs.* time. At the same time, the duration of the linear changes as well as the time required to achieve the plateau decreases.

It is well known that in general, the rate of bonding of some substances is mainly limited either by Fick's Law of diffusion of molecules to the bonding centers or by the rate of reaction of substances with an active center, and as a result, the possibility of describing kinetics of nicotine bonding by the most common theoretical model, i.e., by the diffusive kinetics model, was examined first.

When the kinetics of nicotine bonding are determined by the rate of diffusion of nicotine molecules, then the kinetics of bonding are governed by the Fick Law of diffusion, and the degree of nicotine bonding ($\alpha_B$) obeying this law is proportional to the square root of time, i.e., $\alpha_B = k\sqrt{t}$. In that case, the dependences of $\alpha_B$ on $\sqrt{t}$ must give straight lines

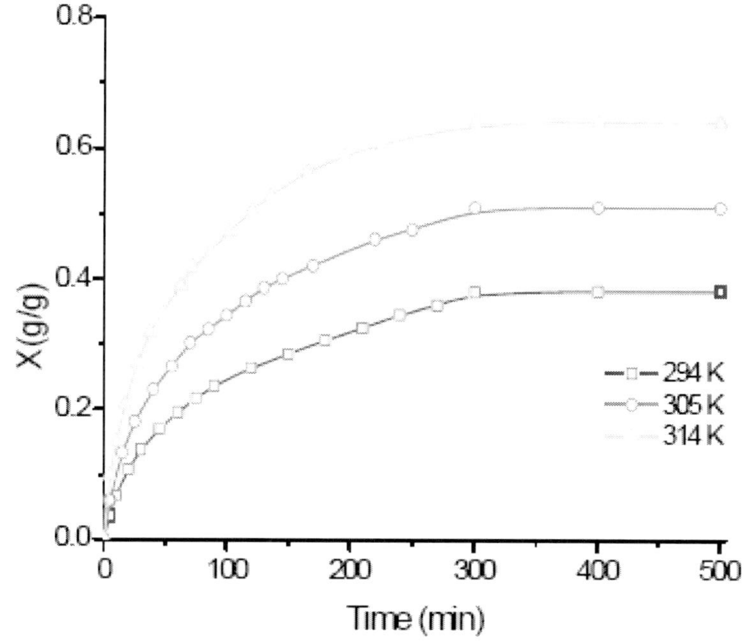


Figure 1. The isothermal kinetic curves of bonding nicotine from water solution at PAM xerogel at different temperatures.

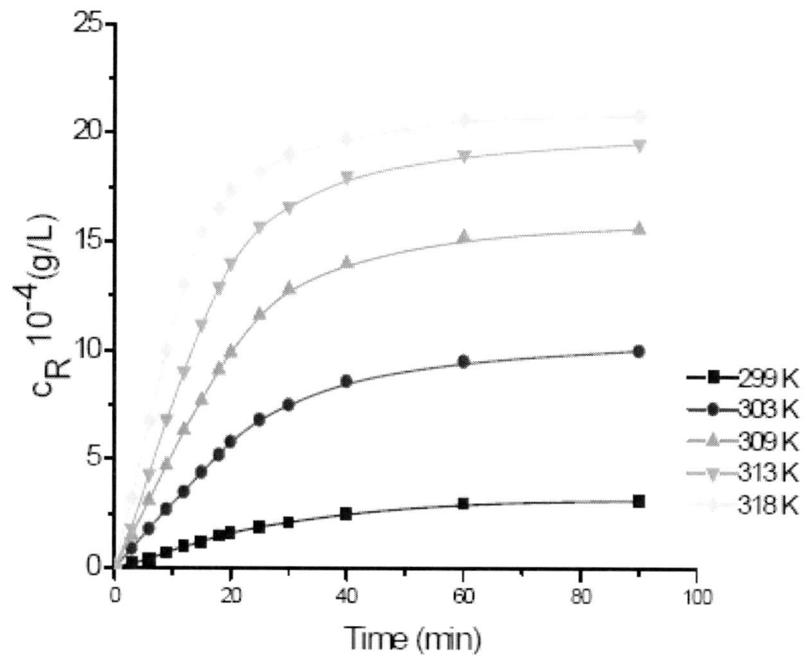


Figure 2. The isothermal kinetic curves of nicotine release from PAM xerogel in distilled water at different temperatures.

The plots of $\alpha_B$ as a function of $\sqrt{t}$ for nicotine bonding at PAM hydrogel at different temperatures are shown in Figure 3.

The plots of $\alpha_B$ as a function of $\sqrt{t}$ deviated from straight lines for all the examined temperatures. These results may imply that the so-called Fickian type of nicotine diffusion into the hydrogel had neither a dominant influence on the kinetics of its bonding to the hydrogel, nor on the changes of the swelling kinetics on temperature within the investigated range of temperatures. For these reasons, it appears that the Fick Law of diffusion is not suitable for describing the investigated kinetics of nicotine bonding to the hydrogel in distilled water.

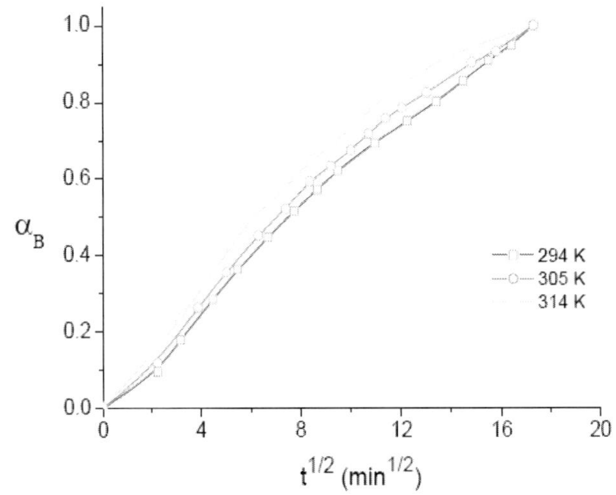


Figure 3. Dependence of $\alpha_B$ on $\sqrt{t}$ for the isothermal nicotine bonding at PAM hydrogel at different temperatures.

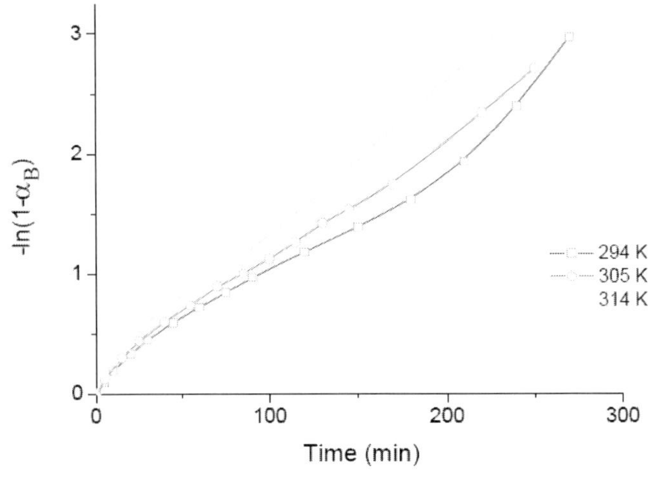


Figure 4. The plots of –ln (1- $\alpha_B$) *vs.* time of nicotine bonding for hydrogel at different temperatures.

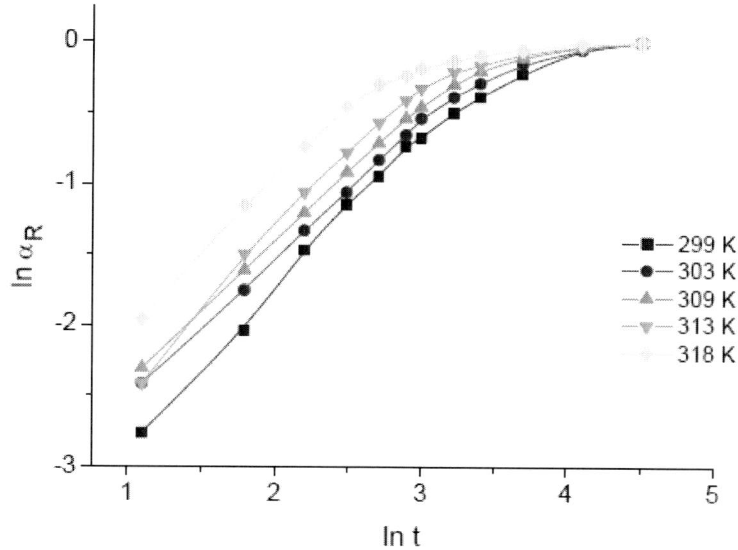


Figure 5. Plots of ln $\alpha_R$ *vs.* ln $t$ for the nicotine release from the PAM hydrogel at different temperatures in distilled water.

In the case when the kinetics of nicotine bonding at PAM hydrogel is controlled by the rate of nicotine bonding onto the active centers, it can be described by the Equation: $\alpha_B$ $\alpha_B = 1-\exp(-kt)$, and then the plot of -ln (1-$\alpha_B$) *vs.* time would be linear. Plots of -ln (1-$\alpha_B$) *vs.* time, for the nicotine bonding to the investigated hydrogel at different temperatures, are shown in Figure 4.

Based on the results presented in Figure 3, the plots of –ln (1- $\alpha$ $\alpha_B$) *vs.* time of nicotine bonding gave straights lines only in certain ranges of the swelling process. Thus, it was possible to conclude that the presented model is not appropriate for describing the examined kinetics of nicotine bonding.

Most commonly, in the up-to date literature, the kinetics of a drug release from the hydrogels can be described by the semi-empirical Peppas Equation: $\alpha_R = kt^n$. In the case when the kinetics of nicotine release from the PAM hydrogel , a dependence of ln $\alpha_R$ *vs.* ln $t$ would be linear. Plots of ln $\alpha_R$ *vs.* ln $t$ for the nicotine release from the PAM hydrogel at different temperatures in distilled water are shown in Figure 5.

It is clear from Figure 5 that the plots of ln $\alpha$ *vs.* ln $t$ gave straights lines in certain ranges of the process, maximally up to the the $\alpha_R$ =0.6. Thus, only for that range of release, it was possible to model the examined kinetics with the above-mentioned Peppas Equation.

Because the commonly used models in up-to date literature cannot be used to properly describe the kinetics of both bonding and the release of nicotine, the "model-fitting" method was applied to effectively determine the kinetics model [29, 30]. For this reason, the experimentally determined conversional kinetics curves of nicotine bonding and release "$\alpha = f(t)$)" were transformed into the so-called "experimentally conversional normalized curves " $\alpha_{exp} = f(t_N)$, where $t_N$ is normalized time, which were then compared with the model's normalized conversional curves. The isothermal normalized conversional curves of nicotine bonding and release are presented in Figure 6.

As can be seen, the normalized conversional curves of nicotine bonding and release significantly differ from one to the other, while within the same process they are of identical shape at all of the investigated temperatures.

The evaluated independence of the normalized conversional curves of nicotine bonding and release processes on temperature imply the unique mechanism of both nicotine bonding and release. By application of the "model-fitting" method, it was found that the nicotine bonding can be modeled by kinetics model D-2, while the nicotine release can be modeled by kinetics model R-3 [29].

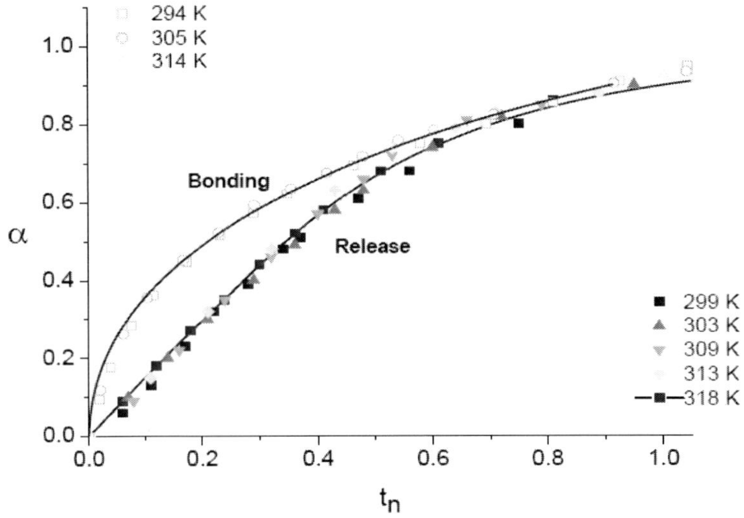


Figure 6. The isothermal normalized conversional curves of nicotine bonding and release.

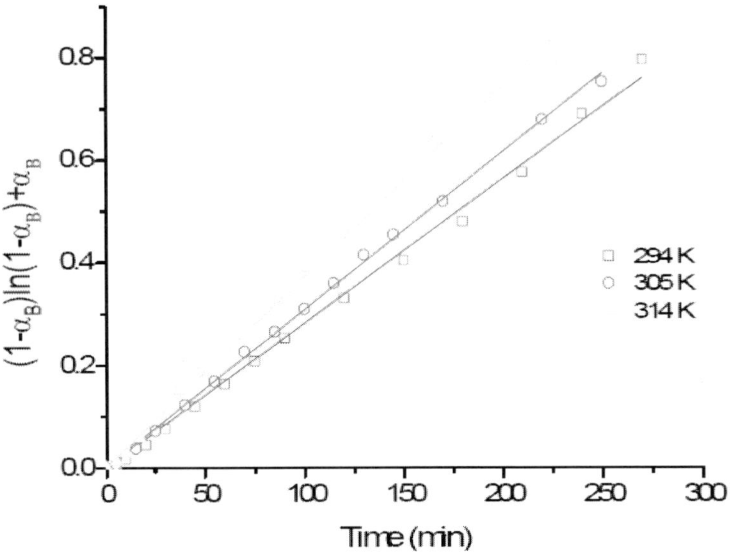


Figure 7. Dependence of $[(1-\alpha_B)\ln(1-\alpha_B) + \alpha_B]$ on bonding time for different temperatures.

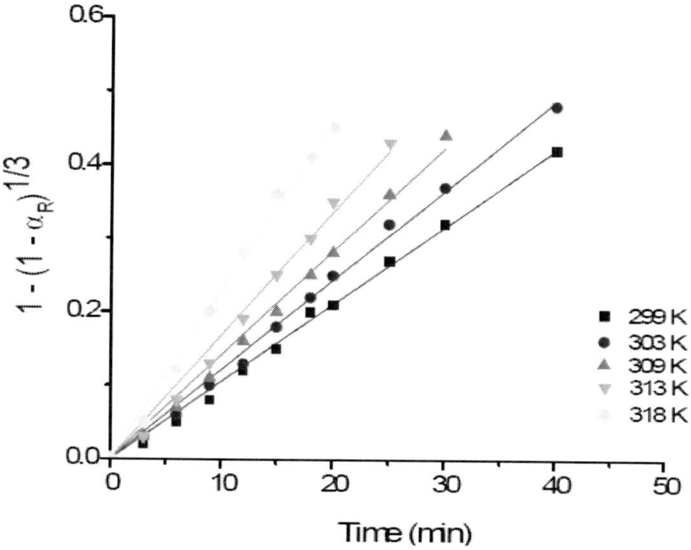


Figure 8. Dependence of $[1-(1-\alpha)^{1/3}]$ vs. release time for different temperatures.

**Table 2. The rate constants of nicotine bonding and release and their kinetic parameters**

| Nicotine bonding | | | Nicotine release | | |
|---|---|---|---|---|---|
| T, K | $k_B$, $min^{-1}$ | Kinetic parameters | T, K | $k_B$, $min^{-1}$ | Kinetic parameters |
| 294 | 2.82 | $Ea_{,B}$= 10.0 ±1.5 kJ/mol | 299 | 1.07 | $Ea_{,R}$= 28.0 ±1.0 kJ/mol |
| | | ln $A_B$=1.62± 0.2($min^{-1}$) | 303 | 1.22 | ln$A_R$=8.0± 1.0($min^{-1}$) |
| 305 | 3.08 | | 309 | 1.41 | |
| | | R=0.962 | 314 | 1.68 | R=0.962 |
| 314 | 3.72 | | 318 | 2.28 | |

In the case when the kinetics of nicotine bonding at hydrogel can be described by the D-2 kinetics model, a plot of $[(1-\alpha_B)\ln(1-\alpha_B)+\alpha_B]$ *vs.* bonding time would be linear. Also, if the release can be described by the R-3 kinetics model, a plot of $[1-(1-\alpha_R)^{1/3})$ *vs.* release time would be linear.

Plots of $[(1-\alpha_B)\ln(1-\alpha_B)+\alpha_B]$ *vs.* bonding time for the nicotine bonding at the hydrogel at different temperatures are shown in Figure 7, whereas plots of $[1-(1-\alpha_R)^{1/3})$ *vs.* release time, for the nicotine release from the PAM hydrogel at different temperatures, are shown in Figure 8.

The results presented in Figure 7 and 8 show that at all of the investigated temperatures, the dependences of $[(1-\alpha_B)\ln(1-\alpha_B)+\alpha_B]$ $[(1-\alpha)\ln(1-\alpha)+\alpha]$ *vs.* bonding time, as well as the dependences of $[1-(1-\alpha_R)^{1/3})]$ *vs.* release time, give straight lines over a whole range of the examined process of nicotine bonding and release. This verifies that the applied modeling process enables calculation of the kinetic parameters and implies the possible mechanisms of the examined processes of nicotine bonding and release.

The values of the rate constants $k_B$ and $k_R$ were determined from the slopes at the obtained straight lines in Figure 7 and 8. The rate constants, $k_B$ and $k_R$, for the predicted models of nicotine bonding and release, and their kinetic parameters ($E_a$ and ln A) and corresponding correlation coefficients, are given in Table 2.

The values of the rate constant $k_M$ and the values of kinetic parameters for the nicotine release from the PAM hydrogel in distilled water are considerably higher than the ones for nicotine bonding at the same hydrogel. This may be attributed to the different mechanisms of these processes.

The established kinetic models for nicotine bonding and its release makes novel models of mechanisms and kinetics possible, and offers a realistic explanation of the calculated values of kinetics parameters.

## Models of Kinetic Nicotine Bonding to the Hydrogel

The basic assumptions of the novel model of the kinetics of nicotine bonding to the hydrogel are as follows:

- The xerogel of PAM can be assumed as a system which consists of cylindrical pores with an average radius, R, which grows isotropic during the swelling process.
- The nicotine molecule selectively bonds to the active centers at polymer networks which leads to the pore's enlargement, forming a layer of nicotine with thickness X (see Figure 9).
- The growth of the bonded nicotine takes place through the model "layer by layer".
- The bonded nicotine does not form solid solutions with the polymer network.
- The rate of nicotine bonding at active centers of the xerogel network is higher than the rate of diffusion of nicotine.
- The diffusion coefficient of aqueous solution penetration in hydrogel pores is a constant value and does not change with time.
- The rate of growth of the nicotine bonded layer can be calculated using the equation [31]:

$$\frac{dX}{dt} = \frac{D}{j} \cdot \frac{dc_r}{dr} \tag{13}$$

where D is the diffusion coefficient of volume diffusion, $j$ is proportionality constant, and $c_R$ is nicotine concentration in solution at a distance $r$ (R-x < $r$ < R ).

In that case, the degree of nicotine bonding ($\alpha_B$) is given with the Eq:

$$\alpha_B = \frac{n\pi LR^2 - n\pi L(R-x)^2}{n\pi LR^2} \tag{14}$$

where $n$ is the number of pores per unit mass of xerogel and L is the length of pores per unit mass of xerogel.

Figure 9. Model of forming layer in cylindrical pores.

Based on the above equation, the thickness of the layer of nicotine bound to the hydrogel is given by the Eq:

$$x = R\left[1-(1-\alpha_B)^{1/2}\right]. \tag{15}$$

In the case of radial diffusion in cylinder, the expression for Fick's first law [32] is:

$$c_r = \frac{c_1 \ln\left(\frac{R}{r}\right) + c_2 \ln\left(\frac{r}{R-x}\right)}{\ln\left(\frac{R}{R-x}\right)} \tag{16}$$

where $c_1$ is nicotine concentration at surface r=R-x and $c_2$ is the nicotine concentration at surface r=R.

As the rate of nicotine bonding to the active site of xerogel/hydrogel is higher than the rate of nicotine diffusion, it can be accepted that $c_1$=0. In that case, Eq (16) is transformed to Eq (17):

$$c_r = \frac{c_2 \ln\left(\frac{r}{R-x}\right)}{\ln\left(\frac{R}{R-x}\right)} \tag{17}$$

The derivative of Eq (17) leads to the expression:

$$\frac{dc_r}{dr} = \frac{c_2}{(R-x)\ln\frac{R}{R-x}} \tag{18}$$

The substituting of $\frac{dC_r}{dr}$ in Equation (13) with Equation (18) yields :

$$\frac{dx}{dt} = \frac{k}{(R-x)\ln\left[\dfrac{R}{R-x}\right]} \tag{19}$$

where $k = \dfrac{Dc_2}{j}$.

If the derivative of Eq (15) with $\alpha$:

$$dx = \frac{R}{2(1-\alpha)^{1/2}}d\alpha \tag{20}$$

The substituting of ***dx*** in Equation (19) with expression (20) leads to :

$$\frac{d\alpha}{dt} = -\frac{k'}{\ln(1-\alpha)} \tag{21}$$

where $k' = 4k/R^2$.

Integration of (21) leads to the Eq:

$$[(1-\alpha)\ln(1-\alpha)+\alpha] = kt \tag{22}$$

Therefore, the kinetics of nicotine bonding to the hydrogel is controlled with the rate of diffusion of nicotine molecules through the layer of nicotine which is primarily bonded to the polymer network of partially or wholly swollen hydrogel. Low value of activation energy found for the process of nicotine bonding ( Ea= 10.3 kJ/mol) is in agreement with the low value of activation energy required for the nicotine diffusion through the layer of nicotine bonded to the swollen hydrogel, which additionally confirms the above presented model of kinetics of nicotine bonding.

## The Kinetics Model of Nicotine Release from the Hydrogel

The basic assumptions of the kinetics model of nicotine release from the hydrogel are as follows:

- The xerogel particles with the bonded nicotine are spheres with a radius R.
- The penetration of water into xerogel takes place layer by layer in the direction of the center of the xerogel (see Figure 10).
- The nicotine can be released only if the hydrogel is in "contact" with water.

- The rate of nicotine release is much higher than the rate of water uptake into the hydrogel.

Let's assume that thickness of the of swollen layer of the hydrogel is "$x$".
In that case, the volume of the swollen particles of xerogel is given by the expression:

$$V_N = \frac{4\pi}{3}(R-x)^3 \quad (23)$$

If we denote the degree of nicotine release with $\alpha_R$, then the following will be valid:

$$\frac{4\pi}{3}(R-x)^3 = \frac{4\pi}{3}R^3(1-\alpha_R) \quad (24)$$

If we resolve Eq. (24) per $x$ , it yields the following expression:

$$\frac{4\pi}{3}(R-x)^3 = \frac{4\pi}{3}R(1-\alpha_R)^{1/3} \quad (25)$$

If we suppose that the thickness of the hydrogel's swollen layer is proportional to the volume diffusion coefficient of water into the hydrogel (D) and to the swelling time, and inverse to the radius of particle of hydrogel (R), it can be given as:

$$x \approx \frac{k' Dt}{R} \quad (26)$$

where $k'$ is a proportionality constant.

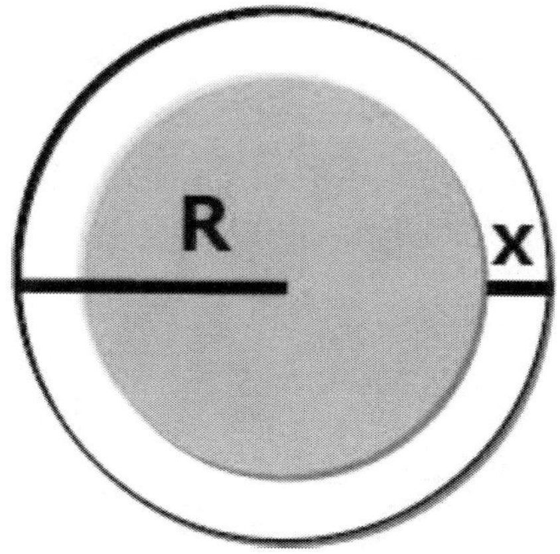


Figure 10. Model of swollen layer growth.

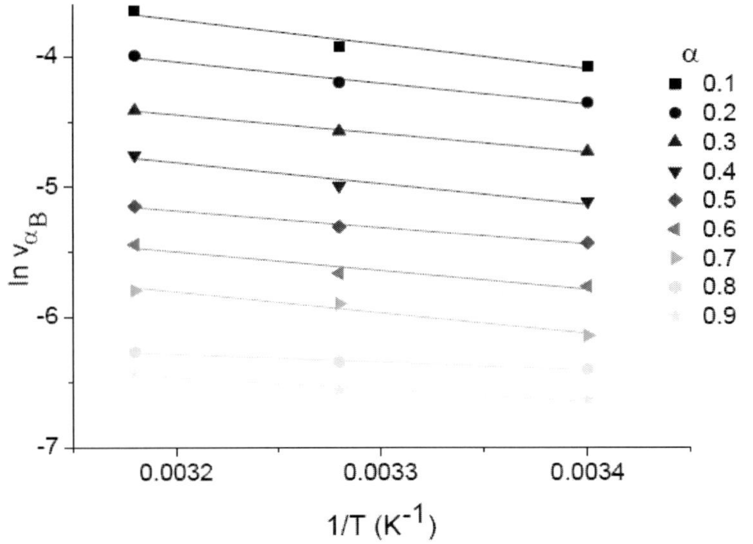


Figure 11. Dependence of $\ln v_\alpha$ on inverse temperature (1/T), for different degrees of nicotine bonding.

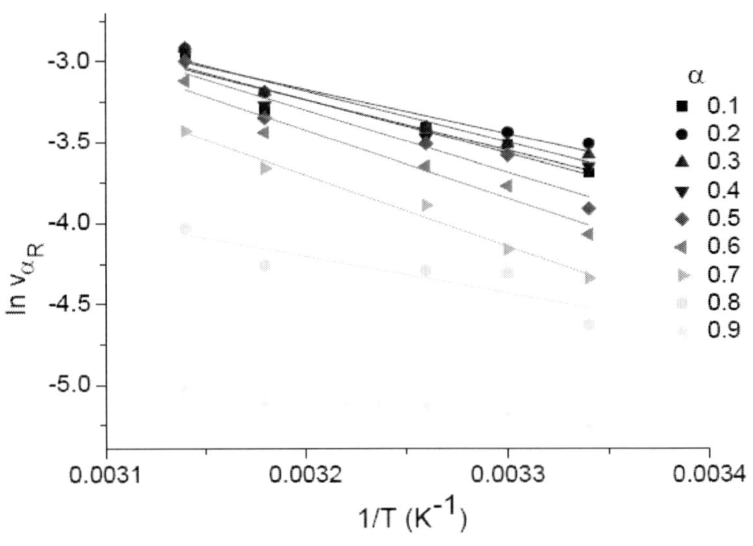


Figure 12. Dependence of ln $v_\alpha$ on inverse temperature ($1/T$) for different degrees of nicotine release.

By the substitution of ***x*** in Equation (25) with expression (26), Equation (27) is obtained:

$$\left[1-(1-\alpha_R)^{1/3}\right]=kt \tag{27}$$

where $k=\frac{k^{'}D}{R}$.

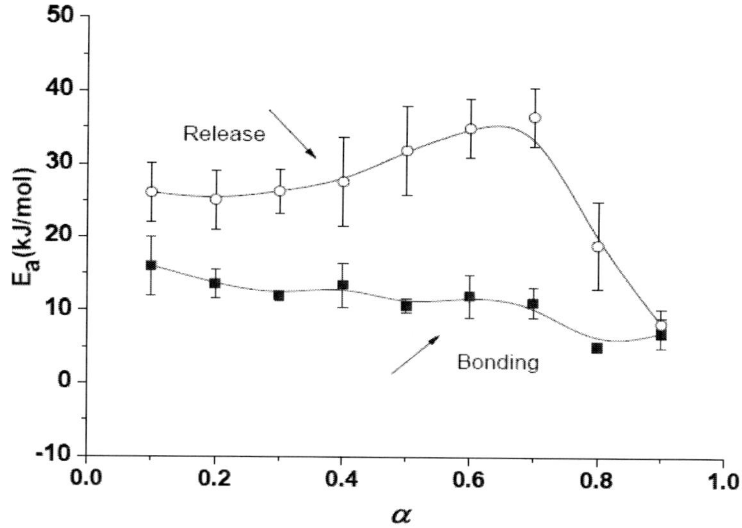


Figure 13. The dependence of $E_{a,\,\alpha}$ on $\alpha$ for the nicotine bonding and release process.

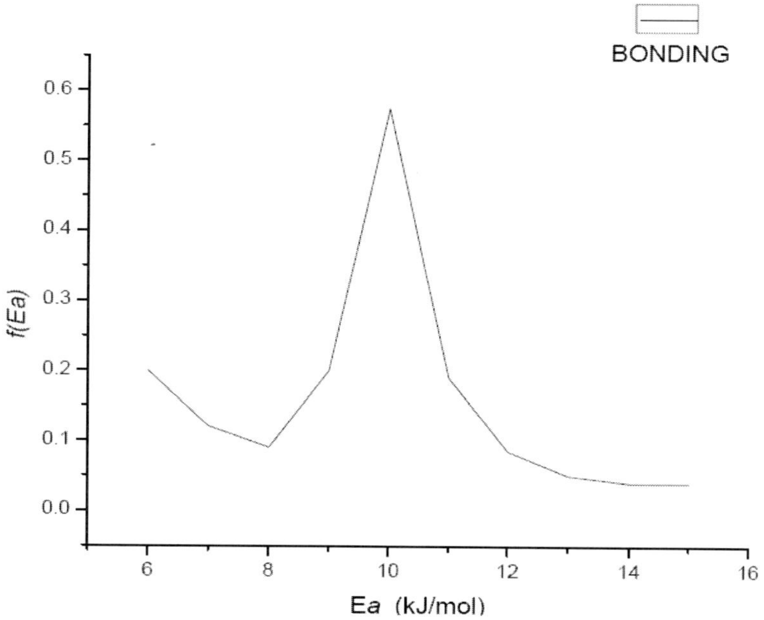


Figure 14. The function of the density distribution for nicotine bonding.

Therefore, the rate of release of bonded nicotine is determined by the rate of the growth of the swollen layer of xerogels particles and a high value of $E_a$=28kJ/mol can be explained as a relationship between high values of Ea required for transition of xerogel from a glassy to viscoelastic state [33], which initiates the swelling process of hydrogel.

With Vyzovkin's [ 34] principle of kinetic complexity and complex shapes of kinetic curves of PAA hydrogel swelling and nicotine bonding , the kinetic complexity of nicotine bonding and release was investigated by application by the conversional method.

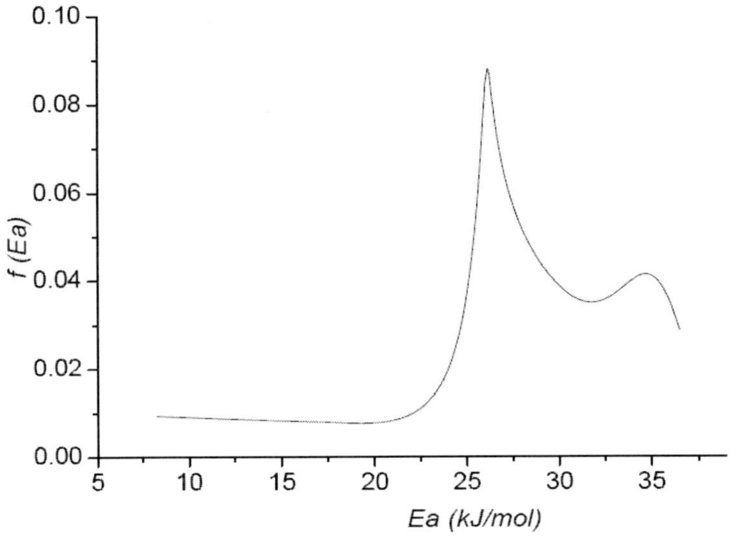


Figure 15. The function of the density distribution for nicotine release.

Figures 11 and 12 show dependences of ln$v_\alpha$ on inverse temperature (1/T), for different degrees of nicotine bonding and release.

The dependences of ln$v_\alpha$ on 1/T give straight lines both in the case of nicotine bonding and release, for each degree of nicotine bonding and release, based on which slope values of $E_a$ were determined. Figure 13 presents a dependence of $E_{a,\ \alpha}$ on $\alpha$ for the process of nicotine bonding and release.

Based on these shown dependences, it may be concluded that both processes of bonding and release are kinetically complex ones, and both $E_a$ values change with the corresponding $\alpha$. The curve of dependence of $E_{a,\ \alpha}$ on $\alpha$ for the nicotine release clearly reveals three characteristic types of changes in $E_{a,\ \alpha}$ on $\alpha$. In the range of $0.05 < \alpha < 0.4$, the value of Ea,α is independent on α, while the increase in α of nicotine release in the range of $0.4 < \alpha < 0.7$ leads to the non-linear increase in the $E_a$. In contrast , for $\alpha > 0.7$, further increases in α leads to a decrease in Ea.

The curve of dependence of $E_{a,\ \alpha}$ on $\alpha$ for the nicotine bonding also reveals three characteristic shapes of changes in $E_{a,\ \alpha}$ on $\alpha$. In the range of $\alpha < 0.3$, the value of Ea,α linearly decreases with the increase in α. For, $0.3 < \alpha < 0.6$, the activation energy is almost independent on α, while for $\alpha > 0.6$, the increase in α leads to the non-linear convexly decrease in the $E_a$.

Therefore, both the nicotine bonding and release are kinetically complex processes consisting of at least three elementary stages and each of them has specific influence on the overall kinetic of nicotine bonding and release.

In order to find out the kinetically dominant stage of the investigated process by application of the method of Muira, the probability function of density distribution of activation energies (f. d. p.) were determined [35].

Figures 14 and 15 present density probability functions of activation energies for nicotine bonding and release, respectively.

On the function of the density distribution for nicotine release, two peaks are clearly distinguished. The first one is sharp and symmetric with a maximum at Ea= 28 kJ/mol and corresponds to the most probable value of activation energy for nicotine release processes. The second one is of a "bell-shape" with a maximum at Ea = 35 kJ/mol. Bearing in mind that the most probable value of activation energy for nicotine release corresponds to the model's value of Ea, we can define the limiting stage of nicotine release, the rate of growth of swollen layer of xerogel, *i.e.*, the rate of phase-transition of xerogel from glassy to viscolelastic stage with a great degree of certainty. The existence of well defined, probable values of Ea and an identification of kinetically limiting stages of the elementary process of nicotine release explains the possibility of describing the kinetically complex processes with a simple model.

The density functions of nicotine bonding processes to the hydrogel has a characteristic sharp symmetric shape with a clear maximum at Ea= 10 kJ/mol. The found shape is characteristic for the kinetically complex process with low energetic heterogeneity, and for the ones with low influence on the overall kinetics. Bearing in mind that as in the case of nicotine release where the most probable value of Ea corresponds to the model's value of Ea, we can once again state that the kinetically limiting stage of the nicotine binding process is the rate of its diffusion through the layer of already bonded nicotine to the hydrogel network.

## CONCLUSION

- It was concluded that the possibilities of describing either nicotine bonding or release by the common kinetics model are limited.
- The new model for the mechanism of nicotine bonding into the hydrogel based on the diffusion of nicotine molecules through the layer of primary bonded nicotine to the polymer network was found.
- The new model for the mechanism of nicotine release from the hydrogel based on penetration of water molecules, layer-by layer, into the nicotine loaded xerogel/ hydrogel was found.
- Physical meanings of the calculated kinetics parameters of nicotine bonding or release are given.
- It was found that both processes of nicotine bonding and release are kinetically complex processes.

Based on the calculated density distribution function, the possibility of describing the kinetics of nicotine bonding and release is explained.

## ACKNOWLEDGMENT

This investigation was supported by the Ministry of Science and Technical Development of the Republic of Serbia, through Project No.172015 OI.

## REFERENCES

[1] Abd El-Rahim, H. (2006). Characterization and possible agriculture application of polyacrylamide sodium alginate crosslinked hydrogel prepared by ionizing radiation. *J. App. Pol. Sci.,* 101 (6), 3572-3580.

[2] Zhang, Y., Perez, P. (2011). Water-in-oil emulsions with hydrogel droplets background. USA Patent 7901 128 B2.

[3] Zheng, T., Liang, Y., Ye, Sh, He, Z. (2009). Superabsoprbent hydrogels as carriers for the controlled release of urea: Experiments and mathematical model describing the release rate. *Biosystems Engineering*, 102 (1), 44-50.

[4] Sohn, D., Kim, D. (2003). Theoretical and experimental investigation of the swelling behaviour of sodium polyacrylate superabsorbent particles. *J. Appl. Polym. Sci.,* 87, 252-257.

[5] Zohuriaan-Mehr, M., Omidian, H., Doroudiani, S., Karibi, K. (2010). Advances in non-hygienic applications of superabsorbent hydrogel materials. *J. Mat. Sci.,* 45(21), 5711-5735.

[6] Buchholz, F. (1998). Application of Superabsoprbent Polymers, In: *Modern Superabsoprbent Polymer Technology*, Buchholz, F. Graham, A. (Ed), Willey-VCH. New York, 251-260.

[7] Sun, X., Zhang, G., Shi, Q., Tang, B., Wu, Z. (2002). Preparation and characterization of water-swellable natural rubbers. *J. Appl. Polym. Sci.,* 86, 3212-3217.

[8] Li, A., Wang, A. (2005). Synthesis and Properties of clay-based superabsoprbent composite. *Eur. Polym. J.,* 41 (7), 1630-1637.

[9] Dzionmwa, G., Wood, C., Hill, D. (1997). Fine coal dewatering using pH- and temperature – sensitive superabsorbent polymers. *Polym. Adv. Technol.,* 8, 767-772.

[10] Bordado, J., Gones, J. (2007). New technologies for effective forsest fire fighting. *Int. J. Environ. Stud.,* 64(2), 243-251.

[11] Zolfaghari, R., Katbab, A.A., Nabavizadeh, J., Tabasi, R.Y., Nejad, M. J. (2006). Preparation and characterization of nanocompositee hydrogels based polyacrylamide for enhanced oil recovery applications. *J. Appl. Polym. Sci.,* 100, 2096-2103.

[12] Teles, F., Fonseca, L. (2008). Applications of polymers for biomolecules immobilization in ellectrochemical biosensors. *Mater. Sci. Eng., (C)* 28(8), 1530-1543.

[13] Raemdonak, K., Demeester, J., Smedt, S. (2009). Advanced nanogel engineering for drug delivery. *Soft Matter, 5,* 707-715.

[14] Sahiner, M. (2007). Hydrogel nanonetwork with functional core-shell structure. *Eur. Polym. J.,* 43(5), 1709-1717.

[15] Peppas, N., Hilt, Z., Khademhosseini A., Langer, R. (2006). Hydrogel in biology and medicine: from molecular principles to bionanotechnology. *Adv. Mater.,* 18, 1345-1360.

[16] Lin, Ch., Metters, A. (2006). Hydrogels in controlled release formulations: network design and mathematical modelling. *Adv. Drug Delivery,* 58, 1379-1408.

[17] Langergren, S. (1898). About the theory of so-called adsorption of solution substances. *K. Sven. Vetenskapsakad Handl.* 24 (4), 1-39.

[18] Ho, Y., Mc Kay G. (1998). Sorption of dye from aqueous solution by peat. *Chem. Eng. J.,* 70, 115-124.

[19] Low, M. (1960). Kinetics of chemisorption of gases on solids. *Chem. Rev.,* 60, 267-312.

[20] Weber, W., Morris, J. (1963) Kinetics of adsorption on carbon from solutions. *J. Sanitary Eng. Div. Am. Soc. Chem. Eng.,* 89, 31-59.

[21] Peppas, N., Bures, P., Leobandung, W., Ichikawa, H. (2001). Hydrogels in pharmaceutical formulations. *Eur. J. Pharm. Biopharm.,* 18(1), 63-88.

[22] Ganji, F., Vasheghani-Farahani, E. (2009). Hydrogels in controlled drug delivery systems. *Iranian Polym. J.,*18(1), 63-88.

[23] Huguchi, T., (1961). Rate of release of medicaments from ointment bases containing drugs in suspension. *J. Pharm. Sci.,* 50, 874-875.

[24] Siepmann, J., Peppas, N. (2001). Modelling of drug release from delivery systems based on hydroxypropyl methylcellulose (HPMC). *Adv. Drug Delivery,* 48, 139-157.

[25] Peppas, N., Sahlin, J., (1989). A simple equation for the description of solute release III, Coupling of diffusion and relaxation. *Int. J. Pharm.,* 57, 169-172.

[26] Hopfenberg, H. (1976). Controlled release polymeric formulations. In: Paul DR, Hares Fw (Ed), ACS Symposium Series, *Vol 33*, American Chemical Society, Washington, DC, 26-31.

[27] Adnadjevic B., Jovanovic J., Krkljus, I., (2008). Isotermal kinetics of(E)-4-(4 metoxyphenyl)-4-oxo-2-butenoic acid release from poly(acryliccid-comethacrylic acid)hydrogel. *J. Appl. Polym. Sci.,* 107(5), 2768–2775.

[28] Flory, P.J. Rehner, J. (1943) Statistical mechanics of cross-linked polymer network. I Rubberlike elasticity. *J. Chem. Phys.,* 11, 521-525.

[29] Brown, M.E., Dollimore, D., Galway, A.K. (1980). *Reaction in the Solid State.* In *Comprehensive Chemical Kinetics.* Ed. Elsevier.

[30] Adnadjevic B., Jovanovic J. (2008). A novel approach of investigation the poly(acrylic acid) hydrogel swelling kinetics in water. *J. Appl. Polym. Sci.,* 107(6), 3579-3587.

[31] Crank, J. (1975). The mathematics of diffusion, $2^{nd}$. Ed: Clarendon Press, Oxford, England, Chapter 5, p.69.

[32] Khawan, A., Flanagan, D. (2006). Solid-State kinetics models: Basics and mathematical fundamentals. *J. Phys. Chem., B,* 110, 17315-17328.

[33] Jankovic, B., Adnadjevic, B., Jovanovic, J. (2011). The comparative kinetics study of non-isothermal and isothermal dehydration of swollen poly(acrylic acid) hydrogel using the Weibull probability function. *Chem. Eng. Res. Design,* 89, 373-383.

[34] Vyazovkin, S. (1996). A unified approach to kinetics processing of nonisothermal data. *Int. J. Chem. Kinet.,* 28, 95-101.

[35] Muira, K., Maki, T. (1995). A new and simple method to estimate f(E) and kO(E) in the distributed activation energy model from three sets of experimental data. *Energy Fuels,* 9(2), 302-307.

# INDEX

## B



## C

## D

## E

## F



## G



## H

## I

## N

## O



## P

## Q



## R

## S

## T

## U



## V

## W



## Y



## Z